# WOMEN

AND THE

# ECONOMY

# WOMEN

AND THE

# ECONOMY

A READER

Edited by ELLEN MUTARI and
DEBORAH M. FIGART

*M.E.Sharpe*
Armonk, New York
London, England

**Library of Congress Cataloging-in-Publication Data**

Women and the economy : a reader / Ellen Mutari and Deborah M. Figart, editors.
    p. cm.
  Includes bibliographical references and index.
    ISBN 0-7656-0995-9 (cloth : alk. paper)  ISBN 0-7656-0996-7 (pbk : alk. paper)
      1. Feminist economics. 2. Women—Economic conditions. 3. Women—
Employment. I. Mutari, Ellen, 1956– II. Figart, Deborah M.

  HQ1381 . W644 2003
  330′.082—dc21

                                                                                2002042802


Printed in the United States of America

The paper used in this publication meets the minimum requirements of
American National Standard for Information Sciences
Permanence of Paper for Printed Library Materials,
ANSI Z 39.48-1984.

BM (c)  10   9   8   7   6   5   4   3   2   1
BM (p)  10   9   8   7   6   5   4   3   2   1

# Contents

**Appendix**

**Appendix**

# Tables and Figures

**Tables**

## Figures

# Preface

*Women and the Economy: A Reader* is designed as a primary or supplementary text for the growing number of courses offered on women's roles in the economy. These courses range from those focused on women and work (both paid and unpaid) to those that incorporate feminist critiques of traditional social science methodologies. Courses on women and work or women and the economy are taught in economics and sociology departments and in interdisciplinary women's studies programs.

Between the two editors, we have taught such courses at Richard Stockton College, Rutgers University, Temple University, Eastern Michigan University, and the New School for Social Research (New School University). We assembled this reader because we found the available texts insufficient for the type of course we had developed for our students. The study of gender, race-ethnicity, and class is interdisciplinary, yet the primary authored or edited volumes available for classroom use are discipline-specific. Further, within economics, the emphasis of the major women and work texts is "neoclassical economics," that is, a mainstream or traditional perspective. Our approach, reflected in this reader, is both heterodox and interdisciplinary. We showcase feminist economic analyses that utilize insights from institutionalism as well as neoclassical economics. The economics chapters are supplemented with chapters by authors from gender studies, sociology, demography, history, philosophy, social and public policy, planning, business studies, and advocacy groups. We have carefully selected newer pieces providing fresh and innovative insights and added a few articles that may be considered "classics."

The primary audience for this reader is undergraduate and graduate students in a variety of majors and degree programs. Though the majority of chapters are reprinted from journals in the economics discipline, for accessibility, our objective has been to minimize the technical content of the readings. This has been achieved through the adaptation of the original articles, without sacrificing the intent and argument of the authors' published versions. Specifically, we have often shortened articles that were rather lengthy in their original form, eliminated most endnotes and footnotes, and cut or adapted tables and figures that were not central to the arguments. The reader is to interpret ellipses [. . .] as text that has been deleted from the original. Those interested in a full-length presentation of the chapter are encouraged to consult the source publication.

The readings are organized by broad topic into seven sections. The structure of these sections is designed to complement and augment some of the standard texts. Each section begins with an introduction by the editors. The introductions lay out background material designed to guide students' reading. Following the chapters in each of the seven sections, there are a range of pedagogical tools for the instructor and the student. A section called "Key Terms" lists the major vocabulary words and phrases that are used in the chapters and are critical to understanding the analyses provided by the chapter authors. This is followed by "Discussion Questions" that can serve as launching points for class discussion, essay assignments, or seminar papers. Optional "Exercises" allow students and instructors to further apply the material learned in the chapter by completing assignments that may require further research. A number of sections include some innovative exercises that involve weaving quantitative reasoning into the study of women and the economy. In exercises designated "Do the Q," we ask students to manipulate and interpret data, visit web sites and analyze relationships among socioeconomic indicators, plot graphs, and conduct an original survey and then analyze the results. Finally, we provide some suggestions for further reading.

We are grateful to Elizabeth Granda and Lynn Taylor, editors at M.E. Sharpe, for believing in our mission, and to Esther Clark from the Editorial Department. The authors with whom we have corresponded and whose work we adapted have supported the project and were cooperative and flexible in reading the adaptations and granting permissions. The copyright holders have also been professional and helpful.

The "Do the Q" exercises were inspired by our participation in a Summer 2002 workshop on "Quantitative Reasoning Across the Disciplines" (QUAD) at Richard Stockton College. Stockton has been an innovator in developing curricula that assist students in seeing links between mathematical concepts and real-world, disciplinary-based applications. We thank the workshop participants (Frank Cerreto, Mark Mallett, Carolyn Routledge, Kathy Sedia, Linda Smith, and Karen York) for piloting our exercises and providing feedback. We would also like to acknowledge the students in our courses throughout the years. They continue to inspire us as teachers and as researchers.

# Section 1

# Methodologies for Studying
# Women and the Economy

Why begin our study of women and the economy with a section on methodology? One of the most important insights that feminist scholars have emphasized over the past few decades is that *how* we go about studying issues in the social sciences can play a large role in the questions we ask and the answers we find. This opening section of three chapters will therefore introduce you to some of the methodologies that have been used to study women and the economy. The focus is both on the theories used to guide research and the techniques used for researchers' investigations.

Because we are interested in women's positions in the economy, we start by considering the role that economics, as a social science discipline, can play in guiding our studies. Unfortunately, according to Myra Strober, in "Rethinking Economics Through a Feminist Lens," the discipline has been dominated by biased ways of thinking. She focuses, in particular, on feminist critiques of neoclassical economics, the dominant school of economics.

Within economics, there are several competing theories, approaches, and methodologies for studying questions of interest. The curricula of most undergraduate programs emphasizes neoclassical economics, the theoretical approach that developed at the end of the nineteenth century. Neoclassical economics defines its mission as the study of choices made under conditions of scarcity or constraint. Rational economic actors (once referred to as "rational economic *men*") make decisions in pursuit of their own self-interest; economics thus emphasizes selfishness over altruism and empathy. Neoclassical economic theory has searched for laws of human behavior under conditions of scarcity and selfishness. In microeconomics, this gives us constructs such as the "Law of Demand" (stating that people will buy more of something when it is cheaper, if all else is held constant). In this respect, economics has modeled itself on the Newtonian school of physics that also dominated

1

the late nineteenth century. By treating the economy as a natural object about which laws can be discovered, neoclassical economists have viewed themselves as objective scientists, rather than engaged citizens attempting to increase economic well-being.

Strober deconstructs each of these assumptions about economics. The work of economists has been flawed by an overemphasis on qualities that society traditionally associates with men. She argues that economics needs to be reformed not only to improve our understanding of women's condition, but to better comprehend economic life in general.

Strober presents a summary of the ideas of feminist economics, a relatively new school of economic thought. However, there are numerous alternative or *heterodox* schools of thought. The term "heterodox" is often used as a synonym for nonneoclassical approaches. If you are an economics student, you may be most familiar with Keynesian or post-Keynesian economics from your macroeconomics courses. A few of the other heterodox schools of economics include institutional economics (emphasizing the influence of habits, social norms, and institutions within the economy), Marxist economics (focusing on class conflict over power and access to resources), and social economics (addressing ethical concerns). Strober points out that many feminist economists draw upon these other heterodox schools, as well as some of the strengths of neoclassical or mainstream methods. This is a theme to which we will return throughout this reader, as neoclassical methodologies are contrasted with heterodox views.

The second selection on methodology is by a sociologist who studies workplace organizations, Joan Acker. Acker analyzes work organizations, rather than disembodied labor markets, as a site for the determination of wages, employment, and working conditions. "Revisiting Class: Thinking from Gender, Race, and Organizations" also provides an overview of important developments within interdisciplinary women's/gender studies. In particular, Acker's contribution examines how feminists have interpreted and utilized the concepts of gender, race, and class in their work. She argues that class has become less salient in feminist scholarship in recent decades. Part of the problem is that traditional Marxist interpretations of class, divorced from gender and race, failed to account for the ways that many workers experienced their economic position. Like neoclassical economics, Marxism was biased by an emphasis on men's experiences and male perspectives. In practice, Acker maintains, class, gender, and race interact in peoples' daily lives in complex ways. We need all three concepts in order to fully appreciate the distribution of resources and responsibilities within work organizations and within society.

Martha MacDonald, in "Feminist Economics: From Theory to Research," addresses some of the practical problems that feminist scholars have encountered in trying to improve their research strategies. Often, they find that the data they need are unavailable because the definitions used by data-gathering agencies are premised on the male-biased theories discussed by the first two authors in this section. For example, economic analysis has focused almost exclusively on market transactions. Because much of the work that women do within their households, on family farms and in family businesses, or as volunteers in the community is unpaid, it has been defined as outside the scope of economic analysis.

Economists also tend to treat households as a "black box," meaning a vessel painted so that the internal mechanisms cannot be seen from the outside. In economics texts, households interact with firms, and the decisions economists predict from these interactions assume that the household can act with a singular sense of self-interest. However, if you accept that men and women may have different amounts of power within households, their interets may not coincide. MacDonald therefore discusses the issues involved in intrahousehold decisions about (1) the distribution of income (New dishwasher or big-screen television? Whose salary pays for child care?), (2) labor allocation (Who does the dishes? Who should work overtime or take off when the kids are sick?), and (3) power relations (Who makes the decisions?). These three areas—the value of unpaid labor, intrahoushold decisions, and power relations—will be revisited in more detail in Section 3 of this reader. Finally, MacDonald discusses the issue of gendered processes in the labor market, a topic to which we will return in Sections 4 and 5. MacDonald makes the important point that economists' quantitative methodologies have focused almost exclusively on discriminatory outcomes such as wage inequality. Feminists are utilizing case studies in order to focus on discriminatory processes as well.

The methodological issues raised by MacDonald, Acker, and Strober highlight the contributions that feminism makes to social science methodologies. The issues they raise will guide our investigation of women in the economy, helping us analyze both women's and men's socioeconomic status.

# 1

# Rethinking Economics Through a Feminist Lens

## *Myra H. Strober*

Feminist economics is a rethinking of the discipline of economics for the purpose of improving women's economic condition. As a by-product (or external benefit) of this rethinking, feminist economics provides an improvement of economic theory and policy.

John Maynard Keynes observed that all too often human beliefs and actions are the result of an outmoded attachment to some archaic economic doctrine. Feminist economics argues that many of economics' core beliefs and policy recommendations are out of date, products of the peculiarities and politics of the periods in which they were developed and products of sexism in the Western world during the past two centuries. Feminist economics provides an impetus for economists to revise these outmoded attachments.

Feminist economics is a radical endeavor. In a discipline (economics) that is still remarkably positivist, feminist economics questions the whole notion of objectivity and argues that what one chooses to work on and how one formulates theories and policy recommendations are dependent upon one's culture, one's position in society, and one's life experiences. Feminist economics not only exposes the hidden political agendas of received economic doctrine, it straightforwardly acknowledges its own economic and political agenda: the improvement of women's economic condition.

Feminist economics is reopening questions that were seemingly answered years ago, much larger questions than those that most economists currently ask—questions about value, well-being, and power. In the process of asking these larger questions, feminist economics challenges several basic disciplinary assumptions: for example, the value of efficiency, the existence of scarcity, the omnipresence of selfishness, the independence of utility functions, and the impossibility of interpersonal utility comparisons. Indeed, feminism's basic assumption, that the oppression of women exists and ought to be eliminated, is a fundamental challenge to the supposed impossibility of interpersonal utility comparisons.

Feminist economics points out that despite economists' protestations to the contrary, economists do in fact make interpersonal utility comparisons and that often these are detrimental to women. Michèle A. Pujol (1992) shows, for example, that A.C. Pigou, the dean of welfare economics, openly argued that women are weaker and lesser than men and was primarily interested in how women's labor in their homes could be used to increase national well-being. Pigou also argued that keeping women's wages lower than men's was "welfare maximizing" (Pujol 1992, p. 151). Clearly Pigou was making utility comparisons and equally clearly he was not concerned in the least with women's utility.

Feminist economics is also interested in economics at a methodological level and provides a careful scrutiny of economics' knowledge claims. For example, it asks *how* economists in fact come to know what they assert is true (Bergmann 1987). It also subjects to examination economists' narrowly quantitative approach, their skepticism about the value of seeking information from interviews, and their insistence that economic analysis and its classroom presentation should be "unemotional" (Strober 1987).

Before looking at an example of feminist economic analysis, I will turn for a moment to what feminist economics is not. Feminist economics is not about essentialism, the doctrine that there are fundamental (essential) differences between women and men. Therefore, it does *not* say that women need a different economics than men. For this reason, feminist economics does not use the terms "masculine economics" or "feminine economics," terms that confuse the issues and perpetuate the stereotypes. The point is that mainstream economics is sexist, not that it is masculine.

Feminist economics is also *not* about fundamental differences between women and men economists and therefore does not hold the view that women economists do economics in a different way from what men economists do, or even that women economists have a special pipeline to understanding women's economic situation. Some of the insights that some women economists have, however, may come from experiences that most men economists do not have. For example, many women economists have a direct understanding of sexism gained through direct personal experiences in academe. Moreover, as bearers and rearers of children, some women economists may be more likely to question economics assumptions of a separative self and selfish utility maximization; but men economists who spend a great deal of time and effort rearing children may also find themselves questioning these assumptions for the same reason. The insights come not from gender, but from experiences. (See Amartya Sen 1992 on the roles that "position" and experience play in human knowledge.)

The questions that feminist economics seeks to answer at this point in its development are what Sen (1987) has called the "ethics" questions in economics (as contrasted to the "engineering" questions). In her comments on the feminist economics papers in the collective volume of Marianne Ferber and Julie A. Nelson (1993), Rebecca Blank (1993, p. 143), indicates that she would like feminist economics to become "a usable alternative model of economic decision-making." This is not the current goal of feminist economics. For the time being, feminist economics is operating at the ethics level of theory and is engaged in rethinking the very foundations of economic suppositions and method.

## A Quick Tour Through the Existing Literature

Feminist economics is hardly monolithic. Its practitioners come from multiple "schools" within economics: mainstream, institutional, and Marxist, to name a few. They also come from various "schools" of feminism: liberal, radical, Marxist, and separatist. Moreover, many feminist economists are as interested in race-gender or race-gender-class as they are in gender alone. Thus, the subject matter of feminist economic writing is extremely varied and wide-ranging.

There have been several phases of feminist economics. The first feminist economists were John Stuart Mill, Harriet Taylor, and Barbara Bodichon (Pujol 1992). Writing in England in the period that covered the 1840s through the 1870s, they theorized women's equality in employment and ownership of property. Mill's (1970) [1869] "On the Subjection of Women," written in 1869 with Taylor as the acknowledged joint author, still stands as one of the classic discussions of women's second-class economic status.

Beginning in the 1890s and stretching through the early 1920s, again in England, economists Millicent Fawcett, Ada Heather-Biggs, Eleanor Rathbone, and Beatrice Webb all took the feminist view in the debate about equal pay for women and men (Pujol 1992). In the United States, just around the turn of the century, Charlotte Perkins Gilman analyzed women's position in the home and pushed the importance of market work for women.

With the rise of the second wave of the feminist movement in the 1960s, a great outpouring of feminist economics appeared, dealing with issues of labor force participation, household work, earnings differentials, occupational segregation, the feminization of poverty, and the economics of child care (see Blau and Ferber 1992 and Bergmann 1986 for reviews). This literature sought to use its new theoretical constructs and empirical findings to improve women's economic position.

Beginning in the 1980s, feminist economists began the current wave of writing, this time concerned not only with women's situation but also with the underlying structure of economics as a discipline. Blau (1981) wrote on the impossibility of value-free scholarship in economics, Bergmann (1987) wrote on the question of how economists come to know what they think they know, and I (Strober 1987) wrote on the role of values and emotions in economics. Marilyn Waring's (1988) book dealt with the negative repercussions for women of the exclusion of nonmarket work from the national income accounts.

The current wave of feminist economic writing accelerated in the late 1980s and early 1990s with emphasis on the sexism inherent in fundamental constructs in economics (i.e., the focus on scarcity and choice, and assumptions of self-interest, separative selves, rationality, and exogenous preference formation). These writings, including those by Paula England, Nancy Folbre, Heidi Hartmann, Ann Jennings, Julie Nelson, Michèle Pujol, and Diana Strassmann, are presented or reviewed in Ferber and Nelson (1993). A more complete discussion of the issues presented in the next section may be found in Strober (1993).

## A Sample Feminist Economic Analysis

Women's interests are disadvantaged by the centrality in economic theory of the concepts of scarcity, selfishness, and competition. The feminist rethinking of these concepts benefits not only women, but also economic theory and policy.

Scarcity, selfishness, and competition are each half of a dichotomy: scarcity/abundance; selfishness/altruism; and competition/cooperation. What economic theory has done is largely to relegate the other half of the dichotomy to a place outside of economic analysis. That is, economics is almost always about scarcity, selfishness, and competition, but rarely about abundance, altruism, or cooperation.

One could argue that these dichotomies have masculine and feminine sides (scarcity, selfishness, and competition being masculine; abundance, altruism, and cooperation being feminine) and that economics has chosen to make central to its analysis the masculine while ignoring the feminine. I do not subscribe to this notion. To criticize the use of dichotomies by employing yet another dichotomy (male/female) is sophistry. Moreover, assigning masculine and feminine characteristics in this way merely perpetuates stereotypes. There is nothing masculine or feminine about any of these attributes, nor am

I persuaded that on average men or women are more or less likely to be characterized by them.

The feminist insight about these dichotomies is that by concentrating on scarcity, selfishness, and competition, economics makes it more difficult to redistribute power and economic well-being. The more those who are among the "haves" are told that the world is characterized by scarcity and that the path to well-being is through selfishness and competition, the less likely they are to behave in ways that foster altruism, cooperation, and a more equal sharing of economic goods and services.

Since women are disproportionately represented among the "have-nots," women stand to benefit from a worldview that is less centrally focused on scarcity, selfishness, and competition. As economics begins to include abundance, altruism, and cooperation in its analyses, there will be more emphasis on redistribution of goods and services and more emphasis on an improvement in women's economic situation. At the same time, economics will have reclaimed a wide range of human economic behavior currently outside the disciplinary purview.

By focusing on scarcity and ignoring abundance, economics chooses to view the glass of economic well-being as half-empty. It could just as easily view it as half-full, for, although in some respects true scarcity exists, in other respects the world is abundant. The choice to elaborate scarcity and neglect abundance takes economists' consciousness off the fact that many problems are not a result of scarcity but of maldistribution. For example, in the United States today there is abundant food; we have sufficient food to feed all Americans. That some Americans (disproportionately women and children) experience malnutrition and hunger in the United States is a result of maldistribution of food, not of scarcity.

Some of the scarcity that economics sees as central is in fact engendered by economic actors, particularly through advertising. Perceptions of relative abundance and economic well-being depend not only on what one has, but also on one's expectations. These expectations are subject to both individual and social control. Economists maintain that an individual's wants, needs, and tastes are independent of those of other individuals, and independent of suppliers of goods and services (demand and supply are, after all, supposed to be independent of one another, derived separately from unrelated factors). But of course, wants are manipulated by suppliers. By failing to look more carefully at both scarcity and abundance instead of simply assuming scarcity, economists act as apologists for advertisers and the businesses that pay them to induce perceived scarcity. This is not to say that, merely by studying abundance, economics can create more of it. Rather, as economics begins to consider both abundance and scarcity, the result will be a better understanding of which problems stem from true scarcity, which from induced scarcity, and which from maldistribution.

Adam Smith saw a world situated in scarcity and populated by selfishness. He was relieved to "discover" that through a competitive economy human selfishness could nonetheless be harnessed for the greater good. Economists treat Smith's observations as universal, but feminist economists, influenced by postmodern theorists, are skeptical of universals. Smith observed a society with a particular culture at a level of well-being far below our own. In not all cultures are people as selfish as they may have been in late eighteenth-century England. Moreover, each society has a choice about which characteristics of its people it wishes to endorse and elaborate and which it wishes to change.

Why does economics have so much to say about selfishness and competition and so little to say about individuals' aspirations for others' well-being or about cooperation? People talk frequently about the Jones effect, but is there no flip side to the Jones effect? Are people never genuinely pleased to see others improve their situation? For example, economics theorizes about backlash from men who are disturbed when some women advance. Are there no men who are pleased to see women's situation improve?

Economics teaches that people feel better off if they use additional income to buy themselves an additional pair of shoes or take an additional vacation, but it does not examine the extent to which people might feel better off if, for example, that additional income were used to provide a single mother with needed medical care. Economics does not inquire, to use economic parlance, how a reduction in the inequality of economic well-being might affect an individual's utility function. And yet many of us, particularly women, would gladly give up some additional market good or service if we could somehow improve the well-being of others so that we could have some physical security when we walk out into the street at night.

Economic theorizing that includes both competition and cooperation will have beneficial effects on women's positions. When white men in power stop seeing women (and minorities) solely as competitors, they can begin to ask fruitful questions about how best to cooperate with them to bring about more creative and productive businesses.

An end to economics' fixation on the importance of competition in creating economic well-being and the discipline's resultant failure to consider cooperation as a mode of motivating and organizing economic activity will also be beneficial for the American economy. As a result of the failure to update Adam Smith, the U.S. antitrust policy is outmoded, and Americans seem ideologically incapable of emulating the best of Japanese industry-government cooperation. Feminist economics may induce economic theorists to stop treating cooperation and competition as dichotomous and start asking intelligent questions about how much of each works best under which conditions.

## Conclusion

It is ironic that a discipline ostensibly concerned with well-being should be called the dismal science. It may be that one of the unanticipated benefits of feminist economics will be a change in that appellation. By challenging economics to take seriously a concern with well-being and encouraging the discipline to rethink its emphasis on efficiency, scarcity, selfishness, and competition, economics may begin to be thought of as a humane discipline interested in such matters as quality of life, cooperation, and equity. Economics might move from a conservative, laissez-faire orientation, protesting the impossibility of interpersonal utility comparisons, to a science that seriously investigates strategies for improving well-being.

Feminist economics may also have significant effects in the methodological arena. If feminist economics is sufficiently influential, it will cause economists to regularly ask themselves *how* they know what they profess to know. Their dissatisfaction with the source of their knowledge may propel them away from the technique of musing (Bergmann 1987) and more toward empirical observation and questioning, away from parsimony for its own sake and the mathematical modeling of abstractions and more toward complex verbal explanations of real economic problems.

Still, these will be by-products of a feminist economics. The primary product will be an improvement in women's situation. Feminist economics will be successful if its analysis causes economists and others to understand the sexist nature of economics and motivates them to change both the analysis and the policy recommendations that flow from it. Feminist economics will be successful if it causes economists and others to put matters of women's well-being on a par with those of men.

## References

Bergmann, Barbara R. 1986. *The Economic Emergence of Women.* New York: Basic Books.
———. 1987. "'Measurement' Or Finding Things Out in Economics." *Journal of Economic Education* 18 (2): 191–201.
Blank, Rebecca M. 1993. "What Should Mainstream Economists Learn from Feminist Theory?" In *Beyond Economic Man: Feminist Theory and Economics,* ed. Marianne A. Ferber and Julie A. Nelson, pp. 133–43. Chicago: University of Chicago Press.

Blau, Francine D. 1981. "On the Role of Values in Feminist Scholarship." *Signs: Journal of Women in Culture and Society* 6 (3): 538–40.

Blau, Francine D., and Marianne A. Ferber. 1992. *The Economics of Women, Men, and Work*. Englewood Cliffs, NJ: Prentice Hall.

Ferber, Marianne A., and Julie A. Nelson, eds. 1993. *Beyond Economic Man: Feminist Theory and Economics*. Chicago: University of Chicago Press.

Mill, John Stuart. 1970. [1897] "On the Subjection of Women." In *Essays on Sex Equality*, ed. Alice S. Rossi, pp. 123–242. Chicago: University of Chicago Press.

Pujol, Michèle A. 1992. *Feminism and Anti-Feminism in Early Economic Thought*. Aldershot, UK: Edward Elgar.

Sen, Amartya. 1987. *On Ethics and Economics*. Oxford: Blackwell.

———. 1992. *Objectivity and Position*. The Lindley Lecture. Lawrence: University Press of Kansas.

Strober, Myra H. 1987. "The Scope of Microeconomics: Implication for Economic Education." *Journal of Economic Education* 18 (2): 135–49.

———. 1993. "Feminist Economics and the Improvement of Women's Economic Condition." Paper presented at the annual meetings of the Allied Social Sciences Association, Anaheim, CA, January.

Waring, Marilyn. 1988. *If Women Counted: A New Feminist Economics*. San Francisco: Harper and Row.

---

Adapted from "Rethinking Economics Through a Feminist Lens," *American Economic Review* 84 (2) (May 1994): 143–47. Reprinted with permission of the American Economic Association.

# 2

# Revisiting Class

## Thinking from Gender, Race, and Organizations

### Joan Acker

The study of gender and organizations, a relatively new focus in feminist social science, has expanded rapidly in the last ten years. However, scholars in this field have not responded very energetically to the strong argument that feminists must not only examine gender patterns in social life, but must also bring class and race into the analysis in order to give a full account of the complexities of individual experiences and social structures. This argument has been widely accepted among feminist scholars since the 1980s, when feminist writers and academics who were also women of color or Third World women began pointing out that most feminist scholarship was actually about white, middle-class, heterosexual women and consequently ignored the lives of women in other class and race situations (e.g., Hull, Scott, and Smith 1982; hooks 1984). The validity of this claim was accepted by many feminist scholars, who then expressed the commitment to studying "gender, class, and race." But it was easier to make the pledge than to carry it out in a thorough way. Researchers could add women of color to a sample, study in depth the experiences of minority or working-class women, or analyze the intersections of gender, class, and race in particular empirical/historical cases, but a conceptual integration of "gender, class, and race" was more difficult to achieve. Considerable progress has been made in theoretically bringing together gender, class, and race (e.g., Collins 1990, 1995; Crenshaw 1995; Glenn 1999). However, a major problem persists: class, although regularly invoked as one of the necessary three, has not been retheorized in a way that facilitates its use in a combined analysis (Acker 1999). . . .

## Why Many Feminists Forgot About Class

Class was the central concept for understanding structurally based inequalities at the time that the present feminist movement emerged in the late 1960s. However, class theories, whether Marxist, structural-functional, or occupational/categorical, could not account for the economic and occupational disadvantages that women suffered in comparison with men in the same class positions. Feminist theorists attempted to modify male-centered class concepts, hoping to more adequately account for women's subordination within what were seen as "general" theories of societal processes. None of these attempts were wholly successful; components of women's class experiences such as sex segregation of jobs, the gender-based wage gap, and the assignment to women of unpaid caring labor could not be attributed solely to class processes such as capitalist exploitation. Class concepts, it became clear, were modeled on social reality as seen from male perspectives and could not be simply reshaped to take into account female reality (Acker 1980; 1999; Sokoloff 1980; Hartsock 1983). Massive amounts of research were being done on sex segregation, the gendered wage gap, practices of discrimination, and women's experiences in the labor force, workplace, and home, but this empirical work did not result in new theorizing about class. Efforts to theorize class within a gender perspective declined as scholars were dissatisfied with the results, and debates over the issues almost disappeared by the mid-1980s (Beechey 1987; Barrett and Phillips 1992). Some discussions of conceptual issues and efforts to formulate new ways of seeing class continued, but these were no longer the heated debates in feminist scholarship, nor did they resolve the difficulties. This meant that the old conceptual formulations that rendered women invisible and that failed to explain different gender situations within class societies persisted. . . .

A number of factors contributed to feminists' forgetting about class. First, the debate had run into a dead end. There was not much more to say. Some of the impasse can be attributed to the type of discourse into which feminists had tried to enter: Marxist feminists had, on the whole, attempted to modify the structural Marxisms that were predominant among intellectuals in the 1960s and 1970s. These were highly abstract theoretical formulations positing relations among conceptual categories in which it was difficult to see any human agency or any concrete, embodied practices involved in making structures (e.g., Wright 1985). Given that these abstractions contained an implicit male point of departure and assumptions about men's working lives, inserting women and, for example, unpaid labor undermined these assumptions and threatened to upset the systematic formulations themselves. An additional problem was, however, that class theory itself was in a crisis, or so numerous male writers had been claiming since the early 1970s (e.g., Giddens 1973). The world of production and capitalist relations was changing as the old industrial working class began to decline and the heavily female service sector rapidly expanded. The old theories seemed inadequate for representing these changes. Anxiety over the adequacy of class analysis does not seem to be directly reflected in feminist discussions, but I think that it contributed to "forgetting."

The political-economic climate also contributed to forgetting about class. In the 1980s, as we all know, there was a shifting of influence and power away from working-class–based interests and toward interests allied with big capital and big organizations. Not that capital had ever been less powerful than labor, but with the Reagan era in the United States, neoliberal economics, and the celebration of free-market capitalism, backed by antilabor legislation, there emerged the powerful argument that capitalism is "the only way." Class relations embedded in capitalist processes, it followed, were part of "the only way." Class relations, including inequality and exploitation, as intrinsic to the fundamental and necessary organization of society, became more legitimate than ever, while gender- and race-based inequalities, at least in public law and public discourse, were illegitimate. Discussions of class, particularly from a Marxist or working-class perspective, began to be cast as irrelevant. What was relevant was how to organize production in the most efficient ways, how to tap the knowledge and creativity of employees, how to use new technologies to the fullest, all in order to win the competitive battles on the world economic stage. The collapse of the Soviet Union and of socialism there and in the eastern European countries furthered the marginalization and irrelevance of class theories linked to socialist discourses. To talk about class was no longer cutting edge, it was old-fashioned. Attacks on class exploitation were out of step. In this climate, many scholars began to develop feminist thinking in other directions, including toward analyses of culture and the ways in which cultural constructions contributed to the reproduction of exclusions and oppressions based on gender, race, ethnicity, sexualities, etc. . . . .

Class relations are, however, still in existence. Economic power, exploitation, and capital accumulation have not disappeared, but are the dominant reality as globalization of production and finance capital has accelerated. Changes in class relations, and gender and race relations as well, are related to changes in production, economic organization, and technologies. Changes in class relations are also related to restructuring and downsizing of welfare states that accompany these economic alterations. Therefore understanding class is as essential as ever for understanding societal problems and individual fates, including the often differing fates of women and men. . . . .

**Rethinking Class from a Feminist Perspective**

My rethinking of class is rooted in a much-modified Marxist understanding of class: "class" refers to economic, including production and distribution, relations of exploitation, power, dominance, and subordination that produce inequalities and contradictory interests. . . . Certain feminist insights that originate in our attempts to comprehend gender can help in rethinking class. These are, first, that class, gender, and race are interrelated in practice; class relations are formed in and through processes that also form gender and race relations. Second, class is best understood as social relations constructed through active practices, not as categories or classifications of people according to socioeconomic characteristics or occupational status. Third, the complexity of class processes come into view when we study them from the viewpoints of different participants within organizations. Finally, we need to expand the notion of "the economic" in order to develop a concept of class that can encompass the economic situations of white women and people of color, as well as contemporary changes in world class structures.

*Class, Gender, and Race as Interrelated and*
*Mutually Constituted*

Feminists have for some time recognized that the diversity of women's experiences cannot be captured by looking only at gender: at least class and race must be part of the analysis. Class, race, and gender interconnections can be traced in the historical development of contemporary capitalism and the organizations through which it functions; these interconnections occur both within and between particular states and nations. The same concrete historical processes produced the particular forms of what we now call class, race, and gender. For example, the slave trade between emerging capitalist powers was integral to the early development of capitalism. Slavery constituted the conditions of exploitation and oppression in which the lives of women and men, both black and white, in the United States were constructed as different and unequal. Slavery was not the only economic organizational form that shaped race, gender, and class relations, but it continues to be a salient one. Slavery was not a mass of free-floating relations; it was organized and occurred within and between organizations as they engaged in production and trade.

The consequences of this history can be seen today in the ways in which class relations in the United States are patterned along lines of gender and race. Such patterns continue, although white women and people of color have begun to enter organizational positions from which they were entirely excluded previously. For example, the "ruling class" within large organizations is still primarily a class of white men, while certain sectors of the "working class" are almost entirely female—clerical workers, cashiers, waitresses—or are almost entirely white and male—skilled trades. Racial patterning of class divisions in work organizations persists, with the exclusion of people of color from certain jobs and positions or their segregation at the bottom of organizational hierarchies.

Class, race, and gender patterns are not just the shards of history, but are continually created and re-created in today's organizations, as people are hired, promoted, or fired, as wages are set, and as managers, supervisors, and workers organize and execute their daily tasks (Acker 1990). Variations in these patterns are great. In some cases, as in an advertising agency studied by Alvesson (1993), class lines are identical with gender lines: all the professionals were men and all the secretaries were young and pretty women. In other cases, such as a college that Don Van Houten and I recently studied (Acker and Van Houten 1999), class lines were not identical with gender divisions. Women were well represented at the upper levels, while clerical workers were almost entirely women and skilled blue collar workers were almost entirely men. In both of these organizations, people of color were excluded, as almost all the employees were white northern Europeans or Americans. White racial privilege guaranteed that in these organizations the jobs, all of which were relatively desirable, were filled by white people.

The interweaving of gender, race, and class is more fundamental than the persistent distributions of men and women, white people, and people of color into particular class-related jobs or positions, for the creation of such positions was frequently through processes in which gender and/or racial vulnerabilities and assumptions played a part. For example, many light assembly jobs appear to have been created for women because women were an available and low-paid labor force and because employers believed that women with their "nimble fingers" were better suited than men for the work. On the other hand, as Reskin and Roos (1990) argue, employers may start to hire women into men's jobs for essentially class-related reasons (e.g., new technology facilitates the lowering of wages in particular jobs and women are more willing than men to take them) and then begin to define these positions as "women's jobs." In some instances, class relations appear to be gender or race relations; the boss-secretary relation is both a class and gender relation. Or the relationship between the medical professional and the worker who cleans the floors in the hospital is very often both a class and a race relation.

Class relations are also constituted in gender and racial images of the organization and the identities of men and women as organizational participants. White working-class masculinity has been defined in terms of earning a living wage, putting in a fair day's labor, and supporting one's family. Working-class solidarity has been, and probably still is, organized around male bonding and these notions of male responsibility. At the other end of the class structure, images of masculinity as competitive, aggressive, and relentlessly focused on individual success have justified the dominance of particular hegemonic masculinities (Connell 1987) as well as the actions of organizations headed by men who at least seem to embody these virtues. While women and men of color now occasionally fill such positions, some evidence exists that their modes of action are congruent with the demands of hegemonic masculinity, incorporated into the demands of organizational performance (Wajcman 1998). . . .

## Class Relations as Active Organizational Practices

Feminist scholars recognized at least fifteen years ago that to understand gender it was necessary to study the concrete activities of women and men, activities through which differences are created and inequalities maintained. . . . Of course, there is a long tradition of the view of class as concrete processes and historically identifiable actions of actually existing people (e.g., Thompson 1963). Contributions to this perspective from an organizational point of view were made by the many labor process studies that followed the publication of Harry Braverman's *Labor and Monopoly Capital* (1974). Since that time, there have been numerous studies of gender relations in work and organizational processes, and many of these can also be read as studies of class. . . . Studies of wage systems (Acker 1989; Steinberg 1992) carried out as part of the pay equity movement in the United States provide examples of widespread, textually mediated managerial practices that replicate class inequalities as well as gender and race inequalities.

Class relations are embedded in regulatory practices originating outside organizational boundaries. They are written into laws, governing practices, and union-management agreements that specify, support, and sometimes limit the power of employers to control workers and the organization of production. Class-based inequalities in monetary reward and in control over resources, power, and authority, and the actions and routine practices that continually re-create them, are accepted as natural and necessary for the ongoing functioning of the socioeconomic system. In contrast, inequality and exploitation based on gender or race are not required by law, although at one time in the not too distant past this was the case in most northern industrial countries. In the United States, a civil war, a civil rights movement, and two mass women's movements extending over a century were necessary to remove these bases for discrimination from the laws of the land. Thus, at the end of the twentieth century in the United States, class exploitation and inequity have far more legitimacy than gender- and race-based exploitation and inequity, which are illegal and defined as discrimination. The legitimacy of class is, at the present time, so self-evident that no one with any political or economic power, at least in the United States, discusses eliminating wage labor and mandating a communal and cooperative organization of production, although many at least claim to be in favor of eliminating gender- and race inequality, discrimination, and segregation.

Wage labor, basic to capitalist class relations, has not always been so widely accepted. As wage work was established in the United States in the nineteenth century, it was called wage slavery, not a fitting occupation for free white men (Perrow 1991; Glenn 1999). The meaning of wage labor was transformed from slavery to the fundamental requirement for masculine self-respect in a process that differentiated free white men from women and African Americans. The identification of wage labor with masculine self-respect has weakened as more and more women have also become wage earners and female self-respect has also become tied to a wage. Thus the legitimacy of class becomes even more entrenched. . . .

Because of the legality of class and the widespread legitimacy of class inequalities, class relations may be more difficult to challenge in work organizations than gender or race relations. However, studies of attempts to reduce or eliminate gender or race inequities in organizations show rather modest results (e.g., Cockburn 1991; Reskin 1998). Gender and race are deeply embedded in organizational history and present processes that reproduce class. Attempts to eliminate gender- and race-based subordination and inequality may necessitate changes in organizational control structures and work processes, threatening existing class as well as gender and race interests. The probable result is that those threatened undermine the change effort.

### Taking the Viewpoints of Different Organizational Participants

Feminists have argued, convincingly, I believe, that to develop knowledge about different women's situations, the social world must be viewed from their diverse standpoints. The standpoints of different organizational participants, both women and men, can provide entry into ongoing class processes within organizations. For example, in a recent study of organization change in which I participated, clerical workers, all women, had a much more critical opinion about inequalities and the possibility for democratic participation in their organization than did professional workers, few of whom could see any inequalities in their workplace. Consciously attempting to take the viewpoint of the relatively more powerless members of organizations, particularly white women and people of color, can make visible the many ways in which class relations are mediated by gender and race. . . .

Taking the standpoints of women or people of color, or of any lower-level organization member, may make visible the "normal violence" of organizational life that serves as a means of control over challenges to class, gender, and racial inequalities. By normal violence I mean the implicit threats (sometimes explicit) and the intimidating behavior of people in positions of power. Temper tantrums, threats of firing or demotion, and summary dismissals are not uncommon events, but ones that may be visible primarily to the targets of attack. Often interpreted by people in the workplace as psychological and individual manifestations of imbalance or deviance, normal violence is systemic, a product of the structures of power and control.

Taking the points of view of different organizational participants may also make visible contradictions for particular individuals or groups between organizational class situations and class affiliations in the larger society. For example, university faculty from working-class backgrounds face a more problematic environment in academia than faculty from upper–middle-class backgrounds (Barker 1995). Or middle-class women may find themselves in jobs such as secretary or research assistant in which they are subservient to men of similar class backgrounds. This was probably more common in the past when women were actively excluded from anything but peripheral, female-segregated positions, but it is still a potential. Another example of a group experiencing contradictory class situations in the United States is physicians, many of whose class situations are changing as the organization of medical care is transformed with the proliferation of managed care organizations. Their class situation as small businessmen/professionals is changing into that of professional wage workers, dramatized now by their increasing organization into labor unions approved by the professional body, the American Medical Association.

### Expanding the Notion of the "Economic"

Feminists have long contended that what counts as "economic" must be broadened to encompass the unpaid but economically valuable work done primarily by women. This implies expanding our notions of the bases for class relations by moving outside the discursive boundaries of existing class theories, which are, it can be argued, constructed from the perspective of capital as well as from the perspectives of working-class men of earlier generations. Although there have been a number of different proposals for expanding these boundaries, one way to do this is to ask, "What are the contours of class processes that become visible when taking the standpoints of unpaid women workers or other people outside ordinary, regular employment?" Taking the perspective of housewives, many single mothers, the elderly poor, the chronically ill, or the unemployed reveals that relations of distribution other than wages, salaries, and profits are essential to survival in industrial societies and thus can be seen as economic and as components of class structuring (Acker 1988). While distribution through wages, profit, interest, and rent, the components of distribution in Karl Marx's writing, are all important, distribution through marriage and other family relationships and through the welfare state are essential economic transfers, and most of these are patterned along lines of gender and race as well as class. Thus private life becomes enmeshed in the processes constructing the gender and race contours of class.

From the perspective of those who are economically disadvantaged, class situations may not be adequately described by the concepts of relations of production/employment and distribution. They may put together their survival, and thus their class situations, through complex maneuvering within and between different organizational locations of production and distribution. For example, single mothers on welfare in the United States may have to combine welfare payments, contributions from ex-husbands or mothers, occasional part-time work, contributions from food banks, and careful sorting through thrift shops to be able to get along. Families may piece together various unsteady low-wage jobs or work in the informal economy with transfer payments, backyard gardens (if they have backyards), and a little hunting (if they live in small towns). Coping strategies on the fringes of the stable wage and transfer economies are highly variable, but are the reality for some people in Western industrial countries and for many more in Third World economies. Any expanded definition of the economy must include these activities if our understanding of class is to be comprehensive enough to be useful.

Private organizations in the United States are major players in political battles over distribution, including income support programs, pension provisions, and the funding of medical care. In the present period in the United States, corporations also influence political decisions that channel government money into corporate purposes, further participating in class processes on a societal basis. I wish to emphasize two points here. First, class processes are political as well as "economic," and placing strict boundaries around these concepts tends to obscure the close connections. Second, in attempting to understand class as related to gender and race within an organizational perspective, we should not lose sight of the fact that organizations are not rigidly bound entities and should not be studied as such. Political conflicts in which large corporations invest large sums of money and influence have consequences for class processes within those organizations and in the surrounding world.

Much of the preceding discussion has implicitly assumed that the changing contours of class, gender, and race are produced in particular organizations located within particular states. Instead, it may be useful to think about large organizations as spanning national boundaries and creating class relations that extend beyond the boundaries of nation-states as well as beyond the boundaries of specific organizations. For example, the movement by managers of large organizations of much of the garment and electronic production out of the western and northern countries has altered class conditions for many women workers in both the industrial north and low-wage countries in the south and in Asia, in the process changing their family and personal lives. These movements of production to new locations increasingly create a new international division of labor and rapidly changing global class processes in which gender, race, and ethnic differences are used by capital as resources for profit maximization. In the process, global inequalities increase. The development of transnational production organizations raises questions about how we should define an organization. Does a corporation such as Nike or Liz Claiborne include within its boundaries the independent Third World manufacturing company whose business is exclusively devoted to producing for Nike or Liz? Does the U.S. company have any responsibility for the terms of labor, the class/race/gender exploitation, in the factory? What are the extended class relations linking a white American worker to the Filipina who sews his shirt? How, concretely, does class, race, and gender privilege operate globally? If we now have a globally dispersed, racially and ethnically fragmented class structure, what are the possibilities for anything like class consciousness and class solidarity? These are a few of the questions raised by the present expansion of organizations. . . .

The use, outlined above, of insights from feminist work on gender for rethinking class produces a multidimensional, highly varying view of class as concretely and historically produced in organizing processes, mediated by race and gender. This view provides one solution to the problem of combining gender, race, and class, a way of beginning to see class, race, and gender as complexly related aspects of the same ongoing practical activities, rather than as relatively autonomous intersecting systems. . . .

## Conclusion

Class relations are created and re-created in the ordinary processes of organizational life. Gender and race relations are closely intertwined with class in these processes. Indeed, what looks like class from one conceptual point of view may look like gender and/or race from another point of view. It follows that to understand gender and race, we must also understand class, and vice versa. Class processes are not simply interior to the rather arbitrary boundaries conventionally set for organizations, but extend outward, shaping what we call "the class structure" of a particular country. At the same time, class processes within organizations are not peculiar to a particular location, but are formed in accordance with surrounding laws, social conventions, and markets. . . .

## References

Acker, Joan. 1980. "Women and Stratification: A Review of Recent Literature." *Contemporary Sociology* 9: 25–35.

——. 1988. "Class, Gender and the Relations of Distribution." *Signs: Journal of Women in Culture and Society* 13: 473–97.

——. 1989. *Doing Comparable Worth: Gender, Class, and Pay Equity*. Philadelphia: Temple University Press.

——. 1990. "Hierarchies, Jobs, Bodies: A Theory of Gendered Organizations." *Gender & Society* 4: 139–58.

——. 1999. "Rewriting Class, Race, and Gender: Problems in Feminist Rethinking." In *Revisioning Gender*, ed. Myra Marx Ferree, Judith Lorber, and Beth B. Hess, pp. 44–69. Thousand Oaks, CA: Sage.

Acker, Joan, and Donald Van Houten. 1999. "Regimes of Inequality: The Gender, Class, and Race Politics of Organizational Change." Unpublished manuscript, University of Oregon.

Alvesson, Mats. 1993. "Gender Relations, Masculinities and Identity at Work: A Case Study of an Advertising Agency." Working Paper, Department of Business Administration, University of Lund, Sweden.

Barker, Judith. 1995. "White Working-Class Men and Women in Academia." *Race, Gender & Class* 3: 65–77.

Barrett, Michèle, and Anne Phillips, eds. 1992. *Destabilizing Theory*. Stanford, CA: Stanford University Press.

Beechey, Veronica. 1987. *Unequal Work*. London: Verso.

Braverman, Harry. 1974. *Labor and Monopoly Capital: The Degradation of Work in the Twentieth Century*. New York: Monthly Review Press.

Cockburn, Cynthia. 1991. *In the Way of Women: Men's Resistance to Sex Equality in Organizations*. Ithaca, NY: ILR Press.

Collins, Patricia Hill. 1990. *Black Feminist Thought*. Boston: Unwin Hyman.

——. 1995. "Comment on West and Fenstermaker." *Gender & Society* 9: 491–94.

Connell, R.W. 1987. *Gender and Power: Society, the Person and Sexual Politics*. Stanford, CA: Stanford University Press.

Crenshaw, Kimberlé Williams. 1995. "Mapping the Margins: Intersectionality, Identity Politics, and Violence Against Women of Color." In *Critical Race Theory: The Key Writings That Formed the Movement*, ed. K. Crenshaw, N. Gotanda, G. Peller, and K. Thomas. New York: New Press.

Giddens, Anthony. 1973. *The Class Structure of Advanced Societies*. New York: Harper & Row.

Glenn, Evelyn Nakano. 1999. "The Social Construction and Institutionalization of Gender and Race: An Integrative Framework." In *Revisioning Gender*, ed. Myra Marx Ferree, Judith Lorber, and Beth B. Hess, pp. 3–43. Thousand Oaks, CA: Sage.

Hartsock, Nancy. 1983. *Money, Sex, and Power: Toward a Feminist Historical Materialism*. New York: Longman.

hooks, bell. 1984. *Feminist Theory: From Margin to Center*. Boston: South End Press.

Hull, Gloria T., Patricia Bell Scott, and Barbara Smith, eds. 1982. *All the Women Are White, All the Blacks Are Men, But Some of Us Are Brave: Black Women's Studies*. Old Westbury, NY: Feminist Press.

Perrow, Charles. 1991. "A Society of Organizations." *Theory and Society* 20: 725–62.

Reskin, Barbara. 1998. "The Realities of Affirmative Action in Employment." Paper presented at American Sociological Association meetings, Washington, DC.

Reskin, Barbara, and Patricia A. Roos. 1990. *Job Queues, Gender Queues*. Philadelphia: Temple University Press.

Sokoloff, Natalie J. 1980. *Between Money and Love: The Dialectics of Women's Home and Market Work*. New York: Praeger.

Steinberg, Ronnie J. 1992. "Gendered Instructions: Cultural Lag and Gender Bias in the Hay System of Job Evaluation." *Work and Occupations* 19: 387–423.

Thompson, E.P. 1963. *The Making of the English Working Class*. New York: Vintage.

Wajcman, Judy. 1998. *Managing Like a Man*. Cambridge: Polity Press.

Wright, Erik Olin. 1985. *Classes*. London: New Left Books.

---

Adapted from "Revisiting Class: Thinking from Gender, Race, and Organizations," *Social Politics* 7 (2) (Summer 2000): 192–214. Reprinted with permission of Oxford University Press.

# 3

# Feminist Economics

## From Theory to Research

*Martha MacDonald*

The feminist critique of neoclassical economic theory is by now well established (Ferber and Nelson 1993; Woolley 1993). While some feminist economists are grappling with conceptual issues, others are engaged in empirical research. They find that the standards for data collection and analysis in mainstream economics create difficulties in dealing with feminist concerns. Issues such as power relations in households and the subtle processes that create the glass ceiling in the work world are not easily investigated and measured. Just as neoclassical theory gives rise to certain methodologies and data needs, so does feminist theory. . . .

Technical problems confront feminist economists in their day-to-day research as they try to collect new kinds of data and measure previously unmeasured economic phenomena. They realize that their graduate training instilled skills for data analysis but not for data collection. Research methodology courses are not part of the typical economics graduate program. Most econometric courses emphasize the theoretical derivations and proofs for the techniques, rather than hands-on practice with secondary data analysis. The challenges of creating primary data—even survey data that might be amenable to econometric techniques are untouched.

This paper discusses the empirical challenges of developing a feminist economics. Empirical approaches are deeply embedded in the underlying assumptions and theoretical framework of a discipline. Thus, for example, economic and sociological methods differ even when the same general issue, such as labor market segmentation, is being researched. Feminist work has drawn attention to the implicit male bias of "objective" social science frameworks. This theme has been applied to neoclassical economics by many feminist economists, who show that the economy analyzed is the visible, male-dominated, public, cash economy, rather than the full range of human economic endeavor (Cohen 1982; MacDonald 1984; Robb 1991; Day 1992; Nelson 1992, 1993; Pujol 1992; Ferber and Nelson 1993; Strassmann 1993; Woolley 1993). The profoundly gendered nature of the economy is not accorded any analytical relevance, and therefore the data are not collected to support an alternative economic analysis. The data collected by statistical agencies and made available for economic analysis bear the direct imprint of the male bias of the discipline. . . .

## Empirical Concerns of Feminist Economics

The different empirical approaches needed to address feminist concerns can be illustrated by discussing three central areas of interest to feminist economics over the years. They are

1. Measurement/valuation of women's unpaid work
2. Intrahousehold issues (distribution of income and resources, labor allocation, decision-making, and power relations)
3. Gendered processes in the paid labor market

These are essential components of an analysis in which gender is a fundamental organizing principle of the economy—an economy that is not limited to the market. . . .

### Measuring/Valuing Women's Unpaid Work

To understand the whole economy, and changes in it, information is needed on subsistence production, informal paid work, domestic production, and volunteer work (Benería 1992; Day 1992). These measurement issues challenge individual researchers and are important in terms of the data collected by national statistical bureaus on gross domestic product (GDP) and labor force activity. Work by Waring (1988) and others (Folbre 1991; Anderson 1992; Aslaksen 1992) shows that gender-biased statistical conventions for the definition and measurement of economic activity and output developed as a result of systematic sexist and patriarchal decisions.

Feminists have challenged these conventions for over two decades and significant progress is now being made in accounting for women's work by national statistical agencies (Benería 1981, 1992). The International Labour Office (ILO) and International Research and Training Institute for the Advancement of Women (INSTRAW) have been instrumental in the initiative to revise national accounting to include unpaid work (Goldschmidt-Clermont 1982, 1987; Dixon-Mueller 1985; Dixon-Mueller and Anker 1988), and the momentum has increased since the Forward-Looking Strategies from the [United Nations] 1985 Nairobi conference on women endorsed the issue. . . .

While feminist economists support these efforts, they raise several concerns. For example, maintaining the integrity of the existing accounts is paramount in the eyes of most economists and statisticians involved. Unpaid work is being added on in satellite accounts, to be used for certain purposes but not for general economic analysis. Furthermore, the need to be consistent with existing accounting practices constrains discussions of how to measure and value unpaid work—the standard is still the market. No significance is accorded to the different social relations and institutional organization of nonmarket work.

Although a case is made that the best way to measure/value unpaid work is by outputs (Goldschmidt-Clermont 1993), the approach being taken by most statistical bureaus is to measure inputs, which means estimating the cost of performing the unpaid work in the market (replacement cost). This requires good time-use data and decisions about the equivalent market labor. Feminists are concerned that time-use surveys will measure only the menial tasks performed and miss the more abstract management function. They are also concerned that the market wages used to value the work will be the undervalued wages of female-dominated occupations. Should the value of child-care services be calculated using the wages of day-care workers or child psychiatrists? Feminists fear that the valuing of unpaid work will reflect the undervaluing of women's paid work.

There are also theoretical concerns about the meaning of aggregating the unpaid and paid economies. The central interest of feminists is the interaction between the two; the unpaid economy is embedded in the measured market economy, but is not an adjunct to it. There is not a simple one-to-one trade-off between the two.

Feminists are also concerned about the uses of the data. Assigning a value in the accounts does not alter the fact that the work is unpaid, and it may convey a false message of recognition. While feminist researchers will certainly be able to use these data, they can also be used to support antifeminist initiatives. There is suspicion about why measuring this unpaid output is suddenly popular. It may be part of the search for better numbers by nation states. GDP measures that used to show growth for the north as the market expanded now show stagnation, as work has shifted from the public sector to the volunteer and domestic sphere, and from the formal to the informal economy. This may be as much the cause of the interest in satellite accounts as two decades of pressure from both academics and the international women's movement (Benería 1981; Goldschmidt-Clermont 1982, 1987, 1990; Dixon-Mueller 1985; Dixon-Mueller and Anker 1988; Eisner 1988, 1989; Waring 1988). Revised GDP figures can sometimes paint a rosier picture.

Another important initiative related to measuring the aggregate economy is the attempt to develop alternative indicators of economic and social well-being. Social indicators are being more widely used, such as the United Nations Development Program (UNDP) Human Development Index (HDI), which combines indicators of national income, life expectancy, and education (UNDP 1992). The UNDP also calculates a gender-sensitive HDI for thirty-three countries. While this initiative is laudable, the index is based on the gender-biased measures of GDP and labor force activity discussed above.

Despite their shortcomings, these initiatives at the national and international level represent major gains. Continuous feminist involvement in the technical issues is necessary, however, to ensure their integrity and usefulness. . . . The goal is not counting and measuring for its own sake, but gathering information that will enable us to understand how the unpaid/informal economy functions and integrates with the cash/market. Who does unpaid work for whom? What do they get in return? What obligations do people feel to family and nonfamily members? What networks of support exist in communities? How does cash support unpaid work and vice versa? Are paid and unpaid work substitutes or complements? How elastic is the provision of unpaid work? In all cases, of course, the gender dimensions of these arrangements are of utmost concern. . . .

### Intrahousehold Issues

Feminist work also emphasizes the importance of intrahousehold processes. This is the second major empirical issue challenging feminist economists. . . . Empirical work on the household has demonstrated significant intrahousehold inequality in the distribution of income and other resources. The women and development literature has emphasized inequality in access to education, food, land, technology, and credit. There is evidence of differential mortality and health for male and female children (Blumberg 1988; Sen 1990). Studies also show that it matters who spends the income in a household (Blumberg 1988; Thomas 1990; Phipps and Burton 1992). . . .

Household decision making, division of labor, and allocation of resources are important factors in the feminist analysis of economic restructuring. In this literature the concern is not with testing economic models of the household but in seeing how the household and the rest of the economy are articulated. How do households respond to external economic pressures, such as price changes for consumer goods, provision of government services, changes in labor market alternatives? How is labor allocated and reallocated? How do the workloads, status, and well-being of family members change? The crucial questions have to do with the gendered division of labor in the home, household labor allocation (market and nonmarket), and the intrahousehold allocation of income and resources. For the most part, this task involves collecting primary data through survey or in-depth interview methods, though it is also necessary to challenge the data that are publicly collected. We need carefully designated national household surveys that are administered on a regular basis (Appleton 1991). Household data must be combined within data on other levels of the economy, preferably disaggregated by gender. . . .

The term "household" has been used uncritically in the above discussion. However, even the definition of the household is problematic conceptually and empirically. The nuclear household is still the implicit, if not explicit, norm in economics. The researcher must be on guard for how such assumptions get built into the data. For example, I conducted a household survey that systematically omitted single-parent households from the sample, and then I fell into the trap of writing about "women" in a universal sense. There is a general awareness of the problems with the concept of household head, both in theory and data collection. There are also many issues in how to define a household unit. Alternative definitions include all those people under one roof, those related, those who share resources. The conventions can be culturally or gender biased.

We must also question this emphasis on the household (however defined) as the unit of analysis. For example, if our interest is to understand nonmarket processes, then social relations much broader than the household are important. The proper unit of analysis to use should be an empirical question, not an assumption. "Intrahousehold decision making/resource allocation" is thus for now only a shorthand for our interest in the personal, gendered, nonmarket relations that are a crucial part of the economy. Unfortunately, secondary data construction norms based on neoclassical economics typically leave us with only two choices for a unit of analysis—the individual, with little information on any of the social relations in which the person is embedded, or the household, with artificial limits set on what relations of pooling, sharing, or exchange are recognized. This is an area that is particularly challenging even when one is collecting primary data.

## Gendered Processes in the Paid Labor Market

Feminist work also emphasizes the importance of gender in understanding the formal labor market. This creates the third empirical challenge to feminist economists. . . . Feminists have participated in the empirical literature on female labor force participation and gender wage differentials and have run into problems with both theory and data in trying to improve on the traditional work in these areas (Blau and Ferber 1986; Brown and Pechman 1987).

[For instance, neoclassical] human capital wage regressions have become increasingly sophisticated, but they shed little new light on inequality. The list of variables is typically very limited; occupational categories are too broad; experience is poorly measured; demand measures are inadequate; and typically there is little information on the individual's family characteristics. Furthermore, the analysis is usually not informed by a knowledge of the feminist literature. Similar data problems are encountered when one analyzes changes in the occupation and industry distribution of female employment. . . .

Secondary data available from national statistical agencies to study women in the labor market are inadequate in many ways.

- There is a preponderance of cross-sectional data and very little panel data.
- The level of aggregation makes it impossible to study issues of segmentation within occupations.
- The use of categories like "personal or family reasons" versus "economic reasons" in labor force surveys embed gender biases in the data.
- Skill measures used (SVP and GED, the specific vocational preparation and training or general formal and informal education needed to perform the job) have been shown to be gender biased (Gaskell 1986; Boyd 1990).
- It is difficult to measure changes in the quality of jobs.

Considering these difficulties, many feminist economists have turned to primary data collection to understand further issues of skill, technological change, occupational segregation, nonstandard work, internal labor markets, and the gendered institutional processes that help explain the differential returns to characteristics identified in wage equations. While specialized survey data can address some of these issues, using either household or employee samples, case study methodology is also useful in the analysis of the labor process within firms. These case studies usually combine qualitative and quantitative data. Only rarely do the data lend themselves to sophisticated econometric techniques. Usually they involve key informant interviews with managers, union representatives, and workers, as well as observation of day-to-day process in the firms and access to company records, if possible.

These case studies lie outside the traditional methodology of neoclassical economics and are criticized for being nonrepresentative and subjective. Certainly one has to guard against making unwarranted generalizations from such studies. . . . Poorly conducted case studies do not further feminist interests and will never achieve respectability in economics. Until case study methodology is recognized within economics, however, it will fail to develop sophistication. This is a vicious circle for feminist economists and other labor economists interested in the labor process and institutional issues. One approach to these dilemmas with both secondary and primary data is to use a mixture of methods, including secondary data analysis, employee surveys, and in-depth interviews with employers and employees.

Additional challenges are faced when one tries to focus on the household, not simply the individual worker, in studying gendered processes in the labor market. Secondary data sets usually do not have equal detail on the activities or incomes of all household members. Lengthy, expensive questionnaires are needed to address these issues in primary surveys, and the choice of respondent is problematic. In-depth interviews are useful for getting proper detail, but they then limit one to qualitative analysis. Despite these problems, a household focus is essential in understanding issues like the gender effects of changes in location of economic activity. What kind of migration is required? Are women able to take advantage of new opportunities? How do families respond to these changes? How are patterns of remittances among extended family members affected? These and other questions facilitate an understanding of a labor market made up of male and female household members, not lone individuals.

## Conclusion

This paper has summarized the central empirical concerns of feminist economics. Feminist economics necessarily challenges the data and methods of economics. Data collected by national statistical agencies directly reflect the gender biases of neoclassical theory. National income and product or GDP accounts measure market production; household income and expenditure surveys do not collect information on intrahousehold access to resources; labor force surveys reflect a nation of the "typical"—that is, male—worker: the lone individual. Feminists are challenged to work creatively with these data to tease out a gender analysis. They are also working to force changes in the data collected, for example, through revised GDP accounts and household panel data with more information on intrahousehold differences in resource access and work load.

Primary data collection is also an important component of feminist economics research. While specialized surveys may lend themselves to standard econometric techniques, other more qualitative methods necessarily place the researcher outside the economic mainstream. There are many challenges in perfecting alternative methodologies and constructing new data. This kind of empirical economics is not easier, contrary to popular belief in the profession.

Clearly, both economic theory and methodology have to change if they are to serve feminist purposes, and the changes are interactive. We should not put new wine in old bottles. As economic theory becomes broadened by feminist insights, so too will economic methodology be enhanced. Just as econometrics developed in response to the needs of modern economics, so too will new methodologies and refinements of the old gradually emerge as feminist economists turn more and more from conceptual to technical issues.

## References

Anderson, M. 1992. "The History of Women and the History of Statistics." *Journal of Women's History* 4 (1): 14–36.

Appleton, S. 1991. "Gender Dimensions of Structural Adjustment: The Role of Economic Theory and Quantitative Analysis." *IDS Bulletin* 22: 17–22.

Aslaksen, I. 1992. "National Accounting and Unpaid Household Work: A Feminist View on the Concept of Value in Economics." Paper presented at the Conference on Feminist Economics, American University, Washington, DC.

Benería, L. 1981. "Conceptualizing the Labour Force: The Underestimation of Women's Economic Activities." *Journal of Development Studies* 17: 11–28.

———. 1992. "Accounting for Women's Work: The Progress of Two Decades." *World Development* 20: 1547–60.

Blau, F.D., and M.A. Ferber. 1986. *The Economics of Women, Men and Work.* Englewood Cliffs, NJ: Prentice Hall.

Blumberg, R. 1988. "Income Under Female Versus Male Control." *Journal of Family Issues* 9: 51–84.

Boyd, M. 1990. "Sex Differences in Occupational Skill: Canada, 1961–1986." *Canadian Review of Sociology and Anthropology* 27: 285–315.

Brown, C., and J. Pechman. 1987. *Gender in the Workplace.* Washington, DC: Brookings Institution.

Cohen, M. 1982. "The Problem of Studying Economic 'Man.'" In *Feminism in Canada: From Pressure to Politics,* ed. A. Miles and G. Finn. Montreal: Black Rose Books.

Day, T. 1992. "Women's Economic Product: Unmeasured Contributions to Measured Output, Or the Perils of Woman-Blindness." Paper presented at the Canadian Economics Association meetings, Charlottetown, Price Edward Island.

Dixon-Mueller, R. 1985. *Women's Work in Third World Agriculture.* Women, Work and Development 9. Geneva: International Labour Office.

Dixon-Mueller, and R. Anker. 1988. *Assessing Women's Economic Contributions to Development:* Training in Population, Human Resources and Development Planning. Geneva: International Labour Office.

Eisner, R. 1988. "Extended Accounts for National Income and Product." *Journal of Economic Literature* 26: 1611–85.

———. 1989. *The Total Incomes System of Accounts.* Chicago: University of Chicago Press.

Ferber, M.A., and J.A. Nelson, eds. 1993. *Beyond Economic Man: Feminist Theory and Economics.* Chicago: University of Chicago Press.

Folbre, N. 1991. "The Unproductive Housewife: Her Evaluation in Nineteenth Century Economic Thought." *Signs: Journal of Women in Culture and Society* 16: 436–84.

Gaskell, J. 1986. "Conceptions of Skill and the Work of Women: Some Historical and Political Issues." In *The Politics of Diversity,* ed. R. Hamilton and M. Barrett. Montreal: Book Centre.

Goldschmidt-Clermont, L. 1982. *Unpaid Work in the Household: A Review of Economic Evaluation Methods.* Geneva: International Labour Office.

———. 1987. *Economic Evaluations of Unpaid Household Work: Africa, Asia, Latin America and Oceania.* Geneva: International Labour Office.

———. 1990. "Economic Measurement of Non-Market Household Activities: Is It Useful and Feasible?" *International Labour Review* 129: 279–99.

———. 1993. "Monetary Valuation of Unpaid Work." Paper presented at the Statistics Canada International Conference on the Measurement and Valuation of Unpaid Work, Ottawa.

MacDonald, M. 1984. "Economics and Feminism: The Dismal Science." *Studies in Political Economy* 15: 151–78.

Nelson, J. 1992. "Gender, Metaphor and the Definition of Economics." *Economics and Philosophy* 8: 103–25.

———. 1993. "Value Free or Valueless? Notes on the Pursuit of Detachment in Economics." *History of Political Economy* 25: 121–45.

Phipps, S., and P. Burton. 1992. "What's Mine Is Yours? The Influence of Male and Female Incomes on Patterns of Expenditure." Working Paper No. 92–12, Economics Department, Dalhousie University.

Pujol, M. 1992. *Feminism and Anti-Feminism in Early Economic Thought.* Aldershot, UK: Edward Elgar.

Robb, R.E. 1991. "Gender and Economics: Some Issues." Paper presented at the Canadian Economics Association meetings, Kingston, Ontario.

Sen, A. 1990. "Gender and Cooperative Conflicts." In *Persistent Inequalities,* ed. I. Tinker. New York: Oxford University Press.

Strassmann, D. 1993. "Not a Free Market: The Rhetoric of Disciplinary Authority in Economics." In *Beyond Economic Man: Feminist Theory and Economics,* ed. M.A. Ferber and J.A. Nelson. Chicago: University of Chicago Press.

Thomas, D. 1990. "Intra-Household Resource Allocation: An Inferential Approach." *Journal of Human Resources* 25: 635–64.

United Nations Development Program. 1992. *Human Development Report.* New York: United Nations.

Waring, M. 1988. *If Women Counted*. San Francisco: Harper Collins.

Wilson, G. 1991. "Thoughts on the Cooperative Conflict Model of the Household in Relation to Economic Method." *IDS Bulletin* 22: 31–6.

Woolley, F. 1993. "The Feminist Challenge to Neoclassical Economics." *Cambridge Journal of Economics* 17: 485–500.

---

Adapted from "Feminist Economics: From Theory to Research," *Canadian Journal of Economics* 28 (1) (February 1995): 159–175. Reprinted with permission of the *Canadian Journal of Economics*.

# Section 1

# Appendix

**Key Terms**

capitalism
class
dichotomies (or dualism)
essentialism
feminist economics
gender
race-ethnicity
rationality
utility, and interpersonal utility comparisons

**Discussion Questions**

1. What are some major questions and issues that would be addressed by studying the economy from a feminist perspective? How do these differ from more traditional perspectives?
2. If students and scholars are concerned about the economic status of women, how would attention to class and race-ethnicity add strength to their analyses? Give one or two examples on specific topics.
3. How does a feminist analysis expand the notion of what counts as "economic" or "economic activity"?
4. What are some empirical concerns for those interested in a feminist approach to the economy?

**Exercise**

1. Here is an essay that you can write at any point during the academic term. The nature of the assignment will change slightly—specifically, whether you integrate readings and which readings are incorporated—depending on when in the academic term you embark upon the project. In a narrative essay, describe your "foremothers'" own work experience and family history, as well as your own plans for labor market participation. Compare and contrast your experiences and plans for the future with (a) those of your mother or an equiva-

lent female role model, and (b) one or two grandmothers or an older family member. (For men in the class, also include a short discussion of male forefathers or the equivalent.) In your essay, consider the social, cultural, political, and economic factors affecting this personal history, including marital status, race-ethnicity, income or class background, geographic location, the health of the overall economy at the time(s), the number and age of children in the home, and gender role expectations appropriate to the period.

## Further Reading

Barker, Drucilla K. 1995. "Economists, Social Reformers, and Prophets: A Feminist Critique of Economic Efficiency." *Feminist Economics* 1 (3): 26–39.

DeVault, Marjorie L. 1999. *Liberating Method: Feminism and Social Research*. Philadelphia: Temple University Press.

Ferber, Marianne A., and Julie A. Nelson, eds. 1993. *Beyond Economic Man: Feminist Theory and Economics*. Chicago: University of Chicago Press.

Hewitson, Gillian J. 1999. *Feminist Economics: Interrogating the Masculinity of Rational Economic Man*. Cheltenham, UK: Edward Elgar.

Nelson, Julie A. 1996. *Feminism, Objectivity and Economics*. New York: Routledge.

Peterson, Janice, and Doug Brown, eds. 1994. *The Economic Status of Women Under Capitalism*. Aldershot, UK: Edward Elgar.

# Section 2

# The Rise and Fall of
# Separate Spheres

In order to understand the position of women in the economy today, we need to be aware of the past. The attitudes of today's employers, political leaders, and policy makers have been shaped by the world of their parents and their childhood. Today's laws, employment policies and practices, and social institutions were often developed to respond to the perceived problems and issues of the time in which they were written. For this reason, institutional economists view the process of historical change as slower than many textbook economic models would indicate. Since social norms, institutions, customs, and habits of thought are rather rigid and slow to change, it is unlikely that the organization of economic life will necessarily be rational or efficient. And yet change does occur. The opportunities and constraints that women face today are quite different from those faced by their mothers, grandmothers, and great-grandmothers.

The five chapters in this section were chosen to provide snapshots of the world of your foremothers. In particular, they focus on how women's lives have changed along with major economic transformations such as industrialization and the development of a service-based economy. They demonstrate that the organization of the economy that we often think of as "traditional"—that is, the separation of paid employment from household labor—was a by-product of the process of industrialization. Production moved out of the household with the transition from agriculture and small artisan production to factory-based manufacturing. This new world of production became identified as a male sphere, while women's place was defined as the home. Yet, as Deborah Figart, Ellen Mutari, and Marilyn Power discuss in "Breadwinners and Other Workers," the ideal of separate spheres—a male breadwinner and female homemaker—always had many exceptions and became less and less representative of family structure over the course of the twentieth century. The authors define several of the economic indicators used to describe women's and men's economic status, including *labor force distribution*, *labor force participation*, *occupational segregation*, and the gender-based *wage gap*.

The construction of separate spheres during industrialization is analyzed comparatively (across countries) by William Rau and Robert Wazienski. Their chapter on "Industrialization, Female Labor Force Participation, and the Modern Division of Labor by Sex" introduces three alternative hypotheses about the impact of industrialization on women. They test two of the hypotheses using cross-sectional data from 1960 and 1970. Their findings support the argument that women's employment diminishes in the early phases of industrialization and increases with the growth of the *post-industrial* service sector. In the following chapter, economic historian Wayne Lewchuk probes behind the quantitative evidence with a case study of employment at Ford Motor Company from 1903 to 1930. "Men and Monotony" vividly demonstrates how life in mass production manufacturing came to be considered a man's world. This case study is particularly important because the automobile industry became the linchpin of U.S. economic growth during the postwar period.

The final two chapters in Section 2 scrutinize the period when women's labor force participation and attachment dramatically increased. In "Exploring the 'Present Through the Past,'" Claudia Goldin studies a specific subset of U.S. women: college graduates. She tracks several cohorts of educated women, identifying different life patterns during changing historical circumstances. Barriers to combining good jobs and a fulfilling family life have diminished, but still shape the opportunities available to educated women. Philip Cohen and Suzanne Bianchi also focus on a subset of women, married women. Their chapter, "Marriage, Children, and Women's Employment," argues that we must go beyond simple labor force participation to examine hours of work. The extent of married women's hours has important implications for attitudes toward single women from various class and racial-ethnic backgrounds. Like Goldin, they focus on the constraints women face in blurring the boundaries between the separate spheres.

# 4

# Breadwinners and Other Workers

## Gender and Race-Ethnicity in the Evolution of the Labor Force

*Deborah M. Figart, Ellen Mutari,
and Marilyn Power*

Many of us take for granted that most people, male or female, will hold down jobs for much of their lives. Waged work is so much a normal part of our lives that we forget that it was once a controversial activity. During the early days of U.S. nationhood, the Jeffersonian ideal was a relatively self-sufficient farmer who owned land, worked his farm with his family, and produced most necessities at home. In pursuit of this ideal, the territory of the United States was expanded westward, repeatedly displacing the Native American inhabitants, to carve out farms for European American settlers. Given access to land, who would choose to submit themselves to an employer or risk unemployment due to changed fortunes or mere whim? Wage labor was scarce. In its place was slavery or indentured servitude. In the South, those who could afford not to do their own labor often kept slaves. People who could not pay the fare to come to the United States, debtors, and some criminals were sold as indentured servants to work until their monetary or social debts were repaid, a temporary form of bondage. In the urban areas of the North, independent artisans (for example, silversmiths, cobblers, and blacksmiths) took on apprentices and journeymen who lived with the family until they could set up their own business.

Industrialization, beginning around the 1820s, led employers to search out new sources of labor, in particular people who would work for wages. Some of the pioneers in waged work were young, white, single daughters of farm families. Sons were used in the fields or were migrating west, mothers ran the household, and fathers certainly would not submit to the indignity of employment. But time could be allocated in girls' lives between their training in household crafts and their future as farm wives for the earning of money to raise their families' standards of living, pay off farm debts, or build dowries. In some of the first factories, girls spun thread, just as they had done at home. Young women were also sent to work as domestic servants in the homes of wealthier families.

However, as the availability of land declined while industrialization expanded over the course of the nineteenth century, the nature and meaning of waged work began to change. "Heavy" industries developed, including railroads, iron and steel, and oil refining. Paid employment became defined as a man's world and, more specifically, as a white man's world. New definitions of whiteness and of masculinity went hand in hand with the growth of men's work. The expansion of capitalism coincided with the creation of a working-class masculinity based on "wage-earning capacity, skill and endurance in labor, domestic patriarchy, and combative solidarity among wage earners" (Connell 1993, p. 611). This was a "hegemonic" form of masculinity—that is, it was the cultural ideal of the moment, even though not every male was a married, heterosexual breadwinner. Correspondingly, a "cult of domesticity" (or "cult of true womanhood") originating in the early to mid-nineteenth century insisted that women's virtue was found in submissiveness, purity, piety, and a unilateral focus on home and family.

Under this male breadwinner ideal, a young girl from a family of modest means might spend a few years contributing to her family's income before she got married. The jobs that she could respectably hold were few. Once married, the cult of domesticity dictated that she should concentrate on the private sphere of home and family. This cultural mandate was enforced by marriage bars, which were employer policies to fire women once they married—unless, that is, they were the daughters of immigrants, immigrants themselves, or African Americans and other women of color. Public opinion countenanced the employment of married working-class immigrant women and women of color, as well as a few middle-class women that historian Lynn Weiner refers to as "women of rare talents" (1985, p. 104).

The dominant (or hegemonic) model of gender relations—based on a male breadwinner and a female, full-time homemaker—never became the norm for African American women. In a major study of black women's experiences since slavery, Jacqueline Jones (1986) establishes that African American women typically began self-sustaining work around age fifteen, stayed in the labor force when married and raising children, and worked through middle age. The necessity of paid labor by married African American women reflected, in part, the constraints imposed by racism against black men. For the first hundred years after slavery, relatively few African American men earned wages sufficient to support a family, a so-called *breadwinner wage* or *family wage* (Jones 1986; Amott and Matthaei 1996). In addition, employers, including the white women who hired black women as domestics, viewed African American women as workers first, to the detriment of their family life. Thus, black women were, by their circumstances, defined as "less than a moral, 'true' woman" (Giddings 1984, p. 47).

This definition was not passively accepted. There is evidence that African American women, both working-class and middle-class, forged an alternative set of gender norms. Two studies of the history of black women since the nineteenth century—one focusing primarily on working-class women (Jones 1986) and one focusing on middle-class women (Landry 2000)—agree that African American women defined their lives in terms of interrelated commitments to family, community, and paid employment. According to Landry, "just as a particular ideology of white womanhood influenced white wives' employment decisions, so too a particular ideology of black womanhood, developed within the black community, shaped black wives' orientation to paid work" (2000, pp. 30–31). Rather than embracing the male breadwinner model, African American women posited a "co-breadwinner" model.

## Labor Force Participation: The Twentieth Century's Gradual Revolution

Compared with a century ago, today, women of all racial-ethnic groups are more likely to be employed and spend many more years of their lives working for wages. Women's increased wage labor has been a gradual, but pivotal revolution. The first indicator typically used to demonstrate this trend is *labor force composition*, or the percent of the total paid labor force in the United States that is made up of women.[1] Imagine the total labor force as a pie. The total pie is divided into two parts, the portion of the labor force that is male and the portion that is female. Table 4.1 depicts the changing labor force composition. At the beginning of the twentieth century, 81.7 percent of the total labor force was men and only 18.3 percent was women. In other words, eight out of ten labor force members in 1900 were men. Change in these proportions was slow until the 1940s. Thus, paid work was largely a male domain, with pockets of employment for women.

The composition of the labor force began to change during World War II, with women representing a steadily growing proportion of the labor force. To fill the growing need for wartime workers, women, as new labor force entrants or as crossovers from female-dominated jobs, replaced the men who had entered the military. These women, typified as "Rosie the Riveter," gained

Table 4.1

**Labor Force Composition, 1900–2000** (in percent)

| Year | Female | Male | Year | Female | Male |
|------|--------|------|------|--------|------|
| 1900 | 18.3 | 81.7 | 1960 | 32.1 | 67.9 |
| 1910 | 21.2 | 78.8 | 1970 | 37.2 | 62.8 |
| 1920 | 20.5 | 79.5 | 1980 | 42.6 | 57.4 |
| 1930 | 22.0 | 78.0 | 1990 | 45.2 | 54.8 |
| 1940 | 24.3 | 75.7 | 2000 | 46.6 | 53.4 |
| 1950 | 27.8 | 72.2 | — | — | — |

*Notes:* The labor force equals employed plus unemployed. The years 1980–2000 are the civilian labor force, otherwise total labor force.

valuable experience and access to better wages in the wartime factories and defense plants, and many sought to remain in the labor force following the war. At mid-century women were 27.8 percent of the labor force; by the end of the century, women were 46.6 percent of the labor force. The labor force today has almost as many women as men. The doubling of women's share since 1940 is referred to as a process of "feminization" of the labor force.

The other statistic that expresses the growing involvement of women in the workforce is the *labor force participation rate*. For the labor force participation rate, the pie or denominator is all women (or all men) rather than the total labor force. The labor force participation rate is the number of women (or men) in the labor force divided by the number of women (or men) in the population who are over the age of sixteen, that is, "eligible" for work. This ratio is expressed as a percent. (Sometimes the total population, including the armed forces and people in prisons and other institutions, is the denominator; more commonly today, the civilian, noninstitutional population is used.)

In 1900, only 18.8 percent of all women were in the labor force compared with 80.0 percent of men. Since then, men's and women's rates have moved in different directions. As we can see from Figure 4.1, women's labor force participation rate rose steadily while the labor force participation rate of men gradually fell. The increases in women's labor force participation rate accelerated in the second half of the twentieth century, especially in the 1960s and 1970s. In 2000, the rate stood at 60.2 percent. This means that six out of ten women over the age of sixteen were employed or were actively seeking work. In contrast, men's labor force participation rate peaked at 81.3 percent in 1910 and gradually declined, reaching 74.7 percent in 2000. Men in their

Figure 4.1 **Total Labor Force Participation by Gender, 1900–2000**

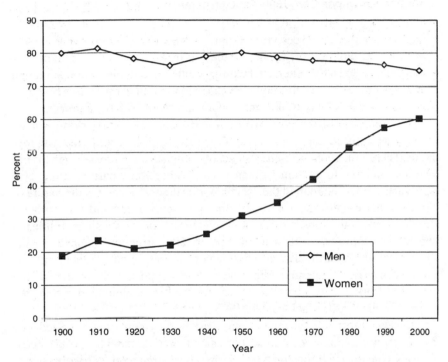

prime earning years remained at work. Younger men pursued higher education while older men retired earlier, pulling down the overall rate.

Some secondary research culled from decennial U.S. census data provides a telling story about the role of race-ethnicity and class. According to historian Julia Kirk Blackwelder, at the turn of the last century, the labor force participation rates for women whose parents immigrated to the United States and those who had immigrated themselves were higher than the rate for white women of native parentage (1997, pp. 14–15). The labor force participation rate of single white women in 1900 was only 21.5 percent in contrast with 34.3 percent for those whose parents were born overseas and 60.9 percent for those who were themselves foreign-born. Additionally, African American women consistently had higher labor force participation rates than white native-born women across all marital groups. For example, divorced black women had a labor force participation rate of 82.2 percent in 1900 compared with 26.0 percent of married and 47.4 percent of single black women. Bart Landry (2000) notes that in some urban labor markets, the percentage of married black women working for pay was as high as 65.0 percent. High rates of immigration and the migration of southern blacks to northern cities brought new sources of waged labor to urban industries.

The movement of new groups of women into the paid labor force has been called a "subtle revolution" (Smith 1979, p. 2) and a "quiet revolution" (Blackwelder 1997, p. 3) because it is not traceable to any abrupt event. In fact, there were multiple factors leading to the rise in women's labor force participation, and these factors interacted with each other in complex ways. Although some economists reduce this complex causation to a linear narrative based on changes in either supply or demand, we favor a more eclectic approach.

The expansion of the post–World War II economy clearly drew women into the labor force, especially in rapidly growing clerical and sales employment. Therefore, some economists and sociologists have looked to the types of jobs available to explain women's rising labor force participation. This approach, sometimes called the "suitable jobs theory," says it is the nature of the jobs that employers want to fill that generates a demand for women's employment. If the jobs involve tasks related to women's responsibilities in the home, employers hire women. Specifically, structural changes in the economy led to both increased employment in traditionally female professions such as teaching and nursing and also new opportunities in clerical and technical work where shortages of qualified workers enabled women to gain entry (Goldin 1990; Blackwelder 1997).

However, women's movement into paid employment cannot be reduced to a primary explanatory variable such as increased demand in specific occupations. One reason is that the types of jobs considered women's work change over time (see Reskin and Roos 1990). When an occupation is expanding or labor markets are tight, employers are forced to take "less desirable" groups of workers. Often, they redefine the necessary qualifications and characteristics of the job to explain or rationalize the presence of this new group. The growth of occupations traditionally designated for women is therefore only a secondary factor in the growth of women's employment.

The steady commodification of more and more of the production that once occurred in the home is also key to the story. People work in order to meet certain monetary needs that are socially defined and tend to escalate in capitalist economies. This was especially true during the postwar period (1945–1973), when U.S. economic growth was predicated upon rising domestic consumption linked to gains in productivity. A culture of consumerism influenced the social context in which economic decisions were made. As the standard of living considered normal and desirable for working- and middle-class families increased and included more purchased commodities, additional income from family members was needed.

Some scholars, such as Barbara Bergmann (1986), maintain that women were available for paid employment because the arduous household production performed by their mothers and/or their mothers' servants was being replaced by purchased commodities. Household appliances and other labor-saving devices in the home made cooking, washing, cleaning, and shopping easier. This argument assumes a fixed amount of housework that can be reduced through technological innovation. Far from being fixed, however, social standards regarding housework are quite fluid. In addition, the increase in household purchases itself raised the amount of time spent on household maintenance and record-keeping. Therefore, it is not clear that the total volume of housework has diminished over time, although the nature of the work has changed.

Finally, transformations in social attitudes and gender culture are crucial, especially in prompting the growing proportion of white, married mothers in the workforce in the second half of the twentieth century. Declining birth rates, wrought in part by the availability of birth control, and rising divorce rates had tremendous implications for women's expectations regarding marriage and motherhood. The impact of the women's movement should not be underestimated. Gender ideology changed profoundly in concert with women's labor force participation. The idealization of the male breadwinner family lost its dominance, although it did not completely fade away.

## Marriage, Children, and Women's Work

Differences in the trends in labor force participation rates by marital status are indicative of shifting gender norms. In 1900, the labor force participation rate of single women (43.5 percent) was more than double the rate for all women (20.6 percent). This was the era of the "working girl," who contributed to her family's earnings while preparing for her future role as wife and mother. Even in 1940, on the eve of World War II, the participation rate of single women was 45.5 percent compared with 13.8 percent for married women with a husband present. However, the era of the working girl would evolve into a world where working mothers became a cultural norm. A sweeping change in married women's work behavior took place following World War II. The civilian labor force participation rate of married women rose considerably, from 13.8 percent in 1930 to 61.2 percent in 1999.

African American women have always had higher labor force participation rates than white women. But, as shown in Figure 4.2, the gap was wider in the first part of the century. The labor force participation rates of black and white married women began to converge after the Great Depression of the 1930s and narrowed significantly in the 1940s. This convergence was primarily due to white women's increased labor force attachment—that is, more

Figure 4.2  **Labor Force Participation Rates of Married Women, Husband Present, by Race**

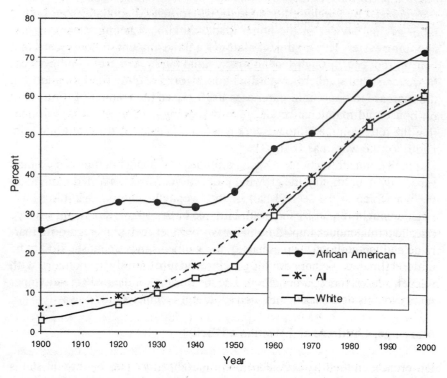

continuous participation over the life cycle. While the rate for African American women more than doubled in the twentieth century, the labor force participation rate for white women increased more than ten times, from 6 percent to 62 percent. Since 1970, white and black women's labor force participation rates have increased at roughly the same pace.

The decade of the 1950s exposes a particularly important finding. It is often assumed or perceived as common knowledge that married women left the labor force after World War II to make room for returning veterans. The 1950s is sometimes termed the decade of the "nuclear family." However, Figure 4.2 reveals a steep increase in the labor force participation rate for married women; in fact, the rates of increase (or slopes) for white and for black married women were steeper in the 1950s than in any other decade. Although women lost well-paid jobs in war industries, they fought to stay in the labor market, even if this meant lower-paid women's work.

In the early decades of the century, as we have seen, white women's relationship to the labor force largely depended on whether or not they were married. By mid-century, the ages of a woman's children was pivotal. Women with

Table 4.2

**Labor Force Participation Rates of Married Women, Husband Present, by Presence and Age of Children** (in percent)

| Year | No children < 18 years | Children 6–17 years | Children < 6 years |
|------|------------------------|---------------------|--------------------|
| 1950 | 30.3 | 28.3 | 11.9 |
| 1955 | 32.7 | 34.7 | 16.2 |
| 1960 | 34.7 | 39.0 | 18.6 |
| 1965 | 38.3 | 42.7 | 23.3 |
| 1970 | 42.2 | 49.2 | 30.3 |
| 1980 | 46.0 | 61.7 | 45.1 |
| 1985 | 48.2 | 67.6 | 53.4 |
| 1999 | 54.4 | 77.1 | 61.8 |

young children were less likely to work in paid employment than women with school-age children. As noted by historian William Chafe (1991), caring for children full time during the preschool years was now seen as fulfilling women's responsibilities as mothers even if they returned to the labor force once their children began kindergarten. Employment, especially part-time employment that did not conflict with after-school care, was now deemed socially acceptable.

The gap between women with preschool children and women with older children narrowed beginning in the 1970s. This trend is exhibited in Table 4.2. The labor force participation of women with children aged six to seventeen years increased from 28.3 percent in 1950 to 77.1 percent in 1999, a relative increase of 172 percent. There was an even greater surge of labor force participation of married women with young children under the age of six. From 1950 through 1999, there was a more than fivefold increase (11.9 percent to 61.8 percent). The age of the working mother had arrived.

The data in the early decades in Table 4.2 reflect what economists have called an intermittent labor force participation. Working women once had a bimodal distribution over their work lives, shaped like a letter M, as in Figure 4.3. That is, young women began to work from age sixteen through nineteen, then tended to drop out during the childbearing years of twenty to thirty-four, then returned to work when their children were grown or in school. Three clusters of women by age in the postwar United States illustrate this M-shaped distribution—women in 1950, 1960, and 1970. By 1980, women had a more continuous labor force participation rate until near retirement; in 1990, the distribution took on the shape of men's labor force behavior over the life cycle. More and more women with children sought to balance work and family, boosting their labor force attachment.

The increase in women's labor force participation and attachment has in-

Figure 4.3  **Women's Labor Force Participation Rates by Age, 1950–1990**

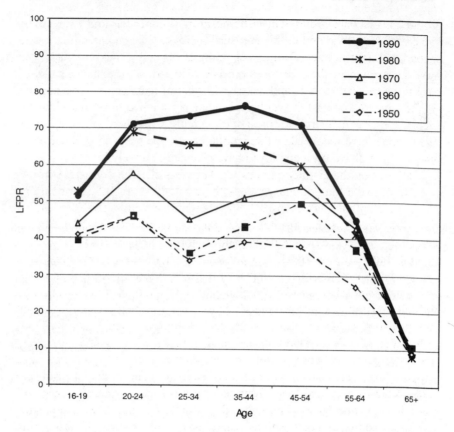

deed been a social revolution, perhaps subtle, perhaps not. This revolution has redefined what it means to be a worker, a breadwinner, and even a wife and mother. Yet the sexual division of labor within the home remained intact. As feminist economists Teresa Amott and Julie Matthaei have argued, "Although the relationship between productive and reproductive labor was changing in this way, the sexual division of labor between the two did not change—if anything, it became more extreme" (1996, p. 297). Acknowledging that women still do the majority of the unpaid housework and child care, we focus our attention on their jobs in the labor market.

## The Ongoing Problem of Occupational Segregation

Technological and industrial change have played a role in the kinds of jobs available to both men and women over the last century. The shift from an agriculturally based economy to manufacturing and then to the service sector can also be seen as the extension of the market into more and more forms of production that once occurred in the home. From goods to services, from clothes and cars to fast food and child care, such increased commodification has re-shaped the labor market. Further, beginning at the end of the nineteenth century, the growth in the size of enterprises also led to an expanded clerical workforce to keep records and increased layers of management and supervision to maintain control. Nevertheless, women remained in a small subset of occupations and industries for most of the century. Compared with the impressive change in women's labor force participation, the kinds of occupations in which women have been employed have changed relatively little.

We focus on the distinction between African American and white women since these were the dominant racial-ethnic categories in U.S. national data during much of this period. In 1910, for example, nine out of ten black women were employed in either farming (52.0 percent) or private household service (38.5 percent). These two fields were the major occupations for white women as well, but only employed 29.3 percent of white women workers. White women had more occupations open to them, working in clerical and sales positions as well as low-paid blue-collar operator and laborer positions. Clerical and sales positions required more education, and an expensive wardrobe, and they provided a cleaner work environment. Therefore, such jobs were financially inaccessible to poorer women and reinforced a class distinction between "respectable" women's jobs and lower-status occupations. Even when African American women had access to education and financial resources, cultural biases excluded them from occupations involving face-to-face contact with customers and clients. In other words, African American women were screened out of occupations where they were "visible" in serving the public or working in proximity to a white male boss (Jones 1986; Chafe 1991). A small group of white women found employment in professional and technical fields, but this was less than 12 percent. Women managers, white or black, were rare. Women who worked did so largely from necessity and for the most part toiled in relatively low-status and low-paid occupations.

By 1940, technological improvements in agricultural production meant that labor requirements were reduced. The use of servants and other private household workers also declined as electric appliances made housework less physically demanding and as former domestics found increased access to other, "better" jobs. For white women, their share in private household employment began falling in the 1940s; for black women, it was a decade later. Black women began to shift out of private household work and into clerical, sales, and service work in the 1950s, but even more rapidly in the 1960s and 1970s. White women also moved into these same job categories at a swift pace with the growth of bureaucracies and paperwork in the 1940s and 1950s. By the end of the twentieth century, the single largest broad occupational category employing both black and white women was clerical and sales work. The second most predominant job category for black women was service work, while white women moved into professional and technical work.

Neither black nor white women have been able to break down the entry barriers into skilled blue-collar craft occupations. No more than 2 percent of all working women, white and black, were employed as craft workers throughout most of the twentieth century. When women did obtain jobs in manufacturing, they were relegated to lower-paid and less unionized operator and laborer positions. These jobs typically involved repetitive assembly in textiles, apparel, food processing, and small electrical appliances. With the flight of manufacturing jobs overseas in the 1970s, even these inroads were undermined as women machine operators lost their jobs along with other factory workers.

A job is generally considered to be feminized or "female dominated" if 70 percent of the incumbents are female and "male dominated" if less than 30 percent of the incumbents are female. This is demonstrated by looking at the percentage of workers in an occupation who are women. While *occupational distribution* indicates the influence of sectoral change on the types of jobs women hold, *percent female* in an occupation evaluates women's parity with men. Clerical work is a dramatic example of work that was resegregated, or "feminized," in the twentieth century. Clerical workers were 24.2 percent female (male dominated) in 1900 and 73.6 percent female (female dominated) by 1970. More than nine out of ten private household service jobs were and still are held by women, with imperceptible changes over time. In contrast, skilled blue-collar craft work remains the preserve of men, primarily white men. Even less skilled blue-collar occupations, operators and laborers, remain male dominated.

What we consider to be typically female professions—for example, teaching, nursing, social work, and librarianship—were also feminized early in the twentieth century. As white-collar work grew over the course of the century, women made more inroads into professional and managerial jobs. Over time, the broad category of professional and technical workers has been relatively gender integrated (neither male dominated nor female dominated), although the kinds of professional and technical jobs held by women and men are quite different. In the 1970s, women, especially white women, entered professional fields that were formerly male bastions, including law and medicine. This occurred, however, as some of the autonomy in these professions began to diminish. Large law firms, medical and legal clinics, and health maintenance organizations pushed out the sole practitioners. Independent

Figure 4.4 **Gender-Based Wage Ratio and Wage Gap** (median annual earnings of full-time workers in current dollars)

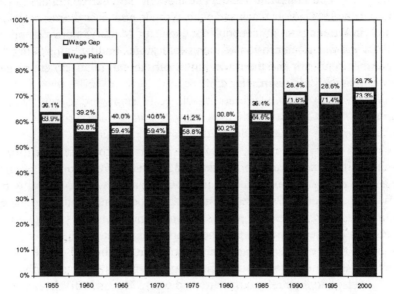

pharmacies were replaced by chains. Even more dramatic than the change in the professions is the increase in the percentage of managers who are women. What was an overwhelmingly male-dominated profession, 4.4 percent female in 1900, became an integrated occupation, 45.3 percent female in 2000. However, once again women are overrepresented in fields that have been redefined as requiring "feminine" skills: marketing, human resources, and public relations. Men, on the other hand, predominate in production, financial management, and other areas providing a fast track up the corporate hierarchy. Women managers, especially women of color, have experienced obstacles to advancement within firms, a problem evoked by the image of a "glass ceiling."

These constraints are reflected in the gender-based wage gap. The wage gap is an overall measure of the difference between men's and women's earnings. To determine the wage gap, first the female-to-male wage ratio is calculated by dividing the median (or average) earnings of women by the same gauge for men. If men's and women's earnings were the same, the ratio would equal 1.00 or 100 percent. But women earn less than men on average, so the gender-based wage ratio is less than 100 percent. The gap is equal to the difference between the wage ratio and 100 percent. For example, in 1955, the wage ratio, based on median annual earnings, was 63.9 percent and the wage gap was 36.1 percent. Figure 4.4 traces the gender-based wage gap from 1955 to 2000. Notice that the gap widened from 1955 to 1965 and was stable in the late 1960s. The gap gradually narrowed in the late 1970s. The most marked narrowing of the gap occurred in the 1980s. Policy analysts such as the Institute for Women's Policy Research in Washington, DC, report that over half of this "improvement" in the 1980s was due to an erosion of men's real wages (that is, controlling for inflation). At century's end there was still a substantial, relatively stable gap between what men and women earn.

## Conclusion

The patterns of women's employment reflect broad economic transformations and shifting boundaries of gender and race-ethnicity. Work for wages, once a mark of degradation, became an important means of provisioning for family needs. A century ago the preferred mode of gender relations relied upon a male breadwinner, temporary employment spells for young, single women, and married women's full-time domestic labor. Immigrant women and women of color had continuous labor force participation. Over the course of the twentieth century, white married women, especially those with young children, redefined their relationship to paid work. The growth of the service sector, rising consumption standards, and shifting gender ideology all contributed to legitimating women's paid employment. Men and women, white and nonwhite, work, but not in the same places. Occupational segregation by gender and race-ethnicity have maintained hierarchies. Hierarchies are also reinforced by relative wages for different groups.

## Note

1. The majority of the labor force statistics cited in this chapter are from annual volumes of the U.S. Census Bureau's *Statistical Abstract of the United States*. Specific information can be found in Figart, Mutari, and Power (2002, chapter 2).

## References

Amott, Teresa, and Julie Matthaei. 1996. *Race, Gender, and Work: A Multi-cultural Economic History of Women in the United States*, revised edition. Boston: South End Press.

Bergmann, Barbara R. 1986. *The Economic Emergence of Women*. New York: Basic Books.

Blackwelder, Julia Kirk. 1997. *Now Hiring: The Feminization of Work in the United States, 1900–1995*. College Station: Texas A&M University Press.

Chafe, William H. 1991. *The Paradox of Change: American Women in the 20th Century*. New York: Oxford University Press.

Connell, R.W. 1993. "The Big Picture: Masculinities in Recent World History." *Theory and Society* 22: 597–623.

Figart, Deborah M., Ellen Mutari, and Marilyn Power. 2002. *Living Wages, Equal Wages: Gender and Labor Market Policies in the United States*. London: Routledge.

Giddings, Paula. 1984. *When and Where I Enter . . . : The Impact of Black Women on Race and Sex in America*. New York: William Morrow.

Goldin, Claudia. 1990. *Understanding the Gender Gap: An Economic History of American Women*. New York: Oxford University Press.

Jones, Jacqueline. 1986. *Labor of Love, Labor of Sorrow: Black Women, Work, and the Family from Slavery to the Present*. New York: Vintage Books.

Landry, Bart. 2000. *Black Working Wives: Pioneers of the American Family Revolution*. Berkeley: University of California Press.

Reskin, Barbara F., and Patricia A. Roos, eds. 1990. *Job Queues, Gender Queues: Explaining Women's Inroads into Male Occupations*. Philadelphia: Temple University Press.

Smith, Ralph E., ed. 1979. *The Subtle Revolution: Women at Work*. Washington, DC: Urban Institute.

Weiner, Lynn. 1985. *From Working Girl to Working Mother: The Female Labor Force in the United States, 1820–1980*. Chapel Hill: University of North Carolina Press.

---

This original chapter draws extensively from chapter 2 of Deborah M. Figart, Ellen Mutari, and Marilyn Power, *Living Wages, Equal Wages: Gender and Labor Market Policies in the United States*. London: Routledge, 2002. Adapted with permission.

# 5

# Industrialization, Female Labor Force Participation, and the Modern Division of Labor by Sex

*William Rau and Robert Wazienski*

There are descriptions of how industrialization changes the division of labor, but controversies still exist regarding its effect on the sexual division of labor. While research on the effects of industrialization on female labor force participation has grown rapidly since Ester Boserup's (1970) pathbreaking work, no consensus exists on how industrialization has changed the division of labor by sex. Instead, there are three competing positions in the literature: the *emancipation hypothesis*, the *U-hypothesis*, and the *constancy hypothesis*. Our purpose is to present evidence supporting the U-hypothesis, a position arguing for decreases in female labor force participation during the early phases of industrialization and then subsequent increases among more developed or industrialized nations. . . .

The emancipation hypothesis (Shorter 1973) posits a direct relationship between industrialization and increasing employment and "freedom" for women. Shorter argues that patriarchy reigned supreme in preindustrial Europe, with women's submission to husbands or fathers a result of patriarchal control of the household economy. But patriarchy disintegrated, Shorter holds, when women went to work in factories. Impersonal labor markets fostered a new mentality of self-interest among women. Factory employment allowed young women in particular to escape the social confines of work at home. More important, the economic self-sufficiency brought by wage labor greatly diminished the ability of men to control women.

Scott and Tilly (1975) reject Shorter's argument and present a more complex relationship among industrialization, women's work, and emancipation. While noting exceptions, they see a curvilinear relationship between industrialization and female labor force participation. Since most goods in preindustrial societies were produced in the home, women were able to combine work with child rearing and other domestic chores. Preindustrial farms were both highly diversified and labor-intensive, so women had "their" work to do. But as farms become more specialized and mechanized with industrialization, the importance of women's labor is greatly reduced. At the same time, the production of many goods moves from the home to the factory, a new work milieu that is often restricted to men. Thus women's employment diminishes during early industrialization and does not improve until changes in family structure occur and the growth of white-collar service occupations follow in the postindustrial period. Davis (1984) charts this transition in terms of movement from the so-called traditional "breadwinner" system to the emergence of a more contemporary "egalitarian" system in more industrialized economies. The overall process, as presented by Scott and Tilly (1975), is called the *U-hypothesis*.

Bose (1987a, 1987b) argues that women always worked and that Scott and Tilly's curvilinear pattern is a statistical artifact due to the underenumeration of women's work activity during industrialization. This is called the *constancy hypothesis*. Bose (1987a) and other scholars (Conk 1978; Deacon 1985; Waring 1988) show that census officials in the United States, England, and Australia formulated definitions of gainful employment in the late nineteenth century that excluded a wide variety of work activities through which women earned money or contributed labor to family farms and businesses. Bose (1987a) reestimated women's employment rate in 1900 for the total economy (formal and informal) using the Public Use Sample for the 1980 census. When the concept of gainful employment as defined by the 1980 census is applied to 1900 census data, she finds that a minimum of 49 percent of women were gainfully employed at the turn of the century. While these estimates do not capture a good deal of factory outwork and "off-the-books" employment, they do indicate that there is no meaningful difference in the employment rate for women in 1900 relative to that of 1980 once women's work in the informal economy is counted.[1]

The constancy hypothesis is supported by those who pin much of the growth of the service sector in postindustrial nations to the commercialization of reproductive work (child care, cooking, cleaning). This work, once done by women at home, moves into the formal economy, where it is done once again by women. Wilensky (1968) calls this *Parkinson's law for women*: Paid employment expands to fill women's time for leisure. As a result, women work at least as many hours today as at any time in the past (see also Berch 1980).

One problem with much of the research on the effects of industrialization and female labor force participation (FLFP) is that it is too specialized or focuses on only a few nations to address the issue. In this article we try to overcome some of these problems by examining occupational data on sixty-two nations in different stages of industrial development. The main effort is to determine which hypothesis may best describe the effect of industrialization on FLFP. . . .

## The Industrial Transition

We intend to demonstrate how industrialization induces the U-shaped pattern by changing the distribution of work tasks and occupations toward those dominated by men. Our starting point is Table 5.1, which gives the degree of sex specialization among work tasks in the preindustrial societies. These data are from Murdock's Standard Cross-Cultural Sample of 185 Preindustrial Societies (Murdock and Provost 1980). This sample was designed to incorporate the full range of social and economic diversity found in preindustrial societies and therefore contains societies from every cultural and geographic region of the globe. Table 5.1 dramatically reveals the monopoly men have held over manufacturing activities in every part of that globe. The Murdock and Provost male dominance index for the transformation of bone, stone, wood, and metal runs from 95 to 100 percent. This monopoly was balanced, however, by the lesser monopoly of women over household-based tasks (weaving, spinning, pottery making, etc.) and their substantial role in agricultural work, the central activity in most of these societies. Hence women were economically indispensable in preindustrial societies.

All this changes with industrialization. In the demographic transition, high birth rates and declining death rates led to rapid population growth. An analogous dislocation is seen in the industrial transition. Here, work moves from subsistence agriculture to mechanized farms and factories; women have highly visible and significant work roles in the first setting but not in the second. This transition increases occupational opportunities for men while decreasing them for women. We can summarize the effects of the industrial transition as follows.

First, the industrial transition radically reshapes the distribution of work tasks in favor of men. Manufacturing tasks monopolized by men in preindustrial times grow in number and significance. Second, household tasks become less important economically, since many goods once produced by women in the household are now manufactured more efficiently in factories.

Table 5.1

**Degree of Sex Specialization for Work Activities Among 185 Pre-Industrial Societies** (in percent)

| Task | Percent male | All male | Mostly male | Equal | Mostly female | All female | N |
|---|---|---|---|---|---|---|---|
| Smelting ores | 100 | 100 | | | | | 37 |
| Metalworking | 99 | 99 | 1 | | | | 86 |
| Lumbering | 99 | 97 | 3 | | | | 139 |
| Woodworking | 99 | 97 | 2 | 1 | 1 | | 164 |
| Boatbuilding | 97 | 92 | 3 | 3 | | 1 | 91 |
| Stoneworking | 96 | 92 | | 8 | | | 73 |
| Work in bone | 95 | 87 | 9 | 2 | | 2 | 82 |
| Mining/quarrying | 94 | 89 | 3 | 6 | | 3 | 35 |
| Land clearance | 90 | 68 | 24 | 4 | 2 | 1 | 139 |
| Soil preparation | 73 | 49 | 20 | 10 | 13 | 7 | 134 |
| Crop planting | 54 | 19 | 25 | 23 | 18 | 14 | 141 |
| Harvesting | 45 | 7 | 26 | 24 | 24 | 18 | 141 |
| Crop tending | 45 | 17 | 18 | 18 | 23 | 24 | 131 |
| Milking | 44 | 31 | 4 | 17 | 4 | 44 | 48 |
| Care of small animals | 36 | 20 | 8 | 14 | 12 | 45 | 97 |
| Loom weaving | 32 | 27 | | 7 | 9 | 57 | 88 |
| Fuel gathering | 27 | 15 | 7 | 7 | 14 | 57 | 185 |
| Manufacture of clothing | 22 | 13 | 3 | 9 | 11 | 64 | 122 |
| Potterymaking | 21 | 13 | 5 | 6 | 6 | 70 | 105 |
| Dairy production | 14 | 14 | | | | 86 | 28 |
| Spinning | 14 | 8 | 3 | 4 | 5 | 79 | 91 |
| Laundering | 13 | 8 | | 6 | 12 | 74 | 66 |
| Water fetching | 9 | 2 | 2 | 5 | 8 | 82 | 160 |
| Cooking | 8 | | 1 | 1 | 34 | 64 | 184 |

*Source:* Murdock and Provost (1980, p. 293).

Initially, a number of these factory jobs are typed as women's work and provide employment for mostly young, unmarried women. However, as the factory system spreads and technological innovations change work tasks, many of these jobs are reallocated to men. Third, the same process occurs in agriculture. Tasks once done by or with women are mechanized and recast as men's work. Most often, farm women continue to work by assisting their husbands or fathers during peak labor periods, but these contributions are often ignored by census enumerators. Such oversight was much more difficult when women commanded independent roles in the highly diversified farms of the premechanical era. Finally, the structural transformation of agriculture reduces women's chances for other kinds of work tied to agriculture. When women controlled vegetable, fruit, milk, egg, or poultry production, they also typically controlled the marketing and exchange of these products. Control over certain agricultural tasks gave women access to the marketplace. Eliminate the former, and you eliminate the latter. This is what happened to women during industrialization and the enclosures in England (Pinchbeck 1930). A similar process appears to be occurring in areas of the third world today (Boserup 1970; Gladwin and McMillan 1989).

The male monopoly over production means that men also will monopolize management in production, and both the number and importance of managers grow rapidly as industrialization lends itself to the bureaucratic consolidation of separate businesses (Bendix 1963; Chandler 1977). One of the firmest beliefs in sex role stereotypes is that women should not supervise men. In the past, supervisors of male-typed occupations also have been men. Industrialization is therefore a double-edged sword. As the marginalization of women in agriculture cuts them off from a variety of trading and commercial activities, their exclusion from production extends into management. In sum, the industrial transition systematically privileges the work roles of men while devaluing those of women. Women continue to labor, but their contributions become less visible because official definitions exclude work in the informal economy, where women are relegated. The structural transformation of the economy strongly favors men as it brings increasing significance to specialized, bureaucratically organized occupations.

## Data and Methods

The International Labour Office's (ILO) *Yearbook of Labour Statistics* is our data source. Starting with 1960 and concluding with the 1970s, we selected all nations with occupational data for both women and men ($N = 62$) at two points in time (see Table 5.2). . . . [T]his period precedes the internationalization of the women's movement and the accelerating movement of large American, European, and Japanese corporations into developing nations. We wanted to study this period without the complications of recent sociocultural, economic, and technological trends. . . . ILO data are suitable for a test of the emancipation and U-hypotheses but do not contain the kind of information needed for a test of the constancy hypothesis. The latter requires labor force surveys with definitions of work that included women's contributions outside the formal economy. . . .

Industrial level is measured through the percentage of the workforce in nonagricultural occupations. These percentages are classified into deciles where ten categories of equal intervals reflect the percent of the workforce in nonagricultural occupations. Nations fall into one of these groups (deciles) along a continuum of industrialization. A *mature* industrial nation is defined as having more than 50 percent of its workforce in nonagricultural occupations. An *early* industrial nation is defined as having less than 50 percent of its workforce in nonagricultural occupations.

We measure FLFP by the percentage of women in all occupations. The seven occupational groups classified by the ILO include (1) farming, (2) manufacturing, (3) sales, (4) service, (5) clericals, (6) professionals, and (7) administrators. This classification scheme presents a problem. With only seven occupational aggregates, it is difficult to accurately represent changes in the sex composition of occupations during industrialization. Women are often heavily concentrated in a small number of occupations, and seven aggregated categories conceal such concentration. For example, 90 percent of all women professionals in India in 1971 were either nurses or school teachers (Anker and Hein 1985). Nonetheless, these data provide some powerful insights into how industrialization affects the sexual division of labor.

**Results**

Table 5.3 gives means by industrial decile for female labor force participation (FLFP). . . . Other than a minor inconsistency in the fifth (41–50 percent) decile, the means for FLFP are decidedly curvilinear. FLFP decreases through the sixth decile. Thereafter, it increases to a plateau in the ninth and tenth deciles. Correlations for industrial level and FLFP provide added support for the curvilinear hypothesis. For all nations, industrial level and FLFP correlate at 0.20. When we separate nations into early and mature industrial groupings, however, correlations double in size and signs change to reflect the curvilinear pattern in Table 5.3. The correlation of industrial level with FLFP is –0.45 for early industrial nations ($N = 39$) and +0.41 for mature industrial nations ($N = 85$). In sum, both means and correlations support the U-hypothesis. . . .

The industrial revolution pivots on the transfer of labor from farm and village to factory and city. The big shift moves labor off the land and into a welter of manufacturing occupations. For women, this exchange is the proverbial "stacked deck." Women disappear from the fields, but they do not reappear in manufacturing. The mirror-image symmetry of farm and manufacturing is the underlying cause of the decreasing employment of women during the first phase of industrialization. Given the sheer size of these two occupations, large numbers of women have little alternative but to retreat from the labor market.

The exclusion of women from manufacturing is so universal that [it] merits close examination. Initially, differences are not great, but as industrialization proceeds, the percentage of male production workers increases *six times*

Table 5.2

## List of Nations with Industrial Level and FLFP for the 1960s and 1970s

|  | IND60 | FLFP60 | IND70 | FLFP70 |
|---|---|---|---|---|
| Antigua | 77.0 | 40.2 | 85.9 | 38.7 |
| Argentina | 80.4 | 22.0 | 84.6 | 25.0 |
| Barbados | 74.8 | 41.1 | 84.1 | 39.3 |
| Belgium | 92.2 | 27.5 | 95.2 | 30.1 |
| Brunei | 64.9 | 16.8 | 87.3 | 17.4 |
| Canada | 87.7 | 27.8 | 92.3 | 33.5 |
| Chile | 70.7 | 14.1 | 77.3 | 21.3 |
| Costa Rica | 50.3 | 16.7 | 62.4 | 16.9 |
| Czechoslovakia | 78.7 | 41.1 | 87.9 | 44.7 |
| Denmark | 81.7 | 31.7 | 89.1 | 37.3 |
| Dominican Republic | 35.0 | 11.3 | 46.8 | 23.0 |
| Ecuador | 42.6 | 16.6 | 50.7 | 17.2 |
| Egypt | 45.3 | 5.3 | 51.5 | 5.7 |
| El Salvador | 38.9 | 17.9 | 42.7 | 21.4 |
| Finland | 64.7 | 39.5 | 79.8 | 42.3 |
| France | 79.0 | 35.1 | 83.3 | 35.3 |
| Ghana | 38.9 | 39.9 | 42.6 | 44.7 |
| Greece | 44.5 | 32.3 | 58.9 | 28.0 |
| Greenland | 62.2 | 29.0 | 80.8 | 31.0 |
| Guatemala | 35.2 | 12.6 | 43.3 | 14.0 |
| Guyana | 64.9 | 22.7 | 69.8 | 26.9 |
| Honduras | 30.3 | 12.7 | 39.4 | 15.7 |
| Hong Kong | 92.6 | 28.9 | 95.9 | 33.5 |
| Hungary | 66.1 | 35.1 | 82.0 | 41.2 |
| India | 26.9 | 31.6 | 24.8 | 22.3 |
| Ireland | 64.0 | 26.0 | 73.9 | 25.9 |
| Japan | 67.6 | 39.1 | 80.8 | 39.1 |
| Jordan | 61.9 | 5.9 | 88.6 | 7.3 |
| Libya | 57.6 | 4.7 | 78.0 | 7.0 |
| Luxembourg | 84.8 | 27.0 | 92.4 | 26.1 |
| Malaysia-Sabah | 22.7 | 30.2 | 38.0 | 29.2 |
| Malaysia-Sarawak | 18.5 | 37.4 | 27.2 | 36.8 |
| Malaysia-West | 42.4 | 25.0 | 49.4 | 30.2 |
| Mauritius | 62.0 | 17.8 | 67.8 | 20.1 |
| Mexico | 46.5 | 17.9 | 61.8 | 19.0 |
| Morocco | 37.9 | 11.2 | 43.7 | 14.7 |
| Netherlands | 88.9 | 22.9 | 93.2 | 25.5 |
| Netherlands Antilles | 98.0 | 26.4 | 99.0 | 32.7 |
| New Caledonia | 61.2 | 27.7 | 64.3 | 33.2 |
| New Zealand | 85.3 | 25.3 | 88.2 | 30.0 |
| Nicaragua | 41.0 | 20.1 | 51.9 | 21.5 |
| Norway | 80.4 | 23.1 | 88.1 | 28.3 |
| Panama | 49.3 | 19.9 | 61.1 | 24.6 |
| Paraguay | 42.8 | 23.4 | 48.6 | 21.7 |
| Peru | 48.4 | 22.1 | 56.8 | 20.2 |
| Philippines | 33.9 | 24.7 | 45.1 | 31.3 |
| Portugal | 56.3 | 18.3 | 67.1 | 26.2 |

| | | | |
|---|---|---|---|
| Singapore | 92.0 | 18.2 | 95.7 | 24.4 |
| South Africa | 67.5 | 22.3 | 68.9 | 30.2 |
| South Korea | 33.6 | 28.8 | 48.8 | 35.5 |
| Sri Lanka | 47.8 | 20.4 | 54.7 | 25.7 |
| Sweden | 86.4 | 29.9 | 92.0 | 35.6 |
| Switzerland | 88.6 | 30.1 | 91.9 | 33.8 |
| Syria | 47.3 | 7.3 | 49.1 | 10.7 |
| Thailand | 17.1 | 48.7 | 17.6 | 47.6 |
| Trinidad and Tobago | 79.1 | 26.3 | 86.3 | 28.4 |
| Tunisia | 58.7 | 6.1 | 62.5 | 18.7 |
| United States | 93.4 | 32.6 | 96.8 | 36.9 |
| Uruguay | 80.8 | 25.1 | 82.2 | 29.1 |
| Venezuela | 65.4 | 18.5 | 90.1 | 21.4 |
| West Germany | 85.9 | 36.2 | 91.7 | 36.0 |
| Yugoslavia | 42.8 | 35.5 | 53.1 | 36.9 |

*Source:* International Labour Office (1985).

faster than the percentage of women. The pattern is so unequivocal that it conjures up the image of a fork in the road with men taking one path and women taking another.

Management is even more sex-segregated than manufacturing. For all nations, men command 85 percent of the total manufacturing jobs in comparison with 89 percent of the jobs in management. Further, the difference between male and female managers increases at an accelerating rate with increases in industrial level. Thus, the occupation most responsible for shaping and governing the workforce as a whole falls under the near exclusive sway of men.

It is the interrelated changes across farming, manufacturing, and managerial occupations that give rise to the modern sexual division of labor, but employment in manufacturing is the heart of the matter. If the producing occupations are the crucible of the industrial age, then men use this vessel to cast the industrial order in their own image. Societies do have the option of attempting to emphasize services during development. This decision could increase employment opportunities for women. However, while there are some instances of successful service-led development, these appear to be the exception rather than the rule. . . .

## Discussion

Our examination does not support the emancipation hypothesis; our findings do support the U-hypothesis. We have seen that early industrialization decreases FLFP by removing women from agriculture while excluding them from manufacturing and management. Exclusion from manufacturing and

Table 5.3

**Industrial Decile and Means for Female Labor Force Participation**

| Industrial decile | FLFP |
|---|---|
| 11– 20 | 44.6 |
| 21– 30 | 26.7 |
| 31– 40 | 21.3 |
| 41– 50 | 22.2 |
| 51– 60 | 18.4 |
| 61– 70 | 24.6 |
| 71– 80 | 27.8 |
| 81– 90 | 30.3 |
| 91–100 | 30.1 |

*Source:* International Labour Office (1985).

management is most significant because they lie at the very center of the industrial order. By shifting most work into man's sphere, the industrial transition deprives women of a role in the institution-building stage of modern societies. It is here that we find the origins of the modern sexual division of labor. In this sense, it is critical that solutions for increasing women's participation in the manufacturing sector be found *early on* if developing nations wish to avoid reinforcing the advantages that industrialization offers to men.

It is important to stress that we do not dismiss the effect of nonoccupational factors (e.g., fertility, education of women, income inequality) on FLFP. Rather, we wish to bring attention to forces inside the division of labor that also merit attention. Further research needs to examine the effect of different paths of industrialization on FLFP. Since there are two approaches to industrialization (Rau and Roncek 1987), one emphasizing manufacturing and the other service industries, and since these two approaches are strongly confounded with industrial level, different strategies and rates of industrialization also may affect FLFP and a host of other factors related to the well-being and status of women in society. . . .

[I]ndustrialization in the developing world may depart from the historical pattern described here. The traditional conceptions of women's work roles are most likely to be carried forward into an emerging industrial economy when traditional or indigenous agents guide the process of industrialization. Since the 1970s, however, multinational corporations (MNCs) have moved a large percentage of their labor-intensive manufacturing to export zones in the Third World. In the process, they have generated a good deal of employment for women. This employment is hardly emancipating. Women are largely relegated to repetitive, unskilled, and low-paying assembly operations (United

Nations 1985). In some instances, their status is not much improved over that of women textile workers in the "Satanic mills" of Marx and Engels.

Nonetheless, MNCs create employment for women that might not have been available had job growth been controlled by local entrepreneurs or government officials. And if MNC-induced industrialization continues to spread, the U-shaped pattern documented here may be "flattened" or even disappear. A crucial issue, therefore, is whether this employment gives women a secure and stable foothold in the industrial order or whether it represents, as in the past, a temporary interlude. If history is allowed to repeat itself, these women, like women textile workers in early nineteenth-century Britain and New England, may help build a house from which they are evicted.

Finally, there is a clear need to change definitions of work in census and labor force surveys so that women's contributions to the total economy are recognized and recorded accurately. Nonetheless, more power, pay, and status go with work in the formal economy. If, during industrialization, large numbers of women spend more time in reproductive activity or in unrecognized or devalued work in the informal economy, then they are also shunted into work located on the lowest rungs of modern stratification systems. In other words, future research should show the U-shaped and constancy hypotheses to be complementary, with the former describing productive labor in the formal economy and the latter describing productive and reproductive labor in the economy as a whole. In the interim, our analysis lends support to the U-hypothesis and suggests the importance of considering the occupational distribution of the workforce when attempting to account for comparative differences in women's labor force participation.

## Note

1. The United States was a well-established industrial nation by 1900; over half of its labor force was already in nonagricultural occupations. Given the argument presented here, the forces working to exclude women from the formal economy would have been much stronger two or three decades earlier. It is likely that examination of data from 1870–1880 would show a much larger percentage of women in the informal economy during this period than in the 1900s.

## References

Anker, Richard, and Catherine Hein. 1985. "Why Third World Urban Employers Usually Prefer Men." *International Labour Review* 124: 73–91.

Bendix, Reinhart. 1963. *Work and Authority in Industry: Ideologies of Management in the Course of Industrialization*. New York: Harper & Row.

Berch, Bettina. 1982. *The Endless Day*. New York: Harcourt, Brace, Jovanovich.

Bose, Christine E. 1987a. "Devaluing Women's Work." In *Hidden Aspects of Women's Work*, ed. C.E. Bose, N. Sokoloff, and R. Feldberg. New York: Praeger.

———.1987b. "Dual Spheres." In *Analyzing Gender*, ed. B.B. Hess and M.M. Ferree. Newbury Park, CA: Sage.

Boserup, Ester. 1970. *Women's Role in Economic Development*. London: Allen and Unwin.

Chandler, Alfred D., Jr. 1977. *The Visible Hand: The Managerial Revolution in American Business*. Cambridge: Harvard University Press.

Conk, Margo A. 1978. "Occupational Classification in the United States Census: 1870–1940." *Journal of Interdisciplinary History* 9: 111–30.

Davis, Kingsley. 1984. "Wives and Work: The Sex Revolution and Its Consequences." *Population and Development Review* 10: 397–417.

Deacon, Desley. 1985. "Political Arithmetic: The Nineteenth-Century Australian Census and the Construction of the Dependent Woman." *Signs: Journal of Women in Culture and Society* 11 (Autumn): 27–47.

Gladwin, Christina H., and Delia McMillan. 1989. "Is a Turnaround in Africa Possible without Helping African Women to Farm?" *Economic Development and Cultural Change* 37: 345–69.

International Labour Office. 1985. *Yearbook of Labour Statistics*. Geneva: International Labour Office.

Murdock, George P., and Cathrina Provost. 1980. "Factors in the Division of Labor by Sex." In *Cross-Cultural Samples and Codes*, ed. H. Barry III and A. Schlegel. Pittsburgh: University of Pittsburgh Press.

Pinchbeck, Ivy. 1930. *Women Workers and the Industrial Revolution, 1750–1850*. New York: F.S. Crofts.

Rau, William, and Dennis W. Roncek. 1987. "Industrialization and World Inequality: The Transformation of the Division of Labor in 59 Nations, 1960–1981." *American Sociological Review* 52: 359–69.

Scott, Joan W., and Louise Tilly. 1975. "Women's Work and Family in Nineteenth-Century Europe." *Comparative Study of Society and History* 17: 36–44.

Shorter, Edward. 1973. "Female Emancipation, Birth Control, and Fertility in European History." *American Historical Review* 78: 605–40.

United Nations Centre on Transnational Corporations. 1985. *Women Workers in Multinational Enterprises in Developing Countries*. Geneva: International Labour Office.

Waring, Marilyn. 1988. *If Women Counted: A New Feminist Economics*. San Francisco: Harper & Row.

Wilensky, Harold L. 1968. "Women's Work: Economic Growth, Ideology, Structure." *Industrial Relations* 7: 235–48.

Adapted from "Industrialization, Female Labor Force Participation, and the Modern Division of Labor by Sex." *Industrial Relations* 38 (4) (October 1999): 504–21. Reprinted with permission.

# 6

# Men and Monotony

## Fraternalism as a Managerial Strategy at the Ford Motor Company

*Wayne A. Lewchuk*

> Mr. Ford's business is the making of men,
> and he manufactures automobiles on the side
> to defray the expenses of his main business.

—*Rev. S.S. Marquis, Director, Ford Sociology Department, 1915–1921*

> One of the most priceless possessions still retained by modern
> man is what is called manhood. . . . Would you be a MAN—
> free, proud, independent, POWERFUL? Then get together with
> your fellow worker, ORGANIZE YOURSELF, and you will be
> in a position to proudly look into the eyes of foremen, straw
> bosses, and all the world and say: I AM A MAN.

—Auto Worker News, *October 1927, p. 4*

Until very recently, the shop floor of America's leading automobile manu-
facturers, and the unions that bargained for those who worked there, were
the domain of men. For example, throughout the interwar period, the level of
female employment in production departments hovered around 1 percent at
the Ford Motor Company. At its massive River Rouge complex outside of
Detroit, Ford employed over 70,000 men but not one woman in a production
department in the early 1940s. This chapter examines why this was the case.

I will argue that as the production process became more capital intensive and integrated, the importance of converting labor time into a steady stream of effort increased. But converting time into effort became more difficult as work became increasingly unskilled, repetitive, and monotonous and as workers, especially male workers, became alienated from their tasks. For men, this alienation was partially the result of the growing gap between the nature of work under mass production and the gender norms of skilled men who, building on their and their fathers' experiences in craft shops, associated independence and decision-making power at work with masculinity. At Ford, the attempted solution to this problem went far beyond simply raising wages to compensate for the deterioration in working conditions. The increase in wages was part of a broader strategy to reconstruct the concepts of masculinity inherited from the nineteenth century. The new focus was on hard work and making useful products in the company of other men. Fraternalism replaced paternalism as a managerial strategy to convert labor time into effort, a strategy that limited employment opportunities for women.

Research during the 1970s and 1980s directed at understanding the experiences of women at work is now having a profound impact on our understanding of men at work. Two critical themes have emerged. First, a deeper understanding of the role of women within the family, kin networks, and the "informal economy" can illuminate the relationship of women to work and work-based organizations. This is described as a "gender model" as distinct from a "job model," which explains behavior on and off the job by looking only at work-based experiences. Second, these studies suggest that gender norms change over time and are socially constructed as men and women interact in their daily lives.

The literature on gender and work encourages us to think of men and women as bringing both economic and gender interests to the workplace and to acknowledge that patterns of conflict and cooperation between employers and employees need to be studied in terms of both sets of interests. For example, in the case of men, their role within the production process has implications for their status and authority in the larger society and within the family. Furthermore, although male managers and male workers may have opposing economic interests in some contexts and complementary ones in others, they remain men throughout. The possibility of male workers participating in the restructuring of work contrary to their economic interests in order to protect their gender interests must be considered. From this perspective, managerial strategies are gendered strategies, in the sense that they will build upon existing gender norms in pursuit of economic objectives. I will later argue that in some cases employers try to change these norms in order to achieve their economic goals. . . .

In what follows, the focus is the American automobile industry and the workshops of Henry Ford between 1903 and 1930.[1] During this period, a technology based on a predominantly skilled male workforce was displaced by one employing large numbers of less-skilled but still predominantly male workers, who were machine paced and subjected to an extreme division of labor. Ava Baron has argued that periods of major technical change can create a crisis in masculinity, "a crisis for men workers both as men and as workers" (1987, p. 61). She has shown how the late nineteenth-century introduction of the linotype machine in the printing trades reshaped social norms regarding how men should work and how hard they should work. Building on these insights, I suggest that a similar crisis occurred during the transition to mass production in the automobile industry. How the crisis was resolved may shed light on how Ford revolutionized labor productivity standards and why other automobile producers, especially those in Europe, had difficulty matching Ford's success.

### The Automobile Industry as a Male Domain

One of the critical points made in the literature on women at work is that the social construction of gender norms gives substance to concepts of masculinity and femininity. Ava Baron (1991), Sonya Rose (1992), and Elizabeth Faue (1991) have shown how lived experiences, interpreted through the lenses of language and discourse, shape and give meaning to gender identities and how men and women come to understand their roles in society. In this section I examine how gender norms interact with more conventional economic forces to shape the gender division of labor and why women and men rarely work together on the same tasks in a workplace. . . .

During the first stages of the Industrial Revolution in both Britain and the United States, women readily found employment in industries such as textiles (Dublin 1975; Kessler-Harris 1982; Rose 1987, 1991). In Massachusetts in 1840, 40 percent of the entire industrial workforce was female (Goldin 1990). Women found their way into the British hosiery, carpet, and silk trades and worked many of the new steam-powered looms (Rose 1992). However, in other trades, employers either made no effort to use women or were prevented from doing so by organized men. In the lace trades in Britain, men worked the new machines for making lace, whereas in the United States, attempts by employers to use women on the new linotype machine were successfully resisted by men. The spread of mass production created new opportunities for employing women, and in industries such as electrical goods, women were employed in large numbers. But even here variations can be found, with firms like Philco in the United States relying more heavily on men than their competitors (Cooper 1991).

The automobile industry, despite major changes in technology between 1903 and 1930, employed very few women in the United States. At first, a number of Detroit firms did turn to low-wage female workers during the shift to mass production. Hudson began employing women in 1910 when it built special facilities for them in their new plant and may have employed as many as 5,000 women by the mid-1920s. In 1927 women trimmers were employed at Murray, which supplied bodies to Ford. At Studebaker, women were employed in large numbers on drill presses, lathes, and internal grinders, and they could be found on the assembly line at the Piquette plant in the 1920s.

However, by the late 1920s, before the onset of the Depression, many automobile employers lost their early enthusiasm for employing women. A study by the Women's Bureau [of the U.S. Department of Labor] in 1928 charged that employers showed little interest in exploring how the labor of women could be more effectively used in automobile plants. The study concluded:

> Throughout the interviews . . . there was little to indicate that anything scientific in the way of personnel work had been undertaken to find which jobs were suitable for women. . . . Managers who were progressive and alert to changes in machinery, to new ideas in sales and advertising policies, when they turned to personnel problems, especially those affecting the employment of women, were likely to revert to rote reasoning. (U.S. Department of Labor 1928, p. 233)

By 1941, the purge of women from the plants of Detroit's major assemblers was almost total. In 1942, when women were brought into the plants in large numbers on war work, they tended to work in isolation from men in predominantly female departments. Once the war ended, women were quickly "invited" to leave the automobile plants and to return to the home, thereby maintaining the masculinity of the industry (Milkman 1987; Kossoudji and Dresser 1992).

At Ford there was never any great interest in employing women. The spread of mass production was associated with a gradual decline in the proportion of women production workers. . . . What explains the low level of female employment in this industry, the trend away from women in the late 1920s and early 1930s, and the absence of women on the shop floor at Ford? The question is even more puzzling if one accepts contemporary opinion that trends in technology after 1910 reduced the strength and knowledge requirements for working in automobile plants, opening possibilities for employing more women. . . .

The cost-effectiveness of employing women on mass-production tasks in the automobile industry is supported by observations that, when employed, they were as productive as men, but paid much less. According to the *Auto Worker News* in December 1927, "They [women] can do many of the operations as well as men, but they get much less money for doing the same work." Nancy Gabin (1990) has shown that women doing identical jobs as men earned from one-half to two-thirds of the male wage rate. Nor is it plausible to suggest that Ford needed to maintain maximum flexibility in allocating labor and hence resisted hiring women who may have been ill-suited for half of all positions. By 1917 nearly one-fifth of the workforce at Ford was classified as crippled or physically substandard and, one suspects, as limited in the number of jobs they could do as able-bodied women might have been.

A number of recent studies have pointed to the role of labor laws and factory legislation in restricting industrial wage work for women. However, a study of the automobile industry in the United States in 1928 dismissed this explanation. Conditions in the industry already exceeded most of the standards imposed by law, and there were no restrictions in Michigan on night work by women. Instead, it was argued, "In no other industry studied was there found such violent prejudice [by employers] against women's employment because of the mere fact that they were women. It is this prejudice that is a stronger force than any legislative requirements in closing opportunity to women in such occupations" (U.S. Department of Labor 1928, p. 220).

Ruth Milkman (1987) has argued that Ford's decision to follow a high-wage and high-effort strategy, abandoning at least temporarily the more traditional strategy of employing the least costly labor time available, precluded the employment of women. She suggests that even during periods such as the 1930s, when firms were more concerned about minimizing costs, the dominant ideology that in times of high unemployment men should be offered jobs first shaped hiring policies. There is little doubt that the general acceptance of male priority in employment had negative consequences for women seeking work, especially in times of high unemployment. It is less obvious why the decision to pursue a high-wage policy in 1914 should close the door to women seeking jobs. Ford could have increased the wages of women relative to their alternative opportunities and extracted more effort from them as well. They were almost certainly available, even outside war years, given their employment in the thousands by other Detroit assemblers mentioned above. Had Ford employed women at high wages, there is no reason to believe that the effort-to-earnings ratio of women would have been less attractive than that of men on many jobs. But there is no evidence anywhere in the Ford archives of an attempt to hire women during this period, nor of their unsuccessful use in production departments. It was an option that simply was not considered.

In the remainder of the chapter, I show that women were excluded from production not because men were being paid a high wage, but rather because it was unclear if time could be converted into effort as efficiently in a mixed-gender workforce. The exclusion of women was part of a broader strategy by Ford to reshape masculinity along lines more consistent with conditions in a mass-production factory. Ford consciously excluded women from the workplace and created a fraternal system, a men's club, to help male workers adjust to a world of monotonous repetitive work. In the process, Henry Ford and his managers shifted both gender norms at work and standards of labor productivity; they also helped to remodel the family and the role of working-class men in society. The Ford strategy gave real meaning to Marquis's claim that "Mr. Ford's business is the making of men."

## Masculinity in the Pre-Mass Production Period

In order to understand why Henry Ford might have believed that the conversion of male time into effort would be more difficult with a mixed-gender workforce, despite evidence that on individual tasks women were a cost-effective alternative, it is useful to look more closely at the norms of masculinity in effect at the end of the nineteenth century and how work in the new mass-production plants was incompatible with these gender norms. Our current understanding of working-class masculinity is shaped by studies of nineteenth-century British and, to a lesser extent, North American skilled male workers. . . .

Keith McClelland's study of the mid-nineteenth-century British "representative artisan" suggests that such a worker was a man in control of his life and worthy of respect. In the words of a British miner in 1873, a man wanted "the independence of the workshop, and he wanted to be able to pursue his work in such a manner and under such a condition that it should not be a degradation to him in his eyes. He wished to be independent in following his ordinary daily occupation" (McClelland 1989, p. 172). Many of these values were taught during an apprenticeship when boys learned the mysteries of a trade, appropriate attitudes toward employers, male codes of sexual conduct, and male social responsibility. In the process, a boy went through a period of "unfreedom" from which he emerged a free and independent man, that is, "one of the lads." Many crafts in North America continued the tradition of apprenticeships. Armed with new technical skills, boys proved their masculinity by defending their right to a decent standard of living and autonomy in applying their skills (Baron 1991). . . .

The introduction of linotype technology in the printing trades led to conflict between employers wishing to employ less expensive women and male printers trying to defend the masculinity of their trade. The men argued that printing was men's work because it combined intellectual and manual labor and that the traditions of tramping, social drinking while waiting for work, and an aggressive shop-floor culture made printing unsuitable for women. In the end, the men maintained control of the trade, but only by redefining their masculinity on the basis of how hard they could work. Gradually the *quantity* of work a man could do became as important as alleged advantages in intellectual capacity in defining masculinity among printers (Baron 1987, pp. 62–65).

Race also forced some American men to redefine the basis of their masculinity. Dolores Janiewski (1991) explores the contradictions between a southern male view of society—where it was claimed that white men loved to control, whereas blacks loved to be controlled—and the reality of the developing southern economy in which more and more white male workers were directly controlled by white employers. She argues that the physical segregation of black and white workers was in part a response to these tensions. What emerged was a cross-class brotherhood of white men that allowed white wage-earning males the illusion of superiority over blacks in southern society, despite their loss of autonomy. . . .

There is thus no single set of characteristics that defined masculinity in North America or Britain during the process of modernization, and clearly gender norms were reconstructed in various ways as technology changed the nature of work. However, at least for early twentieth-century North American men, the themes of control, skill, autonomy, and independence were important in how they defined their masculinity. The centrality of these themes to the gender identities of workingmen created serious problems for employers in the American automobile industry as they tried to make the transition to mass production and the institutionalization of work that was regimented, boring, and monotonous. This transition created a crisis for workingmen not only in respect to their patterns of work, but also in respect to the ways they constructed their identities as men. It remains to show in detail how Ford responded to this crisis not only by hiring new workers from regions less affected by the norms of male craftworkers and paying his workers a premium to accept the new conditions, but also by setting out to change male notions of appropriate manly work in line with the realities of mass production and monotonous, repetitive tasks.

## Masculinity and Mass Production at the Ford Motor Company

In the pre-mass production period, Ford relied heavily on skilled male workers and had little choice but to leave them a degree of control over how vehicles were assembled. These workers played a key role in suggesting improvements in the production process and had some control over getting tools and fixtures designed for their tasks. The social organization of work was paternalist, with Henry Ford visiting the shops frequently and knowing most workers by their first names. The spread of mass production and the transition to an unskilled workforce created both new problems and new possibilities for converting time into effort. In 1910, about 60 percent of Ford's workforce were classified as skilled mechanics. By 1913, skilled workers comprised only 28 percent of the workforce, and by 1917 they represented only 8.6 percent of all employees (Meyer 1981). Skilled workers had been replaced by unskilled assemblers and machine tenders, many of whom were machine paced after the introduction of the moving assembly line in 1913. For men, the new conditions of work undermined any sense of control or independence on the job, what had been the key characteristics of manly work among skilled workers. . . .

Henry Ford and his managers pointed to the removal from workers of virtually all decision-making power as a great social advance. R.L. Cruden (1929) claimed that in the 1920s, Ford tour guides boasted about the simple and repetitive nature of work at Ford. They claimed that Ford workers were well suited to such an arrangement and that "most of the workers have had little or no schooling . . . . They have never been taught to think; and they do not care to think . . . . All of which means that they get to like their monotonous jobs." Ford argued that "the vast majority of men want to stay put. They want to be led. They want to have everything done for them and to have no responsibility" (Ford 1923, p. 99). . . .

Although Ford may have believed that his male workers were indifferent to the loss of skill and autonomy, one of the few accounts by a contemporary autoworker paints a different picture. In 1914, Frank Marquart, then a young factory hand, but eventually a key player in the rise of the United Auto Workers (UAW), recounted how the boys and men employed in the industry would pass their time in the local saloon, talking shop, each trying to impress the others with how important his job was and how much skill it required (Marquart 1975, p. 12). In fact, the introduction of mass production at Ford coincided with growing labor relations problems. As early as 1908, as employment levels grew, the company began experiencing problems converting labor time into effort and experimented with time studies and profit-sharing plans. By 1913, daily absenteeism reached 10 percent of the workforce and the annual turnover rate was 370 percent (Meyer 1981, p. 83). Arthur Renner, who began working at Highland Park in 1911, recalled that during this period, relations between male workers were fractious. It was not unusual to see five or six fistfights in progress while walking from one department to another. Detroit workers were also looking to unions to defend their interests. Raff (1988) argues that at least part of Henry Ford's motivation in doubling wages in 1914 was to ensure that the Wobblies [union] did not gain a foothold in his shops. The high rates of turnover, the turmoil on the shop floor, and the growing interest in unions suggest that existing male workers were less than enthusiastic about the new conditions of work under mass production.

In 1914, Ford moved to stabilize his workforce by effectively doubling real wages to five dollars a day. Turnover rates fell to a fraction of their pre-1914 levels. Raff and Summers (1987) have argued that the payment of five dollars a day was more than simple compensation for the new working conditions. The long queues of men seeking employment at Ford before and after wages were raised suggests that the company was paying them above their opportunity cost in 1914 in return for stability and more effort, that is, an "efficiency wage." However, according to Raff (1988), it is difficult to explain the doubling of wages in terms of the factors stressed in the efficiency wage literature. Neither turnover costs, the need to control shirking, nor the ability to select only the most able workers warranted the doubling of wages. Raff accepts that the wage increase improved the morale of workers and led to higher productivity, but argues that the timing and the magnitude of the pay increase were determined by the company's desire to keep newly active unions such as the Wobblies out of the Ford plants.

### Hard Work, Useful Products, and Masculinity

There remain, however, troubling questions about the five-dollar day, the high effort norms at Ford, and the absence of women that, I argue, a gendered analysis can help resolve. One of the problems is that many of the factors that Raff suggests motivated the payment of a higher wage in 1914 remained in place through the 1930s, by which time the premium offered by Ford had eroded in real and relative terms. Why Ford would raise wages 100 percent to combat unions who rarely succeeded in raising wages more than 20 or 30 percent is also puzzling. In addition, the payment of a premium to men does not help us explain the absence of women. All of the reasons given by Raff for paying men more money apply equally to women. If keeping the union out was the main reason for paying the higher wage, one might have expected Ford to employ women, which would have compounded the organizing tasks of the union by forcing it to face a mixed-gender workforce. Any argument that seeks to identify the reasons behind the five-dollar day needs to explain why only men could profitably be employed at a wage above their opportunity cost and why a male-only workforce was the most effective way of preventing unionization.

A reinterpretation of changes taking place at Ford during this period suggests that the five-dollar day was one component of a broader strategy to revise norms of masculinity in keeping with the new conditions of work. The first signs of a tendency to extol the virtues of work in Ford shops in order to sustain labor productivity appeared in 1908, when the *Ford Times*, a company magazine, encouraged workers to take a new approach to their jobs, offering them a New Year's Eve resolution that included an exaltation of the "gospel of work" and affirmed the need "to keep the head, heart, and hand so busy" that a worker would not have time to think about his troubles. It suggested that "idleness is a disgrace" (December 15, 1908). Obviously such messages from management to workers were not particularly novel, and they could be applied to women as well as men, although in fact Ford was employing only men in this period. It is the focus on *how much* work, rather than the intrinsic characteristics of work and the skill needed to execute it, that marks the beginning of a campaign that would eventually redefine masculinity on the job.

The campaign to promote monotonous and repetitive work as masculine intensified with the introduction of the moving assembly line. Again, the focus was not on the skill requirements and inherent qualities of work at Ford, but rather on the virtues of working hard and the usefulness of the products being produced. An appropriately titled but short-lived company publication, *The Ford Man*, suggested in 1917 that

> The nobility of labor rests in the practical merit of the product, it makes. . . . A common complaint against modern labor is that it breeds dissatisfaction. This complaint cannot be lodged against Ford workers. . . . Even when the extreme specialization of the work obliges the man to make the same motion over and over again, the monotony of the action has not smothered the consciousness or the importance of his task. . . . He is building something that is a benefit to humanity and why should not his work be a pleasure. (September 20, 1917, pp. 2–3)

In 1919, the paper again stressed the importance of making useful articles, claiming that "anyone working for an organization that has good working conditions, is paying good wages, and is making a thing that people need can be sure that he is in a good calling" (September 3, 1919, p. 2). This was a theme that Henry Ford would stress in his autobiographies, where he claimed, "There is one thing that can be said about menial jobs that cannot be said about a great many so-called more responsible jobs, and that is, they are useful and they are respectable and they are honest" (Ford 1923, p. 278). In focusing on the usefulness of the Model T, Ford was both tapping an undercurrent of American populist culture that stressed the usefulness of work and reflecting pressing material demands in a developing economy.

Again, the strategy calling for more work and pride in producing a utilitarian product could have been applied equally to men or women. However, other evidence suggests that these characteristics were being promoted as components of a new masculine respectability. Effort and speed came to be identified as laudable features of working at Ford, affirming the positive self-image of workers as men. Those who could not work at the expected pace were ridiculed and characterized as suitable only for women's work, such as cutting ribbons. . . .

## The Production of Family Men

A careful reading of the implementation of the five-dollar day, and the adoption of the eight-hour day, reveals that these were more than an attempt to motivate through the cash nexus. Not only was Ford raising wages, he was also promoting a particular vision of men and women at work, in the home, and in society—a vision that he hoped would enable and motivate his male workers to work harder (see May 1982). When the new wage standard was introduced in early 1914, it applied only to men. Its objective was, in the words of a contemporary Ford manager, "to help men to be better men and to make good American citizens and to bring about a larger degree of comfort, habits and a higher plane of living among our employees by sane, sound and wholesome means" (letter dated January 26, 1914, to C.L. Gould). . . .

With the higher wages, men were expected to provide for their families and participate more fully in family life. In return, their status within the household would be enhanced. Ford argued that "if a man feels that his day's work is not only supplying his basic need, but is also giving him a margin of comfort and enabling him to give his boys and girls their opportunity and his wife some pleasure in life, then his job looks good to him and he is free to give it his best" (Ford 1923, p. 120). Men were encouraged to buy homes and life insurance and were discouraged from drinking outside the home or taking in boarders. . . .

To J.R. Lee, Ford's first personnel manager, the five-dollar day was a comprehensive strategy that linked together monetary inducements to effort, the home as a nurturing center enabling high effort, and the redefinition of masculine work as labor that required abnormal effort. In 1914 Lee wrote, "Mr. Ford believes, and so do I, that if we keep pounding away at the root and the heart of the family in the home, that we are going to make better men for future generations, than if we simply pounded away at the fellows at their work here in the factory" (cited in Meyer 1981, p. 124). . . . This point is elaborated by Martha May in her analysis of the five-dollar day:

> Ford's family wage implicitly recognized the contribution of women's domestic labor to a stable and secure family life. In all likelihood, Ford believed that women's contribution was greatest in their emotional, nurturing, and motherly roles. This emphasis on psychological rather than material comfort parallels the arguments of many Progressive reformers, who saw the female emotional, affective role as a necessary aspect of family life which should be supported by adequate wages. (May 1982, p. 416) . . .

## A Community of Men

Accompanying the increase in wages was a campaign to promote the Ford Highland Park plant as a fraternal community, a male club. The company publication *Ford Man* was a key contributor to this new campaign; its stated objective was "to cultivate and establish the broadest fellowship among Ford workers through understanding each other." It stressed that "the Ford shop is a community in which all kinds of men" could be found (September 20, 1917, pp. 2, 3). Marquis, in a piece on the "Eight Hour Day" [from the Ford Archives], asserted that "The attitude of the Ford Motor Company toward its employees is not paternal, but fraternal. . . ."

Employment policies also reflected the climate of community and fraternalism being developed at Ford. The changes implemented went much further than the rationalizing of hiring procedures in 1913 and the removal of the foreman's autocratic power. In 1914, when demand for vehicles fell, married men were given preference over single men for employment. Ford's stated policy was "to give employment to those who are in the greatest need. As a result, a slight preference is given to married men, or single men who have others totally dependent upon them for support, although single men with no dependents are not barred." . . . Over time, however, this practice created ill feeling and opportunities for abuse; it was among the reasons that the unionization campaign was eventually successful. . . .

Even the limited employment of women after 1919 contributed to the restructuring of Ford as a fraternal community where men supported each other for the common good. "Like the substandard men, the women are employed not because they are women. Most of the Ford women are wives or daughters of Ford men who have been in some way temporarily or permanently disabled. A woman whose husband is an active worker in the factory cannot obtain employment in the Ford plants" (Li in the R.W. Dunn Collection at the Reuther Library). . . .

Although not the main focus of this chapter, it is worth discussing briefly the role of male workers in supporting the new norms of masculinity. Male workers and the unions that tried to bargain for them were generally supportive of the gender hierarchy implicit in the fraternalist strategy. In the early 1920s, union papers such as the *Auto Worker* carried articles discussing alleged differences between men and women. One article suggested that women were less suitable for factory work than men because women valued employer approval more than the size of their paycheck, which led them to "unconsciously expanding energy which is unpaid for" (December 1920, p. 13). . . . Gabin (1990), in her study of women and the UAW, argues that men viewed women as less than equal partners in the drive to organize the auto industry and that men were supportive of a gender hierarchy that ensured their access to high-paying jobs. Union organizers called on male workers to vote for their union to raise wages and to restore their manhood. When employers refused to raise wages, the union dressed a number of men in women's clothes, symbolizing their understanding of how the level of wages differentiated men from women. . . .

One might have expected that if Ford was trying to run a men's club, it would have been exclusively a white men's club. This was not the case, for in 1919, following Packard's lead, Ford began hiring large numbers of blacks and quickly became the largest employer of blacks in the area. Although many found jobs in dirty and dangerous parts of the plant, Ford opened all areas of employment to blacks, including the apprenticeship schools. Employment at Ford became a mark of superiority, and it was not unusual to see black workers wearing their Ford badges on their lapels on Sundays. To Ford, blacks were quiet, compliant, and loyal, both needing guidance and willing to be guided. However, racial conflict was a serious problem; it has even been claimed that in the late 1920s the possibility of laying off all black workers was seriously considered, given the amount of unrest in the shops. . . .

## Conclusion

The implementation of mass-production technology at Ford brought with it a heightened managerial focus on effort levels. A capital-intensive integrated system could be profitably employed only by sustaining high and stable levels of effort on the part of workers. However, enforcing such requirements was problematic. The new technology generated tensions for some men as it removed many of the attributes of work prized by skilled male workers in the nineteenth century. The evidence presented in this chapter indicates that Ford went beyond raising wages and tightening up supervision to ensure an adequate supply of effort. There was a conscious attempt by management to revise notions of masculinity. Through company papers, public speeches, and employment policies, a new ideal of what a man was supposed to be—at work, within the family, and in society—was promoted. Working hard—in the company of other men, on a useful product, and being paid well for it—would make Ford workers manly, even though the work itself was repetitive, boring, and devoid of many of the elements of autonomy and control that were characteristic of nineteenth-century skilled labor. The Ford strategy balanced economic and gender interests as it reached beyond the workplace to shape relations of men in the household and in society at large. The loss of control, independence, and status at work was compensated by gains in the household and in the rest of society. The exclusion of women from the Ford shops was a component of this strategy. . . .

## Note

1. The author draws extensively from material in the Ford Archives in Dearborn, Michigan. For detailed citations, see the original article.

## References

*Auto Worker*, Chicago. Various dates.
*Auto Worker News*, Detroit. Various dates.
Baron, Ava. 1987. "Contested Terrain Revisited: Technology and Gender Definitions of Work in the Printing Industry, 1850–1920." In *Women, Work, and Technology*, ed. B. Wright, pp. 58–83. Ann Arbor: University of Michigan Press.
———, ed. 1991. *Work Engendered: Towards a New History of American Labor*. Ithaca, NY: Cornell University Press.
Cooper, Patricia. 1991. "The Faces of Gender: Sex Segregation and Work Relations at Philco, 1928–1938." In *Work Engendered*, ed. Ava Baron, pp. 320–50. Ithaca, NY: Cornell University Press.
Cruden, R.L. 1929, June 12. "No Loitering: Get Out Production." *The Nation*, p. 698.
Dublin, Thomas. 1975. "Women, Work, and the Family: Female Operatives in the Lowell Mills, 1830–1860." *Feminist Studies* (Fall): 30–39.
Faue, Elizabeth. 1991. *Community of Suffering and Struggle: Women, Men and the Labor Movement in Minneapolis, 1915–1945*. Chapel Hill: University of North Carolina Press.
Ford Archives, Greenfield Village and Henry Ford Museum, Dearborn, Michigan.
Ford, Henry. 1923. *My Life and Work*. Garden City, NY: Doubleday, Page.
*Ford Man*. Various dates. Ford Motor Company.
*Ford Times*. Various dates. Ford Motor Company.
*Ford Worker*. Various dates. The Ford Shop Nuclei of the Worker (Communist) Party of America, Detroit, Michigan.
Gabin, Nancy. 1990. *Feminism in the Labor Movement: Women and the United Auto Workers, 1935–1975*. Ithaca, NY: Cornell University Press.

Goldin, Claudia. 1990. *Understanding the Gender Gap*. New York: Oxford University Press.

Janiewski, Dolores. 1991. "Southern Honor, Southern Dishonor: Managerial Ideology and the Construction of Gender, Race and Class Relations in Southern Industry." In *Work Engendered: Towards a New History of American Labor*, ed. Ava Baron, pp. 70–91. Ithaca, NY: Cornell University Press.

Kessler-Harris, Alice. 1982. *Out to Work: A History of Wage-Earning Women in the United States*. New York: Oxford University Press.

Kossoudji, Sherrie A., and Laura J. Dresser. 1992. "The End of a Riveting Experience: Occupational Shifts at Ford After World War II." *American Economic Review* 82 (2): 519–25.

McClelland, Keith. 1989. "Some Thoughts on Masculinity and the 'Representative Artisan' in Britain, 1850–1880." *Gender and History* 1 (Summer): 164–77.

Marquart, Frank. 1975. *An Auto Worker's Journal: The UAW from Crusade to One-Party Union*. University Park: Pennsylvania State University Press.

May, Martha. 1982. "The Historical Problem of the Family Wage: The Ford Motor Company and the Five Dollar Day." *Feminist Studies* 8 (Summer): 399–424.

Meyer, Stephen, III. 1981. *The Five Dollar Day: Labor Management and Social Control in the Ford Motor Company, 1908–1921*. Albany, NY: SUNY Press.

Milkman, Ruth. 1987. *Gender at Work: The Dynamics of Job Segregation by Sex during World War II*. Urbana: University of Illinois Press.

Raff, Daniel M.G. 1988. "The Puzzling Profusion of Compensation Systems in the Interwar Motor Vehicle Industry." Photocopy, Harvard University, Cambridge, MA.

Raff, Daniel M.G., and Lawrence H. Summers. 1987. "Wage Determination Theory and the Five-Dollar Day at Ford." *Journal of Economic History* 48 (June): 387–99.

Reuther (Walter P.) Library. Wayne State University, Detroit, MI.

Rose, Sonya O. 1987. "Gender Segregation in the Transition to the Factory: The English Hosiery Industry, 1850–1910." *Feminist Studies* 13 (Spring): 163–84.

———. 1991. "From Behind the Women's Petticoats: The English Factory Act of 1874 as a Cultural Production." *Journal of Historical Sociology* 4 (March): 32–51.

———. 1992. *Limited Livelihoods: Gender and Class in Nineteenth-Century England*. Berkeley: University of California Press.

U.S. Department of Labor, Women's Bureau. 1928. *The Effects of Labor Legislation on the Employment of Women*. Bulletin no. 65. Washington, DC: Women's Bureau.

---

Adapted from "Men and Monotony: Fraternalism as a Managerial Strategy at the Ford Motor Company." *Journal of Economic History* 53 (4) (1993): 824–56. Reprinted with permission of Cambridge University Press.

# 7

# Exploring the "Present Through the Past"

## Career and Family Across the Last Century

*Claudia Goldin*

. . . The past and the present are linked in many ways. Institutions survive over time; individuals, themselves, carry the past into the present. Over somewhat longer intervals, cohorts inherit the past from previous, often overlapping, generations (parents and teachers influence children; experienced managers guide younger workers). Responses to exogenous shocks are thereby transmitted from one generation to the next. But these transmissions are often slowed or altered, as in a game of telephone, by the previous generations (I will elaborate on this below). It is incumbent on all economists to situate their subjects and questions temporally to comprehend whether they are observing transient events or phenomena of greater significance.

The example I will use for examining the "present through the past" is the current discussion regarding whether women, particularly those who have graduated from four-year colleges, are able to combine career and family. Even though the educational and employment barriers faced by previous generations of women have been substantially reduced, many college women today are concerned. They would like to achieve career and family concurrently but fear they will not achieve one or the other or else will accomplish both serially with many years in between. But in the absence of historical data, we do not know how much change has already been generated. What were the demographic and labor force histories of college women across the past century? And if there was change, what generated it?

Using U.S. federal census population data, alumnae and Women's Bureau surveys, and the National Longitudinal Survey (NLS) of young women, I

Table 7.1

## Five Cohorts of College Graduate Women: Career and Family

| Cohort | Year graduating from college | Percent married by age 25–34 | Percent ever married with no births by age 35–44 | Career or job (C or J) family (F) combination |
|---|---|---|---|---|
| 1 | 1900–1919 | <50.0 | >30.0 | F or C[a] |
| 2 | 1920–1945 | 61.3 | 23.8 | J then F[a] |
| 3 | 1946–1965 | 82.1 | 8.6 | F then J[a] |
| 4 | 1966–1979 | 74.4 | 19.1 | C then F[b] |
| 5 | 1980–1995 | <68.5 | — | C and F[b] |

*Source:* Goldin (1997).
*Notes:*[a] Characterization of attained combination.
[b] Characterization of desired combination.
For column 3, data for cohort 5 end with women born around 1960, and data for cohort 1, when it was 25–34 years old, are not available. Marriage data for cohort 1, when it was 45–54 years old, support a figure of less than 50 percent for its 25–34-year-old marriage rate. For column 4, data are not available for cohort 1; the earliest data show 27.9 percent of women born in 1900 had no births by age 44. Cohort 5 is too young for data to be available for column 4. Column 2 entries are approximations based on age (graduation is assumed to take place at age 22); columns 3 and 4 are taken at the midpoint of the range of cohort birth years.

have pieced together the career and family histories of college women during the past century (Goldin 1997). Five cohorts emerge from the data in terms of economic and social change (see Table 7.1). The first cohort considered (graduating from 1900 to 1919) attained either *"career or family,"* rarely both. Fully 50 percent either never married or, if they did marry, did not have children. Yet the occupation of choice, for those without family, was teaching in the primary or secondary grades. The second cohort (graduating from 1920 to 1945) married at higher rates, had far more children, and attempted to defy social norms and have a career. The vast majority, however, eventually attained what I characterize as *"job, then family."* Despite their initial career desires, they did not remain in the labor force for long, rarely achieving careers.

The third cohort (graduating from 1946 to 1965) emerged as young adults just after World War II, became the mothers of the baby boom, and, later, sparked the revival of feminism in the late 1960s. The era was one of a rebirth of family in which college women participated along with the rest of America. I characterize this cohort as attaining *"family, then job."* For those graduating in the late 1950s, marriage occurred early (60 percent married before or during their first year after college) and was virtually complete (82 percent married by age thirty-four). Children were plentiful for those who married (about 90 percent had a first birth by age forty-four). The labor force participation rate of this cohort was low when they were in their twenties and thirties. College, for many of these women, was a good place to meet a college man, for the sex ratio in college was at its historic high point (2.3 men to 1 woman in 1950; 1.7 to 1 in 1955). The total rate of return to college for these women consisted, by my calculations, of two nearly equal parts: higher earnings in the labor market and a higher (husband's) income from the marriage market.

Finally, the fourth cohort (graduating from 1966 to 1979) is the most recent whose fertility, marriage, and labor force histories can be traced into their forties. Almost 30 percent of this group had not yet had a first birth by the early 1990s, and most had delayed marriage substantially. By using the NLS, I can calculate the percentage who achieved "*career and family*" by their late thirties and early forties. Although the definitions of both can be debated, between 13 percent and 17 percent reached the elusive goal of family and career by age forty-four, where family is defined as having a child, and career is defined as reaching some income goal per unit time for several years in succession (full-time employment is not required, however). The comparable number for their male counterparts is around 60 percent. But many of the women who achieved *career* in this cohort did so by delaying *family*, and that which is delayed is often not achieved.

The population of college women (and men) expanded substantially over the period considered, but selection into college does not appear to have generated the changes just noted. A socially and economically more homogeneous population (Radcliffe women) had nearly identical labor market and family histories to those in the larger group.

Even though the youngest cohort that can be studied did not reach the goal of full equality with its male counterparts, there was substantial change over time in the degree to which career and family were achieved by college women. The most important causes of change were the greater acceptance in the labor force of married, not just college, women and the reduction in employment barriers for all women (e.g., in the professions) and particularly for married women (see Goldin 1990 on the decline of "marriage bars"). Further, none of the major demographic changes were specific to women with more education; rather, the ups and downs of fertility and marriage existed throughout the population.

I model each of these changes as altering a "lifetime budget constraint," incorporating both income-earning and family-building as the uses of time. Thus the time allocation of the first cohort of college women was limited to either full-time income-earning or full-time family-building (the corner solutions), whereas the second and third cohorts responded to the filling in of the choice set, created by their being permitted to work after marriage. Most recently, the fourth cohort has been faced with the most complete choice set thus far, one that includes the possibility of both family and career. These transformed choice sets have been a legacy from one generation to the next. Each generation inherited the reduced barriers won by, or simply occurring in, the previous one and passed on new gains to the next. But the overlapping generations of grandmothers, mothers, and aunts may also have impeded change, for they often had a stake in the current system. Only by careful study of many generations of college women can one comprehend the reasons why change has taken so long and why current concern about career and family demonstrates just how much change there has been.

## References

Goldin, Claudia. 1990. *Understanding the Gender Gap: An Economic History of American Women*. New York: Oxford University Press.

———. 1997. "Career and Family: College Women Look to the Past." In *Gender and Family Issues in the Workplace*, ed. Francine D. Blau and Ronald G. Ehrenberg. New York: Russell Sage Press.

Adapted from "Exploring the 'Present Through the Past': Career and Family Across the Last Century," *American Economic Review* 87 (2) (May 1997): 396–99. Reprinted with permission of the American Economic Association.

# 8

# Marriage, Children, and Women's Employment

## What Do We Know?

*Philip N. Cohen and Suzanne M. Bianchi*

One of the well-known economic trends of the past several decades is an increase in women's labor force participation, particularly among married women with children. Although the trend is well established, there is no consensus as to its causes or consequences. With regard to causes, some argue that constraints such as low male earnings have propelled women into the marketplace, while others highlight expanding opportunities for women. Consequences are also contested, and the changing economic role of women is central both to debates about fairness and gender equity and to debates about family values and children's well-being.

In this chapter, we reexamine the *extent* of involvement in paid work for women in general and married women in particular, for both substantive and methodological reasons. Our substantive interest grows out of a renewed focus on paid work and child care that is related to welfare reform. Although welfare reform has concentrated attention on single women with children, we argue that married mothers' allocations of time to paid work also are central to the welfare debate, as these women often appear as a de facto comparison group. Hence, it is important to have a clear picture of both how much married mothers currently work for pay and how much that has changed over time. We develop our argument about the interrelationship of married women's labor market activity and welfare reform in the next section of this chapter.

The data we use, from the March Current Population Surveys (CPS), constitute the main source of information on trends in women's paid work. . . . We describe changes in hours and weeks of paid employment, focusing on trends for all women, for married women, and for married mothers of young children. We show that, depending on the universe and reference period one uses, widely different estimates of married women's "attachment" to the labor force may be calculated. The range of estimates creates ambiguity and complicates assessments of competing claims about women's "commitment" to market work.

Finally, to address the question of whether women's market involvement has responded more to constraints or to opportunities, we model the relationship between the extent of a woman's employment (as measured by annual hours of paid work), on the one hand, and marriage, young children, the woman's level of educational attainment, and her access to other income (for example, her husband's earnings), on the other. We do not view women's labor supply as unfettered; indeed, we find that women continue to work more when they have less access to other sources of income. However, the *trends* in the relationship between labor supply and predictor variables such as education and other income are more consistent with an "opportunities" than with a "constraints" interpretation. We conclude by speculating about the implications of our findings for the combination of paid work and child rearing among poor single mothers.

**Work and Welfare**

The year 1996 saw landmark legislation that is changing the face of welfare support for poor single mothers in the United States. The Personal Responsibility and Work Opportunity Reconciliation Act emerged from a long debate about the purpose and potential negative incentives of welfare. With the imposition of time limits on the receipt of welfare and a strong emphasis on moving recipients from welfare to work, the act implicitly endorses a model of mothering of young children that looks quite different from the one behind the establishment of the 1935 Social Security Act (with its widows' pensions) and the Aid to Dependent Children (later, Aid to Families with Dependent Children) programs that were the centerpiece of the welfare system.

Originally, mothers who had lost the wage support of the father of their young children because of his early death (or who were indigent because the child's father deserted the family or was unwilling or unable to financially support his children) were supported, at least at some minimal level, so that they could remain *out of the labor force* to nurture and raise their children. The Personal Responsibility and Work Opportunity Reconciliation Act is based on a quite different model of motherhood: a "good mother" locates child care for her young children and finds a job, perhaps after some additional job training, by means of which she can financially support herself and her children. Given the wage rates that many, if not most, single mothers on welfare can expect to command even after job training, the new model requires full-time, year-round market work for former welfare mothers if they are to have a realistic hope of keeping their families above the poverty level (in 1998 dollars, $13,133 for a mother living with her two children). The new scenario for poor mothers—sufficient paid work, in conjunction with fathers' responsibility to support their children—is in part dictated by the more general changes that have occurred for all mothers (see McLanahan and Casper 1995; Spain and Bianchi 1996).

Labor force rates for married mothers have risen rapidly in recent decades, and many see this increase as connected to what has happened to men's wages. Researchers have noted the dramatic widening of wage inequality among workers (Karoly and Burtless 1995; Gottschalk and Smeeding 1997) and the stagnation or, in the case of the least skilled, the substantial decline, in the real wages of men (Juhn, Murphy, and Pierce 1993; Levy 1995). The suggestion is that, increasingly, married women "need" to work to compensate for the labor force difficulties of their husbands, and as the "choice" of married mothers to stay out of the labor market and rear their own children becomes more and more constrained, it appears reasonable that single mothers, too, are subjected to similar constraints.

Although many more married women with young children work for pay nowadays than in the past, married women continue to exercise a variety of options in the way they balance work and family. For example, as we shall show, in any given year, most married women with preschoolers do not negotiate full-time, year-round jobs together with family responsibilities. Thus, the question arises—to the extent that the trends for married women have influenced the welfare debate, is it realistic to expect *single* mothers to combine full-time paid work and child care?

A second concern is that the focus on men's declining wages may have led to a view of changes in married women's market work as primarily the result of economic constraints. But have economic forces compelled married women to work more than they really want to? In actuality, the view that married women's economic roles have expanded more from "push" than "pull" factors is not clearly established. For example, although one recent study estimates that at least half of the increase in women's earnings relative to men's results from men's declining wages (Bernhardt, Morris, and Handcock 1995), others question this interpretation (Cotter, DeFiore, Hermsen, Kowalewski, and Vanneman 1997).

Economists who have investigated whether a woman's own wage-earning potential and occupational opportunities or whether her lack of prospects of financial support from another person (for example, her husband) are more likely to encourage her labor force participation tend to find that changes more often reflect expanding opportunities. For example, Claudia Goldin (1990) argues that, over time, married women's labor force participation has become less responsive to their husband's earnings. And Chinhui Juhn and Kevin M. Murphy (1997) contend that, although in the aggregate the increase in wives' employment would seem to compensate for the decline in their husband's earnings, this needs-based interpretation does not square well with the fact that labor force gains have been largest for wives married to highly educated, high-earning husbands.

In sum, we see the trends in paid work for women—particularly married women—as providing a context in which expectations are developed for single mothers. We raise two questions. First, are we overestimating how dramatic the march toward paid work—especially full-time, year-round paid work— has been for *married* mothers of young children? Second, is an explanation of changes in married women's labor force participation that emphasizes "push" factors, such as the decline in male earnings, a correct or useful way to interpret the trends? There is an interesting irony that attaches to the received view of married women's labor supply: emphasizing need factors rather than opportunity structures for married women strengthens the rationale for why (single) welfare mothers should be propelled into the labor force.

## Data and Methods

The data we employ in this study are from the March CPS microdata for the years 1978 through 1998. Two reference periods are used in the March survey: respondents are asked about their work schedules in the week preceding the survey and about weeks and hours worked in the previous year. [W]e distinguish two universes: all women and women workers (women who were employed at least one hour in the previous week). . . . In addition, we estimate tobit regressions of annual hours of paid work for prime working-age women (25–54), for each year from 1978 to 1998. The regressions help establish the extent to which the changes over time represent compositional shifts or changes in the forces that affect women's labor force participation directly. The regression model includes dummy variables for four categories of family: married women with spouse present and with children under six, married women with spouse present and without children under six, women with no spouse present and with children under six, and women with no spouse present and without children under six (the excluded category). . . . To evaluate the effect of other available income on women's decisions regarding employment, we add a variable for other family income. . . .

## Methodological Issues

The most commonly used indicator of women's market involvement is the percentage of women who are in the paid labor force in a given week. The labor force concept encompasses not only those who actually worked for pay in the reference week, but also those who had a job, but, for various reasons, were not actually working in the week before the survey and those who did not have a job, but were actively looking for work. By the mid-1990s, more than three-quarters of women aged twenty-five to fifty-four (women in the "prime working ages," when school attendance is usually complete and retirement has not yet begun) were in the labor force. By contrast, in 1960 the percentage was 43 percent, and in 1970 it was 50 percent (Spain and Bianchi 1996).

Although commonly used, the labor force participation rate gives little sense of how much time workers commit to paid work. As noted earlier, March CPS data employ two reference periods: how much respondents worked for pay in the week before the March survey (typically, the week in March containing the twelfth) and how much the respondent worked in the year preceding the survey. More individuals work some hours for pay over the course of a year than are in the labor force at any one particular time during the year. Hence, the "last year" reference period yields higher employment rates than the "last week" reference period.

With the CPS, it is also possible to calculate employment measures using all women as the base for rates or using only employed women. For illustrative purposes, the following tabulation displays the percentage of women working full-time, year-round, based on the cross-classification of the two universes (all women and women employed the previous week) by the two reference periods (last week and last year), for two age ranges in March 1998:

### Reference Period

| Universe | Last week | Last year |
| --- | --- | --- |
| Aged 16–64 | | |
| All women | 43.9 | 42.3 |
| Employed women | 67.6 | 61.4 |
| Aged 25–54 | | |
| All women | 51.2 | 50.2 |
| Employed women | 72.2 | 67.1 |

Shown in the tabulation are the percentages that would be classified as having a full-time commitment to market work. Not surprisingly, fewer women meet the criterion of working full-time when the reference period is an entire year than when it is just one week.

It is common to assess full-time work status not for all women, but as a percentage of *working* women. The second row of figures for each age group provides these estimates: when we restrict the universe to women who were employed at the time of the survey, 68 percent of them were full-time workers the previous week, and 61 percent were estimated to have worked full-time, year-round the previous year. The important point is the large gap separating the four estimates, any of which could be taken to indicate women's attachment to full-time work. In 1998, 42 percent of all women had worked full-time during the preceding year, whereas 68 percent of women who were employed the week before the survey put in a full-time workweek—a difference of more than 25 percentage points. (Estimates are higher if the age range is restricted to twenty-five to fifty-four, but the range between these estimates is still 22 percentage points among "prime" working-age women.)

Competing claims about whether women are committed to market work or just responding to economic need can be substantiated or refuted by opportunistically choosing a particular reference period and subgroup. The foregoing tabulation reminds us that, given the range of estimates of full-time attachment to market work (from 42 percent to 68 percent in 1998), it is probably not surprising that the views on women's motivations about market work (as well as the evidence cited in support of each view) continue to be discussed, debated, and disputed. On the one hand, those who want to suggest that women would really rather be in the home have only to point out that just 42 percent of women worked full-time, year-round, according to the March 1998 CPS. On the other hand, those who wish to emphasize women's commitment to market work can refer to the 72 percent of working women aged twenty-five to fifty-four who were employed full-time in March 1998. Our goal here is primarily to emphasize how important it is to understand the array of reference periods, universes, and age groups—as well as the trends in each—that are used in assessing women's participation in market work.

**Trends in Women's Employment**

. . . Is juggling work and family more pressing for women today than thirty-five years ago? The answer is "yes and no": yes, in that proportionately more adult women are engaged in the juggle; no, in that the number of weekly hours of paid work that an employed woman must balance with other commitments has not increased dramatically—it is a little, not a lot, higher than twenty years ago.

Table 8.1 [profiles changes in women's hours and weeks of paid work] for women aged twenty-five to fifty-four; in addition, the table describes married women and married women with children under age six. [T]here is no

Table 8.1

**Hours and Weeks of Paid Work for Women by Demographic Characteristic**

| All women | All | | Married | | Married with children < 6 years | |
|---|---|---|---|---|---|---|
| | 1978 | 1998 | 1978 | 1998 | 1978 | 1998 |
| Previous year | | | | | | |
| Average weeks | 27.5 | 36.8 | 25.2 | 35.8 | 17.5 | 30.9 |
| Percent employed ≥ 1 weeks | 65.7 | 79.4 | 62.0 | 77.7 | 50.5 | 70.5 |
| Percent employed FTYR | 32.4 | 50.2 | 26.9 | 46.1 | 14.3 | 34.7 |
| Annual hours | 1,002 | 1,415 | 884 | 1,339 | 583 | 1,094 |

| Employed women* | All* | | Married* | | Married with children < 6 years* | |
|---|---|---|---|---|---|---|
| | 1978 | 1998 | 1978 | 1998 | 1978 | 1998 |
| Previous year | | | | | | |
| Average weeks | 43.5 | 47.3 | 42.4 | 47.2 | 36.0 | 45.4 |
| Percent employed FTYR | 54.4 | 67.1 | 48.5 | 63.3 | 33.2 | 54.0 |
| Annual hours | 1,596 | 1,830 | 1,501 | 1,779 | 1,215 | 1,625 |

*Note:* *Employed women worked one or more hours the week prior to the survey.

question that married mothers' attachment to market work has increased greatly since 1978. Trends are similar for married women, married mothers of young children, and all women, with one important exception: working married women with children under age six have increased the number of weeks they work per year—and consequently their annual hours—more substantially than have all women (or all married women).

By 1998, half of all women in the prime working ages were employed full-time, year-round; in comparison, 46 percent of married women and 35 percent of married mothers of young children did so. We estimate that in 1998, around 65 percent of married mothers of preschoolers were not full-time, year-round workers. This is by no means a picture of married mothers abandoning the rearing of their own children so that they can commit themselves to market work. Rather, there has been a ratcheting up of attachment to market work, but with the norm— at least in terms of modality—continuing to be something other than full-time, year-round work for married mothers during their children's preschool years. . . .

**Explaining the Trends**

Although half of women are still not full-time, year-round workers, their involvement in market work has moved steadily upward. There are two competing explanations for this trend: compared with past experience, women have increased opportunities for earnings and occupational attainment that they seek to realize, or, alternatively, women have increased needs because male wages stagnated and desired standards of living rose.

If women increasingly work because opportunities have expanded, we might expect to see a decline in the effect of other income—particularly their husbands' earnings—on women's labor force participation. We might also view an increasing correlation between educational attainment and labor force participation as suggestive of increased opportunities for women, for it is likely that the most highly educated have gained the most in terms of opportunity structures in the labor market over the previous two decades.

On the other hand, if women's increased commitment to paid work is in response to men's labor force difficulties, we might expect access to other income to remain a strong predictor of the extent of women's employment. If, instead, it is primarily need that drives women's labor force participation, we should see a stable or increasing effect of other income, and we should see labor force rates remain high among those with less education, who presumably have more need for income.

## Findings

. . . Relative to unmarried women without children (the omitted category in the regression models), both married mothers and single mothers commit far fewer hours to market work, but the differential has declined significantly over the past two decades. In the late 1970s, married women without young children worked for pay significantly fewer hours than their single counterparts, the models show, but by the late 1990s, there was no longer a significant difference in hours of labor force participation attributable to marriage among these women. . . .

With respect to the question of what drives women's increased attachment to paid work, the coefficients on education and on the other income variables are illuminating. Relative to those without a high school education, both high school- and college-educated women have become increasingly likely to commit hours to market work over time. Coefficients for high school graduates rose from about 500 in the late 1970s to 700 or more in the late 1990s. College-educated women in the 1970s were predicted by the model to work about 800 hours more than those without high school diplomas, but more than 1,000 hours more by the late 1990s. And although access to other income continues to depress women's labor supply, between the late 1970s and the late 1990s the coefficient for other income declined by almost half.

These findings certainly do not constitute conclusive proof that expanding opportunities explain women's increased labor supply, but they are consistent with an increased emphasis on "pull" factors, especially for women with high levels of education.

## Conclusion

Women have reached the point at which marriage in itself has relatively little effect on their labor supply, although access to other income, which, for married women, is primarily earnings from their spouse, continues to exert a downward pressure on women's allocation of time to paid work. This effect of other income is diminishing, however: not unlike what happened earlier for men (Juhn, Murphy, and Pierce 1993), educational differentials in the labor supply of women have grown over time, widening the gap between better educated and less educated women, but giving the former more market work opportunities.

Similarly, children exert less of a downward pressure on women's labor supply in the 1990s than they did in the late 1970s, but the effect of having pre-school-age children on annual hours is substantial. Increasingly, American women seem to exchange some hours of caring for their own children for hours of paid work, but married mothers remain a long way from a situation in which most of them remain committed to full-time, year-round market work.

It is important to emphasize the current level, as well as the trend, of the extent of married mothers' work, especially when one considers current welfare reform. Rather than being in step with levels of employment of married mothers, current reforms require paid-work efforts on the part of single mothers that put them substantially ahead of the curve.

Given the relatively low rates of full-time, year-round labor force attachment of married mothers, what are the implications of a model of full-time, year-round work for poor single mothers? Certainly, poor women have far less access to any other source of income for their children. Also, placing children in nonparental child care settings is far more common in 1998 than it was when Aid to Families with Dependent Children was introduced. But given the low rates of full-time, year-round labor force participation of married mothers, most of their young children are probably not spending exceedingly long periods in nonparental care settings. Hence, the new model for mothers currently on welfare, who would almost certainly have to work full-time, year-round to support a family, embodies child care arrangements that have not yet become typical.

# References

Bernhardt, Annette, Martina Morris, and Mark S. Handcock. 1995. "Women's Gains or Men's Losses? A Closer Look at the Shrinking Gender Gap in Earnings." *American Journal of Sociology* 100 (September): 302–28.

Cotter, D.A., J.M. DeFiore, J.M. Hermsen, B.M., Kowalewski, and R. Vanneman. 1997. "Same Data, Different Conclusions: Comment on 'Women's Gains or Men's Losses? A Closer Look at the Shrinking Gender Gap in Earnings.'" *American Journal of Sociology* 102 (January): 1143–54.

Goldin, Claudia. 1990. *Understanding the Gender Gap: An Economic History of American Women.* New York: Oxford University Press.

Gottschalk, Peter, and Timothy M. Smeeding. 1997. "Cross-national Comparisons of Earnings and Income Inequality." *Journal of Economic Literature* 35 (June): 633–87.

Juhn, Chinhui, and Kevin M. Murphy. 1997. "Wage Inequality and Family Labor Supply." *Journal of Labor Economics* 15 (January): 72–97.

Juhn, Chinhui, Kevin M. Murphy, and Brooks Pierce. 1993. "Wage Inequality and the Rise in Returns to Skill." *Journal of Political Economy* 101 (June): 410–42.

Karoly, Lynn A., and Gary Burtless. 1995. "Demographic Changes, Rising Earnings Inequality, and the Distribution of Personal Well-being, 1959–1989." *Demography* 32 (August): 379 406.

Levy, Frank. 1995. "Incomes and Income Inequality." In *State of the Union: America in the 1990s.* Vol. 1, *Economic Trends*, ed. Reynolds Farley. New York: Russell Sage Foundation.

McLanahan, Sara, and Lynne Casper. 1995. "Growing Diversity and Inequality in the American Family." In *State of the Union: America in the 1990s.* Vol. 2, *Social Trends*, ed. Reynolds Farley. New York: Russell Sage Foundation.

Spain, Daphne, and Suzanne M. Bianchi. 1996. *Balancing Act: Motherhood, Marriage, and Employment among American Women.* New York: Russell Sage Foundation.

Adapted from "Marriage, Children, and Women's Employment: What Do We Know?" *Monthly Labor Review* 122 (12) (December 1999): 22–31.

# Section 2

# Appendix

**Key Terms**

breadwinner wage (or family wage)
commodification
constancy hypothesis
cult of domesticity
emancipation hypothesis
female-dominated occupation; male-dominated occupation
feminization of the labor force
hegemonic masculinity
industrialization
informal economy vs. formal economy
labor force composition
labor force participation rate
male breadwinner family
occupational segregation
postindustrial
U-hypothesis
wage gap
welfare reform

**Discussion Questions**

1. Based on the readings, why does women's labor force participation have a U-shape as industrialization occurs? What forces inhibit women's involvement in paid employment? Using the U.S. experience, what factors contribute to the rising part of the U? Discuss supply vs. demand and push vs. pull factors.
2. Why have industrialization and mass-production manufacturing traditionally been a male domain? Compare and contrast the explanations offered in two chapters: (a) Rau and Wazienski; and (b) Lewchuk.
3. How did both labor unions (fraternalism) and management (Henry Ford) in the automobile industry maintain and redefine masculinity at work? What role did technology play in gender relations?

4. How did women from different "cohorts" in the twentieth century balance work/career and family? Were they able to have both simultaneously, or did they make sacrifices? Explain.
5. How has women's paid work been affected by race-ethnicity, marital status, the presence of children, and the age of their children? What implications do these trends hold for single mothers?
6. Rau and Wazienski deliberately chose only data from 1960 and 1970, rather'than later years. Why? Do you think that the U-hypothesis would still hold true in a newly developing country today? Discuss.

### Exercises

1. *"Do the Q."* In the article by Rau and Wazienski, Table 5.3 shows the curvilinear (or U-shaped) relationship between the degree of industrialization (industrial decile) and female labor force participation. To see this relationship graphically, copy the table into a spreadsheet program such as Microsoft Excel. (Note: you may have to insert an apostrophe after each decile range so that the software program reads 11–20 as a category rather than as a date.) Use the "chart" function to plot a line graph. Can you see the U? Which industrial decile does not seem to fit the U-shape pattern? Reflecting on the chapter and your graph, summarize what the U-hypothesis means in words.
2. Interview some women who graduated from high school or college after 1980. How have they attempted to reconcile their paid work and family life? Compare and contrast your findings with the women in earlier cohorts studied by Claudia Goldin.
3. *"Do the Q."* When you see a percentage in a table, can you discern what was measured to calculate the percentage? Recall that percentages are derived from fractions, dividing the numerator by the denominator and multiplying by 100. In the chapter by Cohen and Bianchi, it is crucial to notice whether each percentage in Table 8.1 is a proportion of all women, employed women, employed married women with children under six years of age, etc. In the table, there are three rows of percentages. Each percentage defines a group (the denominator) and a subgroup (the numerator) and compares them. For example, in the first column of data, you see the number 65.7 in the second row. The group is "all women in 1978" and the subgroup is "those women who were employed for at least one week." We can interpret this to mean that 65.7 percent of all women were employed at least one week in 1978.

a. Which rows of Table 8.1 contain percentages? Describe, in words, the group and subgroup for each of the percentages in the table. Can you draw a Venn diagram (a circle within a circle) to represent the group and subgroup? Can you write, in words, the numerator and denominator for each case, too?

b. Write a sentence to present a finding about each percentage in the table.

c. You can also calculate the *absolute change* in percentage points from 1978 to 1998 by subtracting the 1978 percentage from the 1998 percentage. Which group had the highest absolute change?

d. Compare this with the *relative change* (the percent change). Take the absolute change and divide by the starting value (in 1978); then divide by 100. Which group had the highest relative change?

4. The wage gap can be costly to women over the course of their work lives. The AFL-CIO's Working Women Department, in conjunction with the Institute for Women's Policy Research, has developed a statistical program to calculate how much the pay gap would cost over a lifetime of work. The formula is based on your earnings (or expected earnings in an occupation), your age group, and your level of education. To use the calculator, follow the links of "How Much Will the Pay Gap Cost YOU?" at www.aflcio.org/women/index.htm.

## Further Reading

Amott, Teresa, and Julie Matthaei. 1996. *Race, Gender, and Work: A Multi-cultural Economic History of Women in the United States*, revised edition. Boston: South End Press.

Blackwelder, Julia Kirk. 1997. *Now Hiring: The Feminization of Work in the United States, 1900–1995*. College Station: Texas A&M University Press.

Connell, R.W. 1993. "The Big Picture: Masculinities in Recent World History." *Theory and Society* 22: 597–623.

Goldin, Claudia. 1990. *Understanding the Gender Gap: An Economic History of American Women*. New York: Oxford University Press.

Wootton, Barbara H. 1997. "Gender Differences in Occupational Attainment." *Monthly Labor Review* 120 (4): 15–24.

# Section 3

# Households and Social Reproduction

The view of economic life in most textbooks centers on two economic processes: production and distribution. Firms produce goods and services for sale in markets where they are purchased by households for private consumption. Feminists have long argued that this narrow focus omits an important sphere of economic life, the unpaid work that takes place within the household. In fact, some of this work is another form of production. Many of the goods and services purchased are not ready to be directly consumed. Food needs to be cooked into meals. People grow flowers, fruits, and vegetables in their gardens. Services such as laundering clothes, cleaning the house, and fixing broken toys are often produced in the household.

However, as our economy has grown, more and more of this work is embedded in the products we buy. Generations ago bread was baked from scratch; today we usually buy presliced loaves. Convenience foods need only be popped in the microwave. Some clothes are sent out to be cleaned. Most of us do not know how to repair the high-tech toys we now play with, such as computers, DVD players, and video game devices. As we saw in Section 2, this commodification process was both a cause and an effect of women's increased labor force attachment.

There is another form of work that is also associated with the household, the work of *social reproduction*. Social reproduction refers to the daily and intergenerational renewal of human society. Biological reproduction of the next generation is only a part of this process. Children must not only be born, they must be nurtured and educated. On a daily basis, adults as well as children need to be "reproduced." That is, we use up energy each day that needs to be replenished with food and rest. We also may find ourselves emotionally drained and in need of caring attention to recharge ourselves. The production that takes place in the market economy could not take place for long if human beings were treated as completely disposable resources, although it may seem that some exploitative employers who pay low wages and over-work their labor force forget this.

Despite U.S. women's increased involvement in paid work (described in Section 2), unpaid production in the household and especially the caring labor involved in social reproduction are still largely women's "separate sphere." In fact, many women still specialize in this form of work for at least part of their lives. Barbara Bergmann takes a strong position about the dangers of such specialization in a classic article, "The Economic Risks of Being a Housewife." Her lively piece is humorous in tone, yet her point is absolutely serious. She believes that women who specialize as homemakers put themselves in a weak economic position. A full-time homemaker lacks *bargaining power* compared with her spouse because she would be financially weak if the relationship dissolved.

To understand Bergmann's chapter, you will need a brief background on the economist whose work she is critiquing, Gary Becker. Becker won the Nobel prize in economics in 1992 because he used the tools of neoclassical economics—rational decision making in order to maximize happiness—to explain areas of human life that others thought were outside the scope of economic analysis. Becker studied, among other areas, the decisions to marry, have children, and get divorced, pioneering the "new home economics." He also applied a concept from economic trade theory called *comparative advantage* to the division of labor within households. Just as the level of production in the world economy is supposed to be better off if countries specialize in producing one product and trade for others, Becker argued that a household will be better off if one member (the higher wage earner) specializes in paid employment and another specializes in home production. For this to be true, however, you must assume that members of the household, or at least the head of the household, are altruistic and share the benefits equally. Therefore, neoclassical theory assumes one type of human behavior—selfishness—in market transactions and an entirely different type of behavior within families.

Nancy Folbre and Julie Nelson make this last point in their chapter, "For Love or Money—Or Both?" They also probe the implications of the commodification of social, emotional, and caring work for the future well-being of our society. While Bergmann's contribution focuses on the downside of specializing in homemaking under our current arrangements, Folbre and Nelson capture the social value of this sphere of economic life. They also document the hidden secret behind much of the economic growth associated with industrialization in market economies: when the same amount of production is commodified instead of performed at home, the economy appears to be growing though "consumers" are no better off. Most importantly, Folbre and Nelson present two sides of a debate over the benefits and drawbacks of commodifying caring work. Can work remain caring if it is done for pay? How can we reorganize this work to alleviate the stress of working women's "double day"?

Of course, if more of the caring work were shared within the household, the burden on working women would be reduced. Yet time use studies demonstrate that the redistribution of homemaking tasks has been negligible compared with the trend toward women's paid employment. Marianne Ferber and Lauren Young investigate whether we can have hope for more egalitarian future arrangements in "Student Attitudes Toward Roles of Women and Men." This survey of Harvard undergraduates indicates that these young men and women have relatively egalitarian value systems, although the male students still view care of preschool children as primarily women's responsibility. Ferber and Young also critique Becker's analysis of comparative advantage, arguing that he neglects the inhibiting effect of gender ideology and institutionalized social norms. As long as housework remains socially devalued and participation in paid employment reaps respect and monetary awards, it will be difficult to encourage men to increase their participation in work at home.

In the final chapter of this section, Jane Wheelock and Elizabeth Oughton explore the nature of the household in greater depth. In "The Household as a Focus for Research," they argue that institutional economics provides better insights into economic activities such as production, reproduction, consumption, and socialization of children than do neoclassical analyses of rational individuals. Rather than treating the market and the household as entirely separate spheres with different modes of behavior, the authors see the household as positioned at the center of concentric circles, encompassing the social environment. Although often taken to be synonymous with the nuclear family, the household can, in fact, take different forms. Household structure therefore varies historically and cross-culturally. The larger economic, political, and social environment can affect changes in household structure. The task for us is to find the forms that will enhance the well-being of the members of our households and the members of our society.

# 9

# The Economic Risks of Being a Housewife

*Barbara R. Bergmann*

To be a housewife is to be a member of a peculiar occupation—one with characteristics quite different from all others. The nature of the duties to be performed, the form of the pay, the methods of supervision, the tenure system, the "marketplace" in which "workers" find "jobs," and the physical hazards are all so different from conditions found in other occupations that one tends not to think of a housewife as belonging to an occupation in the usual sense. Yet being a housewife certainly meets the *American Heritage Dictionary*'s definition of an occupation, as "an activity that serves as one's regular source of livelihood." In fact, to be a housewife is to be a member of the largest single occupation in the U.S. economy. Thus, it is certainly both legitimate and interesting to compare the advantages and disadvantages of the housewife's source of livelihood with those of other sources of livelihood.

Few economists have studied the economic aspects of being a housewife. Gary Becker's (1973) economium to the advantages of the division of labor between spouses addresses some of the issues, but its perspective seems to be that of a male member of a "traditional" family. More recently, Marianne Ferber and Bonnie Birnbaum (1977), as well as Clair (Vickrey) Brown (1981) have made contributions in which the interests of each family member are recognized as distinct. In this paper, I focus on the economic risks of the housewife occupation, which are shown to be very high relative to those of other occupations.

## Characteristics of the Housewife Occupation

### *The Duties*

The housewife's occupational duties—which we will define as the things she needs to do to keep her job—usually include cooking, dish washing, housecleaning, laundry work, child care, and a "personal relations" component, which includes sexual relations. Both the sexual and nonsexual components of the duties are sources of economic risk. The nonsexual component of housewives' duties is broadly the same as the duties of paid domestic servants, although the housewife usually has more discretion than the servant and a more responsible role with respect to the children and the finances. A housewife whose "job" ends, either at her own discretion or that of her husband, will probably have to enter some other occupation at least for a time. She will be faced with the fact that the alternative occupation most like the one she has left, and the one for which she has the most fitting recent experience, is one with both low pay and low status. Most housewives who lose their job or who quit do not become domestic servants. However, they will be at a disadvantage in the job market relative to their age group because of the failure in the eyes of employers to build up, during their service as housewives, that part of their human capital thought to be most serviceable on nondomestic jobs.

The sexual component of the housewife's duties also contributes importantly to the risks of the job. Like the airline stewardess [flight attendant], part of the housewife's job is being attractive. Unlike the flight attendant, however, the housewife's duties clearly include cohabitation. The woman who considers entering a housewife job, usually from a paid job, knows that cohabitation is a condition of keeping it, and considers the attractiveness of her suitor (or her husband, if she is already married) in deciding whether to accept the "job offer." Of course, sexual cohabitation in this context forms a perhaps vital part of the intimacy of the marriage relationship, with its presumption of caring, consideration, and long-run commitment. It is usually, at the outset at least, considered a highly valued fringe benefit rather than an onerous duty. However, the sex component of the housewife's duties, and the children who may appear as a result of it, make it difficult to go from one "job" to another within the occupation. The fact that the law makes marriages more costly and difficult to dissolve than are other employee-employer relationships also contributes to the difficulty of going from one housewife job to another.

The housewife's attractiveness to her husband can be thought of as a component of the human capital needed for her job, and she may be in the position of seeing this part of her portfolio of assets wane in value either gradually or suddenly. Her husband's attractiveness to her may also suddenly or gradually diminish, reducing the value of the intimacy fringe benefit, possibly changing it from positive to negative. These possibilities obviously make for high risk both with respect to "working conditions" and tenure.

Another component of a housewife's human capital that contributes to the value of her work is her identity as the mother of the husband's children, and thus as the person usually assumed to be most fitted to give them attentive and loving care. As the number of children born to marriages has on average diminished, and as the number of years in which a married couple has preschool children in the home has diminished, this component of the housewife's human capital disappears faster, leaving her more open to the threat of displacement from her "job."

As Ferber and Birnbaum (1977) have pointed out, the decline in the value of the housewife's services in the home occurs at a time when her husband's earnings and status are usually growing. The discrepancy in the economic position and in the social and sexual opportunities of a housewife and the man to whom she is married typically grows as they go through their forties.

### Physical Hazards

The home is a risky place both for men and women. In 1977, 15.1 million women and 14.4 million men were injured in the home, while 2.4 million women and 9.0 million men were injured in paid jobs. Accidents are not the only source of injury; the chance of physical damage to women because of intentional human violence is far from negligible. A recent survey for the U.S. Department of Justice (1979) found that 4.1 percent of women living with a husband or male partner at the time of the survey had experienced severe physical abuse from him within the last twelve months and 8.7 percent had experienced it at some time. Severe physical abuse was defined as "being kicked, bit, or hit with a fist, being hit with an object, being beaten up, being threatened with a knife or a gun, or having a knife or a gun used against them." If in addition to the above, we include those women who had something thrown at them, or were pushed, grabbed, shoved, or slapped, the proportion who experienced violence so defined comes to 10 percent for the previous twelve months, while 21 percent had experienced violence so defined at some time. Surveys that ask women about violent attacks on them by men living with them probably produce an underestimate of the extent of violence—they leave out women who have left their husbands, and attacks that women are ashamed to report.

In most occupations, physical assault on the job will be likely to result in criminal penalties for the perpetrator, but violence against housewives by their husbands results in few charges—the Justice Department survey found that only 9 percent of violent incidents are reported to police and only 4 percent go to court. Police in most jurisdictions simply do not consider such attacks as criminal.

## The Pay

The "pay for housewives" advocates, such as Carol Lopate (1974), tend to ignore the fact that the housewife does receive a return for her work, perhaps because all or almost all of the pay takes the form of noncash benefits. Like the noncash benefits workers in other occupations get, they are untaxed. The housewife's pay consists of room, board, a clothing allowance, medical care, all-expenses-paid vacations, and the benefits she gets out of her own domestic services. . . .

The noncash nature of the housewife's pay creates problems for her if conditions on her job are such that she wants to quit the marriage. It may be difficult or impossible for her to accumulate a cash reserve that would carry her through until she finds some other source of livelihood, usually a job in another occupation. If she can make such an accumulation, it may have to be done by stealth. The "live-in" feature of the housewife's job increases the difficulty of quitting by increasing the size of the accumulation needed to change jobs. In most other occupations, a person quitting a particular job does not have to move out of his or her present living quarters at the time of the quit—such a person can usually live for a while on the goodwill built up with the landlord and on the stocks of staples in the kitchen. It is conjectured that the reason a wife who is beaten by her husband may stay with him is that she has no place to go—and no resources to establish a place to live apart for herself and for any children she may intend to take with her. Even in less dire circumstances, the practical difficulty of setting up a new household may result in the imposition on and toleration by the housewife of circumstances few workers in other occupations are subject to.

## The Economic Risks the Housewife Runs

If a risky activity is defined as one with a high variability in payoff, then the housewife's occupation is one of the riskiest. The variability of the housewife's pay is larger than the variability of her husband's, because it includes variation due to the possibility that the marriage will end and that the pay she gets from him will cease. In this latter case, she may after a time be able to find a new job either as housewife or in some other occupation providing similar or even improved pay, but there will in most cases be a drop in economic status that is severe and prolonged.

Samuel Preston (1975) has estimated, based on disruption rates experienced in 1973, that 44 percent of marriages will end in divorce. The U.S. Census Bureau (1976) found the median interval between first marriage and divorce for women to be 7.3 years in 1975, which means that a substantial proportion of divorced women will have had relatively long marriages, and the housewives among them will have spent a substantial number of years out of the labor force. About 41 percent of the divorced women responding to the census had not remarried, and for those who had remarried, there was a median interval of three years between divorce and remarriage.

We may deduce from the census data that on average a married woman runs a risk of divorce each year of above 2 percent. The risk of getting divorced in a year is far lower than the risk an employed person runs of suffering a spell of unemployment in a year, which was on the order of 14 percent in 1975. However, leaving or losing a job, difficult as that may be, is usually far less of a personal and financial trauma than ending a marriage is likely to be for a housewife. An important part of the financial trauma may relate to the expenses for children, since economic support from the husband for them will in a high proportion of cases disappear simultaneously with financial support for the wife. The Census Bureau (1979) reports that three-quarters of the mothers who were separated or divorced from their child's father received nothing from the father. Only 8 percent received $1,000 or more per child. Alimony is available with any regularity to an even smaller group.

The power that a husband now has to terminate his marriage to a housewife and thus to reduce considerably her standard of living and her status has effects on those housewives whose marriage has not terminated. First of all, there is the worry that the marriage may terminate. Second, the husband may use the implicit or explicit threat of leaving to achieve a dominance in the relationship, to the detriment of the housewife's feelings of well-being. Thus, the increasingly well-known risk of a bad outcome has the effect of reducing the value of a "good" outcome.

### The Euthanasia of the Housewife?

If the housewife occupation has all of the disadvantages I have cataloged, why have so many people "chosen" it over other occupations? The answer, of course, is that all the people who "chose" it were women, and being women their alternatives were even worse, or were made to seem worse. In the past, the occupation of housewife had the character of a caste into which one was placed at birth. The socialization that female children received (and still receive) that makes membership in the housewife caste seem attractive and inevitable has been documented by Judith Long Laws (1979). The ideology of romantic love and the "Prince Charming" legend have played a part. For adult women, leaving the caste was discouraged by employment discrimination, by the social stigma attached to being a never-married or divorced woman, and by social pressures on wives not to seek paid employment.

In the era prior to the industrial revolution, most women worked on farms and contributed heavily to the output of goods in addition to providing housekeeping services. The housewife caste, in the sense of an occupational group devoting itself exclusively to domestic service, was greatly enlarged by the industrial revolution. As jobs off the farm were created, real wages for men got to a level such that many men were able to afford the services of a live-in domestic servant, who also served as a wife. This development segregated women's productive activities, but probably improved women's lives considerably. As technological change has proceeded further, the real value of cash wages available to women, although continuing to be far below men's wages, has reached a level such that the alternatives to continued membership in the housewife caste have grown more attractive. Thus the same trends that caused the housewife occupation to grow are now causing it to shrink.

Although some women continue to enter the occupation of housewife directly from school and remain there for their lifetime, most women have only a spell as full-time housewives, starting at the birth of their first child. The number and lengths of women's spells in the housewife occupation are decreasing, and an increasing number of women are managing to get through a lifetime with no spell at all.

The decline in size of the housewife occupation will mean that some of the functions this occupation currently serves will disappear, and others will be served in other ways, through the purchase of market services and through the greater participation of husbands and children in providing domestic services. Isabel Sawhill (1977) has posed the question of whether the world would be a better or worse place if there were no full-time homemakers. Although economists do not usually ask such questions about products or occupations that changing technology or tastes have caused to decline, the question is in the minds of many and is becoming a political issue. It is certainly true that, from a narrow point of view, a system in which the homemakers are women with impoverished alternatives serves the comfort and interest of men and male children, and the short-run comfort of female children. However, just as few would say that discrimination against blacks makes the world a better place, or even a better place for whites, so increasingly many are unwilling to say that a world of poor opportunities for women is a better place, or even a better place for men.

# References

Becker, G. 1973. "A Theory of Marriage: Part I." *Journal of Political Economy* 81 (July/August): 813–46.

Brown, C. (Vickrey). 1981. "Home Production for Use in a Market Economy." In *Rethinking the Family: Some Feminist Questions*, ed. B. Thorne. New York: Longman.

Ferber, M.A., and B.G. Birnbaum. 1977. "The 'New Home Economics': Retrospects and Prospects." *Journal of Consumer Research* 4: 19–28.

Laws, J.L. 1979. *The Second X: Sex Role and Social Change*. New York: Elsevier Science.

Lopate, C. 1974. "Pay for Housework." *Journal of Social Policy* 5: 27–31.

Preston, S.H. 1975. "Estimating the Proportion of American Marriages That End in Divorce." *Sociological Methods and Research* 3 (May): 435–60.

Sawhill, I.V. 1977. "Homemakers: An Endangered Species?" *Journal of Home Economics* (November): 18–20.

U.S. Bureau of the Census. 1976. "Number, Timing, and Duration of Marriage and Divorces in the United States: June 1975." *Current Population Reports*, Series P 20, No. 297. Washington, DC: U.S. Government Printing Office.

———. 1979. "Divorce, Child Custody, and Child Support." *Current Population Reports*, Series P 20, No. 84. Washington, DC: U.S. Government Printing Office.

U.S. Department of Justice. 1979. *A Survey of Spousal Violence Against Women in Kentucky*. Law Enforcement Assistance Administration, July.

---

Adapted from "The Economic Risks of Being a Housewife," *American Economic Review* 71 (2) (May 1981): 81–86. Reprinted with permission of the American Economic Association.

# 10

# For Love or Money—Or Both?

## Nancy Folbre and Julie A. Nelson

The connections between the world of money and profit and the world of care and concern are of great importance to society. Traditionally, the "public" world of markets and government was the realm of men, while the "private" realm of family and social relationships was entrusted to women. While some of women's tasks were largely instrumental—cleaning and cooking, for example—many tasks contained more personalized and emotional components. Women were in charge of children, elderly, and the ill; maintaining personal relationships; offering emotional support, personal attention, and listening; embodying (or so it was understood) sexuality. This social contract is changing. As women move increasingly into the world of paid work, many of these traditional intimate tasks are being performed in relationships that include the explicit movement of money. Paid child care, nursing homes for the elderly, talk therapy, and phone sex are just a few examples. What are economists to make of this trend?

. . . Whether commentators celebrate the movement to the market or bemoan it, the use of unexamined assumptions and outdated rhetoric is endemic to the literature. An a priori judgment that markets must improve caregiving by increasing efficiency puts the brakes on intelligent research, rather than encouraging it. Likewise, an a priori judgment that markets must severely degrade caring work by replacing motivations of altruism with self-interest is also a research stopper. We develop a more open and balanced framework for addressing issues of love and money. We also evaluate the potential benefits and costs of the movement to the market and outline important areas for research and action. The future of social, emotional, and caring work has tremendous implications for human well-being. While such work may have been thought of as intellectually uninteresting because it was "naturally" abundant in supply, the profound changes taking place in gender norms sharply call into question the wisdom of continuing to neglect this area of study.

## The Shift from Family to Market

### The Dependency Burden

The sweep of demographic change has transformed the relationship between the family and the economy—and vice versa. Once upon a time, child rearing contributed to the family labor force and could be easily combined with income-generating activities such as farm labor and industrial home work. It also consumed a large share of economic resources. Times have changed. Birth rates have declined dramatically over the long run in the United States, as in most other countries. In 1860, the total fertility rate (the number of live births a woman could expect to have, given age-specific birth rates) was 5.2. By 1900, it had fallen below 4. In 1997, it was 2 births per woman. Meanwhile, life expectancy at birth has increased from forty-seven years in 1900 to almost 77 in 1997.

These demographic changes have reduced the aggregate burden of child raising while increasing the burden of elder care. The meaning of the term "dependent" has changed enormously over time. Still, the percentage of the population that is under eighteen combined with the percentage that is over sixty-five—traditionally termed the "dependency ratio"—is an important indicator of the amount of time, energy, and money the working age population must devote to nonworkers. [T]he percentage of the population under the age of eighteen has steadily declined in the United States, with a countervailing trend toward an increase in the share of the population sixty-five and over. . . .

Of course, the specifics of dependency are very different for a five year-old, a fifteen-year-old, a healthy sixty-five-year-old, and an ailing ninety-year-old. Even if individuals aged sixty-five to seventy-five are economically dependent in the sense that they receive Social Security and Medicare, this age group has also seen recent improvements in health and activity levels. The number of individuals eighty-five and older, who tend to require very high levels of direct care, is projected to grow from about 1.6 percent of the population to about 4.6 percent between 2000 and 2050.

### Labor Force Categories

We use the somewhat anachronistic term "homemaking" to describe women's nonmarket work because it conveys the nature of the caring activities inter-

Table 10.1

**The Decline of Full-Time Homemaking in the United States, 1870–2000**

|  | Homemakers as percent of all women workers | Women in paid jobs as percent of all women workers | Homemakers as percent of all workers |
|---|---|---|---|
| 1870 | 70.2 | 29.8 | 40.1 |
| 1900 | 64.4 | 35.6 | 35.6 |
| 1930 | 59.7 | 40.3 | 34.1 |
| 1960 | 56.0 | 44.0 | 29.1 |
| 1990 | 32.7 | 67.3 | 22.0 |
| 2000 | 29.5 | 70.5 | 16.4 |

*Source:* U.S. Census Bureau.

twined with the household production involved. Both men and women typically combine some homemaking activities with paid employment. However, many women have historically specialized in full-time homemaking. Historical research and early census surveys show that women worked about the same hours per week providing goods and services for family members as paid workers did in their formal jobs (and women typically worked many more hours when young children were present in the home).

If we assume that women devoted about as much productive effort to paid and unpaid work combined as men did to paid work, we can construct estimates of the total labor force, including both paid and unpaid workers (Folbre and Wagman 1993; Wagman and Folbre 1996). Assuming that 85 percent of all women sixteen and over were engaged in productive (paid or unpaid) work and that those who did not have paying jobs were full-time homemakers, we can trace the historical shift in the use of women's time. Table 10.1 shows that in 1870, about 40 percent of the entire productive labor force (paid and unpaid, male and female) was made up of full-time homemakers. This percentage has declined along with increases in the relative importance of paid employment among women, with the biggest change coming between 1960 and 1990. By 2000, homemaking had declined substantially, but still involved over 16 percent of all workers and about 30 percent of all women workers.

Many of the women entering wage employment have moved into jobs considered socially appropriate for women, contributing to a persistent pattern of occupational gender segregation (Blau 1998; Reskin and Roos 1990). Many have shouldered responsibilities that involve paid care for others, leading

Table 10.2

**The Rise of Professional Care Service Industries** (in percent)

|  | Professional care services | Domestic and personal services | Other services | Agriculture, fishing, and forestry | Manufacturing, mechanical, and construction |
|---|---|---|---|---|---|
| 1870 | — | — | 10.4 | 53.5 | 22.7 |
| 1900 | 4.0 | 9.3 | 16.7 | 37.6 | 30.1 |
| 1930 | 7.1 | 10.7 | 28.7 | 21.7 | 31.6 |
| 1960 | 11.9 | 6.6 | 40.7 | 9.4 | 31.4 |
| 1990 | 17.6 | 4.0 | 45.7 | 2.8 | 25.1 |
| 1998 | 19.2 | 3.4 | 52.1 | 2.7 | 22.7 |

*Sources:* U.S. Census Bureau; U.S. Bureau of Labor Statistics, *Employment and Earnings.*

to segregation by industry as well as occupation. To illustrate this trend, it is helpful to create a category we will call "professional care services" by combining the standard industrial classifications of "Hospitals," "Health Services except Hospitals," "Educational Services," and "Social Services." Table 10.2 puts employment in this category in the context of the overall labor market. In 1900, about 4 percent of all workers were employed in professional care services. By 1998, about one-fifth of the paid labor force was engaged in a professional care industry. . . . Today, hospitals and schools should now count as much in forming our image of wage employment as factories and construction sites.

Women remain concentrated in professional care industries. Of all women in paid employment, 31.3 percent were employed in these industries in 1998; women constituted 46.2 percent of the paid labor force over age sixteen, but 76.3 percent of those employed in "Hospitals," 79 percent in "Health Services except Hospitals," 68.7 percent in "Educational Services," and 81.8 percent in "Social Services" (U.S. Bureau of Labor Statistics, *Employment and Earnings*, January 1999, Table 18). The ways in which these care industries are structured will have especially important implications for women workers, as well as for the welfare of children, the sick, and the elderly. We will return to these implications later.

*Time Use Studies*

An alternative way of tracing the shift of caring activities into the paid labor market focuses on the changing patterns of time use. Canada and Australia, as well as most countries within the European Union, now conduct regular surveys based on detailed time diaries. Unfortunately, what we know about time use trends in the United States is based on relatively small and unrepresentative surveys, and often based on stylized questions rather than detailed time diaries.

A theme emphasized in much of the historical literature on time use is "the endless day"—homemaking seems to expand whatever time is available, and standards of cleanliness and quality have ratcheted up over time (Cowan 1980). Another probably more important factor is the high income elasticity of·demand for homemakers' services. Technological innovation has clearly reduced the time necessary to perform many domestic tasks. In 1975, for instance, homemakers worked about thirty hours less per week in preparing meals and cleaning up than they did in 1910 (Lebergott 1993, p. 59). On the other hand, standards of quality have gone up and activities such as shopping have become much more time-consuming—partly because more money is being spent.

The decline of fertility and the expansion of education have reduced the total amount of time devoted to child care. But in an analysis of historical time use data, Bryant and Zick (1996a, 1996b) show that parents may also have increased the amount of time they spend per child. It seems that paid child care tends to displace "on-call" time when most of parental attention was already elsewhere, rather than primary care time. As families purchase more services, they may reallocate their nonmarket time and effort away from material production toward the personal and emotional. Increased freedom to explore career opportunities outside the home means that the time that women devote to homemaking is given more freely—and perhaps more joyously—than before.

On the other hand, efforts to combine paid work and family responsibilities lead to stresses and strains. Pressure on single mothers has increased, with provision of public assistance now largely conditional on paid employment. When married mothers increase their hours of market work, husbands seldom increase their hours of nonmarket work to help compensate (Hartmann 1981; Bittman and Pixley 1997). The time and effort that women devote to homemaking tend to lower their earnings, even net of effects on labor force experience and job tenure (Hersch 1991; Waldfogel 1997). Widespread awareness of this pattern has contributed to a proliferation of studies of how men and women bargain over the allocation of time and responsibility as well as money in the household (Mahoney 1995; Deutsch 1999).

The difficult circumstances faced by single parents and dual-career families with young children help to explain the heated debate over whether Americans are working longer or shorter hours overall (Schor 1991; Robinson and Godbey 1997). In recent years, leisure time has become more unevenly distributed; surveys suggest a mismatch between individual preferences and work schedules (Jacobs and Gerson 1998), largely generated by the difficulties of combining paid employment with responsibilities for the care of family and community.

## Measurement of Economic Growth

The harder one thinks about nonmarket work, the more arbitrary the conventional picture of economic development begins to seem. The conventional history of economic growth embraces the unsurprising insight that when labor was reallocated from the family, where society did not place a dollar value on output, to the market, where it did, the economy appeared to have grown.

Nonmarket activities valued solely on the basis of labor inputs account for a sizable proportion—between 40 percent and 60 percent—of the total value of all U.S. output (Eisner 1989). Even this striking estimate contains a sizable downward bias, since the market wages being imputed to women homemakers are lowered both by discrimination and by the time and effort put into nonmarket work. Furthermore, "total economic product," which includes the value of nonmarket work, grows at a very different rhythm and rate over time than gross domestic product (Wagman and Folbre 1996). The macroeconomic implications depend largely on relative rates of growth in the market and nonmarket sectors, as well as on methods of imputing a value to nonmarket production. However, it seems likely that conventional estimates that omit such imputations altogether overstate economic growth and exaggerate cyclical variation.

. . . The exercise of imputing market values to homemaker output is based on the presumption of perfect substitutability between home-produced goods and commodities. This presumption is plausible for most material goods and for many services. It matters little to most people, for instance, who vacuums their floors or cleans their toilets.

But purchased services are only partial substitutes for personal services in which the identity of the care provider and the continuity of the care relationship matter. As families purchase more services, they probably reallocate their nonmarket time and effort away from material production toward the personal and emotional dimensions of care. There is good reason to believe that the personal and emotional content of home life is becoming more and more concentrated in a relatively small number of activities, such as sharing meals or telling bedtime stories, for which substitutes cannot be purchased. Past a certain point—which our society has yet to define or negotiate—family time cannot be reduced without adverse consequences for all family members. The greater the role that personal and emotional care play in nonmarket work, the greater the downward bias in market-based estimates of its value. In this sense, the economy itself is forcing economists to think seriously about concepts of care that have never played much role in our disciplinary vocabulary.

## Thinking about Care and Commodities

The word "care" has a dual meaning, on the one hand referring to caring activities, like changing diapers or providing a listening ear, and on the other hand to caring feelings, like those of concern or affection on the part of a caregiver. Caring feelings on the part of the caregiver are assumed to provide a motivation for doing caring activities and to assure the effectiveness of the care received. Ideally, a care recipient should feel authentically "cared for," nurtured, recognized and valued as an individual, emotionally supported, empathetically connected, or, in shorthand, loved. There is a sharp division of views about whether markets, caring feelings, and caring activities are at odds with each other.

To economists who take the view that social, familial, and sexual behavior has always been (at least implicitly) a matter of choice and exchange, as in much of Gary Becker's vision of economics, the movement of caring work into markets may be merely a rearrangement of activities in response to income and relative price changes. No qualitative change need be implied, and if anything, the new arrangements should (ipso facto, since they are a matter of choice) be leading to greater economic efficiency. Such a view recognizes no special category of distinctly personal, intimate human feelings and interactions, and may encourage a Candide-like, best-of-all-possible-worlds complacency in the face of the marketization of care.

Others see the worlds of commodities and of care as being at odds and fear that marketization of care might tend to "crowd out" caring feelings. The concern here is that motivation by money may lead to caring activities being performed to minimum standards, mechanically and impersonally, unaccompanied by the personal love and attention that we believe children need to grow, sick people need to heal, and so on. Such resistance to the movement of caring tasks into the market comes from both sides of the political spectrum. On the left, an abiding suspicion of capitalism leads to a fear that monetization of care will lead to care becoming an impersonal commodity, produced at least cost and sold to the highest bidder (Weisskopf and Folbre 1996; Carruthers and Espeland 1998). On the other hand, many social conservatives decry paid child care, for example, as in all ways inferior to mother-provided care (at least if the mother is married and middle-class), and try to demarcate a special, protected sphere of "family values" (for example, Weber 1994).

Before turning to empirical evidence on this debate, we should broaden the discussion beyond such a priori judgments and think more carefully about movements of money, motivations, and "the market."

### Money Moves in Various Ways

Impersonal, anonymous payments are only one way that money moves. It also moves within personal relationships, as gifts to friends, allowances to children, sharing between spouses, thefts, coerced donations, and so on. We have yet another vocabulary for money that moves toward or from the government, through taxes and transfers, and still other terms for ransoms, reparations, bonuses, tips, rewards, and so on (Zelizer 1995). A parent may be obliged to pay "child support," a movement of money based in the concern to provide for the child, rather than in exchange. Or consider the reparation payments recently given to Asian women who had been forced into sex work by the Japanese military during World War II. The social meaning of these payments reflects a recognition that these women's human rights were fundamentally violated and that they deserve an apology and some form of restitution. But if the only way we understood payment was via the model of exchange, then such payments would be merely delayed wages for prostitution services.

Even when money is explicitly given in exchange for goods or services, the relationship between the participants need not be one of anonymity and ad hoc timing. Child care markets can be examples of "rich" markets in which the movement of money is only one dimension in a complex relationship of child, caregivers, and parents including (when it is going well) elements of trust, affection, and appreciation. Other markets for caring services often have similar dimensions.

### Motivations

What are the motivations of paid caregivers? In some discussions, it seems as if a dichotomy is posed: one works either for love or for money—that is, out of spiritual values, affection, and altruism, or out of crass materialism, self-interest, and greed. Such a dichotomy implicitly assumes, however, first, that market agents' actions spring from their own unquenchable wants, and second, that agents are autonomous and unconnected self-sufficient beings. Neither assumption is useful in this context.

While it has become unfashionable in mainstream economics to talk about "needs," in fact the very human need for basic food and shelter is at the base of most work "for money." In a technologically complex, interdependent market society, we provide for ourselves—or get our "provisioning," in the terms of Nelson (1993)—largely through exchange. The fact that we engage in exchange does not prove that we are insatiable materialists. Most workers are not achieving nor seeking to achieve a hedonistic aim of ever-higher material pleasure or a controlling economic power. . . . .

It may also be helpful in illuminating the question of motivations to distinguish between activities that have complex meanings and motivations, and activities solely motivated by payment. Philosopher Margaret Jane Radin (1996, p. 105), for example, makes this distinction between what she calls "work" and mere "labor":

> It is possible to think of work as always containing a noncommodified human element; and to think of the fully commodified version as labor. . . . Laborers are sellers; fully motivated by money, exhausting the value of their activity in the measure of its exchange value. Laborers experience their labor as separate from their real selves. Workers make money but are also at the same time givers. Money does not fully motivate them to work, nor does it exhaust the value of their activity. Work is understood not as separate from life and self, but rather as a part of the worker, and indeed constitutive of her. Nor is work understood as separate from relations with other people.

Such a distinction recognizes that there can be "giving" elements in what are often thought of as "commodified" exchanges.

Traditional neoclassical economists, of course, might reply that the economics profession has already dealt with these issues by including consideration of nonpecuniary rewards in the theory of "compensating wage differentials." According to this theory, all else equal, jobs with worse working conditions should pay more. Translated to the case of caring activities, it implies that if some people enjoy caring, they will be willing to accept a lower wage to do these activities, essentially taking part of their "pay" in good feelings. However, this analysis relies on the assumptions of core neoclassical theory that agents are assumed to have their preferences exogenously given and to be radically autonomous and self-interested. That is, their identity and tastes are set before they enter the labor market; activities in the market register only as yielding this fixed entity more or less utility. Other social sciences and philosophy, in contrast, have a broader understanding of work and motivation. Distinctions such as Radin's posit that "work" is part of the creation of persons and of the relations with other people that form the interactive environment of people's lives.

Relevant discussion of these issues has also taken place at the juncture of economics and psychology, by scholars such as Bruno Frey (1997, 1998).

Frey looks at empirical evidence on the effects on workers of extrinsic motivation (like pay) vs. intrinsic motivation ("when they undertake an activity for its own sake") (1998, p. 441). He finds that external motivations like pay "*crowd-out* intrinsic motivation if they are perceived to be *controlling* and they *crowd-in* intrinsic motivation if they are perceived to be *acknowledging*" (1998, p. 444, emphasis in original). This insight suggests that too direct a pay-for-specific-services approach to the compensation of caring activities could shift the perceived locus of control outside the worker, so that the activities are no longer "work" in the sense of expressing will and agency and building a relational network, but become merely "labor" motivated by pay alone. On the other hand, if the movement of money is understood as an acknowledgment and appreciation of the worker's own intrinsic motivations, it can strengthen such motivations. . . .

## Implications for Well-Being and Policy

We see women's traditional caring activities being done more and more in relationships that include the explicit movement of money. For evaluating the effects of this change, it is not sufficient to compare idealized conceptions of home and market, nor of love and money. Intelligent evaluation involves a more detailed analysis of the actual structures of caregiving and the level of support caregiving receives.

### Advantages of the Family-to-Market Move

One obvious benefit of creating more public and marketed alternatives to family care is the greater freedom it allows for women, who were traditionally expected to do the bulk of such work, irrespective of their own individual variations of interest and talent. While love was (and is) certainly an element in motivating provision of home-provided care, the historical roles of coercion and quid pro quo exchange should not be forgotten. Historically, many women lacked a viable alternative to providing homemaker, mothering, personal nursing, and sexual services, since labor market barriers denied them an alternative means of self-support. Marriage was close to an economic necessity for a young female.

Decreasing the coercive nature of traditional demands on women can also have positive effects for the recipients of care. The recent reduction in the labor market barriers facing women, and the greater availability of alternative provision of care for the young, sick, and feeble elderly, can mean that care activities, when done in private, may increasingly be done more as a matter of choice and less as a matter of necessity. This should raise the quality of care that is provided in private situations, since those who are totally uninterested or untalented in this area will now opt for other activities, while those who do opt to provide them are more likely to be intrinsically motivated.

In taking the burden of care off particular women, who had been assigned to it by status considerations, the marketization of care could contribute to the costs of care being more widely and equitably distributed, and the provision of care could in some ways be accomplished more effectively. Tasks traditionally done in the home were varied and complex, and there could be advantages to applying increased specialization within each class of activities. A traditional at-home caregiver is a generalist. She (it was traditionally a "she") is not likely to have the knowledge of the developmental stage of four-year-olds possessed by a nursery school teacher (and should she obtain it, by then her child would be five). Nor is she likely to have the medical skills of a visiting nurse, the listening skills of a trained psychotherapist, and so on. Shifting at least some aspects and intensities of caregiving to those with specialized training and experience (and who receive the pay that rewards their investment in skill) should raise the quality of care.

The movement from private to public may have other benefits as well. Because of the relative impersonality of market norms, public provision may enhance some people's sense of being in control of their own lives. Some senior citizens would rather be cared for by a paid "outsider" than a family member, for example, because this enhances their feeling of independence.

Finally, the greater attention to care issues, and the skill requirements of care, may aid in the economic analysis of work and well-being, as we recognize the value of caring work (like empathetic listening) in workplaces in general and, conversely, the value of knowledge and skill in the locations where care is provided. In the movement from private to public, researchers have become more cognizant of what constitutes good care. For example, in the literature on child development, the old contrast between merely "custodial" day care "by strangers" in institutional centers versus "loving care in the home" has been replaced by a more careful analysis that concludes (to put it simplistically) that good care is good, and bad care is bad, wherever it takes place. Children on average seem to benefit, or at least not be hurt, when their mothers engage in paid work (Blau and Grossberg 1992; Harvey 1999). Some studies have found small negative implications of maternal employment for children under the age of one—which may be caused by the fact that good care for infants is very time-intensive and therefore costly for the market to provide—but these effects tend to disappear as the child ages (Blau and Grossberg 1992). Whether at home or at other locations, the importance of relationships, knowledge, and environment in providing effective caregiving is becoming clearer.

## Disadvantages of the Family-to-Market Move

Reliance on markets for the provision of care does pose some significant risks. One concern is whether market competition in these areas will produce high-quality care. Dependents such as children, the sick, and the elderly seldom meet the standards for consumer sovereignty. These dependents do not necessarily know what is best for them. They are easily misled, even abused. Even if they have control over income, they may lack the ability or the information they need to make good decisions as consumers. Payments for their care are often made by third parties, and the time-extensive and highly personal character of care work makes it expensive to monitor quality.

Evidence suggests that quality of care is highly variable. Nursing homes offer a case in point. Many are privately run but receive government payments for care of the indigent elderly through Medicaid. According to *Consumer Reports*, about 40 percent of nursing homes repeatedly fail to pass the most basic health and safety inspections (Eaton 1996). The General Accounting Office (1999) recently reported that government inspections of nursing homes across the country each year show that more than one-fourth cause actual harm to their residents. Turnover rates among nursing home aides are high, amounting to almost 100 percent within the first three months.

Child care suffers from less extreme but still serious quality control problems. A recent comprehensive survey argues that the physical and emotional environment in many child care centers remains relatively poor, partly because of lax regulation in many states (Helburn 1995). Pay levels for child care workers are seldom much above minimum wage, and high turnover rates in the child care industry, averaging about 40 percent per year, preclude the development of long-term relationships between caregivers and young children. Voluntary accreditation by the National Association for the Education of Young Children tends to improve quality. A recent California study, for instance, rated 61 percent of accredited child care centers as good in 1997, compared to only 26 percent of those seeking accreditation the previous year. Nationwide, however, only 5,000 out of the nation's 97,000 child care centers were accredited (Whitebook 1997). Furthermore, many children in paid child care are in small informal family settings, rather than centers, where quality is even more variable. In the rush to expand child care slots to accommodate the exigencies of welfare reform, some states have provided child care vouchers that can be used virtually anywhere, including for unlicensed care, and so may actually have a negative effect on average quality.

Even working-age adults find it difficult to monitor care quality. The number of factors that come into play in choosing the best health maintenance organization, for example, is mind-boggling. Yet increased competition among health care providers creates incentives to cut costs by minimizing hospital stays and nursing care. A recent study published in the *Journal of the American Medical Association* found that several measures of the quality of care are significantly lower in for-profit than nonprofit health maintenance organizations (Himmelstein et al. 1999).

Improved regulation might mitigate such problems for health maintenance organizations. But regulation is no magic wand. It is implemented through a political process that is highly susceptible to rent-seeking and corruption. The nursing home, health, and child care industries devote significant resources to lobbying the members of Congress in charge of regulatory legislation.

A second reason to be concerned about market provision is that care creates important externalities that cannot always be captured in individual transactions. Many people share in the benefits when children are brought up to be responsible, skilled, and loving adults who treat each other with courtesy and respect. Employers benefit from lower monitoring costs when their workers are cooperative, trustworthy, and intrinsically motivated. The elderly benefit if a skilled younger generation of workers generates high Social Security and Medicare taxes. Fellow citizens gain from having law-abiding rather than predatory neighbors.

These gains cannot be captured fully by those who created them. Parents cannot demand a fee from employers who hire their adult children and benefit from their productive efforts. Nor can they send a bill to the spouses and friends of those children for the value of parental services consumed. When child care workers or elementary school teachers genuinely care for their students, they foster an eagerness to learn and willingness to cooperate from which later teachers and employers will benefit. When nurses do a good job, patients' families and employers benefit. Anyone who treats another person in a kind and helpful way creates a small benefit that is likely to be passed along. A growing body of research on social capital shows that an atmosphere of trust and care contributes not only to the development of human capital, but also to economic efficiency (Coleman 1988; Putnam 1993, 1995).

Like other externalities, however, those created by care create an incentive to free ride, to let others pay the costs. In the absence of collective coordination, less than optimal amounts of care will be provided, because care providers are not fully compensated for the social value of their services. Some amount of care for dependents will persist because it is embedded in our genes and reinforced by our culture. But if individuals who respect and fulfill norms of care come to be seen as losers in the competitive economic game, we may see a gradual erosion of the supply of unpaid care services (England and Folbre 2000). There are limits to the substitutability between family and market provision, limits that our society needs to discuss, define, and enforce.

A third concern is the evolution of markets for care themselves, which may be shifting away from "rich" markets embedded in local communities to a "thinner," more impersonal form. Residential mobility and job mobility are high in the United States, making it more difficult to sustain long-term relationships. National for-profit chains have moved into the fields of health and child care provision. Of course, there are countervailing trends: the decreased cost of travel, the emergence of new forms of communication such as e-mail, the use of web cams to monitor child care centers. If policy makers want to make distinctions between market structures that bring out the best in people and those that bring out the worst, we need to develop better ways of studying these and monitoring the evolution of care markets over time.

A fourth concern is that markets may increase freedom of choice about caregiving primarily for middle-class, white, U.S.-born women, while worsening, or at least not improving, the lot of other groups. Employees in all but the most highly credentialed care industries are predominately female and disproportionately people of color, and pay and benefit levels are typically low. The recent political shift (in the guise of "welfare reform") to a belief that putting one's dependents in paid care and taking a job is financially and logistically feasible for all parents has likely worsened the standard of living for women with especially high personal caring responsibilities and low market wages. A predominant ideology that saw women as homemakers may have been severely limiting to their life possibilities. However, it implicitly recognized the importance of caring labor, in a way that recent policies do not.

## Conclusion

. . . The shift of caring activity from family to markets represents an enormous social change. Markets on their own are unlikely to provide the particular volume and quality of "real" care that society desires for children, the sick, and the elderly. The increasing intertwining of "love" and "money" brings the necessity—and the opportunity—for innovative research and action. . . . Economists and policy makers can reevaluate our tools for research, as we reevaluate the roles of individuals, families, firms and governmental bodies in the provisioning of the care that we all, at many times in our lives, so critically need.

## References

Bittman, Michael, and Jocelyn Pixley. 1997. *The Double Life of the Family: Myth, Hope, and Experience*. Sydney: Allen and Unwin.

Blau, Francine D. 1998. "Trends in the Well Being of American Women, 1970–1995." *Journal of Economic Literature* 36 (1): 112–65.

Blau, Francine D., and Adam J. Grossberg. 1992. "Maternal Labor Supply and Children's Cognitive Development." *Review of Economics and Statistics* 74 (3): 474–81.

Bryant, W. Keith, and Cathleen D. Zick. 1996a. "An Examination of Parent-Child Shared Time." *Journal of Marriage and the Family* 58: 227–37.

———. 1996b. "Are We Investing Less in the Next Generation? Historical Trends in Time Spent Caring for Children." *Journal of Family and Economic Issues* 17 (3/4): 385–92.

Carruthers, Bruce G., and Wendy Nelson Espeland. 1998. "Money, Meaning, and Morality." *American Behavioral Scientist* 41 (10): 1384–408.

Coleman, James. 1988. "Social Capital in the Creation of Human Capital." *American Journal of Sociology* 94 (Supplement): S95–S120.

Cowan, Ruth Schwartz. 1980. *More Work for Mother.* New York: Basic Books.

Deutsch, Fran. 1999. *Halving It All: How Equally Shared Parenting Works.* Cambridge: Harvard University Press.

Eaton, Susan C. 1996. "Beyond Unloving Care: Promoting Innovation in Elder Care Through Public Policy." Radcliffe Public Policy Institute, Changing Work in America Series, Cambridge, MA.

Eisner, Robert. 1989. *The Total Incomes System of Accounts.* Chicago: University of Chicago Press.

England, Paula, and Nancy Folbre. 2000. "The Erosion of Care." In *Facing the Twenty-first Century,* ed. Jeff Madrick. New York: Century Fund.

Folbre, Nancy, and Barnet Wagman. 1993. "Counting Housework: New Estimates of Real Product in the U.S., 1800–1860." *Journal of Economic History* 53 (2): 275–88.

Frey, Bruno S. 1997. *Not Just for the Money: An Economic Theory of Personal Motivation.* Cheltenham, UK and Lyme, NH: Edward Elgar.

———. 1998. "Institutions and Morale: The Crowding-Out Effect." In *Economics, Values, and Organization,* ed. Avner Ben-Ner and Louis Putterman, pp. 437–60. New York: Cambridge University Press.

General Accounting Office. 1999. *Nursing Homes: Additional Steps Needed to Strengthen Enforcement of Federal Quality Standards.* March 18, 1999. HEHS-99–46. Washington, DC: U.S. GAO.

Hartmann, Heidi. 1981. "The Family as a Locus of Gender, Class and Political Struggle." *Signs: Journal of Women in Culture and Society* 6 (3): 366–94.

Harvey, Elizabeth. 1999. "Short-term and Long-term Effects of Early Parental Employment on Children of the National Longitudinal Survey of Youth." *Developmental Psychology* 35 (2): 445–59.

Helburn, Suzanne, ed. 1995. *Cost, Quality, and Child Outcomes in Child Care Centers.* Technical Report, Department of Economics, Center for Research in Economic and Social Policy, University of Colorado at Denver.

Hersch, Joni. 1991. "Male-Female Differences in Hourly Wages: The Role of Human Capital, Working Conditions, and Housework." *Industrial and Labor Relations Review* 44 (4): 746–59.

Himmelstein, David, Steffie Woolhandler, Ida Hellander, and Sidney M. Wolfe. 1999. "Quality of Care in Investor-Owned vs. Not-for-Profit HMOs." *Journal of the American Medical Association* 282 (2) (July 14): 159–63.

Jacobs, Jerry A., and Kathleen Gerson. 1998. "Who Are the Overworked Americans?" *Review of Social Economy* 56 (4): 442–59.

Lebergott, Stanley. 1993. *Pursuing Happiness: American Consumers in the Twentieth Century.* Princeton: Princeton University Press.

Mahoney, Rhona. 1995. *Kidding Ourselves: Breadwinning, Babies, and Bargaining Power.* New York: Basic Books.

Nelson, Julie A. 1993. "The Study of Choice or the Study of Provisioning? Gender and the Definition of Economics." In *Beyond Economic Man,* ed. Marianne A. Ferber and Julie A. Nelson, pp. 23–36. Chicago: University of Chicago Press.

Putnam, Robert. 1993. "The Prosperous Community—Social Capital and Public Life." *American Prospect* 13: 35–42.

———. 1995. "Bowling Alone: America's Declining Social Capital." *Journal of Democracy* 6 (1): 65–78.

Radin, Margaret Jane. 1996. *Contested Commodities.* Cambridge: Harvard University Press.

Reskin, Barbara, and Paula Roos. 1990. *Job Queues, Gender Queues.* Philadelphia: Temple University Press.

Robinson, John, and Geoffrey Godbey. 1997. *Time for Life: The Surprising Ways Americans Use Their Time.* University Park: Pennsylvania State University Press

Schor, Juliet B. 1991. *The Overworked American.* New York: Basic Books.

U.S. Bureau of Labor Statistics. Various years. *Employment and Earnings.*

U.S. Census Bureau. 1975. *Historical Statistics of the U.S., Colonial Times to 1970.* Washington, DC: U.S. Government Printing Office.

———. 1998. *Statistical Abstract of the United States* Washington, DC: U.S. Government Printing Office.

———. 1999. *Statistical Abstract of the United States* Washington, DC: U.S. Government Printing Office.

Wagman, Barnet, and Nancy Folbre. 1996. "Household Services and Economic Growth in the U.S., 1870–1930." *Feminist Economics* 2 (1): 43–66.

Waldfogel, Jane. 1997. "The Effect of Children on Women's Wages." *American Sociological Review* 62: 209–17.

Weber, Linda. 1994. *Mom, You're Incredible.* Colorado Springs, CO: Focus on the Family.

Weisskopf, Tom, and Nancy Folbre, eds. 1996. "Debating Markets." *Feminist Economics* 2 (1): 69–85.

Whitebook, Marcy. 1997. *NAEYC Accreditation and Assessment,* available from National Center for the Early Childhood Work Force, 733 15th St. NW, Suite 1037, Washington, DC, 20005.

Zelizer, Viviana A. 1995. *The Social Meaning of Money.* New York: Basic Books.

---

Adapted from "For Love or Money—Or Both?" *Journal of Economic Perspectives* 14 (4) (Fall 2000): 123–40. Reprinted with permission of the American Economic Association.

# 11

# Student Attitudes Toward Roles of Women and Men

## Is the Egalitarian Household Imminent?

*Marianne A. Ferber and Lauren Young*

How do college students in the United States feel about sex roles? This chapter focuses on the results of a survey of a sample of U.S. undergraduate students concerning their attitudes toward the roles of women and men in the labor market and in the home. Learning more about people's views is important because, although mainstream economists emphasize the role of rational choices, behavior tends to be constrained by beliefs about what is or should be normal. Some sociologists even speak of "normative imperatives" (Thornton 1989, p. 889). Others make the more modest claim that traditional beliefs serve to reinforce the tendency of people to maintain habitual practices (Anderson, Bechhofer, and Gershuny 1994) and conclude that there is "lagged adaptation" (Gershuny, Godwin, and Jones 1994). Learning more about the opinions of college students is important because it is the highly educated who have been at the forefront of changing sex-role attitudes (Goldscheider and Waite 1991).

## Background

The issue we are concerned with is that, although the labor force participation of women in the United States rose rapidly after 1950, there appeared to be virtually no change for about twenty-five years in men's participation in homemaking, and there have been only slight changes since 1975 (Gershuny and Robinson 1988). Housework and child care continued to be viewed as woman's responsibility whether or not she also had a paid job. As a result, while employed wives spent considerably fewer hours on housework than full-time homemakers—according to a number of studies in the late 1970s, on average about twenty-six hours compared to fifty-two hours a week— they nonetheless had far less leisure time than their husbands, who devoted only about eleven hours a week to housework (Walker and Gauger 1973; Meissner et al. 1975; Walker and Woods 1976; Gauger and Walker 1980).[1] Not surprisingly, the causes and consequences of this unequal sharing of housework and market work emerged as a central issue in discussions of women's continued low status in industrialized societies (Spitze 1986). The consequences of women's heavy "household responsibilities" have been extensively explored in the literature by psychologists, sociologists, and economists. They frequently include unequal distribution of leisure and hence psychological stress experienced by women as a result of what is termed role overload. They also include discontinuous labor force participation, as well as less than full-time, full-year employment, which in turn have contributed to women's low status in the labor market. In this study, however, the focus is not on consequences of unequal sharing of household responsibilities, but on changing attitudes toward sharing.

A variety of explanations have been offered for the traditional division of labor. One that gained considerable prominence is resource theory, initially proposed by Robert Blood and David Wolfe (1960). This theory focuses on the importance of accumulated resources of a spouse as the source of power within a marriage, which is likely to be used to make the other partner do more of the housework. More recently, Gary Becker's (1973, 1974, 1991) "new home economics" has come to the fore. It is based on the assumption that the adult members of a family allocate tasks according to comparative advantage[2] and thus maximize everyone's well-being. These modern theories are instrumental—that is, they assume that labor is divided in a way that will achieve particular goals—and have discarded the unrealistic earlier view that the gender division of responsibilities is biologically determined. Their assumption that decisions concerning this division of labor are entirely rational has not, however, gone unchallenged.

As Michael Geerken and Walter Gove (1983) suggest, the allocation of tasks within the family is likely to be an attempt to maximize "utility," broadly defined, taking into account the husband's and the wife's resources, but may also take into account the social environment, which specifically includes beliefs about the appropriate sexual division of labor. Many other researchers are also ready to accept the importance of resources and/or of comparative advantage, but in addition emphasize the part played by socialization and sex-role attitudes (Stafford, Backman, and Dibona 1977; Perruci, Potter, and Rhoads 1978; Huber and Spitze 1983; Berk 1985; Ross

1987; Blumberg 1991; South and Spitze 1994). Similarly, Shelley Phipps and Peter Burton (1995) point to the importance of social/institutional factors. Further evidence that gender role attitudes tend to play a part is provided by the substantially more equal sharing of housework among gay and lesbian couples (Blumstein and Schwartz 1983; Larson 1992; Kurdek 1993; South and Spitze 1994; Klawitter 1995). Some critics go so far as to argue that in light of the unequal distribution of work and leisure, it has become "intellectually untenable to view the husband's limited family role as the result of an equitable exchange between husband and wife based on their having different resources" (Pleck 1985).

A reasonable interpretation of the dissonance between rationality and traditional norms is that norms, although themselves shaped by objective conditions, are resistant to change and linger long after they have outlived their usefulness. Or, as Ralph Smith (1979) argues, stereotypes that are often initially based on facts are seldom revised as quickly as the facts change. Hence, we conclude that radical transformations in the economy provided impetus for changes in people's behavior, but a stubbornly persistent gender role ideology, shaped in earlier days, tended to inhibit the needed adjustments. The reason is that most people most of the time act in conformity with their conception of what behavior is normal for and expected by members of their group (Anderson, Bechhofer, and Gershuny 1994). Resistance to change is likely to be all the greater because men have a stake in preserving the status quo within the family. They have much to gain when their wives enter the labor market and bring home a paycheck, but many may see little to gain by doing a larger share of the housework. Gradually, however, some of them may see that they would earn more goodwill from their partner. Also, as organized groups agitate for change, and as individual nonconformists are increasingly willing to deviate from traditional norms, it becomes easier for others to do so as well. Thus, eventually, norms may be expected to change, and this in turn should make further changes in behavior easier.

### Evolution of Women's Roles

It is not difficult to understand how the traditional view of women as homemakers became established. True, in preindustrial, agricultural economies both women's and men's work centered in and around the home, the family was the economic unit, and women as well as men worked in the family enterprise. At the same time, however, families were large and life expectancy was short. Most women were pregnant or nursing virtually all of their adult lives and therefore tied largely to the homestead and its immediate vicinity, where they baked the bread, spun the cloth, and raised much of the food consumed by the family. In other words, they were responsible for the housework, although these women were also full-fledged economic partners who worked on farms and in shops, frequently took in boarders, and among the poorest often did paid homework as well. With the coming of the industrial revolution, however, men increasingly worked in factory or office away from home, and the work of middle-class wives came to be entirely confined to the household, except for volunteer work, particularly common among those affluent enough to have hired household help. It was then that the view of women as consumers rather than producers came into full flower as the "cult of true womanhood" (Welter 1978). It is well known, of course, that poor women in the United States, particularly African Americans and immigrants, frequently did work for pay in addition to taking care of their own households, but this was generally regarded as a necessary evil, and most of these overworked women understandably aspired to achieving the middle-class "housewife" status.

Thus the domestic sphere was, more than ever, viewed as women's responsibility. At the same time, with the growth of the money economy, housework was relegated to low status, and women came to be seen as dependents rather than partners. Hired household workers as well as those who performed work previously done in the household, from laundresses and short-order cooks to those who cared for infants and children, were among the least well-paid members of the labor force, as they continue to be to this day. Another symptom of the low esteem in which housework has been held is the scant attention it has received from social scientists; for a long time, economists ignored it entirely. They not only failed to include the value of housework done by family members in calculations of gross domestic product, but frequently failed to acknowledge this omission; in the United States the value of housework is not taken into account when calculating the poverty line for a family; nor were working conditions of paid domestic workers studied, although this was at one time one of the leading occupations for African American women. Similarly, as Huber and Spitze (1983) point out, sociologists preferred to study the attitudes, values, and daily activities of autoworkers, skid-row bums, medical students, and soldiers. Huber and Spitze also note that not a single entry in the 1968 *International Encyclopedia of the Social Sciences* refers to housework.

### Recent Developments in the United States

It is not surprising, then, that men were less than eager to participate more fully in what were seen to be unimportant, not to say demeaning, activities. There may also be other reasons why most women, as well as men, tend to prefer market work to housework, except for child care (Juster 1985); much of it tends to be repetitive (furniture needs to be dusted and floors swept again and again), it often shows few long-term results (even the most elaborate meal is consumed in one sitting), and it is performed in isolation from other adults. Clinging to the traditional notion that this is women's work was an easy way for men to justify their resistance to doing more of these chores. It is more surprising that, for a long time, many women also tended to accept this view or, at least, resigned themselves to it.

John Robinson (1977) found that in 1965–66 only 19 percent and in 1973 only 23 percent of women said that they would like their husbands to help more with housework.[3] Pleck (1985) reports that in 1970 only 30 to 35 percent (depending on level of education) of a national sample of both men and women thought men should do more housework, that in 1974 only 30 to 35 percent of young people thought willingness to do housework was an important quality for a man, and that in a local sample from the state of Washington in 1976, no more than 2 percent of either men or women thought that husbands and wives should be equally responsible for housework. With the growing feminist movement of the 1970s, however, women came to aspire to more egalitarian arrangements. While recent surveys (e.g., Willinger 1993) still show that men are more reluctant to accept a larger role for themselves in the household than they are to accept women's greater role in the labor market, it appears that eventually they are not likely to be entirely immune to women's demands for justice (Goode 1992).

This willingness to recognize that women's claims are reasonable may well help to explain why there has finally been a perceptible shift in opinions over the last twenty years. Numerous surveys indicate that an increasing proportion of both men and women tend to believe husbands should do a larger share of housework and child care, and there is considerable evidence that this trend has been greatest among the young and the highly educated (Huber and Spitze 1983; Goode 1992). Whether one shares Goode's view that this has been a surprisingly marked change in attitudes or shares the frustration of many feminist writers because the changes have been so modest is really a question of seeing the glass as half full or half empty. In any case, although it must be recognized that a change in attitudes is not necessarily tantamount to changing behavior, husbands may be expected to gradually become less resistant to greater participation in homemaking.

The evidence is less than overwhelming, but at least small changes in the division of household work became apparent during the late 1970s (Pleck 1985). According to one report, men spent only about 17 percent of their total work time on housework in the 1960s, and for over a decade there appeared to be virtually no change in that proportion; by the mid-1980s it had, however, risen to 30 percent (United Nations 1991). This does amount to a perceptible increase, even taking into account that it was in part caused by a decline in the number of hours men spent in the labor market. Similarly, the ratio of time men spent on housework as compared to women rose during this period. In 1987, among those working in the labor force, men spent 57 percent as much time on domestic chores as women, compared to 46 percent in 1975 (Shelton 1992), albeit much of the larger ratio was due to women doing less household work when they entered the labor market, rather than to men doing a great deal more of it (see, for instance, Huber and Spitze 1983; Hochschild 1989). Also, according to Robinson (1988) and Pleck (1985), by the 1980s the total amount of work women and men did, paid and unpaid, was about the same. Overall, then, there is evidence of change, but it is equally clear that there is a need for considerably more change if something approximating real equality is to be achieved.

**The Survey**

*The Sample*

In order to learn to what extent the views of the young and highly educated today differ from those that were accepted by the general population of earlier years, we conducted a survey of undergraduates at Harvard University. As noted earlier, examining the views of a group of college students is instructive not only because a large proportion of young people in the United States go to college and because a disproportionately large number of women who have attended college will enter the labor market. As mentioned previously, college students have also been in the vanguard of change concerning sex-role attitudes in the United States. It should be noted, of course, that Harvard students are not representative of all college students in the country, because they are considerably more likely to come from wealthy families and hence, undoubtedly, also expect to be in a very high-income bracket after they set up their own households. This must be kept in mind when interpreting their answers to questions concerning the sharing of homemaking responsibilities, because they would also be expected to anticipate purchasing many goods and services less affluent women and men produce themselves. The sample is, nonetheless, a useful one because it is representative of an influential segment of the college population.

The first step in this survey was to distribute approximately 300 questionnaires at one of the university residence halls during the spring semester of 1993–94. We expected that this approach would enable us to reach a representative cross-section of students in various majors. The response rate of 43 percent did not, however, provide a large enough sample. Therefore, we distributed 140 additional questionnaires in a large intermediate undergraduate microeconomics class, because we expected, as it turned out correctly, that the students would be willing to fill them out and return them. In this manner we obtained a total sample of 268, although we must note that not all respondents answered all the questions, so that the total number of responses for individual questions is somewhat lower.

. . . The sample obtained is reasonably representative of Harvard undergraduates. The proportions of men and women are virtually identical, but this is somewhat less true for the various racial and ethnic groups. Most notably, there is a larger proportion of Asian and Pacific Islander Americans in the sample, and a smaller proportion of individuals who failed to provide information concerning their race/ethnicity. . . . As would be expected, the sample is far less representative of the total population of the country. . . .

Our survey focused on the students' views about appropriate sharing of household and market work between men and women. This was not intended to imply that all the respondents would or should anticipate having heterosexual relationships; rather we wanted everyone's opinion of what the division of labor among such couples ought to be.[4] We then went on to ask questions concerning their own expectations for labor force participation and sharing household work, both when young children are and are not present in the household. We also asked about their mother's labor force participation, and their mother's and father's occupation. In addition to these questions, we obtained the usual classifying information, including sex, race and ethnicity, religion, and country of origin, as well as their year in college, and their college major.

### Attitudes and Expectations of the Students

The most striking aspect of our findings can be summed up very simply: a large majority of both men and women profess to have very egalitarian attitudes. First, 83 percent of women and 81 percent of men agreed that both husband and wife should be employed full-time when there are no preschool children in the household; as few as 4 percent of women and 9 percent of men specifically thought that only the husband should be employed full-time. While as many as 89 percent of men and 81 percent of women thought that only one partner should be employed full-time when there are preschool children present, a far smaller number, 18 percent of women and 28 percent of men, specifically thought that the wife should be the one to work less than full-time. Second, as seen in Table 11.1, both men and women expect to do almost equal amounts of housework and think that approximately equal sharing is fair. Furthermore, when asked how much housework and child care each should do when only one of the partners works for pay full-time, the answer is not very different, whether it is the wife or the husband who works full-time. Finally, women as well as men expect to spend virtually all of the next thirty years in the labor market, on average 29.3 years and 29.9 years respectively, albeit the amount of time women expect to be employed part-time is significantly greater, 6.9 years as compared to only 2.7 years for men.

Even so, some other findings are also worth noting. Although for the most part the differences in expectations between women and men when both partners are employed full-time are quite minor, they are consistently in the traditional direction and are statistically significant in all cases at the 1 percent level, except for the amount of housework they expect to do when there are young children in the household. Furthermore, in all the instances (not only those shown in Table 11.1, but also in all others), women expect to do at least slightly more household work than do men under comparable circumstances. However, counter to the usual belief that men are more willing to spend time with children than on household chores, the differences are somewhat larger for child care. This may be explained by the emphasis in our questionnaire on preschool children; it is entirely likely that men are more inclined to help children with schoolwork and to participate in scouting activities than they are to feed or bathe an infant. To the extent this is true, it would also explain why a somewhat larger proportion of these men with otherwise very egalitarian views believe that it is the wife who should be employed less than full-time when there are preschool children in the household. In addition, one reason why a larger proportion of women than men prefer for both partners to be employed full-time when there are preschool children in the household may be that these women suspect that they would be the ones who would end up being the part-time employees.

Finally, another consistent pattern of differences is that in all cases men, on average, plan to do a slightly smaller proportion of housework and to provide slightly less child care than they consider fair, while the opposite is true for women. We had been concerned, when developing the questionnaire, that the respondents would be reluctant to give different answers to these two sets of questions, and in fact the divergence between their responses is not very large. Nonetheless, the existence of even a small divergence suggests that at least some of these students themselves still expect their behavior to be somewhat more traditional than their attitudes are, and confirms the lingering influence of tradition even among young and highly educated people.

Further examination of the data raises a more troublesome question. Economists are notoriously suspicious of putting credence in what people say, as

Table 11.1

## What Percent of Work Students Expect to Do, What They Consider Fair

|  | Men | Women |
|---|---|---|
| Percent of housework the respondents expect to do when both partners are employed full-time and there are no preschool children in household | 47.2 | 55.5 |
| Percent of housework the respondents consider their fair share when both partners are employed full-time and there are no preschool children in household | 48.2 | 50.9 |
| Percent of housework the respondents expect to do when both partners are employed full-time and there are preschool children in household | 49.6 | 52.0 |
| Percent of housework the respondents consider their fair share when both partners are employed full-time and there are preschool children in household | 50.9 | 47.5 |
| Percent of child care the respondents expect to do when both partners are employed full-time and there are preschool children in household | 44.8 | 59.5 |
| Percent of child care the respondents consider their fair share when both partners are employed full-time and there are preschool children in household | 45.4 | 52.8 |
| Percent of housework the respondents expect to do when only husband is employed full-time and there are no preschool children in household | 29.9 | 70.1 |
| Percent of housework the respondents expect to do when only wife is employed full-time and there are no preschool children in household | 68.7 | 30.7 |
| Percent of child care the respondents expect to do when only husband is employed full-time and there are preschool children in household | 31.1 | 67.1 |
| Percent of child care the respondents expect to do when only wife is employed full-time and there are preschool children in household | 63.7 | 35.6 |

opposed to what they do. The data in Table 11.2 suggest that in this instance the suspicion is justified, at least as far as the men in our sample are concerned. While women's plans for years of full-time employment are, on the whole, consistent with their stated preferences for full-time employment,

Table 11.2

**Number of Years Men and Women Expect to Work Full-Time During the Thirty Years After Leaving School by Attitude Toward Full-Time Employment of Husband and Wife**

| | Number of years expected to be employed full-time | | | |
| --- | --- | --- | --- | --- |
| | Men | N | Women | N |
| When there are no preschool children present, it is preferable: | | | | |
| (a) for both parents to be employed full-time | 27.3 | 121 | 23.3 | 90 |
| (b) for only one to work full-time, either one | 28.1 | 13 | 16.9 | 15 |
| (c) for only the husband to be employed full-time | 27.4 | 14 | 22.5 | 4 |
| (d) for only the wife to be employed full-time | 17.5 | 2 | — | — |
| When there are preschool children present, it is preferable: | | | | |
| (a) for both parents to be employed full-time | 26.9 | 16 | 27.4 | 19 |
| (b) for only one to work full-time, either one | 27.1 | 87 | 21.9 | 72 |
| (c) for only the husband to be employed full-time | 27.9 | 44 | 18.2 | 18 |
| (d) for only the wife to be employed full-time | 23.8 | 4 | 30.0 | 1 |

men expect to be employed full-time virtually all of the thirty years after leaving school, regardless of their stated preferences about one partner working only part-time. Further, those who prefer for only one partner to be employed part-time, but claim that it could be either one, expect to be employed for marginally more years than those who prefer that both partners be employed full-time. Because of these inconsistencies among the responses of male respondents to different questions, we conclude that it would clearly be a mistake to accept the answers to this survey entirely at face value.[5] On the other hand, as already noted in the introduction, it is significant that these students overwhelmingly at least believe that they ought to give very egalitarian answers. We shall return to this issue once more in the concluding section. . . .

## Discussion and Conclusion

The sample used in this research was clearly not chosen because it is representative of the general population or even of all college students, but, as noted earlier, it does represent a rather influential segment of U.S. society. Further, we asked students about their attitudes and expectations not because they are likely to coincide entirely with their actual behavior, but rather because evidence from previous research suggests that attitudes do influence behavior over time. Evidence from our own sample that the mothers of these young women are disproportionately represented in the labor force, and that the daughters of employed women plan to spend somewhat more time in the labor market than do those whose mothers are full-time homemakers, further suggests that the attitudes and behavior of parents influence their children as well. Hence, it is all the more plausible to conclude that the very egalitarian views expressed by these students themselves portend well for the future.

It would, however, be a mistake to assume that this means the arrival of the millennium is imminent. Therefore, several cautionary comments made earlier deserve to be emphasized once more. First, this sample is not representative of the whole population. Second, it would be unrealistic to overlook the possibility that the answers the respondents gave to some extent represent what they thought they ought to say, rather than what they really think. Last, but not least, even their own answers suggest that actions will not always coincide with their intentions.

## Notes

1. It should be noted that even the most carefully collected data on household work are not expected to be entirely reliable. Not only are people's memories imperfect, but their estimates may be influenced by their desire to live up to their own beliefs of what they ought to be doing. For obvious reasons, surveys that rely on reports of one spouse about time spent by the other spouse are likely to be even less accurate.

2. The simplest case for Becker's model can be made when each family member has an absolute advantage in one sphere; for instance, A can earn $10 an hour in the market and produce a meal at home in one hour that is worth $8, while B earns $7 an hour in the market and can produce a meal at home in an hour that is worth $8. However, given the assumptions in this model, it will still pay to specialize when one has an absolute advantage in both spheres. If the situation for A is the same as described above, but B can earn only $4 in the market and produce a meal at home that is worth $5, it is still most efficient for A to be in the labor market and for B to stay home and cook the meal. For a fuller explanation and a critique of this model see, for instance, Francine Blau and Marianne Ferber (1992, pp. 36–48).

3. The same survey showed that for African American women the figure in 1973 was a substantially higher 37 percent. This may well be related to the fact that, in the 1970s, they were somewhat more likely to be in the labor force and considerably more likely to work full-time than white women.

4. In fact, it would have been interesting to ask about plans for gay/lesbian relationships as well, but experience with a recent survey of university and college faculty in Illinois, where virtually no one answered in the affirmative when asked whether they ever had a same-sex partner, suggested that little information would

be obtained (Ferber and Loeb 1997). It would, nonetheless, be useful to add such a question in future surveys in order that no one feel excluded, but also because it is to be hoped that over time increasingly more people will feel free to be more open about such relationships.

5. There is no evidence to suggest that we need to be equally suspicious of the answers the women gave.

## References

Anderson, Michael, Frank Bechhofer, and Jonathan Gershuny. 1994. "Introduction." In *The Social and Political Economy of the Household*, ed. Michael Anderson, Frank Bechhofer, and Jonathan Gershuny, pp. 1–16. Oxford: Oxford University Press.

Becker, Gary S. 1973. "A Theory of Marriage: Part I." *Journal of Political Economy* 81 (4): 813–46.

———. 1974. "A Theory of Marriage: Part II." *Journal of Political Economy* 82 (3): 1063–93.

———. 1991. *A Treatise on the Family*. Cambridge: Harvard University Press.

Berk, Sarah F. 1985. *The Gender Factory: The Apportionment of Work in American Households*. New York: Plenum Press.

Blau, Francine D., and Marianne A. Ferber. 1992. *The Economics of Women, Men, and Work*. Englewood Cliffs, NJ: Prentice Hall.

Blood, Robert O., and David M. Wolfe. 1960. *Husbands and Wives*. Glencoe, IL: Free Press.

Blumberg, Rae L. 1991. *Gender, Family, and Economy: The Triple Overlap*. Newbury Park, CA: Sage.

Blumstein, Philip and Pepper Schwartz. 1983. *American Couples*. New York: William Morrow.

Ferber, Marianne A., and Jane W. Loeb, eds. 1997. *Academic Couples: Problems and Promise*. Champaign: University of Illinois Press.

Gauger, William, and Kathryn Walker. 1980. *The Dollar Value of Housework*. Information Bulletin No. 60: Ithaca: Cornell University, New York State College of Human Ecology.

Geerken, Michael, and Walter R. Gove. 1983. *At Home and at Work: The Family's Allocation of Labor*. Beverly Hills, CA: Sage.

Gershuny, Jonathan, and John P. Robinson. 1988. "Historical Changes in the Household Division of Labor." *Demography* 25 (4): 537–52.

Gershuny, Jonathan, Michael Godwin, and Sally Jones. 1994. "The Domestic Labour Revolution: A Process of Lagged Adaptation." In *The Social and Political Economy of the Household*, ed. Michael Anderson, Frank Bechhofer, and Jonathan Gershuny, pp. 151–97. Oxford: Oxford University Press.

Goldscheider, Frances K., and Linda J. Waite. 1991. *New Families, No Families? The Transformation of the American Home*. Berkeley: University of California Press.

Goode, William J. 1992. "Why Men Resist." In *Rethinking the Family*, ed. Barrie Thorne and Marilyn Yalom, pp. 131–47. New York: Longman.

Hochschild, Arlie R. 1989. *The Second Shift: Working Parents and the Revolution at Home*. New York: Viking.

Huber, Joan, and Glenna Spitz. 1983. *Sex Stratification: Children, Housework, and Jobs*. New York: Academic Press.

Juster, F. Thomas. 1985. "Preferences for Work and Leisure." In *Time, Goods and Well-Being*, ed. F. Thomas Juster and Frank P. Stafford, pp. 333–51. Ann Arbor: Institute for Social Research, University of Michigan.

Klawitter, Marieka M. 1995. "Did They Find Each Other or Create Each Other? Labor Market Linkages between Partners in Same-Sex and Different-Sex Couples." Paper presented at the Meeting of the Population Association of America, April.

Kurdek, Lawrence A. 1993. "The Allocation of Household Labor in Gay, Lesbian, and Heterosexual Married Couples." *Journal of Social Issues* 49 (3): 127–39.

Larson, Kathryn. 1992. "Economic Issues Facing Lesbian Households." Paper presented at the annual meeting of the International Association for Feminist Economics, Washington, DC.

Meissner, Martin E., E.W. Humphreys, S.M. Meiss, and W.J. Scheu. 1975. "No Exit for Wives: Sexual Division of Labour and the Cumulation of Household Demands." *Canadian Review of Anthropology and Sociology* 12 (4): 424–59.

Perruci, Carolyn, Harry R. Potter, and Deborah C. Rhoads. 1978. "Determinants of Male Family-Role Performance." *Psychology of Women Quarterly* 3 (1): 53–66.

Phipps, Shelley A., and Peter S. Burton. 1995. "Social/Institutional Variables and Behavior within Households: An Empirical Test using the Luxembourg Income Study." *Feminist Economics* 1 (1): 151–74.

Pleck, Joseph H. 1985. *Working Wives, Working Husbands*. Beverly Hills, CA: National Council on Family Relations, Sage.

Robinson, John P. 1977. *Changes in America's Use of Time*. Cleveland, OH: Communications Research Center, Cleveland State University.

———. 1988. "Who's Doing the Housework?" *American Demographics* 10 (12): 24–8, 63.

Ross, Catherine E. 1987. "The Division of Labor at Home." *Social Forces* 65 (3): 816–33.

Shelton, Beth A. 1992. *Women, Men, and Time: Gender Differences in Paid Work, Housework, and Leisure*. New York: Greenwood Press.

Smith, Ralph E. 1979. "The Movement of Women into the Labor Force." In *The Subtle Revolution: Women at Work*, ed. Ralph E. Smith, pp. 1–29. Washington, DC: Urban Institute.

South, Scott J., and Glenna D. Spitze. 1994. "Housework in Marital and Nonmarital Households." *American Sociological Review* 59 (3): 329–47.

Spitze, Glenna D. 1986. "The Division of Task Responsibility in U.S. Households: Longitudinal Adjustments to Change." *Social Forces* 64 (33): 689–701.

Stafford, Rebecca, Elaine Backman, and Pamela Dibona. 1977. "The Division of Labor Among Cohabiting and Married Couples." *Journal of Marriage and the Family* 39 (2): 43–54.

Thornton, Arland. 1989. "Changing Attitudes Toward Family Issues in the United States." *Journal of Marriage and the Family* 51 (4): 873–93.

United Nations. 1991. *The World's Women, 1970–1990: Trends and Statistics*. New York: United Nations.

Walker, Kathryn, and William Gauger. 1973. *The Dollar Value of Household Work*. Information Bulletin No. 60. Ithaca: Cornell University, New York State College of Human Ecology.

Walker, Kathryn, and Margaret Woods. 1976. *Time Use: A Measure of Household Production of Family Goods and Services*. Washington, DC: American Home Economics Association.

Welter, Barbara. 1978. "The Cult of True Womanhood, 1820–1860." In The American Family in Social-Historical Perspective, 2nd ed, ed. Michael Gordon. New York: St. Martin's Press.

Willinger, Beth. 1993. "Resistance to Change: College Men's Attitudes Toward Work and Family in the 1980s." In *Men, Work, and Family*, ed. Jane C. Hood, pp. 108–30. Newbury Park, CA: Sage.

---

Adapted from "Student Attitudes Toward Roles of Women and Men: Is the Egalitarian Household Imminent?" *Feminist Economics* 3 (1) (Spring 1997): 65–83. The web site for *Feminist Economics* can be found at www.tandf.co.uk/journals. Reprinted with permission of Taylor & Francis Ltd.

# 12

# The Household as a Focus for Research

*Jane Wheelock and Elizabeth Oughton*

> Give all thou canst; high Heaven rejects the lore
> Of nicely calculated less or more;
> So deemed the Man who fashioned for the sense
> These lofty pillars.

*—Wordsworth, "Inside of Kings College Chapel, Cambridge"*

Institutional economists have played a major role in criticizing "rational economic man," a concept that Wordsworth was one of the first to ridicule. Less thought has been given to what economic agent might usefully replace this timeworn abstraction. In this paper, we investigate the strengths and weaknesses of using the household as an alternative economic agent. We are concerned with developing a set of tools for conditions of economic change. Since most individuals live in households,[1] we argue that an analysis starting at the level of the household, and the individuals within it, enables researchers to tackle a broader and more relevant research agenda than one based on the maximizing individual.

. . . For consumption as well as labor supply decisions, the crucial unit is not the individual, but the household. Indeed, the term "individual" is misleading because it conjures up the idea of isolation from the social and historical setting. Nor does it distinguish between men and women. Also, once we look at people in households, it becomes apparent that they have a variety of motivations besides narrow economic gain: actions may be based on traditional or patriarchal reasoning; people have a need for dignity and self-respect, and a need to care and nurture. Actions can also be based on reciprocity or cooperation between people. . . .

## Locating the Household

The use of the household as the focus for the analysis of economic behavior is not without its difficulties, and at this point we need to clarify some of the conceptual issues—the opportunities and limitations of this approach. From the outset, we reject the idea of the household being synonymous with the nuclear family, which, as Harris (1981) has pointed out, has been taken to be a very widespread institution. Even within Britain, where the popular belief is that the nuclear family is the main basis of the household, more recent official approaches have tried to broaden the concept. The 1991 U.K. census defines a household as a single person living alone or a group who may or may not be related living, or staying temporarily, at the same address, with common housekeeping. British official definitions of the family, on the other hand, are restrictive, as it is assumed that families cannot span more than two generations. Thus, in general grandparents and grandchildren cannot belong to the same family within a household unless the children are being looked after by the grandparents in the absence of the parents. This is too limited as it excludes one example of precisely the type of relationships in which we are interested.

Roberts (1991, p. 62) proposes a definition based upon function, with the household being "the basic unit of society in which the activities of production, reproduction, consumption and the socialisation of children take place." Most importantly from our perspective, this definition neither requires members of the household be coresident nor be related through kinship or marriage. A further definition, based upon the functional activities of the household and of particular use in the analysis of policy effects, is Messer's: "that group of people, their relationships and activities, who acknowledge a common authority in domestic matters, a 'budget unit,' or 'a group who have a common fund of material and human resources and rules for practices and exchange within it'" (1990, p. 52).

This is a useful working guide to the identification of the household, the basic social unit of the society, a unit that is bounded by common agreement on the management of its resources, both the management of resource inflows into the household and their use and distribution. This concept can be used anywhere at any time. In practice, though, it will produce households of very different types depending on place, culture, and history. By different types we mean that the membership of the household may be characterized by individuals with very different relationships, kin or nonkin, depending upon the specific context. The definition of the household creates a boundary, a recognizable and accepted border to the household as a social unit. We agree with Wallerstein and Smith that "the bounding of households is itself an historical process which not only can but must be analysed, as it is probably the key process in the functioning of householding and is what integrates this structure into the larger network of structures that constitute the capitalist world-economy" (1992, p. 14).

## Modeling the Household

. . . How, then, can we conceive the factors affecting the livelihood decisions of the household? Identifying the household was the first step. Within the household framework, describing individuals' movements between the formal, informal, nonmarket, and social economy is the second. And, finally, the goal is to analyze the movements and the factors affecting peoples' decisions to change the combinations of their productive and socially reproductive activities. It is through this third area of analysis that we can start to pursue the idea of households generating livelihood strategies.

We will outline briefly some relationships between the monetized and the nonmonetized activities of the household and the points at which the individual's position in the household, their own personal characteristics, and their position within wider groups may affect decisions about those activities.

Let us imagine a household made up of individuals who have available to them an initial endowment of resources. The household is embedded in a society that is itself composed of more aggregate orderings. We can further imagine the household at the center of concentric areas accounting for the economic, political, sociocultural, and physical environments. Changes in any of these environments may affect any or all of the other environments. The household objective is to sustain itself within this changing world. . . .

Wallerstein and Smith (1992) propose five different types of "income" that the household uses in order to do this: wages, market sales, rent, transfers, and subsistence. Wages, market sales, and rent may be cash or kind income and may be generated by what we have referred to as the marketed sector in either the formal or the complementary economy. Transfers and subsistence move us into more rocky terrain. This classification does not entirely capture the value of the activities of the nonmarketed economy. As Wallerstein and Smith themselves note, transfers may not be pure income flows to the household at all, in that they are not necessarily a reward for work. They may be receipts that are part of gift giving or reciprocal transactions that may or may not be obligatory. It then becomes relevant to ask whether such transfers should be classified as a production or consumption activity. The ability to participate in such social activities in turn may be important in maintaining the status of the household within the community, affecting its future productive and consumption opportunities. The subsistence activities to which Wallerstein and Smith refer are not the primary activities of production, but are activities to maintain the home and family. Wallerstein and Smith list as examples food processing and home maintenance and improvements. Such activities can be seen as producing "income" for the household, but the motivations to carry them out may well not be economic.

All members of the household except the very young or the very old may participate in some or all of these activities. All members of the household will be involved in consumption activities. Neoclassical models have used consumption of goods and services as a proxy for welfare. We need to ask, though, whether consumption is a satisfactory measure of the output of the household. We would argue that the well-being of household members is also affected by factors such as recognition, appreciation, love by others, feelings of self-worth, participation in the community, and so on. Just as we have noted above that receiving gifts may not be straightforwardly classed as an income flow into the household, so giving may not be a straightforward act of consumption (see Douglas 1982). Thus, the "income"-generating activities that each individual participates in will be mediated by the desire for these outcomes as well as the (assumed) objective output of consumption. . . .

How, then, does the notion of a strategy fit with this framework? The formal definitions of strategy include the idea of rational decision making applied to long-term plans. This concept raises difficulties with respect to the study of households. Rationality requires comparison with a single dimensional yardstick. Yet, as has been pointed out, the activities of households are multidimensional: behavior that is rational in economic terms may not be rational for the nurturing objectives of the household. Similarly, religious activity and commitment may be "rational" within the cultural sphere, but not economically.

Rationality, then, is not an appropriate defining criterion of household strategies. . . . This gives further weight to our argument for adopting an institutionalist approach to the study of household behavior. The social, local, regional, and environmental networks and context within which the household is embedded will contribute to determining the circumstances under which choice is made and a strategy devised. Most importantly, we can expect these contexts to change over time.

What is clear is that the concept of the household is not useful when abstracted from the complex of relations that extends beyond it (Evans 1991). The concept of the household is inevitably fluid, particularly at a time of rapid economic change. The institutionalist method ensures that these relations are incorporated into the analysis. Furthermore, it permits the explicit character of gender relations and the temporal characteristics of the object of the study to be explored.

## A Method of Analysis: The Institutionalist Approach to the Household

The neoclassically based new home economics school made a refreshing (though, as we have already argued, limited) attempt to look inside the household, seeing the family as more than a unit of consumption. In the mid-1960s, Gary Becker used opportunity cost to explain household divisions of paid and unpaid work (Becker 1965). His questioning of the stereotype of the family as private and noneconomic was continued, in a different form, in the largely Marxist domestic labor debate of the 1970s. Participants also looked at the unpaid production role of women but in terms of its role within capitalism (see Close and Collins 1985). From a very different perspective, which looks at the household as an institution, it is also possible to show that what Stanfield (1982) calls "substantive institutional analysis" has much to contribute to developing an economics of the household (see Greenwood 1984).

What does an institutionalist approach provide? How far has the institutionalist analysis of the household actually developed, and what still remains to be done? The methodology of institutionalism lends itself, first, because it looks at power and at power relations. It therefore moves away from the atomistic individualism that ignores the household as a family unit whose overall structure, including that of gender and age, is crucially important.

Second, the focus on cultural processes and the social construction of knowledge encourages questions about the nature of rational choice when people form and maintain households together. It is therefore possible to look at how the institutions of the household and of the labor market interact with each other, asking what choices households make about their work strategies and how members divide their time between paid work in the formal economy and unpaid work in the complementary economy.

Third, institutionalists examine the processes of evolutionary change. Such an approach encourages analysis of how the relation between the household and the economy evolves over time. For the individual household, movement through the life cycle of marriage, birth of children, and the children eventually leaving home introduces a dynamic element into family work strategies and household behavior. But structural economic changes, such as rising female participation in the labor market or increased male unemployment, can also influence the behavior of different household members. There are thus crucial causal links between the formal and the complementary economy, mediated by changing household work strategies. . . .

As Waller and Jennings (1991) point out, there are two further advantages to substantive analysis, though neither of them have necessarily been achieved in practice. One is to address the importance of the links between market and nonmarket activities, which is difficult for formalist economic accounts to include. The second is that gender roles can be unpacked, for "reification of the market in formalist economics constitutes the acceptance of our current prioritization of gender roles as appropriate and natural" (Waller and Jennings 1991, p. 490). This approach, then, examines the "economic character" of the household, arguing that economic motivation must be examined in a household, rather than in an individual context. The economic character of the household can be built up from a study of the ways in which judgments about values are made. Such judgments are made in the context of the dynamic process of technological accumulation.

Comparative research on the household, based on a substantive institutional approach, could thus be put into effect with a number of specific research objectives. The first objective would provide a material basis for subsequent interpretation of behavior. It would identify and compare household strategies for the organization and planning of resource use and exploitation within and outside the household. This would include the intergenerational transfer of resources, the application of market and nonmarket labor, temporal aspects of consumption, and gender. Investigation of the commonalties and differences in the diffusely felt experience of livelihood could thus be undertaken.

Second, it would be important to examine the way in which intrahousehold relations, gender, and conjugal and kinship status affect and are affected by the economic activity of the household. This would contribute to a theoretical model of household economic behavior that is sensitive to the embeddedness of eco nomic behavior within a social, cultural, and political context. Such a model would need to be responsive to the gender of the individual; his or her position within age or alternative hierarchical structures of the household; and his or her specific contribution, both actual and potential, within the formal and the complementary economy. An understanding of the process of decision making, whether explicit or implicit, would be vital.

Third, one would need to gain understanding of the process of the economic socialization of individuals within households. This involves examination of the development of economic values and beliefs within the household: the way in which these have been inherited or adapted from the previous generation, and the form in which they are passed on to children. It also means asking how people within households build their economic understanding of a changing economic context (Gudeman and Rivera 1990).

Last, what are the processes for sustaining and reproducing the household? Past behavior, present strategies, and plans for the future illuminate the decision-making process, where differing weight would be given to individuals within the household. Responses to risk and uncertainty in terms of intergenerational transfers in the form of inheritance, dowry, gifts, and provision for old age are important, as is the tension between individual acquisition and long-term reproduction.

## Conclusion

We have adopted the household as the unit of analysis because of the strengths and opportunities it offers as a starting point for both our theoretical and empirical studies. Our methodology is not limited to the domestic sphere, but if we are to understand the "personal, gendered, non-market relations that are a crucial part of our economy" (MacDonald 1993, p. 13), then the "household" effectively describes a concentration of actors and activities that we can use both to lead us into the wider economy and to a better understanding of the behavior of individuals. The analysis of the household is not in itself a methodology, but a description of a level of analysis.

As we have argued, the household as a unit of analysis is particularly appropriate to the institutionalist approach that we adopt. Social institutions and norms provide guidelines for behavior not covered by contracts to buy and sell. As Elson notes:

> *the gap* has to be filled by a mixture of mutuality, goodwill, trust, and power, coercion, and submission—a kind of "moral economy" interacting with the monetary economy, embodied in routines, habits, customs, linking economic agents through co-operative networks as well as through cash. (1993, p. 245)

Households are not universal in their form. Identifying and setting a boundary around the household unit will depend upon the cultural context, and the way in which decisions are made and resources allocated and shared will be "logically inseparable from the issue of household boundaries" (Wilk 1989, p. 27). The cultural context will similarly determine the form and nature of the household's relationships with other households and individuals and with the wider, formal economy. The household can be envisaged as a node in a multilayered web or as the locus for a number of networks of relations: economic, social, and technological. The household as a unit and its individual members are embedded and implicated in these networks.

The institutionalist method recognizes that the roles of men and women, their ability and willingness to command and distribute resources, and the rate at which these abilities and relations change will be strongly determined by the social context. To draw closer to an understanding of the social provisioning process, the ways in which women and men create and maintain their livelihoods, and achieve lives of "human flourishing,"[2] we should focus our analytical tools on the multidimensional dialectic of the economy. An economics of the household must not exclude a spiritual dimension.

## Notes

1. There can, of course, be a one-person household.
2. The term "human flourishing" was suggested to us by Chang-Woo Lee based on the use of this Korean term in his doctoral thesis. We are grateful.

## References

Becker, G. 1965. "A Theory of the Allocation of Time." In *The Economics of Women and Work*, ed. A.M. Amsden, pp. 52–81. Harmondsworth: Penguin Books.
Close, P., and R. Collins, eds. 1985. *Family and Economy in Modem Society.* London: Macmillan.
Douglas, M. 1982. *In the Active Voice*. London: Routledge and Kegan Paul.
Elson, D. 1993. "Gender Aware Analysis and Development Economics." *Journal of International Development* 5 (2): 237–47.
Evans, A. 1991. "Gender Issues in Rural Household Economics." *IDS Bulletin* 22 (1): 51–59.
Greenwood, D. 1984. "The Economic Significance of 'Women's Place' in Society: A New-Institutionalist View." *Journal of Economic Issues* 18 (2): 613–22.
Gudeman, S., and A. Rivera. 1990. *Conversations in Colombia: The Domestic Economy in Life and Text.* Cambridge: Cambridge University Press.
Harris, O. 1981. "Households as Natural Units." In *Of Marriage and the Market: Women's Subordination in International Perspective*, ed. K. Young, C. Wolkowitz, and R. McCullagh. London: CSE Books.
MacDonald, M. 1993. "The Empirical Challenges of Feminist Economics: The Example of Economic Restructuring." Paper presented at the International Conference on Feminist Perspectives on Economic Theory, Amsterdam, The Netherlands, June 2–5.
Messer, E. 1990. "Intra-Household Allocation of Resources: Perspectives from Anthropology." In *Intra-Household Resource Allocation*, ed. B.L. Rogers and N.P. Schlossman. Tokyo: United Nations University Press.
Roberts, P. 1991. "Anthropological Perspectives on the Household." *IDS Bulletin* 22 (1): 60–64.
Stanfield, J.R. 1982. "Towards a New Value Standard in Economics." *Economic Forum* 13 (Fall): 67–85.

Waller, W., and A. Jennings. 1991. "A Feminist Institutionalist Reconsideration of Karl Polanyi." *Journal of Economic Issues* 25 (2): 485–97.

Wallerstein, I., and J. Smith. 1992. "Households as an Institution of the World-Economy." In *Creating and Transforming Households*, ed. J. Smith and I. Wallerstein. Paris: Cambridge University Press.

Wilk, R.R. 1989. "Decision Making and Resource Flows Within the Household: Beyond the Black Box." In *The Household Economy: Reconsidering the Domestic Mode of Production*, ed. R.R. Wilk. Boulder, CO: Westview.

---

Adapted from "The Household as a Focus for Research," *Journal of Economic Issues* 30 (1) (March 1996): 143–59. Reprinted with special permission of the copyright holder, the Association for Evolutionary Economics.

# Section 3

# Appendix

## Key Terms

bargaining power
caring labor
commodification
compensating wage differentials
externalities
family
gross domestic product
household
new home economics
provisioning
sexual division of labor
time use study

## Discussion Questions

1. What are some of the arguments made both for and against paying for housework and child care?
2. Why is Barbara Bergmann's argument about the risks of specializing in housework still relevant today?
3. Why is "caring" an economic activity? Would caring change if it were motivated by the pursuit of profit, and, if so, how?
4. Who does the housework and other aspects of social reproduction? Has this varied over time? Does it vary by age, marital status, class, or race-ethnicity? Does the division of labor in the home differ in gay and lesbian households? How would you determine this?
5. What would you consider to be a fair distribution of household labor for different types of households or families?
6. Using Wheelock and Oughton's definition of a household, who is in your household? Is it the same as your family (or kin)? What are some of the diverse household structures among people you know?
7. How might a feminist or institutionalist model of the household or household behavior differ from a traditional or neoclassical economic framework?

## Exercises

1. *"Do the Q."* The U.S. Department of Labor's Bureau of Labor Statistics is developing an American Time Use Survey (ATUS). The survey will measure the amount of time people spend doing activities besides paid work, including time devoted to child care, commuting, and socializing. Data collection begins in January 2003, and the first annual estimates will be published in mid-2004. Until we have national data, researchers must rely on their own surveys. Complete a time diary for one week. Account for the time in half-hour (thirty- minute) intervals and make sure that you allocate all 24 hours per day and all 168 hours in the week. How much time do you spend in six specific activities: in class and studying; at paid employment; sleeping; housework/social reproduction; tending to personal hygiene (showering, dressing, styling, etc.); and personal time for leisure, exercise, and socializing? Summarize the raw data in your time diary on Worksheet #1 below. The worksheets should then be reproduced for each member of the class. You will be using these worksheets to analyze time use among your peers.

   a. Use Worksheet #2 as a model to construct frequency tables for each of the six activities. To fill in the table, you will need to "bin" your data, meaning you will group your responses into the hours ranges in Worksheet #2. What do the frequency tables tell you about time use by class members?

### Worksheet #1
### Summary of Time Diary

| Activity | Day 1 | Day 2 | Day 3 | Day 4 | Day 5 | Day 6 | Day 7 | Total hours |
|---|---|---|---|---|---|---|---|---|
| Class/Study | | | | | | | | |
| Paid job | | | | | | | | |
| Sleeping | | | | | | | | |
| Housework | | | | | | | | |
| Hygiene | | | | | | | | |
| Personal | | | | | | | | |
| TOTAL | 24 | 24 | 24 | 24 | 24 | 24 | 24 | 168 |

About you:    Female _____ or Male? _____ Age? _____
Other information (decided by class):

## Worksheet #2
### Frequency Table

Activity: _____

| Ranges | Frequency | Relative frequency | Cumulative frequency |
|---|---|---|---|
| < 10 hours | | | |
| 10–19 hours | | | |
| 20–29 hours | | | |
| 30–39 hours | | | |
| 40–49 hours | | | |
| 50–59 hours | | | |
| 60+ hours | | | 1.00 |

*Frequency* refers to the number of students whose answer falls within a given range. If you add all the frequencies, the total should be the number of students who filled out time diary summaries.

*Relative frequency* is the frequency divided by the total number of students responding to the survey (*n*); this will be a decimal (or you can translate it into a percentage).

*Cumulative frequency* adds the relative frequencies of the current and lower ranges. The cumulative frequency of all the categories will always equal 1 (or 100%).

    b. Now return to the set of Worksheets #1. Calculate the class average (mean), class median, and class mode (most common response). Which of these three measures seems to best represent the class? Is the mean skewed by any unusual "statistical outliers"?

    c. Compare and contrast the class mean and median by: (1) gender, (2) traditional vs. nontraditional age students, and (3) any other salient category.

    d. What does this exercise teach you about the process of collecting and analyzing time use data?

2. Do a short attitudinal survey of your peers to find out how much housework and child care they will be demanding of their spouses or partners. Construct your questions to parallel the possible responses in Table 11.1 of Ferber and Young's chapter. Be sure to code each survey for the sex of the person answering. Are your findings different from those in their study?

3. *"Do the Q."* For this exercise, you will gather and compare longitudinal (time-series) data on several important indicators. One of the major internet sites to begin a search for national data is called "FedStats," the gateway to statistics from over 100 U.S. federal agencies. At the FedStats web address www.fedstats.gov/, you will find an option for alphabetically arranged topic links from A to Z. For example, if you click on "M" and then "Marriage," you will find yourself at the National Center for Health Statistics. One technique to quickly evaluate trends is to glance at tables to see if there are any patterns over time. This is sometimes called "eyeballing" the data.

   a. Describe any trends that you see in the following three variables available through FedStats: (1) marriage rates, (2) divorce and annulment rates, and (3) birth rates. Where are the peaks and valleys? Discuss when they occur and place them in the context of social, political, and economic trends.
   b. Does there seem to be a positive or negative relationship (correlation) between any two of these variables?
   c. Thinking back to the employment trends presented in Section 2, can you infer anything about the relationship among the household variables in this exercise and labor force participation rates by gender since 1940?
   d. What surprised you in looking at this data? What questions were left unanswered? What other data would you have liked to consider?

## Further Reading

Bianchi, Suzanne M., Melissa A. Milke, Liana C. Sayer, and John P. Robinson. 2000. "Is Anyone Doing the Housework? Trends in the Gender Division of Household Labor." *Social Forces* 79 (1): 191–228.

Folbre, Nancy. 1994. *Who Pays for the Kids? Gender and the Structures of Constraint*. London: Routledge.

———. 2001. *The Invisible Heart: Economics and Family Values*. New York: New Press.

Heath, Julia A., David H. Ciscel, and David C. Sharp. 1998. "Too Many Hours—Too Little Pay: The Impact of Market and Household Hours on Women's Work Lives." *Journal of Economic Issues* 32 (2): 587–94.

Jefferson, Therese, and John E. King. 2001. "'Never Intended to Be a Theory of Everything': Domestic Labor in Neoclassical and Marxian Economics." *Feminist Economics* 7 (3): 71–101.

Williams, Joan. 2000. *Unbending Gender: Why Family and Work Conflict and What to Do About It*. Oxford: Oxford University Press.

# Section 4

# Mainstream Approaches to Labor Market Outcomes

Women continue to lag behind men in most indicators of employment status. As we have already learned, women, on average, earn lower wages than men. They tend to be segregated into occupations traditionally associated as "women's work," such as clerical employment, teaching, social work, nursing and health care technician fields, retail sales, and food service. Despite gains into professional and managerial occupations, women are often clustered into positions or job titles with lower status, less authority, and fewer promotional opportunities—a phenomenon called *intraoccupational segregation*. Married women, especially those with young children, are less likely than their spouses to be employed in full-time, year-round jobs. Men's and women's standing is *unequal*.

But is it *inequitable*? How do we define equity? Is it unequal outcomes or unequal opportunities? In assessing men's and women's employment status, economists and other social scientists rely primarily on measurable outcomes such as wages. But unequal outcomes need not indicate discrimination, and the existence of discrimination by individual employers is much harder to "prove." This has left some social scientists skeptical about the extent of discrimination against women and other groups. They argue that men and women voluntarily make different choices about the role of paid work in their lives and this means that they enter labor markets on different terms. Other social scientists accept that discriminatory attitudes exist in the broader culture. But they argue that the competitive forces of market capitalism should erode discrimination in the long run.

The four chapters in this section present mainstream theoretical perspectives on women and the economy, with an emphasis on explaining the gender-based wage gap. All of these perspectives are grounded in neoclassical labor market theory. According to this theory, rational employers will hire workers only when the value of their contribution to the firm's productivity is greater than (or at least equal to) their wages. Therefore, the more productive the worker, the higher the wage she or he can command in labor markets.

The three approaches represented are called (1) human capital theory, (2) tastes and preferences theory, and (3) statistical discrimination theory. Human capital theory highlights the supply side of the labor market, meaning the characteristics of the workers who are trying to sell their time (or labor power). The 'concept of *human capital* is meant to parallel the economic concept of physical capital, the plants and equipment used to produce goods and services. Better technology in a firm's physical capital will make it more productive. Human capital makes workers more productive. Formal education such as college, training, and experience on the job are all good ways of investing in your human capital.

Human capital theory was first developed as a rationale for government expenditures on education in order to boost the nation's productivity. It was applied to the issue of the gender-based wage gap by economists such as Jacob Mincer and Solomon Polachek. In this reader, philosopher Michael Levin provides a provocative (and less quantitative) example of the human capital argument. "The Earnings Gap and Family Choices" offers reasons, rooted in essential differences between the sexes, why women might have less human capital than men, justifying the differences in their wages. Catherine Weinberger presents a rebuttal to this position in her chapter, "Race and Gender Wage Gaps in the Market for Recent College Graduates." The methodology she uses, isolating wage differentials between young workers with similar educational investments and years of experience, aims to demonstrate quantitatively the existence of wage discrimination.

The second theoretical approach was developed by Gary Becker, the economist associated with the new home economics described in Section 3. Becker acknowledges that employers may have an irrational taste or preference for a particular type of worker, such as white men. Or they may adapt to the discriminatory attitudes of their workers or customers. This will affect the demand for particular types of workers. But these employers will have to pay higher wages to indulge in this preference and therefore will have to charge a higher price for their product. Smart customers who shop according to price will go to the rational, gender- and race-blind firm where prices are lower. Competition should eventually put the discriminating employer out of business. If the industry is not competitive, however, discrimination might persist longer. Ann Schwarz-Miller and Wayne Talley test the Becker hypothesis about the effects of competition in their study of "Motor Bus Deregulation and the Gender Wage Gap."

Statistical discrimination theory was also developed by neoclassical economists, including Edmund Phelps and Kenneth Arrow. This approach presumes that employers cannot always sort out the best potential workers among individual job applicants. They have *imperfect information*. To compensate, they generalize about groups of workers. Even if the generalization is statistically true about the average of the group, it may not be true about the individual job applicant. Statistical discrimination is therefore a form of discrimination against that individual. Sometimes the generalization does not even fairly represent the group average, but is based on a small, but noticeable, group of statistical outliers. Ivy Kennelly, in her sociological study of employer attitudes toward African American women, found that employers openly stated these discriminatory assumptions. In particular, employers characterized African American women as "That Single-Mother Element." Statistical discrimination may be harder to eliminate than an irrational taste or preference, since imperfect information means that competitive markets are not always efficient. However, this approach, like other neoclassical theories, locates discrimination in market failure; by implication, a perfectly competitive capitalist economy with perfect information should erode discrimination.

# 13

# The Earnings Gap and Family Choices

*Michael Levin*

We live in an age that tends to treat the most innocent phenomenon as a "problem" to be "solved" by "public policy," which means the intrusive machinery of the state. So it has proven with the "wage gap" separating men and women—it is touted by feminists as one more proof of the oppressiveness of Western society and the inequitability of the free market.

The factual basis of the feminist case is that the income of the average full-time working female is approximately 59 percent of that of the average full-time working male. Indeed, the gap has actually widened slightly over the last thirty years (see Treiman and Hartmann 1981) despite the passage in 1963 of the Equal Pay Act, which mandated equal pay for men and women doing the same jobs. (The failure of the Equal Pay Act to collapse the wage gap is taken by feminists to show not that discrimination is not and never was primarily responsible for the wage gap, but that discrimination is even more insidious and subtle than they thought.)

Of course, once this is stipulated to be a "problem," the range of "solutions" becomes limited to measures for making the average wages of full-time working men and women numerically equal. What is more, a number of subproblems arise that invite their own subsolutions. The clear tendency for jobs to segregate by sex, for example, must be met by attempts to "integrate" women into "nontraditional" jobs. Feminists see this as critical because, they claim, the percentage of women in an occupation correlates negatively with the wages that occupation pays. This claim, which in effect has the market penalizing women for being women, is based on statistical studies of jobs that agree with respect to some fixed set of variables controlling job characteristics and "human capital," but differ with respect to the proportion of women performing them—a technique that obviously ignores the possibility of unidentified variables that affect wages and correlate with sex.

However the "wage gap" is construed, it becomes a "problem," an occasion for action, only given some antecedent presumption favoring numerical equality. And, indeed, the view that numerical equality is somehow the "natural" state, with deviations therefrom requiring special justification, is very common. Its proponents characteristically describe any such deviation as "inequitable," "a failure of parity," or the like.

Yet even in these terms it would seem that there is far less to the wage gap than meets the eye fixed on slogans, for the average full-time working woman is not the economic equivalent of the average full-time working man. She works on average 35.7 hours per week, for example, while he works on average 44 hours per week (O'Neill and Braun 1981). There are marked differences in job tenure—a reasonable proxy for experience. In 1978 the average male had spent 4.5 years with his current employer, the average female 2.6 years. June O'Neill has, in fact, assembled variables that correlate differentially with males and females and that explain 90 percent of the wage gap. Since the wage gap is not a case of equals getting unequal returns, it is absurd to describe it as an inequity: it is explainable on reasonable economic grounds not involving invidious discrimination.

## Women's Different Responsibilities

Most economists I have consulted agree that the difference between male and female labor force participation is due largely (not entirely) to the fact that women see themselves as more responsible for household chores than men, for much of the male/female difference disappears when men are compared to single women (Sowell 1976). In 1971, for example, the wage ratio for strictly single Canadian women to Canadian men in the age cohort thirty and up was 99.2 percent (Block 1982). Women, most especially married women, are less willing to put out the energy needed to work their way up the career ladder, and they tend to see their income as supplementing that of their husband, the breadwinner. As a side effect, women seem more prepared to gravitate toward jobs, such as those in the clerical area, that permit repeated entry and exit without exacting a great economic toll.

Indeed, it is simply a mistake to say that women are thereby crowded into occupations lacking prestige (and thereby suffer the economic consequences of holding unprestigious jobs), since on the average female sex-typed jobs are slightly more prestigious than male sex-typed jobs (Gottfredson 1981).

Men may go after the most prestigious jobs, but they also settle for the least prestigious, while most "female" jobs, like typist or manicurist, have middling prestige. The consequences of the different expectations men and women bring to marriage and their relation to careers are virtually limitless.

To take a final example, the oft-cited average difference in salary between male and female college instructors can be explained by assuming (a) that the husband's career preferences are determinative in a two-instructor household, and (b) that, since female instructors like females generally tend to marry up, a greater proportion of female instructors marry male instructors than vice versa. Female instructors must thus compromise their career ambitions more often in deference to their mates than must male instructors (Maxwell, Rosenfeld, and Spilerman 1979).

To say that women sacrifice market earnings to household activities is of course not to say that female energy devoted to the family is less valuable than energy spent earning wages. The manifold activities of mothers sustain society, yet these activities cannot register as high-priced market commodities because they lack exchange value. The price attached to anything, labor included, is the measure of its capacity to secure other goods and services in barter. From an econometric point of view, mother love has the disadvantage of being fixed on a small number of unique objects and therefore is not exchangeable. I would pay a young mother handsomely if for five mornings a week she would transfer her love of her own infant to my children. Unfortunately, she does not regard children as fungible, so the routine services she is willing and able to provide for others are worth perhaps $5 an hour to a stranger like me. Mother love falls outside the gross domestic product (GDP) not because society undervalues it—only feminists undervalue mother love—but because mother love cannot figure in exchange.

If the wage gap is a product of preference, how can it be construed as discriminatory? True, when women gravitate to secretarial work they depress its wage, in the sense that secretarial wages would rise if there were fewer female secretaries and males did not take up the slack—but this is only to observe that supply and demand is at work in this situation as elsewhere. So long as nobody forces women to be secretaries, so long as what brings women to the "pink-collar ghetto" are their own life choices and skills (such as the greater female knack for repetitive tasks), just where is the inequity?

## Feminist Explanations of the Wage Gap

I would let these rhetorical questions rest except that the feminists take them so seriously and even supply what they think is a compelling answer. Feminists occasionally speculate about actual conspiracies to "herd" women into pink-collar jobs and "keep women's wages down," but the preferred feminist explanation of the wage gap is a straightforward application of the general feminist indictment of society: sex-role conditioning has handicapped women by persuading them that their main task in life is not wage labor but child rearing and that the best jobs are not "for them" even should they decide to work. Thus brainwashed, women of course subordinate career aspirations to family, tend to leave work when their children are young, and so on. Unmarried women, for their part, are conditioned to see the office as a hunting ground for husbands.

In short, according to feminists, the choices women make merely perpetuate the evil of "sexism." Even an observer as shrewd as June O'Neill writes: "One could also classify as discrimination the pervasive cultural factors that have led to different roles for men and women and that shape the extent to which women are able to devote themselves to a career outside the home" (O'Neill and Braun 1981, p. 63). In the words of Nancy Barrett,

> Economic gender roles in the traditional family work against economic parity in several ways. First, of course, they perpetuate gender-based stereotypes and stereotypical self-images. . . . Second, women's household responsibilities compete for time and energy with labor force activities; while for men, household (financial support) responsibilities are complementary to labor force activities. . . . The relative positions of men and women in the labor force are not the outcomes of supply and demand in the conventional sense. Rather, they are the outcomes of a complicated set of traditional expectations that have to be analyzed in a model in which gender confers a set of distinct property rights on certain activities. (1982, pp. 163–64)

Both citations—drawn, incidentally, from writers who so far as I know do not unambiguously endorse characteristic feminist policy demands—deploy the two central feminist assumptions: (a) that economic gender roles are the result of *socially induced* expectations, and (b) that action based upon such "stereotyping" is discriminatory. I will consider these assumptions presently, but I would note now that "second-stage" feminists—*arrivistes* who claim to acknowledge gender differences without abandoning feminism—tend to agree with standard feminists that present economic gender roles are discriminatory, even while admitting that these roles reflect biologically programmed preferences. . . .

Yet even before turning to the origin and justification of the sexual division of labor, it is worth stressing the senselessness of virtually all talk of the economic disparity of men and women, and of all comparisons between women and blacks or other isolable social groups. Despite the feminist representation of men and women as hostile camps in a war for the world's goods, the simple fact is that *men and women marry*. The battle of the sexes is distinguished chiefly by the degree of collaboration.

That the world's men and women share a common fate puts that 59 cents figure in a quite new light; since the woman making 59 cents may be married to the man making one dollar, she will gain nothing if some government exertion raises her income at the expense of his. Their joint income will remain the same at best and probably fall, since state intervention exacts a cost from everybody.

**Biology Is Key**

... But the main trouble with the feminist diagnosis of the economic division of labor is its disregard of biology. The sexual division of labor has been a permanent feature of society because it expresses innate psychological differences between the sexes. This division has been a permanent feature of society. It is sometimes suggested that the home/work division of labor, and even the "nuclear family," were created by the industrial revolution, but this suggestion is misleading at best. In every society of which there is any record, men and women have paired off (sometimes polygamously, to be sure) to rear children in a family unit. Granted, fewer people live with their grandparents and aunts and uncles in industrialized urban settings than in pastoral, rural settings—which may seem like an indictment of urban society until one remembers that a staple of literature of two centuries ago was the young man who wanted nothing more than to escape the confinement of his "extended family" and make his way by himself in the big city.

Moreover, in every society of which there is any record, men have carved a distinctive niche for male activities. If women have gathered berries, then men have hunted. Women in every culture have been the ones responsible for child care and allied domestic tasks, while men have pursued extrafamilial activities. Wage labor may be a recent invention, but not this division of responsibilities. What was introduced by the industrial revolution, and more particularly the railroad and later the automobile, was commuting. Never before had men daily traveled tens of miles away from their homes to do productive work. Never before had the locus of productive work been so disconnected from the home. Yet whether or not commuting has changed the psychosocial character of work, it has not changed the basic sexual division of social tasks.

Any such cultural universal as the sexual division of labor suggests a nonsocial, biological cause, and indeed it is as certain as anything in science can be that men and women do differ in the abilities and, more importantly, the motivations they bring to paid labor and everything else. Neurologists are now reasonably sure that females are born with a greater capacity for fine motor coordination and tolerance for repetitive tasks (McGuinness and Pribram 1976). These innate capacities translate in adulthood into measurable differences in skills highly prized by a highly "technical" society. According to a recent study commissioned by the [U.S.] Department of Defense (1982), men score considerably better than women in mechanical ability.

But much more important than any innate difference in abilities is the difference in competitiveness that men and women bring to the labor market. Men are more competitive than women, which is to say more apt to do whatever is needed to get ahead, whatever "getting ahead" happens to be under the circumstances. This disposition, called "dominance aggression" by physiologist John Money, is perhaps the determinative factor in economic sexual differentiation. Men, more willing to put out the energy required to dominate in extrafamilial pursuits—success in the world of work is such a pursuit—tend to go further in such pursuits. Not all men are prepared to make such efforts, but most of those so prepared are men, which is why most of those who excel in the hierarchical, competitive, rationalized world of the free market are men. For better or worse, money is a symbolic measure of others' estimate of one's worth to them, so that the impulse to compete and dominate will manifest itself as an impulse to seek activities for which remuneration is highest. . . .

It would be a gross error to suppose that women are simply less competitive than men but like men in every other motivational respect. Women have their own nurturant and cooperative drives that deflect energy away from the sort of competition favored by the economic marketplace. Greater female concern with nurturing one's young has an obvious adaptive advantage, since a woman can reproduce only a few dozen times at most to a man's thousands. Liberated female mammals, as heedless of their offspring as male mammals tend to be and as feminists would like human females to be, went extinct a long time ago. The care of young children puts a premium on patience and above all empathy—and, given the helplessness of human children for the first few years of their life, a complete absorption in the child to the exclusion of extrafamilial pursuits. Once again, there will be women who do not experience these impulses, but they will remain in the minority and the basic institutions of human society will continue to coalesce around the impulses felt by the majority of women.

It may seem a long step from these general motivational differences between the sexes to the particulars of "sex-role stereotyping." There may be a gene for nurturance, not for washing the dishes. In fact, however, "sex roles" as we know them are just further consequences of the underlying general sex differences, given unavoidable environmental contingencies. As Steven Goldberg (1977) has noted, there is a feedback loop between biologically given sex differences and the social roles they create. People, particularly parents, notice that on the whole boys and girls act differently. This perception is frozen in the more categorical maxim "boys do one sort of thing, girls another," which maxim then informs parental expectations about boys and girls.

Since boys and girls are expected to act differently, they are socialized to act differently,·and when this socialization *takes*—socialization that emphasizes the differences in gender behavior—the original maxim is confirmed and is deployed in another round of socialization. In this way, biological sex differences are magnified. It will not do to call this process "oppressive," since people are simply exercising their perfect right to form generalizations on the basis of experience, and if the object of the feminist exercise is to prevent the formation of "stereotypes," it will once again involve massive interference with the socialization of children by parents.

Role differentiation is, in any case, a rational solution to the problems of day-to-day life that most couples adopt spontaneously. Since the mother is taking care of the children at home while the father is at work, it stands to reason—to the reason of the people actually involved, if not to the reason of feminists—that Mom be responsible for keeping the home clean and preparing the meals. Somebody must do these things, after all. As children do not dematerialize after a year or two on Earth to let Mom "return to her career and fulfill herself," this modus vivendi crystallizes over time. I would add that, in my view, it is not out of the question that some innate female nest-building drive plays a role in the development of the sexual division of labor as well.

## The Wage Gap as a Result of Choices

In saying that the wage gap—if not the precise figure of 59 percent—is justified because it arises out of the free choices of individuals following biologically given impulses, it is crucial that we be clear about the kind of justification this is. I am not arguing that people ought to follow their biological impulses. In themselves, biological impulses are not good or bad; they are simply there. Nor am I arguing that the sexual division of labor works better than any other. I have no idea whether this is so, although it would be amazing if nature were so inefficient as to make each sex best at what the other sex prefers to do. Nor, finally, am I arguing that men deserve economic preeminence because they want it. Wanting something creates no title to it at all.

Rather, I see the sexual division of labor and its broad statistical contours justified not by its intrinsic character, but precisely because it is the result of uncoerced, free human choice. Left to their own devices, responding to the contingencies of the environment and the unalterable constraints of the human condition, men and women in modern technological society develop skills that tend to be exchangeable in a ratio of roughly 6 : 10. In other societies the ratio might be different. There is nothing intrinsically admirable about this figure. It is perfectly all right, not a "problem," because it came about in a perfectly proper way.

The wage gap does not mean a denial of "equal opportunity" in any reasonable sense that can be attached to that much abused slogan. Women certainly have opportunities equal to those of men in the sense that there are *no laws preventing* women from undertaking any activity available to men. Women certainly have opportunities equal to those of men in the sense that even private discrimination against women is now expressly forbidden by federal law. The average woman may not have the training of some hypothetical male counterpart, but training and like advantages are *means* that one uses to exploit an opportunity, not opportunity itself. Equality of opportunity must never be confused with equality of means. Few of us have the financial means to purchase a ticket for the Concorde, yet we all have the opportunity to do so.

Nor will it do to say that women have less opportunity than men in light of their family responsibilities. A woman who sacrifices a career for her children has *chosen* one of many paths that she might take, in much the way that a man who gives up a career in sports to join the military has chosen to forgo one path open to him. In neither case has any external force foreclosed any choices.

Finally, it borders on the idiotic to say that women lack equal opportunity because they are less interested than men in pursuing careers. Only feminists are so uncomfortable with feminine impulses as to regard these impulses as alien impositions on women. I have spoken to feminist mothers (generally in the academic world) who do profess that "society made me have children" to the detriment of their careers and demand some sort of social recompense for their sacrifice, quite forgetting that having a child is a joint decision with one's husband. (Possibly these women were talked into having children against their will, but most women are not that extraordinarily weak-minded.)

This strange view that children are something that happens to women out of the blue (at society's behest) usually prefaces a demand that "society" let women climb the career ladder just like men while also having children. This is not a demand for equal opportunity at all but a demand to be protected from the consequences of one's choices, in this case the effects on one's wage-earning power of devoting a crucial portion of one's life to children. This is a request for special privileges. A man who takes a few years off to follow his guru to the Himalayas does not and cannot expect society to guarantee him academic tenure upon his return.

The incessant feminist message that a career is as vital (perhaps more vital) to mental health as a family has created a generation of women ever regretting the road not taken. This message has made women who spend full time with their children think they have cheated themselves. This message has burdened women who sacrifice children for work with deeply unsatisfied biological drives. No matter which way they turn, these women feel cheated and discontented.

## Conclusion

So I am skeptical about "solutions" to the wage gap problem because I do not see it as a problem at all. . . . Direct government intervention to eliminate the wage gap takes the form of equal pay laws and, more recently, a court decision under Title VII of the Civil Rights Act that uses the comparable worth slogan. The widening of the pay gap in the last three decades shows not only the patent failure of the Equal Pay Act to accomplish what it was supposed to accomplish, but the general tendency of government action to exacerbate problems (or situations). Given the premise that increased government intrusion in the market and the growth of government generally in the last three decades have fueled inflation and made it harder for one wage-earner to support a family, there is a simple explanation for the small but real growth in the wage gap. Women who entered the labor force in 1955 were more likely to do so for some positive reason, whereas proportionately more women who enter the labor force today do so out of perceived economic necessity. Women who entered the labor force in 1955 were thus more inclined to drive harder bargains than their counterparts today, thereby driving wages up.

If this is so, the one public policy that will "help working women," and indirectly tend to the sort of statistical economic parity so prized by feminists, is a return to the sort of prosperity that allows a single wage to support a family. This outcome would "liberate" the woman of the house to take a paid job or not, as she saw fit, to be a bit more choosy, and to earn a better wage if she did choose to enter the labor force. I have no magic formulas to offer in that regard except further tax cuts, and corresponding cuts in government spending so that deficit financing does not reintroduce inflation through the back door.

## References

Barrett, Nancy S. 1982. "Obstacles to Economic Parity for Women." *American Economic Review* 72 (2): 160–65.

Block, Walter. 1982. "Economic Intervention, Discrimination and Unintended Consequences." In *Discrimination, Affirmative Action, and Equal Opportunity*, ed. Walter Block and Michael Walker. Vancouver, Canada: Fraser Institute.

Goldberg, Steven. 1977. *The Inevitability of Patriarchy*, 2d ed. London: Temple-Smith.

Gottfredson, Linda. 1981. "Circumscription and Compromise: A Developmental Theory of Occupational Aspirations." *Journal of Counseling Psychology*, Monograph 28, November 6, pp. 545–79.

Maxwell, Gerald, Rachel A. Rosenfeld, and Seymour Spilerman. 1979. "Geographic Constraints on Women's Careers in Academia." *Science* 205 (September 21): 1225–31.

McGuinness, Diane, and Karl Pribram. 1978. "The Origins of Sensory Bias in the Development of Gender Differences in Perception and Cognition." In *Cognitive Growth and Development*, ed. Morton Bortner, pp. 3–56. New York: Brunner/Mazel.

O'Neill, June, and Rachel Braun. 1981. *Women and the Labor Market: A Survey of Issues and Policies in the United States*. Washington, DC: Urban Institute.

Sowell, Thomas. 1976. "'Affirmative Action' Reconsidered." *Public Interest* 42 (Winter): 47–65.

Treiman, Donald J., and Heidi I. Hartmann, eds. 1981. *Women, Work and Wages: Equal Pay for Jobs of Equal Value*. Washington, DC: National Academy Press.

U.S. Department of Defense. 1982. *Profile of American Youth: 1980 Nationwide Administration of the Armed Services Vocational Attitude Battery*. Washington, DC: Office of the Assistant Secretary of Defense for Manpower.

---

Adapted from "The Earnings Gap and Family Choices," Chapter 12 of *Equal Pay for Unequal Work*, ed. Phyllis Schlafly. Washington, DC: Eagle Forum Education & Legal Defense Fund, pp. 125–39. Reprinted with permission of the Eagle Forum (see www.eagleforum.org).

# 14

# Race and Gender Wage Gaps in the Market for Recent College Graduates

*Catherine J. Weinberger*

Women and black men have lower average hourly earnings than white men with the same number of years of education. Part of these "wage gaps" may be due to labor market discrimination, whereas part may be due to differences in productivity between the typical members of different demographic groups. For example, it is often suggested that the racial wage gap reflects a tendency for black students to receive a lower quality of education than white students with the same number of years in school. Similarly, it has been suggested that women lack the mathematical ability to pursue college degrees in more remunerative technical fields and that women choose to pursue degrees in fields where the associated careers are compatible with their anticipated family responsibilities. In all these examples, adding appropriate controls to the wage equation for the type and quality of education attained should reduce or eliminate the estimated wage gap.

One approach is to control for the occupation of employment. If we believe that labor markets allocate individuals to the jobs for which they are best suited, then occupation is a good proxy for an individual's productivity and preferences. Adding controls for occupation significantly reduces estimated race and gender wage gaps. . . . The limitation of this method is that occupation is a labor market outcome. Occupational assignments may themselves be affected by labor market discrimination (Brown, Moon, and Zoloth 1980; Blau 1984; Bielby and Baron 1984; Ferber and Green 1991; Gill 1994).

If so, then occupation measures neither an employee's productivity nor preferences, and differences in occupation cannot be used to "explain" differences in wages.

An alternative approach is to control carefully for the skills and preferences that an individual takes into the labor market. For example, estimates of the wage differential between white male and white female recent college graduates are reduced by about one-half when controls for four to eight broad college major categories are included in the wage equation (Polachek 1978; Daymont and Andrisani 1984; Eide and Grogger 1992; Rumberger and Thomas 1993; Eide 1994). Given that increasingly detailed designations of an individual's occupation lead to diminishing estimates of the gender wage differential, an interesting question is whether increasingly detailed measures of the type and quality of education will reduce estimated wage gaps between white men and other groups of young recent college graduates.

While many economic studies focus on differences in outcomes between white men and white women or between black men and white men, this study examines wage outcomes for men and women who identified themselves as white, black, Hispanic, or Asian. This broader focus can reveal relationships in the data that would otherwise not be recognized. . . .

This study uses a unique sample of recent college graduates. The *1985 Survey of Recent College Graduates* reports the earnings, exact college major, college grade point average, and educational institution attended for over 8,000 young college graduates. The sample includes several hundred graduates who identified themselves as black, Asian, or Hispanic.

Each individual in the sample completed a four-year bachelor's degree in an academic field one to two years before the 1985 survey date. These young graduates have very low levels of previous work experience and are homogeneous with respect to the number of years of education completed. College major, college grades, and the college attended represent both exceptionally detailed measures of the type and quality of education attained and an indication of the ability of each graduate to work productively at the broad range of tasks involved in completing college coursework. In addition, college major provides an indication of each graduate's occupational preferences. (For example, in this sample 74 percent of female education majors but only 2 percent of other employed women are employed as teachers.) This sample therefore provides a unique opportunity to observe whether race and gender wage differentials remain after controlling very carefully for the education, productive ability, and preferences an individual takes into the labor market.

The limitation of this analysis is that it examines the wage differential in only a small sector of the economy. This analysis does not even begin to explore whether earlier discrimination affected the educational attainments of these college graduates or of their less educated age-mates. In particular, black and Hispanic young people are much less likely than white young people to become college graduates and enter this sample (Berryman 1983). This analysis has nothing to say about whether individuals with more or less education face comparable wage differentials or what will happen to these wage differentials as the cohort ages.[1] However, this data set provides a unique opportunity to learn whether wage differentials can be found even in the markets for these highly and equally educated young men and women.

**The Data**

. . . The data set is very well suited to determine the average wages of graduates with a given college major. Surveyed individuals were asked to identify their college major from a list of over 300 major fields and subspecialties, of which 246 are represented in this sample. The level of detail includes, for example, thirty-two types of biology major, nineteen types of business major, fifty-five types of education major, and twenty-five types of engineering major. Collapsed major categories are used in some of the analysis, and these categories are business, communications, computer science, economics, education, engineering, humanities, mathematics, nursing, science, social sciences (other than economics), and "other."

Research about which colleges open the doors to higher-paying jobs is at a very early stage. There is statistical evidence that graduates of the most selective private colleges earn higher wages than graduates of other colleges (Brewer, Eide, and Ehrenberg 1996), but knowledge about the relative returns to attending the majority of colleges is speculative. Existing rankings of "college quality" are based on various characteristics of schools that may or may not lead to higher wage jobs. In addition, these rankings are not complete orderings.

In this analysis, a separate dummy variable for each of the 388 colleges represented in the sample was included in the wage equation. These variables control for the relative valuation by the labor market of graduates from each institution. This is the best available information about whether attendance at a particular college tends to be remunerative. Factors that influence this valuation may include instructional quality, the quality of the students admitted, the prevailing campus work ethic, and the reputation of the institution. Local labor market conditions also may affect this estimate, if graduates are geographically constrained. (The current geographic location of the graduates is not recorded in the survey. Each graduate was assigned to one of nine census regions based on the location of the college attended.)

College grade point average is self-reported. Self-reported grades are generally accurate, with no gender difference in the tendency to inflate self-reported grades (Freeberg 1988; Maxwell and Lopus 1994). Therefore, we do not expect the estimated wage gaps to be affected by misreported grades. College grade point average was recoded from a categorical variable ("mostly A's," "3.75," "about half A's" and half B's," "3.25–3.75," etc.) to a continuous variable. All ranges were recoded to the midpoint of the range.

The graduates are grouped demographically by gender and into the following five subgroups: non-Hispanic white ($N = 5025$), non-Hispanic black ($N = 403$), Asian or Pacific Islander ($N = 157$), Hispanic ($N = 349$), and American Indian or Native Alaskan ($N = 18$). Because of small sample size, estimated means and coefficients for the last group are not reported. However, this group was included in the computation of returns to nondemographic characteristics.

Employment data were gathered for the week of April 29, 1985. Respondents had the option of reporting wages or earnings on an hourly, daily, weekly, monthly, or annual basis. Hourly earnings are computed from whatever wage or income figures were reported and from reported hours worked per week. Those reporting their occupation as "teacher" and their salary on an annual basis were assumed to earn that salary in only ten months.

Two separate variables reflecting work experience are included in the analysis. The first is actual full-time work experience prior to receiving the bachelor's degree, excluding summer or other temporary jobs. This question was specifically asked of the graduates in the survey. The second is postdegree experience, defined as time elapsed since college graduation, which varies from ten to twenty-two months in this sample. This "potential experience" variable is a common proxy for work experience. A final labor market variable included in the analysis is hours worked per week.

All analysis contained in this paper is weighted by the "final adjusted weight" constructed by the National Center for Education Statistics (NCES) to adjust for oversampling of graduates of certain demographic groups, institutions, and college majors.

## Observations on the Sample

... Of the 5,952 graduates in this sample, men earn 18 percent more per hour than women ($9.07 for men and $7.70 for women). Hispanic men have the highest average hourly earnings ($10.02), followed by Asian men, white men, Asian women, Hispanic women, black men, white women, and black women ($7.08). ...

Only 20 percent of the male Hispanic graduates have a college-educated parent, compared with 44 to 52 percent for all other groups of men and 32 to

55 percent for all groups of women. Hispanic male college graduates come from families with much less educated parents than black male college graduates. In this sample, female Hispanic graduates come from families with more educated parents than male Hispanic graduates. For Asian and black women, the relationship is reversed; those from families with less educated parents are more likely than their brothers to complete college.

White, black, and Hispanic women in this sample are much more likely than men to have a degree in low-paying fields such as education, humanities, or social sciences and much less likely to have a degree in the high-paying fields of engineering or computer science. However, Asian women in this sample are at least as likely as white men to have studied engineering, math, computer science, or science, and yet they earn lower average wages than white men.

The groups are more similar in the other characteristics used in this analysis. On average, the men are seven months older than the women by the time they complete college. Hispanic men are the oldest at the time of graduation (25.3 years), followed by Asian men, black men, Hispanic women, white men, Asian women, black women, and white women (23.6 years). For college graduates in their twenties, there is no established relationship between age at college completion and labor market productivity.

The men have an average of only five months more work experience than the women before completing college, with no significant variation between groups. All groups of graduates have an average of about one year and one month postgraduation experience. Relative to the typical worker in the U.S. labor force, the amount of both pre- and postgraduation work experience is very small for every member of this sample.

## Methodology

. . . If wages depend only on the type and quality of education, then the following equation describes the true relationship between human capital and wages for all demographic groups:

$ln$ (wage) $= f$(work experience, hours/week) $+ g$ (type and quality of college education)

. . . In this analysis, [the following] equation is estimated:

$$ln \text{ (wage)} = f \text{ (work experience, hours/week)} + g$$
$$\text{(type and quality of college education)} +$$
$$C_1 * \text{white female} + C_2 * \text{black female} + C_3 * \text{Asian female} +$$
$$C_4 * \text{Hispanic female} + C_5 * \text{black male} + C_6 * \text{Asian male} +$$
$$C_7 * \text{Hispanic male}$$

If type and quality of education are measured perfectly, then $-C_i$ is the estimated percentage wage disadvantage of a typical member of group $i$ relative to a white man with the same human capital. If wages depend only on human capital, and if human capital is measured perfectly, then the $C_i$ will equal zero. . . .

The controls for human capital included . . . are predegree work experience, postdegree experience, college grade point average, and hours worked per week. . . . This analysis also will determine whether, on average, women and nonwhite men earn less than white men with the same type and quality of education. Labor market discrimination can be broadly defined as a mechanism that causes individuals with the same productive characteristics but different ascriptive characteristics to be valued differently in the labor market. Where coefficient $C_i$ is nonzero, even with the best controls, then it is likely that the graduates in group i face labor market discrimination.

## Results

### Discussion of General Results

Table 14.1 reports the results of the regression analysis.[2] . . . The coefficients on experience, college grade point average, and hours worked per week are statistically significant. As might be expected, the return to a year of postdegree work experience is higher than the return to predegree experience. Also as expected, higher college grades lead to higher wages. However, the return to working longer hours is negative. . . .

After controlling for the 388 institutions attended and 246 narrowly defined college majors, white male and Hispanic male college graduates have a 10 to 15 percent wage advantage over white, black, and Asian women and black and Asian men. Discussion of the effects of increasingly fine controls for college major, geographic region, and college attended on the estimated wage differential for each of the seven groups follows.

### White Women

For white women, differences in broadly defined college major explain nearly half the estimated wage disadvantage relative to white men. Adding further controls for narrow college major, geography, or institution attended has absolutely no additional affect on the estimated 9 percent white female wage disadvantage. This means that within a broad college major category, women do not choose less remunerative majors on average. It also means that, on average, white women and white men attend colleges whose graduates are similarly valued.

Table 14.1

**Regression Results** (standard errors in parentheses)

| Variable | Coefficient | Standard errors |
|---|---|---|
| White women | −.10 | (.01) |
| Black women | −.15 | (.03) |
| Asian women | −.15 | (.05) |
| Hispanic women | −.06 | (.04) |
| Black men | −.09 | (.04) |
| Asian men | −.14 | (.04) |
| Hispanic men | .01 | (.05) |
| Hours | −.006 | (.001) |
| Predegree experience | .013 | (.002) |
| Postdegree experience | .06 | (.02) |
| Grade point average | .07 | (.01) |
| Neither parent has college degree | −.015 | (.009) |
| | | |
| 388 school controls? | Yes | |
| Sample size | 5,952 | |
| $R^2$ | .3987 | |

*Notes:* Dependent variable is the natural log of hourly earnings. The reference demographic group is non-Hispanic white men.

### Black Men and Women

For black men, controls for college major and institution attended have no effect on the 9 percent estimated wage disadvantage relative to white men. This means that black male college graduates, on average, choose equally remunerative college majors as white men. In addition, black male college graduates attend colleges whose graduates are as highly valued in the labor market as the colleges attended by white men. Because these black male and white male college graduates come from families with similar levels of education, it is not surprising that their educational attainments are similar in type and quality.

Unlike black men, black women attend colleges whose graduates are less valued by the labor market, on average, than those attended by white men. This difference may reflect the fact that the black women in this sample came from less affluent families. Like white women, black women have less remunerative college majors than white men. However, black women have somewhat less remunerative college majors than white men within as well as between broad college major categories. Altogether, controls for college major and the educational institution attended explain two-fifths of the black female wage disadvantage relative to white men, reducing the estimated wage disadvantage from 25 percent to 16 percent. This remaining wage gap is still the largest of any demographic group.

### Hispanic Men and Women

Hispanic male college graduates earn somewhat more than white men until controls for college attended are included. After controlling for type and quality of college education received, the Hispanic male recent college graduates in this sample face no wage disadvantage relative to white men.

Like Hispanic men who complete college, Hispanic women attend colleges whose graduates are highly valued by the labor market. Controls for college major reduce the estimated wage disadvantage faced by Hispanic women from 11 percent to zero. However, further controls reveal that there is a 6 percent gap relative to white men who attended the same college. The 6 percent estimated wage disadvantage faced by Hispanic women has a large standard error. Therefore, we can conclude only that Hispanic women probably face some wage disadvantage and that it is no larger than that faced by other women.

### Asian Men and Women

For Asian men and women, controlling for college major and institution attended reveals a hidden wage disadvantage. Asian men and women tend to choose more remunerative college majors, to live in higher-wage geographic regions, and to graduate from colleges with better-paid graduates than other men and women. All these factors contribute to relatively high average wages. However, Asian men and women actually face the same 10 to 15 percent wage disadvantage as white women, black women, and black men relative to white male graduates of the same institution and college major.

### Further Discussion

How big is a 10 to 15 percent wage disadvantage? As a point of reference, the wage disadvantage associated with coming from a family with no college-educated parent is an order of magnitude smaller, 1.5 percent.

Of course, this 10 to 15 percent disadvantage is only an average. Within any group, there are likely to be individuals and subgroups of individuals with a larger or smaller unexplained wage differential. It is likely that the graduates of certain majors and certain colleges face a greater wage disadvantage than other graduates of the same demographic group. This analysis clearly demonstrates that, on average, the typical white or Hispanic male college graduate enjoys a wage premium relative to other graduates with the same type and quality of college education.

## Summary and Conclusion

The question of whether race and gender differentials in pay among individuals with the same number of years of education are due to labor market discrimination or to unobserved differences in career preferences and the type and quality of education attained is difficult to answer. The focus of this chapter is a large survey of recent college graduates. This data set contains extremely detailed information about the productive characteristics and career preferences that an individual takes into the labor market. The available controls include narrowly defined college major, college grades, and the exact educational institution attended by each graduate. This chapter examines the effects on estimated wage differentials of including increasingly detailed controls for the type and quality of education attained.

This analysis shows clearly that among recent college graduates, white women, black men, black women, Asian men, and Asian women all face the same 10 to 15 percent wage disadvantage relative to white men with the same type and quality of college education. If labor market discrimination is defined as a mechanism that causes individuals with the same productive characteristics but different ascriptive characteristics to be valued differently by the labor market, then this is very strong evidence that discrimination operates in the market for recent college graduates.

## Notes

1. The wage differentials estimated between male and female college graduates tend to increase with the time since graduation (Fuller and Schoenberger 1991; Wood, Corcoran, and Courant 1993).

2. Editor's note: This discussion of the results includes highlights of findings from additional models beyond the model depicted in Table 14.1.

## References

Berryman, Sue. 1983. *Who Will Do Science? Trends and Their Causes in Minority and Female Representation Among Holders of Advanced Degrees in Science and Mathematics: A Special Report.* New York: Rockefeller Foundation.

Bielby, William, and James Baron. 1984. "A Woman's Place Is with Other Women: Sex Segregation within Organizations." In *Sex Segregation in the Workplace,* ed. Barbara Reskin, pp. 27–55. Washington, DC: National Academy Press.

Blau, Francine. 1984. "Occupational Segregation and Labor Market Discrimination."

In *Sex Segregation in the Workplace*, ed. Barbara Reskin, pp. 117–43. Washington, DC: National Academy Press.

Brewer, Dominic, Eric Eide, and Ronald G. Ehrenberg. 1996. "Does It Pay to Attend an Elite Private College? Cross-Cohort Evidence on the Effects of College Quality on Earnings." Unpublished paper.

Brown, Randall S., Marilyn Moon, and Barbara S. Zoloth. 1980. "Incorporating Occupational Attainment in Studies of Male-Female Earnings Differentials." *Journal of Human Resources* 15 (Winter): 3–28.

Daymont, Thomas, and Paul Andrisani. 1984. "Job Preferences, College Major and the Gender Gap in Earnings." *Journal of Human Resources* 19 (Summer): 408–28.

Eide, Eric. 1994. "College Major and Changes in the Gender Wage Gap." *Contemporary Economic Policy* 12 (April): 55–64.

Eide, Eric, and Jeff Grogger. 1992. "Omitted-Ability Bias, Major-Specific Wage Premia, and Changes in the Returns to College Education." Unpublished paper, University of California, Santa Barbara.

Ferber, Marianne A., and Carole Green. 1991. "Occupational Segregation and the Earnings Gap." In *Essays on the Economics of Discrimination*, ed. Emily P. Hoffman. Kalamazoo, MI: W.E. Upjohn Institute.

Freeberg, Norman. 1988. "Analysis of the Revised Student-Descriptive Questionnaire. Phase 1: Of Accuracy of Student-Reported Information, College Board Report 88–5." College Entrance Examination Board, New York (ERIC: ED304460).

Fuller, Rex, and Richard Schoenberger. 1991. "The Gender Salary Gap: Do Academic Achievement, Internship Experience, and College Major Make a Difference?" *Social Science Quarterly* 72 (December): 715–26.

Gill, Andrew M. 1994. "Incorporating the Causes of Occupational Differences in Studies of Racial Wage Differentials." *Journal of Human Resources* 29 (Winter): 20–41.

Maxwell, Nan L., and Jane S. Lopus. 1994. "The Lake Wobegon Effect in Student Self-Reported Data." *American Economic Review* 84 (2): 201–5.

National Center for Education Statistics (NCES). 1988. *Employment Outcomes of Recent Master's and Bachelor's Degree Recipients, CS 88–251*. Washington, DC: U.S. Department of Education.

Polachek, Solomon. 1978. "Sex Differences in College Major." *Industrial and Labor Relations Review* 31 (July): 498–508.

Rumberger, Russell W., and Scott Thomas. 1993. "The Economic Returns to College Major, Quality, and Performance: A Multilevel Analysis of Recent Graduates." *Economics of Education Review* 12 (March): 1–19.

Wood, Robert G., Mary E. Corcoran, and Paul N. Courant. 1993. "Pay Differentials Among the Highly Paid: The Male-Female Earnings Gap in Lawyers' Salaries." *Journal of Labor Economics* 11 (3): 417–41.

---

Adapted from "Race and Gender Wage Gaps in the Market for Recent College Graduates," *Industrial Relations* 37 (1) (January 1998): 67–84. Reprinted with permission.

# 15

# Motor Bus Deregulation and the Gender Wage Gap

## A Test of the Becker Hypothesis

*Ann Schwarz-Miller and Wayne K. Talley*

Over forty years ago, Gary Becker (1957) argued that firms in more competitive industries have less ability than other firms (i.e., neither the profits nor the latitude) to discriminate in either wages or hiring. Support for the argument regarding pay practices is found in studies by Heywood (1987) and Peoples (1994), which show that lower industrial concentration correlates with less racial wage discrimination; support regarding hiring is found in studies by Comanor (1973), Haessel and Palmer (1978), Luksetich (1979), and Ashenfelter and Hannan (1986), which show a negative relationship between industrial concentration and the relative employment of minorities and females.

The Becker hypothesis can also be tested within a single-industry framework. Transportation industries, which have undergone systematic change and deregulation, in particular provide fertile ground for such tests. The increase in competition introduced through deregulation should have made it increasingly costly for employers to discriminate in pay and employment practices. . . .

This study provides a test of the Becker hypothesis with respect to labor market discrimination in a deregulated transportation sector, the motor bus industry, by examining the impact of the regulatory environment on relative earnings. However, it differs from previous studies by focusing on the gender wage gap as opposed to the racial wage gap. The presence of a gender-based earnings differential within an industry may be the direct result of pay practices of individual firms that reflect the strength of their discriminatory preferences and latitude to engage in wage discrimination. It may also arise

175

through firm-level employment discrimination that reduces the aggregate demand for female workers and depresses their relative earnings. As others have pointed out (e.g., Heywood and Peoples 1994), the elasticity of labor supply to a firm is crucial in determining the extent to which the employer engages in wage, employment, or both forms of discrimination. The higher the supply elasticity, the greater the degree of employment discrimination and the smaller the effect on wages.

Since the human capital requirements for driving a bus are comparatively low, the elasticity of labor supply to firms in the motor bus industry is expected to be high, though not infinite. It follows that any gender gap emerging under regulation is not likely to have been produced through wage discrimination alone, but to a large extent as the consequence of employment discrimination. Likewise, much of the hypothesized decline in the gender earnings differential after deregulation should be the result of a reduction in employment discrimination. The actual estimation results suggest that the female/ male wage gap of motor bus drivers declined following deregulation, thereby providing the first supportive evidence of the Becker hypothesis with respect to gender discrimination within a deregulated transportation industry. . . .

## The Motor Bus Industry Under Regulation and Deregulation

The motor bus industry consists of privately owned firms (carriers) providing for-hire bus services such as scheduled regular-route intercity passenger service, charter passenger service, charter tour service, retail tour service, and bus package express service. The industry's scheduled regular-route intercity service is dominated by one carrier, Greyhound Lines, which has the only nationwide bus network. By 1990, it accounted for 75 percent of the service's revenues and 43 percent of its passengers (GAO 1992).

The Motor Carrier Act of 1935 placed the industry under the authority of the Interstate Commerce Commission (ICC), which regulated entry, exit, fares, financial activities, and service levels of carriers involved in interstate commerce. Although regulation limited intraindustry competition, the industry experienced a significant decline in market share and financial performance following World War II as more affluent passengers switched to other transportation modes. Seeking flexibility to compete more effectively in the intercity passenger market, the industry sought regulatory reform. In 1982, the Bus Regulatory Reform Act (BRRA) was passed, substituting competitive market forces for regulatory decree in determining fares and service.

Rather than improving, the industry's financial performance grew worse following passage of the BRRA and its miles of service declined even though the number of carriers increased. Faced with competition from new, lower-cost carriers, large incumbent carriers sought cost reductions through franchising and wage concessions and, in the case of Greyhound, consolidating accounting operations, selling bus terminals, as well as reorganizing the company.

Labor cost reduction has been a particular concern. The motor bus industry has historically been highly unionized, with the Amalgamated Transit Union (ATU) representing labor in much of the industry. ICC regulation (e.g., entry and rate restrictions) provided the ATU with the opportunity to acquire more bargaining power than possible in a more competitive environment, with higher union driver wages and union premiums over nonunion wages the outcome (Schwarz-Miller and Talley 1994).

Following the passage of the BRRA, wage concessions to Trailways Lines (the second-largest motor bus firm) and the outcomes of subsequent rounds of labor negotiations at Greyhound coupled with Greyhound's recurring financial difficulties suggest that the union's ability to generate wage premiums was eroding. In 1982, the ATU signed an agreement with Trailways freezing wages below Greyhound's wages. Greyhound, in response, also sought contract concessions. After eighteen months of unsuccessful negotiations and a bitter and sometimes violent thirteen-month strike, Greyhound ultimately succeeded in obtaining most of the wage and benefit concessions requested. In late 1985, further concessions were sought by Greyhound. However, three separate contract proposals were voted down. In response, the Greyhound Corporation sold its domestic bus operations in 1986, ending seventy-three years in the U.S. motor bus industry. The new owners of Greyhound then succeeded in getting the existing driver force to accept a contract based upon 30 cents per mile for senior drivers, down from 37.34 cents a mile for prestrike hires and 32.7 cents per mile for new hires under the 1983 contract (Fravel 1991).

The new management team sought to reverse the decline in ridership by increasing its responsiveness to the market. In July 1987, Greyhound also purchased Trailways, which had previously filed for bankruptcy. The acquisition was approved under Greyhound's professed commitment to industry-wide cooperation and revitalization.[1] By 1989, the ridership of the combined Greyhound and Trailways system was up, and both service and finances were improving. At the end of 1989, labor negotiations were initiated in anticipation of the March 1990 expiration of the existing labor contract, with the ATU seeking a restoration of all wage reductions since 1982 plus significant benefit improvements. The negotiations reached an impasse, and on March 2, the union called a strike. Greyhound continued to operate nationwide, using existing employees willing to work and replacement drivers, which led to widespread violence against property, employees, and customers. The costs and losses in revenue related to the strike ended the company's financial recovery and forced it to file for bankruptcy (i.e., for protection under Chapter 11) in June 1990. The union continued to maintain an official strike status, inflicting further losses on the company, but leading to no earnings improvement for those who returned to work.

In October 1991, Greyhound emerged from bankruptcy protection. The new management team initiated extreme cost-cutting measures, reducing the number of employees, routes, and services and decreasing the bus fleet from 3,700 to 2,400 buses. By the end of 1992, Greyhound had earned a profit, the first since 1989. However, again the success was short-lived; the cutbacks subsequently led to losses in business. For the first half of 1994, Greyhound reported an operating revenue decline of 12.6 percent and a net operating loss of $61.4 million.

This institutional discussion clearly suggests that competitive forces together with weak industry conditions produced strong downward pressures on driver wages during the deregulatory period, substantiated in an empirical study by Schwarz-Miller and Talley (1994). What remains to be seen is whether the decline was accompanied by the hypothesized improvement in the relative wage position of female drivers.

## Data and Wage Model

Current Population Survey (CPS) data of the Bureau of the Census for the years 1973–1995 (except for 1982) are utilized to examine the influence of motor bus deregulation on gender wage differentials of bus drivers. . . . The sample includes individual white motor bus drivers who worked thirty or more hours per week and provides information on usual weekly earnings, usual hours worked, union status, and a set of demographic characteristics. A control group of nontransport operatives is also utilized together with the motor bus driver data for part of the analysis.

[There was an] increase in the share of drivers who are women—from 16.3 percent during the regulatory period to 31.8 percent following deregulation. This result lends support to the contention that women received greater access to jobs in the motor bus industry subsequent to deregulation. [T]he gain in the percentage of women employed after deregulation occurred exclusively in the union sector, providing indirect evidence that women were also differentially obtaining greater access to better-paying jobs. The overall percentage of jobs in the union sector fell from 63.1 to 39.4 over the same period, which is consistent with an increasingly competitive environment favoring lower-wage firms.

The following equation is used to investigate the gender wage differential of motor bus drivers:

$$lnWage = a_1 \text{ FEMALE} + a_2 \text{ DREG} + a_3 \text{ FMDREG} + a_4$$
$$\text{UNION} + a_5 \text{ UDREG} + a_6 \text{ UNEMPL} + \Sigma BX_{ijk} + e_{ij}$$

where the index $i$ represents the $i$th individual and $j$ represents the $j$th year and where $ln$Wage is the natural log of hourly earnings in 1982–1984 dollars. FEMALE, DREG, FMDREG, UNION, and UDREG are binary variables [dummy variables equal to 1 or zero] representing being: (1) a female driver, (2) a driver in the deregulatory period, (3) a female driver in the deregulatory period, (4) a union driver, and (5) a union driver during deregulation, respectively. UNEMPL is the regional unemployment rate, which captures business cycle effects on earnings. The control vector X includes a constant and variables representing years of schooling completed (SCHOOL); years of potential experience, measured by (age – SCHOOL – 5), and years of potential experience squared (EXPER and EXPERSQ); and binary variables equal to 1 if the driver was married (MARRIED) and working in the Northeast (NORTHEAST), South (SOUTH), or West (WEST), as opposed to working in the North Central region of the country.

The coefficients that are central to the test of our hypothesis are $a_1$, which measures the female/male log wage differential during regulation, and $a_3$, which measures the change in the female/male log wage differential in the deregulatory period. If the employers of bus drivers were able to exercise a taste for discrimination during the regulatory period due to the protection from competitive pressures afforded by industry regulation, the coefficient $a_1$ will be negative. If the increased competition during deregulation weakened this ability, the relative earnings position of females should have improved—i.e., $a_3$ is predicted to be positive.

[The regression] equation is also estimated separately for union and nonunion drivers, with the UNION and UDREG variables omitted. Hence, in the union equation, DREG measures the log wage differential for union workers in the deregulatory period relative to the regulatory period and FMDREG measures the change in the log wage differential between female and male union drivers under deregulation. Here, the sign predictions for DREG and FMDREG are negative and positive, respectively.

For the nonunion equation, the interpretations of DREG and FMDREG are the same as in the original union/nonunion equation. The sign prediction for the DREG coefficient is ambiguous. The coefficient of FMDREG, however, is predicted not to differ from zero. We know that the segments of the industry that received artificial protection from competition through regulation were highly unionized. If nonunion firms were disproportionately in less protected, more competitive sectors of the motor bus industry, then wage differentials there should have been small. For this reason and due to the

Table 15.1

**Hourly Earnings Equations for White Bus Drivers, 1973–1995**

| Variable | All | | Union drivers | | Nonunion drivers | |
|---|---|---|---|---|---|---|
| Constant | 1.71* | (17.01) | 2.19* | (16.00) | 1.70* | (13.30) |
| School | .009*** | (1.94) | .014*** | (1.88) | .009 | (1.45) |
| Exper | .006* | (3.80) | .002 | (.92) | .009* | (3.94) |
| Expersq | −.012* | (−3.91) | −.002 | (−.52) | −.019* | (−4.09) |
| Married | .008 | (.36) | −.002 | (−.05) | −.021 | (−.72) |
| Northeast | .059** | (2.38) | .022 | (.62) | .063*** | (1.90) |
| South | −.011 | (−.36) | −.149* | (−3.12) | .058 | (1.39) |
| West | .097* | (3.61) | .040 | (1.02) | .125* | (3.48) |
| Female | −.227* | (−3.21) | −.519* | (−3.94) | −.138 | (−1.63) |
| Dreg | −.241* | (−4.38) | −.201* | (−5.40) | −.266* | (−4.18) |
| Fmdreg | .122*** | (1.66) | .284** | (2.08) | .085 | (.96) |
| Union | .437* | (7.71) | | | | |
| Udreg | .013 | (.21) | | | | |
| Unempl | .006 | (.78) | .002 | (.19) | .003 | (.29) |
| $R^2$ | .384 | | .153 | | .055 | |
| N | 1,483 | | 631 | | 852 | |

*Notes:* t-statistics are in parentheses; *indicates significant at the 1 percent level, **significant at the 5 percent level, and ***significant at the 10 percent level.

continuance of competitive pressures on nonunion firms, no change is predicted in the postregulatory wage differential between females and males.

### Estimation Results

The estimation results bear out the theoretical expectations of the Becker hypothesis. Estimates of the equations for all drivers, union drivers, and nonunion drivers appear in Table 15.1. The gender variable FEMALE is negative in all three equations and highly significant in the pooled and union equations. This result suggests that female motor bus drivers earned considerably less than males prior to deregulation, particularly in the union sector. The union equation indicates that females earned 40.5 percent less than comparable males, while the other two equations indicate that female drivers in general and nonunion drivers earned 20.3 percent and 12.9 percent less, respectively, than their male counterparts in the regulatory period.[2]

Following deregulation, the female/male wage gap narrowed as predicted, even as real male driver earnings declined significantly in the increasingly competitive environment. The most striking improvement in the relative earnings of female bus drivers occurred in the union sector. The coefficient of

FMDREG is positive in all three equations, but largest and statistically significant in the union equation, which indicates a drop in the gender wage gap to 20.9 percent or approximately one-half its prederegulation level. The union equation also reveals absolute wage gains (7.6 percent) by female drivers, contrasting sharply with the 18.2 percent decline in real male hourly earnings. The existence of a larger, more significant gender wage gap in the union sector during regulation and the narrowing of this gap for union but not nonunion drivers during the deregulatory period is consistent with the argument that the effects of the regulatory environment would be most strongly felt in the unionized part of the industry. Overall, these results clearly suggest the growing accessibility of better-paying jobs in the motor bus industry to female drivers under deregulation, as predicted. . . .

One question that has not been directly addressed in this study is the extent to which federal equal opportunity policies may also have been a factor in the improved earnings status of female drivers. Although relatively little documentation is available, government interest in affecting employment practices in the motor bus industry, both by firms and the ATU, appears to have been less intense than for other segments of the transportation sector (Husbands 1998). However, since major policies were in place prior to our prederegulation observation period and the industry was the target of legal suits during that period, it can be inferred that it was the heightened competitive environment and not just the legal framework that played the critical role.

## Conclusion

The empirical findings provide strong support for the hypothesis that motor bus deregulation, by creating an increasingly competitive environment, making discrimination more costly and providing greater incentives for firms to employ female drivers, ultimately led to an improvement in their wage position relative to males. The earnings status of unionized white female drivers relative to white males improved significantly subsequent to deregulation, with female wages increasing even as the wage level for male drivers declined. In the nonunion sector, in which the regulatory environment was expected to have less impact on earnings, the gender gap was smaller to begin with and was virtually unaffected by deregulation. . . .

## Notes

1. Subsequently, numbers of independent bus carriers consolidated terminal facilities with Greyhound, in many cases leaving their own terminals in order to run their buses out of terminals owned or controlled by Greyhound. Terminal consolidations played an important role in revitalizing the industry, since they reduced operating

costs and improved quality of service, as passengers could take the "next bus out" regardless of which carrier provided the service.

2. Percentage differentials are estimated as $(e^a - 1)100$.

## References

Ashenfelter, O. and T. Hannan. 1986. "Sex Discrimination and Product Market Competition: The Case of the Banking Industry." *Quarterly Journal of Economics* 100: 149–73.

Becker, G. 1957. *The Economics of Discrimination.* Chicago: University of Chicago Press.

Comanor, W. 1973. "Racial Discrimination in American Industry." *Economica* 40: 363–80.

Ehrenberg, R., and R. Smith. 2000. *Modern Labor Economics,* 7th ed. Reading, MA: Addison-Wesley.

Fravel, F. 1991. *Background Paper on Accessibility for the Disabled and the Intercity Bus Industry.* Washington, DC: U.S. Government Printing Office.

General Accounting Office (GAO). 1992. *Surface Transportation: Availability of Intercity Bus Service Continues to Decline.* Washington, DC: U.S. Government Printing Office.

Haessel, W., and J. Palmer. 1978. "Market Power and Employment Discrimination." *Journal of Human Resources* 13: 545–59.

Heywood, J. 1987. "Wage Discrimination and Market Structure." *Journal of Post Keynesian Economics* 10: 617–29.

Heywood, J., and J. Peoples. 1994. "Deregulation and the Prevalence of Black Truck Drivers." *Journal of Law and Economics* 37: 133–55.

Husbands, K. 1998. "Commentary on Regulated Industries and Measures of Earnings Discrimination." In *Regulatory Reform and Labor Markets,* ed. J. Peoples, pp. 325–62. Boston: Kluwer Academic.

Luksetich, W. 1979. "Market Power and Sex Discrimination in White-Collar Employment." *Review of Social Economy* 37: 211–32.

Peoples, J. 1994. "Monopolistic Market Structure, Unionization, and Racial Wage Differentials." *Review of Economics and Statistics* 76: 207–11.

Schwarz-Miller, A., and W. Talley. 1994. "Motor Bus Driver Earnings in Regulated and Deregulated Environments." In *Research in Transportation Economics,* vol. 3, ed. B. McMullen, pp. 95–117. Greenwich, CT: JAI Press.

Adapted from "Motor Bus Deregulation and the Gender Wage Gap: A Test of the Becker Hypothesis," *Eastern Economic Journal* 26 (2) (Spring 2000): 145–56. Reprinted with permission of the Eastern Economic Association.

# 16

# "That Single-Mother Element"

## How White Employers Typify Black Women

*Ivy Kennelly*

Affirmative action programs in the United States have come under attack recently as many citizens and politicians argue that racial-ethnic minorities now have the same chances of making it as do whites. A black woman who walks through the door of the human resources department, according to affirmative action foes, has an equal or possibly even better chance of getting the job as the white woman who comes in after her, and they both have the same or better chance as the white man who comes in the next day. According to this argument, any "preferences" for racial-ethnic minorities in employment constitute discrimination against whites.

One of the many important factors that such attacks disregard is that the overwhelming majority of those who make decisions about whom to hire are white. A substantial literature documents that while whites no longer largely subscribe to beliefs that racial-ethnic minorities are inherently inferior to them, whites continue to harbor racist beliefs and make racist decisions. . . . These forms of racism and sexism are less overt than in previous decades, but they still prevail and are arguably even more dangerous than outright slander because they are hidden within the rhetoric of "logic." Most whites in the 1990s vehemently claim that they are not racist or sexist and use a series of rationales, or *sincere fictions*, to explain the decisions they make that are harmful to racial-ethnic minorities and women. These rationales are often based on stereotypes. . . .

In this chapter, I examine the images some white employers use to construct claims about black women in the labor market.[1] . . . In focusing on white employers' claims about black womanhood, I concentrate not on the well-documented outcomes of labor market discrimination, such as differential rates of pay and promotion, but on how employers construct and use the images that may form the basis of it. Because these employers have the power to hire, fire, pay, and promote, their claims can be important for black women's life chances. While I do not have data to link white employers' images of black women with their employment decisions regarding members of this group, I argue that the evidence that shows that these images exist is compelling in itself. My analysis is focused on the previously unexplored intricacies of the single-mother image as used by some white employers. . . .

## Stereotypes as the Basis for Claims

### Stereotypes and Statistical Discrimination

Stereotypes can have deleterious effects for employees and potential employees. If employers subscribe to stereotypes, whether they are gross overgeneralizations or derived more closely from evidence, they may use these views about groups of people to predict the behavior of individuals. Economists have identified the process of using characteristics associated with groups as substitutes for information about individuals as "statistical discrimination" (Thurow 1975; Aigner and Cain 1977; Bielby and Baron 1986; Kirschenman and Neckerman 1991; Moss and Tilly 1991). Basow argues that

> even when a generalization is valid (that is, it does describe group averages), we still cannot predict an individual's behavior or characteristics. Stereotypes, because they are more oversimplified and more rigidly held than such generalizations, have even less predictive value. (1986, p. 3)

Thus, stereotypes are not required to be false. For example, even if employers know that a higher percentage of black women than white women are single mothers—27.1 percent and 4.5 percent, respectively (U.S. Bureau of the Census 1995)—they may still use this information in a stereotypical way that generates inequality. To assume that each black woman who applies for an entry-level job at a firm is probably a single mother and make employment decisions based on that assumed status is to stereotype and engage in statistical discrimination.

Another example of how employers may stereotype individuals based on the characteristics associated with the group to which they belong involves women and rates of turnover. "If women have higher turnover rates, and employers know this, then, based on this gender difference in turnover, they may engage in statistical discrimination" (England and Browne 1992, p. 35) by not hiring women, not paying women as much as men, not promoting women as rapidly as men, or firing women more readily than men. This example indicates that employers assume that "workers will conform to the average performance of others with the same ascriptive characteristics" (Folbre 1994, p. 21). Yet, the assumptions they make are often not correct; women as a group have turnover rates similar to men when controls for type of job and cohort are introduced (Price 1977; Waite and Berryman 1985; Lynch 1991). Using assumptions, whether erroneous or empirically based, about group characteristics as a proxy for individual productivity is a powerful tool employers use to make decisions about workers.

## Stereotypes of Women, Blacks, and Black Women

. . . Stereotypes, both negative and positive, influence the thinking and decision making of employers. For example, employers tend to think about women in the workforce as mothers. As Sokoloff explains, "Once in the labor market, women—all women—are treated as mothers—former, actual, or potential" (1980, pp. 216–17). The cultural image of motherhood, which is not a stereotypically negative image, can still be used by employers in a negative way. Sokoloff argues that if a woman in the labor force has children,

> the rationalization given is that she will be unreliable because of the need to be absent if her children are sick. This apologia persists despite the fact that male turnover and absenteeism rates are similar to women's, the crucial difference being that women have traditionally left the market for lack of child care and other family services, while men have left a particular job for personal advancement. Men's reasons for leaving are always more acceptable, for men are understood as workers; women, on the other hand, are understood as mothers. (1980, p. 219)

This demonstrates how employers construct an image of women in the workplace using the stereotypes surrounding motherhood as some of their primary defining characteristics. Men who work outside the home for pay may also be fathers, but no stereotypes prompt employers to fear that men's parental roles threaten their productivity.

Employers' images of women as mothers tend to be a disadvantage to women for at least three reasons. First, the image is used negatively, as employers associate it with a weak commitment to paid work. Second, employers do not readily evoke a fatherhood image for men nor assume that men with children are worse workers than men without children. Finally, the assumption that all women workers are plagued by the burdens and responsibilities of motherhood is inaccurate. While a large percentage of women in the paid labor force do have children under the age of eighteen, 75.3 percent do not (U.S. Bureau of the Census 1996). Despite this, employers who assume that women in their workplaces are mothers who are less committed workers than men are allowing this stereotype to influence the way they think about members of their workforces. It follows that such thinking would play a part in the decisions they make about whom to hire, fire, promote, and pay better. More precisely, such stereotypical thinking forms the basis for rationales about why members of their workforces should be hired, fired, promoted, or paid better.

In addition to the stereotype of women as mothers who tend to be late to and absent from work, employers evoke racial stereotypes as sincere fictions. Kirschenman and Neckerman (1991) and Wilson (1996) demonstrate how employers subscribe to common stereotypes of black men as lazy, dishonest, involved with drugs, and lacking a work ethic. Different from the way they take motherhood—a generally positive culture image—and make it negative, employers grab onto the overwhelmingly negative stereotypes that U.S. white culture perpetuates about black men. Employers are able to list the characteristics they associate with black men, which they have adopted from the larger racist white culture, and discuss why they feel justified in not hiring black men because of such characteristics (Kirschenman and Neckerman 1991; Moss and Tilly 1995).

Employers conceivably also evoke racial stereotypes of black women, although employers' stereotypes of black women have been given much less scholarly attention than those of black men. Collins (1990) and Mullins (1994) argue that the image of the matriarch surrounds black women and relates to their experiences in both the home and the paid labor market. The matriarch, according to Collins (1990, p. 72), is a single black working woman with children. The image of the matriarch also carries the connotation of an "overly aggressive, unfeminine" woman who spends "too much time away from home" working. She is "the 'bad' black mother" who has to work so much that she "cannot properly supervise her children and is a major contributing factor to her children's school failure" (1990, p. 74). Collins (1990) and Mullins (1994) suggest that this controlling image, sustained by those with the power to define it, is dangerous because it puts the responsibility and blame for the perceived deficiencies in all African Americans, especially men, directly onto black women. . . .

The ways that employers, specifically, use such cultural stereotypes of black women have not been adequately explored in social scientific work. As suggested in the foreword to the book *All the Women Are White, All the Blacks Are Men, but Some of Us Are Brave* (Berry 1982), the focus of scholarly work about women in general is often limited to white women, and work about African Americans in general often only scrutinizes the situations of black men. Black women are merely assumed to be included in one or both of these categories. While there are undoubtedly some aspects of how employers typify women and blacks in general that are relevant to black women, the specific ways employers typify this group deserve distinct attention.

## Methods and Data

The data I use were collected in Atlanta as part of an extensive project, the Multi-City Study of Urban Inequality. Study design involved three components: interviews of household respondents, a telephone survey of employers, and face-to-face interviews with employers. . . .

The employer study was designed to test theories of industrial restructuring and the changing skill needs of employers for "low-skill" workers. Therefore, all of the sample jobs in the employer survey require a high school diploma or less education. Common sample jobs include clerical worker, cashier, and sales representative. The average hourly wage for all jobs combined is $7.93, ranging from $4.25 to $23.08.

Two interviewers, a white woman and a white man, separately conducted face-to-face, structured, in-depth interviews with Atlanta employers in forty-five firms from July 1994 to March 1995, obtaining a 75 percent completion rate in the final sample. The interviews were conducted at the employers' places of business, most often in private offices or rooms, and all interviews were tape-recorded with respondents' consent. Interviewers asked a series of questions focusing on employers' skill demands and their perceptions of the available workforce. . . . Of the ninety-seven interview respondents, 57 percent are white men, 24 percent are white women, 12 percent are black men, 6 percent are black women, and 1 percent are Asian women.

Because I am primarily interested in white employers' images of black women for the current analysis, I use only the interviews of white employers (78 total). Of these, 27 (34.6 percent) respondents are presidents, CEOs, or related positions; 22 (28.2 percent) are human resource representatives; and 29 (37.2 percent) are supervisors of the sample job. Of the white respondents, 23 (29.5 percent) are women, and 55 (70.5 percent) are men. While it is also important to understand black employers' images of black employees, the current data set better allows me to thoroughly analyze white employers' images than to compare those of white and black employers. Since most employers in the United States are white, the analysis of the ways they typify employees is an important component of understanding labor market dynamics. White women and white men were almost equally likely to express views about black women employees that reveal their use of negative racial and gender imagery. As the remainder of the article makes clear, however, some of the most explicit examples of this imagery come from white men.

In my analysis of the transcribed interviews, I employed the open, axial, and selective coding strategies laid out by Strauss and Corbin (1990) and the comparative scheme outlined by Ragin (1994). In the initial coding phases, I noted and recorded repetitive themes in employers' descriptions of workers. I found at this stage that the concepts of family and motherhood came up often in white employers' discussions of women employees and applicants but not as often and in different ways in their discussions of men. In further coding phases where I examined these concepts in different contexts than those I had originally seen, I realized that employers were not simply talking about their men and women employees differently but that they also differentiated between black and white women employees and applicants. In descriptions of white women, many employers referred to motherhood, but when speaking about black women, employers invoked the image of single motherhood. I then reexamined the data to explore the prevalence of this image and to search out deviant cases. Selective coding strategies allowed me to focus more specifically on the category of single motherhood and identify the contexts and ways in which it was used. . . .

Throughout my discussion of the data, I report percentages of employers who typified black women in particular ways, but it is important to note that these percentages do not necessarily correspond with employers' perceptions in the larger population. These qualitative data reveal white employers' accounts of their workforces and are valuable for their portrayal of the complex, nuanced manner in which race and gender stereotypes color the ostensibly objective processes by which some employers evaluate applicants and employees. . . .

### Images of Women

As the literature suggests, one of the most pervasive images white employers held is the woman worker as mother, a role that employers often further associated with tardiness and absenteeism. For example, one human resources manager at an insurance company that is composed of almost half men and half women stated,

> If I look at our attendance record I would in fact not doubt that the people who have been documented and who have been terminated for attendance reasons were women, and those people are primarily out not because they're ill, but because kids are ill or the husband is ill or the parent. (white man, human resources manager, insurance company)

This employer indicated that women—not men—had problematic attendance rates and speculated that women had family responsibilities that detracted from their paid work duties so much that they needed to be fired. Constructing an image of women in which their assumed motherhood is a large liability in the labor market, he left little room for the possibility that women may have been absent for reasons other than family or that men may have ever needed to be off the job for family reasons.

In another example, the interviewer asked a supervisor of clerical workers if the company's hiring procedures had changed any in the past few years, to which the supervisor responded,

> Yes, because there's some questions you can't ask when you're interviewing, you know. Years ago you could ask them anything, you know. "Are you pregnant? Do you have children? Do you have someone to keep your children while you are at work? Are your children sick often?" You can't ask those questions anymore. (white woman, supervisor, insurance company)

This supervisor of employees in a woman-dominated occupation clearly defined motherhood as part of womanhood and alluded to the potential problems this conflation can bring to her workforce.

These examples suggest that women's family responsibilities are one of the primary concerns employers had about women workers. Forty-two percent of white employers, without prompting from interviewers, brought up the images of motherhood and family when they talked about women. Employers often made these characterizations of women as mothers without empirical knowledge of their actual family situations. . . . Seven white employers, three of whom worked for the same company, brought up the notion of family in conjunction with men. The most common comments these employers made were about men having to monetarily support their families, and just one of these employers indicated that men's familial roles could be problematic. Clearly, many white employers' images of parenthood and the effects of parenthood on paid labor market responsibilities differ along gender lines.

## Images of Blacks

White employers in Atlanta characterized black workers negatively in well over two-thirds of the interviews, with images regarding time, skills, education, laziness, and belligerence. For example, an employment manager at a very large organization made this remark regarding black employees, who made up 58 percent of the sample job, data entry workers: "I have noticed maybe a slight difference in the perception of time. Tardiness, a certain degree of tardiness seems more acceptable" (white woman, employment manager, educational institution). . . . Throughout the interview, this employment manager also stressed that she only processes employees' applications and does not "deal with them [the employees] directly," which makes her perception about employee norms somewhat suspect. An administrative specialist in the same organization explained why she thought blacks were not faring well in the labor market:

> It goes back to just education issues, that a lot of blacks are maybe only getting through high school. And whether it is because of economic issues or whether they just don't have the drive, or y'know, a variety of factors. But they don't pursue, I guess, y'know, being more educated than just being able to get by. (white woman, administrative specialist, educational institution)

This employer subscribed to another stereotype, that of blacks' laziness and lack of motivation, as one of the primary causes for their lack of advancement in the labor market. In these examples, employers were doing more than simply reporting empirical differences in black and white workers' levels of productivity. They were invoking stereotypes to make claims that helped them explain the deficiencies they perceive in blacks. Interestingly, both of these employers said that they had very little day-to-day contact with employees, but both were in the position to make hiring decisions about them.

Many white Atlanta employers also expressed their irritation with what they perceived as black workers' tendency to complain, cause problems, and cry "Discrimination!" For example, when asked if she noticed any differences between black and white workers, one area director for teachers' aides, a job filled only by women, responded,

> The insubordination, and what I would almost say belligerence, is maybe more prevalent in blacks than in whites. I think my black employees definitely question much more management than my white employees do. . . . I have more black employee, black complaints than any other type of complaints. They love to complain about their manager. . . . They're more likely to call and complain either about their manager or new company policies or procedures or something they've been asked to do. And they're also more likely to say to me that, it's because they're black. (white woman, area director, child care center)

This employer, one of two white supervisors over a workforce that is 75 percent black, emphatically expressed her irritation with black employees' insistence on "bringing race" into every issue. Throughout the rest of the interview, she repeatedly defended the decisions she had made that only black employees had questioned, which indicated her unwillingness to consider the validity of their concerns. The other supervisor at this organization also commented at length on how she was "constantly getting this racial stuff thrown in my face" (white woman, branch manager, child care center). "It just seems like every time you turn around," she said, "they want to blame things on racial issues." This manager noted that she planned to make some changes in their hiring practices so that they would have "more kind of a 50/50 thing" of white and black employees as compared to the 25/75 ratio they had at the time of the interview. . . .

This characterization of black employees who do not work hard, cause trouble, are late, lie, and then "use race" to try to compensate for those things is probably the strongest example from the interviews of white employers using stereotypes to construct a negative image of blacks. Moreover, this example highlights white employers' resistance to believing that blacks ever experience racial discrimination. Well over half of white interview respondents mentioned a tendency for black employees to "bring race" into all situations, and none of these ever acknowledged the possibility that black employees do often experience racial discrimination. The construction of this image of blacks as complainers who indiscriminately "play the race card" works to ensure that blacks' concerns will not be acknowledged as legitimate. . . .

**Images of Black Women**

Not separate from some white employers' images of women and blacks, but still distinct, are their typifications of black women. . . . One head cashier provided an excellent example of how some employers' perceptions of black women may be distinct from their perceptions of women in general (i.e., white women). Regarding the cashiers she supervised, three of whom were men and twenty-seven of whom were women, she found that "*Men* are more dependable. . . . They don't have as many emotional problems. They're not as emotional and they're, y'know, they seem to be able to come to work more. . . . Women are a little bit harder to work with" (white woman, head cashier, grocery store). Then, when asked about differences between black men and black women specifically, she said, "Between those two . . . I think the *women* are a little bit more dependable. . . . They do most, most of the work." Her perception of black women was vastly different from the first group of women to enter her mind: white women. This example underscores the need to pay specific attention to the ways employers view black women.

Almost a quarter of the white respondents (24 percent) explicitly used the single-mother image at some point in their interviews when referring to black women. An example of an employer using this type of imagery is a superintendent who hired elementary school instructional aides, a job filled solely by women.

> We are pressed to find minority workers in the work force. . . . I think your typical white instructional aide that comes to us has a four-year degree. And [we get] a large number of black single-parent applicants who are not as skilled . . . not educated. (white man, superintendent for personnel, elementary school)

This respondent talked about white applicants and employees without making any reference to their family situations, yet he said that the black applicants he gets are unskilled single mothers. This statement reveals the melding of single motherhood with black women in his claims and a further assumption that single mothers are unskilled and uneducated.

In an additional 12 percent of the interviews, employers linked black women with single motherhood less explicitly than in the example above. For example, an employer may have talked about the topic of race by referring to differences between workers from the "inner city" and the "suburbs," using these words as code words for black and white. The employer may have then talked about how difficult it is to find employees in the inner city (meaning among blacks) because of the high percentage of single mothers there who are on welfare and do not work for pay. Employers in these implicit instances did not always put "black woman" and "single mother" in the same sentence, but throughout interviews they made the connections.

White employers referred to white women, or women generally, as single mothers in only a handful of interviews, while they made these explicit and implicit associations of black women and single motherhood in more than one-third of the interviews. In no cases did employers talk about either black men or white men having sole responsibility for children.

It is important to note that no questions about single motherhood were included on the interview instrument. Employers brought up this imagery on their own, often in conjunction with explicit questions about race. Some of the questions to which responses about single motherhood and black women frequently came up include the following:

- "What skills and qualities do you look for in a worker for [sample job]?"
- "What are the main problems you face with your workforce, thinking specifically about [sample job]?"

- "We've talked to quite a few other managers who say there are significant differences between black and white workers, and I'm wondering what you think. Have you seen these differences?" (Probe: "We do know from other research that blacks and other minorities are doing badly in the labor market. Why do you think that is?") "Do you see any differences between men and women? City and suburban workers?"

In most cases, where white employers used the single-motherhood image to refer to black women, they used it negatively.... However, about 10 percent of white employers who used this image placed it in a positive context, such as how the workplace needs to change to accommodate the needs of single parents. In addition, about 6 percent of all white employers clearly recognized and renounced racist and sexist practices in the workplace that can be especially damaging to black women.

Direct supervisors of workers were the least likely to typify black women as single mothers. About 31 percent of supervisors, 41 percent of human resource representatives, and 41 percent of high-level employers or CEOs brought up single-mother imagery in speaking about black women. This may be important in speaking to the accuracy of such typifications, since direct supervisors presumably have the most contact with employees, yet they were the least likely to typify black women this way. Men and women employers were almost equally likely to typify black women: 35 percent of women and 38 percent of men used the single-mother image. Men were, however, more likely to explicitly use the image.

The single-mother typification is unique to black women. Employers who expressed this image did not follow one simplified form but made claims about black women based on three different but related aspects of the single-mother typification: (1) black single mothers are poor employees because of their family distractions; (2) black single mothers are hard workers, desperate for their paychecks; and (3) black single mothers are deficient parents to all dysfunctional blacks either in the workforce or unemployed. These claims are not mutually exclusive even though they may seem contradictory....

### Single Black Mothers: The Root of Black Problems

When asked why they believed blacks may be doing poorly in the labor market, many white employers asserted that blacks lack certain necessary elements, such as education and morality. Employers often speculated that these perceived deficiencies were the result of being raised by single mothers. While it is true that a larger percentage of black children are raised by single mothers—54.2 percent compared to 17.9 percent of white children (Bennett 1995)—it is unlikely that white employers who made this claim about black workers actually knew which black workers were and were not raised by women heads of household or that they were able to directly compare levels of labor market success with family type.

About 55 percent of white employers who typified black women as single mothers brought up this image in the context of poor mothering skills. Yet this third and most commonly used image of black women, the mothers of the black workforce, reveals a striking paradox that affects black women not only as mothers but also as workers. Half of the employers who made claims about the poor mothering skills of black single mothers also said that black single mothers are poor workers because they are off work too often attending to their children's needs. Regardless of what these employers actually knew about these women's lives and responsibilities at home, they made judgments about black women's adequacy in their public and private roles based on the stereotypes associated with black single motherhood. Weitz and Gordon (1993, p. 33) refer to Merton's (1957) description of "how ethnic groups can be 'damned if they do and damned if they don't': condemned as pushy or sly when they succeed despite discrimination and as lazy or stupid when they do not." These white employers' simultaneous characterizations of black women as bad workers and bad mothers reveals a similar logic.

An example of the paradox in which black women are seen as both poor workers and poor mothers comes from a plant manager of 70 percent black and 30 percent white women order processors. He talked about "single families," "single-parent families," and "single-parent moms" interchangeably. He also talked about space and race in a related way, using the terms "inner city" and "black" as proxies for one another, and he spoke about single mothers only in the context of the problems of the inner city. When asked to identify the single biggest problem with his workers, he replied, "I'd say single-parent moms. [Interviewer: Why?] Missing work. . . . When somebody's sick they've got to go." This comment, within the context of his discussion of the deficiencies in the inner city, identifies black single mothers as the weakest part of his workforce because of their family responsibilities. Paradoxically, he also talked about black single mothers as poor parents.

> The people that I want, it would be hard to get those people to come downtown. And when we get into the inner city, in my opinion, work values change because you're talking about people that are primarily raised in a single family. Very poor environment, don't have a role model that shows them that work is good, that you should do your very best and a good job no matter where it is or who it's for. (white man, plant manager, manufacturing plant)

Continuing to contrast black and white employees, this employer said,

> Well, I have if you're talking about, and I kind of touched on this a while ago, if you're talking about, I think there's a higher percentage chance that if you go in the inner city that a black person is going to come from a single-parent home where there has not been any values taught or work ethic. But where, and I've got several out here, where a black person has come from what I call a, quote, normal home, there is no difference at all. ... I think that the chances that a black person that's living in suburbia, the chances that he's coming from a normal home is greater. And therefore he's, he has the basic values that you want in a person. (white man, plant manager, manufacturing plant)

This employer unabashedly placed the lack of values and work ethic he perceived in his black employees on the shoulders of single mothers. He simultaneously judged black women the worst part of his workforce and the worst kind of parent. Even while admitting that black women work hard, employers do not believe that these women—in the absence of a man—could provide the example of a "good work ethic." There seem to be few means by which black women employees can balance work and family in a way that these employers find acceptable. . . .

With similar themes to those I describe above, more than half of white employers noted that blacks grow up in homes where there is no emphasis placed on education, a large reliance on welfare, no role models (i.e., *fathers* who work), and no mothers around to care for the children. To these employers, the work involvement of the single mother is not seen as a useful role model for her children, especially not for boys. This evidence indicates that in no small measure, black women in the entry-level labor force must face the image of themselves as distracted, desperate, uneducated, unmarried women who are just one step away from welfare and whose deficient parenting abilities generate many of the perceived inadequacies of black workers generally.

## Conclusion

More than one-third of white employers in this sample from Atlanta either explicitly or implicitly spoke about black women in terms of single motherhood. Encompassed in this typification of black women are claims about their tendency to be tardy and absent because of child care responsibilities, their desperation for a paycheck, and their poor mothering skills. The images these white employers used to describe black women applicants and employees were largely negative and often seemed to be based on stereotypes. These stereotypes, when used to typify black women as a group, can provide the basis for statistical discrimination against individual black women. . . .

Stereotypes of black women as single mothers, because of cultural assumptions about single motherhood as an inherently negative state, can make the positive characteristics of individual black women (and of single mothers) invisible. It is likely that these stereotypes are also shaped by class, since professional black women may be less susceptible than black women in entry-level positions to employers' assumptions about their need for money, their responsibilities outside work, and their values. . . .

The white employers who did not typify black women as single mothers often used guarded and carefully chosen language in answering any questions about race. "Let me see, how should I phrase this" was a typical qualifier. Any attempt to glean racial attitudes from whites also produces difficulties in determining whether those who assert egalitarian views really espouse those views or whether they merely do not want interviewers to view them as racist. A number of platitudes, such as "I don't even see race," "I look at each individual," and "People are people," came up among both white employers who did and those who did not typify black women as single mothers, which alludes to the rhetorical character of such responses.

Other white employers, throughout their interviews, seemed genuinely concerned about avoiding the types of stereotyping I have described.

> I don't think it is fair to make, ah, judgments on blacks in general based on the ten or twelve that work for me, or whites in general based on the ten or twelve that work for me. I, I don't think you can do that. I don't think that's fair to either one of them. (white man, supervisor of order processors, manufacturing company)

Employers in this group gave considered and thoughtful responses to questions about race, the wording of which indicated that they may have received diversity training at their workplaces. Indeed, many of these employers came from larger corporations where such training would not be unusual. These white employers had clearly integrated this sort of thinking into their larger attitudes about the labor force, and the consistency of their responses throughout their interviews indicated that they were not simply concerned with appearing politically correct. The success of diversity training programs may only be anecdotal, however, since other white employers in the same companies did make overtly negative claims about blacks in general. . . .

Knowing the content of white employers' stereotypes is important in counteracting them. This evidence indicates that some white employers do not see all racial and gender groups equally. These white employers often see black women as single mothers, and while single motherhood is not inherently negative, the image is confounded in conservative rhetoric that white employers can use in a negative way. Attacks on affirmative action have ignored the fact that whites continue to be in most positions of power in the labor market and that at least some of these employers do harbor racist, sexist views that can disadvantage black women.

## Note

1. I purposely use the term "black" rather than "African American" because I am focusing on white employers' images of members of this racial group. Since the black persons to whom I refer were not able to report their own race, and the possibility exists that they may have origins other than Africa, I avoid using the term "African American" throughout the text.

## References

Aigner, Dennis J., and Glen C. Cain. 1977. "Statistical Theories of Discrimination in Labor Markets." *Industrial Labor and Relations Review* 30: 175–87.

Basow, Susan A. 1986. *Gender Stereotypes: Traditions and Alternatives*, 2d ed. Monterey, CA: Books/Cole.

Bennett, Claudette E. 1995. *The Black Population in the United States: 1994 and 1993*. U.S. Bureau of the Census, Current Population Reports, pp. 20–480. Washington, DC: Government Printing Office.

Berry, Mary. 1982. "Foreward." In *All the Women Are White, All the Blacks Are Men, but Some of Us Are Brave: Black Women's Studies*, ed. Gloria T. Hull, Patricia Bell Scott, and Barbara Smith. Old Westbury, NY: Feminist Press.

Bielby, William T., and James N. Baron. 1986. "Men and Women at Work: Sex Segregation and Statistical Discrimination." *American Journal of Sociology* 91: 800–37.

Collins, Patricia Hill. 1990. *Black Feminist Thought: Knowledge, Consciousness, and the Politics of Empowerment*. New York: Routledge.

England, Paula, and Irene Browne. 1992. "Trends in Women's Economic Status." *Sociological Perspectives* 35: 17–51.

Folbre, Nancy. 1994. *Who Pays for the Kids? Gender and the Structures of Constraint*. New York: Routledge.

Kirschenman, Joleen, and Kathryn M. Neckerman. 1991. "We'd Love to Hire Them, But . . .": The Meaning of Race for Employers." In *The Urban Underclass*, ed. Christopher Jencks and Paul E. Peterio. Washington, DC: Brookings Institution.

Lynch, Lisa M. 1991. "The Role of Off-the-job Training vs. On-the-job Training for the Mobility of Women Workers." *American Economic Review* 81: 151–56.

Merton, Robert K. 1957. *Social Theory and Social Structure*. New York: Free Press.

Moss, Philip, and Chris Tilly. 1991. "Why Black Men Are Doing Worse in the Labor Market: A Review of Supply-side and Demand-side Explanations." Working Paper. New York: Social Science Research Council.

———. 1995. "'Soft' Skills and Race: An Investigation of Black Men's Employment Problems." Working Paper No. 80. New York: Russell Sage Foundation.

Mullins, Leith. 1994. "Images, Ideology, and Women of Color." In *Women of Color in U.S. Society*, ed. Maxine Baca Zinn and Bonnie Thornton Dill. Philadelphia: Temple University Press.

Neckerman, Kathryn M., and Joleen Kirschenman. 1991. "Hiring Strategies, Racial Bias, and Inner-city Workers." *Social Problems* 38: 433–47.

Price, James L. 1977. *The Study of Turnover*. Ames: Iowa State University Press.

Ragin, Charles C. 1994. *Constructing Social Research*. Thousand Oaks, CA: Pine Forge Press.

Sokoloff, Natalie J. 1980. *Between Money and Love: The Dialectics of Women's Home and Market Work*. New York: Praeger.

Strauss, Anselm, and Juliet Corbin. 1990. *Basics of Qualitative Research: Grounded Theory Procedures and Techniques*. Newbury Park, CA: Sage.

Thurow, Lester C. 1975. *Generating Inequality*. New York: Basic Books.

U.S. Bureau of the Census. 1990. *1990 Census of Population, Social and Economic Characteristics*. Washington, DC: Government Printing Office.

———. 1995. *Current Population Survey*. P. 20–499, July. Washington, DC: U.S. Department of Commerce, Economics and Statistics Administration.

———. 1996. *Statistical Abstract of the United States 1996*. Washington, DC: Government Printing Office.

Waite, Linda, and Sue E. Berryman. 1985. *Women in Nontraditional Occupations: Choice and Turnover*. RAND Report R-3106–FF. Santa Monica, CA: RAND.

Weitz, Rose, and Leonard Gordon. 1993. "Images of Black Women among Anglo College Students." *Sex Roles* 28: 19–34.

Adapted from "'That Single-Mother Element': How White Employers Typify Black Women," *Gender & Society* 13 (2) (April 1999): 168–92. Reprinted with permission of Sage Publications, Inc.

# Section 4

# Appendix

**Key Terms**

discrimination
dominance aggression
dummy variable
human capital
intraoccupational segregation
occupational crowding
sexual division of labor
socialization
statistical discrimination
stereotypes
wage gap

**Discussion Questions**

1. What roles do biology and individual choices play in labor force participation, employment, and wage setting? Do you think that men's and women's labor market decisions are biologically determined, or does discrimination exist? Explain.

2. What roles do education (including skill) and experience play in determining relative wages by gender and race-ethnicity? Would investing in college or graduate school and getting good grades eliminate the gender- or race-based wage gap? Would choosing a college major and career in the sciences eliminate the gender- or race-based wage gap?

3. Becker assumes that discriminating employers pay a wage premium (higher than market wage) to white males. Other theories argue that discrimination depresses or lowers the wages of women and racial-ethnic minorities. Which assumption makes more sense to you? Does it matter?

4. How does the example of deregulation of motor bus travel, on Greyhound, for example, support Becker's hypothesis that increased competition reduces the wage gap? After deregulation, was the motor

bus industry truly competitive? How might a lack of competition affect the persuasiveness of the Becker hypothesis? What impact might unionization have had on wage rates and wage gaps?

5.  Give some specific examples of how employers statistically discriminate in hiring and promotion decisions. Besides interviewing employers, how else could a researcher discern the existence of statistical discrimination?

6.  Has statistical discrimination ever played a role in the employment or wage/salary decision of any worker you know?

7.  Prior to 1964, classified or "Help Wanted" ads were segregated by sex. Advertisements read "Help Wanted: Male" or "Help Wanted: Female." While this is now illegal, are there ways that employers and business establishments can still preserve some categories of jobs for mostly men and others for mostly women, and some jobs for mostly whites and others for people of color? How?

8.  What kind of public policy to reduce the wage gap, if any, would be appropriate according to each of the three theories: (a) biological/human capital, (b) Becker's hypothesis, and (c) statistical discrimination?

## Exercise

1.  One way to organize your thoughts about the various pieces that help to build a mainstream theory explaining the economic status of women is to complete the theory matrix provided on page 201. Can you distinguish among the three mainstream views on discrimination?

## Further Reading

Black, Sandra E. 1999. "Investigating the Link Between Competition and Discrimination." *Monthly Labor Review* 122 (12): 39–42.

Blau, Francine D., and Marianne A. Ferber. 1987. "Discrimination: Empirical Evidence from the United States." *American Economic Review* 77 (2): 316–20.

Jacobsen, Joyce P., and Laurence M. Levin. 1995. "Effects of Intermittent Labor Force Attachment on Women's Earnings." *Monthly Labor Review* 188 (9): 14–19.

Polachek, Solomon W. 1995. "Human Capital and the Gender Earnings Gap: A Response to Feminist Critiques." In *Out of the Margin: Feminist Perspetives on Economics*, ed. Edith Kuiper and Jolande Sap, pp. 61–79. London: Routledge.

Tomaskovic-Devey, Donald, and Sheryl Skagga. 1999. "An Establishment-Level Test of the Statistical Discrimination Hypothesis." *Work and Occupations* 26 (4): 422–45.

## Mainstream Theory Matrix

| | Human capital | Tastes/Preferences (Becker hypothesis) | Statistical |
|---|---|---|---|
| Key names? | | | |
| Discrimination? In the short run? In the long run? | | | |
| Causes of occupational segregation? | | | |
| Causes of wage gap? | | | |
| Strengths of this theory? | | | |
| Criticisms, omissions, or weaknesses? | | | |

# Section 5

# Heterodox Approaches to Labor Market Outcomes

The four chapters in this section offer both critiques of and alternatives to the theoretical perspective offered by mainstream theory. All of the contributors to this section accept that discrimination exists. What further unites these four chapters—and differentiates them from the mainstream perspectives in Section 4—is their focus on institutional, rather than individual, discrimination. Institutional discrimination has less to do with short-sighted or ignorant employers adhering to stereotypes and assumptions and more to do with structural features of labor markets and employment practices. Occupational segregation is one example of a structural form of discrimination.

Each of these studies treats discrimination as deeply embedded in social institutions and culture. Competitive market forces, therefore, will not cause discrimination to evaporate in the long run. In fact, employers may even profit from engaging in discrimination. If we assume that discrimination *lowers* the wages of less powerful groups of workers, rather than assuming it *raises* the wages of preferred groups, employers would have to increase the wages of underpaid workers to eliminate discrepancies.

There is good reason to believe that discrimination depresses the wages of working women, even using supply and demand analysis. Barbara Bergmann (whose chapter you read earlier in Section 3) proposed, in a pathbreaking 1971 article, that discrimination "crowds" women and racial minorities into a smaller subset of occupations. According to the crowding hypothesis, the oversupply of workers in these occupations depresses their wages, due to the competition for limited job openings. As you will recall from the readings in Section 2, women, especially women of color, are overcrowded into female-dominated occupations; these occupations pay less, on average, than jobs with similar education and experience requirements. White male workers have always had more occupational choices, so they do not face crowding.

The crowding hypothesis explains the wage gap, but not how occupational segregation occurs. Steven Shulman, in his presentation of "The Political Economy of Labor Market Discrimination," synthesizes several ideas about why firms respond to specific economic, political, and social situations by discriminating against less powerful groups of workers. In addition to the crowding hypothesis, Shulman draws upon institutional theories of "queuing" and "tipping," also explored by Mary King in "Black Women's Breakthrough into Clerical Work." Queuing theory treats the hierarchy between groups of workers as an institutionalized aspect of the social fabric, rather than an arbitrary taste/preference. Shulman also discusses *class struggle* and *job competition effects*. In segmentation theory, employers may benefit from mirroring race and gender hierarchies in the local culture and keeping workers divided against each other. Another name for this strategy is "divide and conquer." Segmentation theory implies that white male workers could be better off if they joined with their coworkers to demand higher wages for all. However, Shulman points out that the class struggle effect is offset by job competition effects, which imply that white male workers themselves benefit from excluding other groups.

Both Shulman and King also examine instances in which firms may change their preferences and provide access to formerly excluded workers. In particular, employers may reassign jobs to less powerful groups at the same time that they *deskill* the jobs, that is, reduce the amount of training and experience needed to do the work. Technological change may facilitate the deskilling process. In other instances, by substituting cheaper workers while changing job requirements, employers can implement another form of "divide and conquer." Economic growth and low unemployment may make white men less available for jobs lower down on the queue. Active enforcement of antidiscrimination laws may also open doors.

There are other reasons for the persistence of the wage gap and the undervaluation of female-dominated occupations. Some of these are explored by Deborah Figart in her chapter, "Gender as More Than a Dummy Variable." Figart asserts that we must search for the answers to questions about why discrimination persists in cultural assumptions about gender and race. Her first four propositions echo much of the heterodox analysis that Shulman also synthesizes. Proposition 5, however, argues that employers do not always behave rationally; that is, they do not always put profit-maximization above other social goals. Employers maintain gender and race hierarchies, and thus occupational segregation, because cultural assumptions about women of all races and about men of color shape their economic decisions. Gender theory therefore augments heterodox economic theories by acknowledging the cultural devaluation of female-dominated occupations, the tasks and skills associated with "feminine" qualities, and workers with family responsibilities. These cultural values lead employers to create segregated jobs and informal task segregation. While quantitative studies that estimate the degree of wage discrimination (such as Weinberger's in Section 4) are important, attention must also be paid to the more subtle processes involved in discrimination.

The study of supermarket checkout clerks by Martin Tolich and Celia Briar provides a vivid example. In "Just Checking It Out," the authors uncover the informal forms of discrimination that do not show up in hiring statistics or paychecks, but do result in differential promotional opportunities and quality of working life. Employers treat the male and female clerks differently not because it is necessarily profitable or divides their workforce. They simply carry unspoken assumptions about men's impatience with staying in one place, women's greater emotive skills, and which employees need to be cultivated for promotions. Equal opportunity policies and competitive market forces have not rooted out these assumptions and consequently have not eradicated the gendered processes at play in workplaces.

# 17

# The Political Economy of Labor Market Discrimination

## A Classroom-Friendly Presentation of the Theory

*Steven Shulman*

Depending upon your point of view, economics is either blessed or cursed with many different theories of discrimination. The main neoclassical models are based on subjective prejudice and statistical discrimination. The alternatives offered by political economy—an eclectic grouping of Marxian, institutionalist, post-Keynesian, and feminist economics—are based on culture and ideology, the exercise of power, class conflict, market incentives, queuing, tipping, crowding, and still others. There is no shortage of ideas even if there is a shortage of relevant data and definitive empirical tests.

Neoclassical [mainstream] economists have the advantage of simplicity. Discrimination in their view can be analyzed with the same tools used to understand all forms of market behavior. Discriminators are either maximizing their utility or minimizing their perceived risk. In so doing, they must face the consequences from nondiscriminatory competitors who make better use of their human resources. For this reason, neoclassical economists rely more on human capital theory than on the theory of discrimination to explain racial inequality.

Political economists have developed numerous critiques of the neoclassical presumption that competition will automatically erode discrimination. But the presentation of the political economy perspective has been hampered by its methodological diversity as well as by the sheer variety of ideas that have been put forward. This has made the neoclassical alternative seem more attractive, at least to students struggling to make sense of a complicated phenomenon.

This chapter presents a possible synthesis, which could be called *the* political economy theory of discrimination. In part, it seeks to show that such a theory exists and is no less cogent or convincing than its neoclassical alternatives. But it is also motivated by the needs of our students to have a straightforward statement of the political economy theory of discrimination. To this end, it summarizes a complicated literature in as simple a manner as possible. It aspires to be intelligible to undergraduates, though it does presume some background with orthodox and heterodox economic theory. Although much of what it says is theoretical, concrete examples are used wherever possible. Its intent is not so much to critique neoclassicism as to present the political economy alternative. . . .

**Institutional Discrimination**

Political economists think about discrimination in a way that connects the past to the present. Genocide, slavery, disenfranchisement, violence, poverty, segregation, and ghettoization are the backdrops for contemporary discrimination. At the same time, the civil rights movement, the women's movement, and other social and political changes have had a great impact on gender and race relations, quantitatively and qualitatively altering the way in which discrimination works. When political economists analyze discrimination, they seek to show how the present reflects the past and yet is different from it.

Like many concepts in both neoclassical economics (e.g., utility or marginal productivity) and political economy (e.g., surplus or power), discrimination cannot be directly observed or measured. Nobody in this day and age admits to discrimination. Although numerous court cases have resulted in findings of discrimination, it is impossible to directly determine how much discrimination exists in the aggregate or how it fluctuates over time. Furthermore, it is frequently difficult to decide what discrimination means or how it should be applied to particular cases.

These empirical and interpretive difficulties have resulted in disagreements over the very definition of discrimination. *Individual discrimination* is carried out as a conscious decision by individuals; this is the type of discrimination focused on by neoclassical economists. They define discrimination in terms of differences in the treatment of equally qualified workers. This presumes that workers can be unambiguously ranked in terms of their qualifications. More often than not, however, qualifications vary in subtle ways between job applicants, opening the door to subjective interpretations about who is more qualified than whom. Employers may honestly deny they have discriminated even when their decision making consistently leads them to prefer white men. For this reason, political economists focus less on the intentions of employers and more on the institutional context within which their decision making takes place.

*Institutional discrimination* occurs when women or minorities are systematically disadvantaged by the rules and incentives of organizations and institutions such as firms, markets, and the government. It can be overt (e.g., the government passes segregation laws) or covert (e.g., employers use irrelevant tests), intentional (e.g., banks redline minority neighborhoods) or unintentional (e.g., employers hire by word of mouth), rational (e.g., unions create barriers to job competition) or irrational (e.g., unions refuse to organize women workers). In all cases, however, the issue has less to do with the decisions of individuals than with the rules and incentives that govern the behavior of economic institutions and, in so doing, disadvantage women and minorities.

Institutional discrimination is a function of concrete circumstances, not arbitrary choices, ahistorical prejudices, or instinctual aversions. As William Julius Wilson puts it, "racial [and, by extension, gender] antagonisms are the products of situations—economic situations, political situations, and social situations" (1995, p. 3). The same could be said about discrimination in general. Institutional discrimination can be understood only in terms of the situations that give rise to it and cause it to change.

Political economists attempt to identify and analyze these situations with four main elements: adaptation, incentives, flexibility, and feedback. Each provides a mechanism by which discrimination can persist in the face of competitive pressures and varying circumstances. Each can also help us understand how discrimination can qualitatively and quantitatively respond to changes in its socioeconomic environment. Each feeds into the next so that the theory becomes progressively more complex as it develops. We will begin with the simplest element, that of adaptation.

## Organizational Adaptation

*Organizational adaptation* refers to the tendency of firms and other organizations to adapt to the social conventions of their external environment. Firms need to work cooperatively with the world around them. They do not want to offend the sensibilities of their workers, their suppliers, their customers, their neighbors, or the government. Consequently, they will establish a division of labor that mimics existing social hierarchies. If white men traditionally exercise authority over women and minorities in society at large, then the same pattern will be followed within the firm. As customary racial and gender patterns change, firms may be able to change their hiring practices, but insofar as these patterns remain fixed, firms will continue to respect them. It is costly, difficult, and risky for them to do otherwise.

Organizational adaptation derives from the essentially conservative nature of firms. Firms may be innovators with respect to technology, work organization, marketing strategies, or product development. But to do so they need stability and predictability with respect to their external relationships. As a result, business organizations will "almost invariably adjust and conform to the pattern of race relations in the given society" (Blumer 1965, pp. 240–41). The neoclassical belief that managerial decision making would be irrational if it took factors such as race and sex into account fails to consider the firm's need to fit harmoniously into its larger environment. As Stanley Greenberg concludes, the belief in a "struggle between businessmen and the capitalist order, on the one hand, and racial privilege and domination, on the other, is wholly imaginary. . . . Business enterprise . . . responds flexibly to socially and politically imposed market and labor constraints . . . and frequently takes advantage of, and at times creates these relationships. . . . Business enterprise in a racial order [is] adaptive and complicit" (1976, p. 219).

Blumer's and Greenberg's arguments with respect to race also hold true with respect to gender. Rosabeth Moss Kanter (1977) shows how gender roles are incorporated into the division of labor at a large corporation. Certain jobs are considered to be "appropriate" for men and others for women, and these barriers are disruptive to cross even though men and women may be qualified for each other's jobs. For example, when a woman is introduced into all-male work groups, communication and cooperation may diminish due to the inability of the men to accept her as an equal colleague. This problem is especially acute in work situations that are nonrepetitive and require frequent decision making, such as in managerial positions. Although the woman may be as qualified and hardworking as her male colleagues, the productivity of the team as a whole will go down. It would therefore be irrational for the employer to integrate the work group. Social norms as well as productive characteristics thereby dictate the allocation of people to tasks.

The racial and sexual division of labor used to be almost universal. Virtually all positions that contained power and authority were filled by white men. Over time, however, it has become somewhat more likely to see women and minorities in these positions, though many believe that they are treated as tokens and excluded from positions of real power. The process of organizational adaptation can respond to changes in the external environment, as the occupational mobility of women and minorities after the Civil Rights Act of 1964 attests.

Nonetheless, once a firm establishes a division of labor, it tends to become entrenched and difficult to change. According to James Baron, "The evidence suggests that social forces and discriminatory cultural beliefs preva-lent when a job or organization is founded condition the way that positions are defined, priced and staffed, becoming institutionalized within the formal structure and informal traditions of the enterprise" (1991, p. 115). Jobs be-come socially identified as male or female, white or black, and though change is possible it is usually slow, costly, and difficult. New forms of segregation may emerge. For example, new job titles may be created for white men to shield them from integration with women and minorities who hold similar qualifications. Women and minorities may be less likely to wield supervi-sory authority than comparable white men. Organizational structure can maintain the race-gender hierarchy even as it responds to external political pressures for change.

Wage patterns tend to follow suit. Donald Tomaskovic-Devey notes that "It is well established that the earnings of both males and females fall as the percentage of females in an occupation rises" (1993, p. 111). He concludes that the same is true with respect to race. Holding the characteristics of both workers and jobs constant, the sheer presence of women and minorities has a depressing effect on wages.

The concentration of women and minorities may be correlated with low pay because jobs have social labels. White men have historically been seen to have a greater need for money than women (who were "secondary earn-ers") or minorities (for whom poverty was the norm). Consequently, jobs that were allocated to women or minorities were paid artificially low wages. For example, clerical workers were mostly well-paid males in the nineteenth century, and clerical work included managerial functions. As corporations grew and their need for both clerical and managerial labor expanded, the two aspects of the job were separated. Managerial work was reserved for men and was highly paid. Clerical work was reserved for women and was poorly paid. This transition was not a biological or technological necessity. Instead, it reflected the way in which firms adapted their labor needs to existing gen-der hierarchies. In this way, they kept wage scales down for the rapidly ex-panding clerical sector while maintaining a division of labor that seemed natural because it reinforced traditional gender roles (Braverman 1974).

If labor were fully mobile, it would be impossible to sustain artificially low wages. The demand for female and minority workers would rise as firms sought to take advantage of low labor costs. Over time, female and minority wages would rise relative to white male wages as a result. But barriers to labor mobility created by adaptive organizational behavior fore-stall this result. Firms are reluctant to contravene social customs. Further-more, once their division of labor is established, it is costly and risky to change. As long as an excess supply of labor is available, firms can fill their higher-paying positions with white male workers without experiencing labor shortages. They therefore face few incentives to take the risks involved in violating social norms.

## Distributional Incentives

Once organizational adaptation establishes a race-gender division of labor, those who benefit by it will resist change. These benefits function as incentives for individuals to act on the basis of their perceived group interest. The interests of different groups rarely coincide. In fact, it is the conflicts of interest experienced by different groups that provide the dynamic element in the political economy analysis of discrimination.

The neoclassical presumption that individuals "pay" to discriminate (as they would to indulge any other taste or prejudice) is turned on its head in the political economy framework. Here discrimination is perceived to be in the interests of those who practice it. It is exactly for this reason that the political economy theory of discrimination does not depend upon personal prejudice. Instead, discrimination is held to be self-sustaining because it generates rewards for those who are willing to discriminate (or at least unwilling to act against discrimination).

Discrimination can benefit employers as a result of *class struggle effects*. Profit-maximizing employers want to minimize the wage bill and maximize their control over the labor process. These goals are difficult to achieve in the face of labor solidarity. If workers recognize that they have common class interests and act together (for example, by organizing a union) to increase wages and to establish their rights in the workplace, then management will face higher costs and lower profits. But if workers fail to recognize their common interests and therefore are unable to cooperate to achieve these goals, then management can retain the upper hand. Management therefore has an incentive to "divide and conquer" its workforce.

Where organizational adaptation provides an external motive for the firm to discriminate, class struggle effects provide an internal motive. Management may assign white male workers to the "best" jobs in order to reduce the chances that they will feel a need to cooperate with women and minority workers who have the most to gain from a wage hike or an improvement in conditions. Women and minorities may blame white male workers as much as management for their problems. If workers fight each other on the basis of race and/or gender, then they will find it that much more difficult to unite on the basis of class to achieve their common goals. As a result, wages for all workers (including white males) are kept down and managerial control is enhanced (Reich 1981).

If class struggle effects were the whole story, all workers would have the same fundamental interests, and racism and sexism would be merely "false consciousness." The solution would then be for all workers to "unite and fight" for higher wages, better working conditions, and other demands. This is a simple and appealing strategy. Unfortunately, it can be confounded by the benefits that discrimination can confer upon white male employees.

White male workers can benefit from discrimination as a result of *job competition effects*. If women and minorities are excluded from the "best" jobs, then white males will face less competition for them. This will improve their chances to earn higher wages, get promoted, and enjoy job security (Shulman 1987). Furthermore, a reduction in job competition for white males means that they will be better positioned to find jobs for their (white male) relatives and friends. They will also be more likely to work among people like themselves with whom they are comfortable and able to communicate. Job competition effects therefore benefit white males in five ways: higher wages, better promotional possibilities, enhanced job security, nepotism, and social comfort.

Job competition effects depend upon the exclusion of women and minorities from consideration for certain jobs. Exclusion can occur as a result of direct or indirect intervention. Direct intervention—e.g., a strike in protest against the hiring of black workers—was more common in the early part of the century. Today, indirect intervention by white male employees is the common method of exclusion. Instead of boldly presenting their demands, white males can exert pressure in a more covert fashion. Women coworkers may be sexually harassed. Black coworkers may be ostracized and ignored or subtly informed that they got their new job due to quotas rather than qualifications. Morale at the workplace plummets and with it productivity.

Management is therefore understandably hesitant to introduce women and minorities into previously all-white male work groups. Even if none of this actually occurs, the fear of it is ever-present. Of course, management is not necessarily loath to discriminate. Aside from benefiting by class struggle effects, management may also feel that it can maintain a positive relationship with its white male workers by encouraging them to feel that they have exclusive rights to certain jobs. This set of shared values and interests between management and workers (in this case, specifically white male workers) is called *hegemony*. It is one means by which management maintains control over the labor process.

It is important to note that class struggle effects and job competition effects have contradictory distributional consequences with respect to employers and white male employees (women and minorities are always hurt by discrimination). Class struggle effects benefit employers and hurt white male employees. Job competition effects benefit white male employees. Their consequences for employers are more complicated. On the one hand, employers may benefit from the hegemonic control over white male workers that discrimination may facilitate. On the other hand, job competition effects may reduce the ability of employers to make best use of their human resources. It also may strengthen labor solidarity among white male workers, which can inhibit managerial control over those workers.

Because class struggle effects and job competition effects have contradictory distributional consequences, it is impossible to make simple statements about who gains from discrimination. The incentive system that sustains discrimination can change with circumstances and can vary from one historical period to another. As a result, discrimination is *flexible* in the sense that it can adjust to changes in economic conditions. This may make it especially difficult to eradicate.

## Flexibility

Neoclassical models of discrimination cannot explain endogenous changes in discrimination. Changes in prejudice and changes in perceived risk—the sources of neoclassical discrimination—cannot be connected in any systematic fashion to changes in economic conditions. These models are static in the sense that they rely on exogenous shocks to explain changes in the degree of discrimination. Furthermore, none of them has much to say about changes in the types of discrimination that women and minority workers may encounter in the labor market.

These are serious drawbacks. It would be astonishing if change did not occur, and the whole point of economic models is (or should be) to explain change. A major advantage of the political economy theory of discrimination is its ability to explain quantitative and qualitative changes in discrimination in terms of changes in its economic environment.

The flexibility of discrimination has three meanings. First, discrimination should change in response to changes in the long-run patterns of economic growth. Second, discrimination should change over the business cycle. Third, discrimination should change in response to government policies. These changes can be understood in terms of incentive shifts, including shifts in the external and internal incentives described in the previous two sections.

Political economists acknowledge that firms face costs from discrimination that can arise either from market pressures or from the government. A refusal to hire qualified blacks can result in higher search costs or higher wage costs in the effort to find qualified white males. It can create inefficiencies in the use of human resources. It can also result in government sanctions if the firm is subject to antidiscrimination and affirmative action laws. This part of the argument is similar to the one made by neoclassical economists. However, costs can also arise from ceasing discrimination. If both continuing discrimination and ceasing discrimination can be costly, then the firm's behavior cannot be theoretically preordained. Instead, it will depend upon the circumstances that balance these costs against each other.

From the discussion in the preceding sections, we can identify five reasons why ceasing discrimination can be costly. In the first place, a decline in discrimination can disrupt traditional patterns of association and authority. These social patterns lie behind the process of organizational adaptation; realigning them is a risky and time-consuming proposition, which may threaten the firm's internal and external stability. Placing minorities and women on par with white men can raise costs because it undermines the notions of fairness on which white male morale and productivity depend. Second, ceasing discrimination can raise wage costs and reduce managerial control due to class struggle effects and the reduction of hegemony. Third, a drop in discrimination can change the rules of internal labor markets. Disrupting the established channels of recruitment, screening, allocation, training, wage setting, and promotion can "raise the inefficiency of the labor force adjustment process, at least in the short run, thereby imposing costs on both the employer and society. Only where the effect of discrimination has been to create a grossly inefficient internal labor market will there by any offsetting benefits" (Doeringer and Piore 1971, p. 136). Increasing competition for a limited set of rewards and changing tried-and-true procedures inevitably create more conflict and risk. Fourth, a reduction in discrimination can increase training costs (a crucial component of labor costs and productivity) if white male workers refuse to train or work cooperatively with their female or minority coworkers. Finally, a decline in discrimination can reduce team efficiency by reducing social homogeneity and with it trust, communication, and cooperation.

Discriminatory practices can therefore be costly and risky to change due to their impact on employers, white male employees, and organizational structure. If it is also the case that discrimination increases costs, then the firm faces a set of contradictory pressures. The direction it is prone to take in the face of this contradiction is determined by the strength of the labor market.

Assume that the economy is moving into a recession. As unemployment rises, more qualified white male workers become available to fill vacancies. Consequently, the hiring of workers need not be foregone, search time need not be expanded, nor must wages be raised if the firm chooses to discriminate against qualified female and minority applicants. The costs of continuing discrimination thus fall. At the same time, the costs of ceasing discrimination rise.

In weak labor markets, workers place a premium on job security. The ability to protect one's job and to maintain some influence over the hiring process becomes increasingly important to white male workers as their occupational alternatives diminish. The significance of informal job distribution channels (i.e., inside information) grows as the availability of jobs declines. White male workers thus face increasing incentives to discriminate as unemployment rises. At the same time, management is willing to accommodate them since the costs of continuing discrimination have declined. Management has an incentive to do so since wage growth will be dampened as a result of class struggle effects. Management is able to meet short-term goals (stability during a downturn) as well as long-term goals (hegemonic control) by allowing the interests of white male labor to supersede those of female and minority workers. The opposite process kicks in during an upturn. The political economy model of discrimination therefore predicts that the intensity of discrimination should rise in recessions and fall in expansions.

The incentives for discrimination will therefore vary with labor market conditions. Of course, the degree of discrimination is also influenced by many other factors, such as laws, popular beliefs, social patterns (e.g., intermarriage), custom, and so on. But economic factors matter as well. For example, the stagnation of wages and the loss of manufacturing jobs since the early 1970s may have exacerbated racial conflict as the competition for "good" jobs increased. The decline of unionism may have reduced labor solidarity and generated class struggle effects. As a result, discrimination can continue to be a problem despite the changes in law and popular attitudes, which would lead us to believe that discrimination has declined since the mid-1960s.

It is also the case that the composition (as well as the costs) of discrimination can respond flexibly to changes in circumstances. Government is a case in point. Job discrimination is against the law and many firms are covered by affirmative action requirements. Yet the effect of these policies may have been to alter the type of discrimination rather than its intensity pure and simple. Although all forms of labor market discrimination are illegal, not all are equally easy to prevent. Employment discrimination in particular is more costly and difficult to monitor than wage or occupational discrimination. Hiring decisions are more subjective than wage or allocation decisions, individual performance has not yet been observed, and labor force comparisons are more problematic than workforce comparisons. If discrimination is outlawed, the effect may be to reduce wage and occupational discrimination but at the same time to increase employment discrimination. This compositional change in discrimination can occur because a decline in wage and occupational discrimination can reduce the traditional demand for female and minority workers. . . .

In this manner, the political economy theory of discrimination is able to explain changes in the intensity and types of discrimination that prevail in the labor market. In so doing, it can help us understand the persistence of discrimination in the face of pressures to eradicate it.

## Positive Feedback

In addition to its ability to respond flexibly to changing circumstances, labor market discrimination is also sustained through its interactions with its own effects. This type of interaction is called *feedback*. Feedback is akin to a vicious cycle. A problem has effects that reinforce the original problem. As a result, the problem becomes self-sustaining.

The four most important types of feedback are perception, socialization, choice, and market interactions. Each provides a means by which discrimination alters the environment within which the labor market operates and thereby reinforces discrimination in the labor market itself. In contrast to flexibility, which provides an explanation for the dynamics of discrimination inside the labor market, feedback provides an explanation for the dynamics of discrimination that connects the labor market to its external environment. We will begin with feedback due to perception.

A half-century ago, Gunnar Myrdal (1972 [1944]) argued that white perceptions of blacks are reinforced by black life conditions. Black poverty (and its associated behaviors) reinforces negative white perceptions, which in turn reinforce discrimination by whites against blacks and hence perpetuate black poverty. In other words, the interaction of perceptions and actions makes discrimination self-reinforcing. Prejudice becomes a self-fulfilling prophecy. For example, white employers may believe that blacks are more likely to be criminals; hence they are less likely to hire blacks; hence blacks [may] become more likely to commit [certain] crimes, since they have no other means of supporting themselves.

Feedback from perception can be compared to the neoclassical model of statistical discrimination. In that model, individuals get treated on the basis of the perceived characteristics of their group. This type of discrimination is not self-sustaining, however, for competition should push employers to use tests and other means of learning about individuals in order to make best use of their human resources. In other words, the statistical discrimination model leads to a convergence of expectations with reality. Feedback from perception, in contrast, leads to a convergence of reality with expectations.

Socialization is another source of feedback. Discrimination may change the conditions in which children develop into adults and in so doing perpetuate itself. . . . Mary Corcoran and Paul Courant (1986) argue that labor market discrimination against women discourages parents from raising girls to specialize in wage work. When girls grow up, their standard of living will depend more on their husband's job than on their own job, in part because discrimination lowers female wages relative to male wages. Consequently, parents will raise girls to specialize more in finding a suitable husband than in finding a suitable job. As a result, women will exhibit different work behaviors than men, and employers will be encouraged to continue segregating women and men within labor markets and career paths.

The third avenue by which feedback occurs is through choice. Choice is traditionally considered to be the domain of neoclassical economists, but this is only so because they take choice to be exogenous. It depends solely on given preferences. In political economy, however, choice is endogenous in the sense that it can be influenced by the availability of opportunities. For example, if job discrimination lowers the returns to education, then blacks and women may choose to get less (or a different type of) education than white men. Elaine McCrate (1990) argues that black teenagers may be more likely than white teenagers to get pregnant because their future job opportunities (before pregnancy) are lower. Consequently, the opportunity cost of teenager birth is lower for blacks than for whites. These are examples of the way in which choices can respond to circumstances and in so doing reinforce the circumstances.

Finally, feedback can occur as a result of interactions between the job market and other markets, especially the housing market. For example, residential segregation may result in job discrimination if blacks are physically or socially isolated from job vacancies. If jobs move from the cities to the suburbs, and if blacks are locked into the inner cities as a result of housing discrimination and a lack of transportation, then they are in an unequal position (in comparison to whites) to compete for jobs. Or they may lack access to information about job vacancies, or job vacancies may be traditionally filled by the recommendations of existing employees. In situations such as these, blacks and whites are on unequal footing in the labor market as a result of discrimination elsewhere in society. . . .

## Conclusion

In the political economy paradigm, capitalism incorporates, transforms, and ultimately reproduces discrimination. This does not mean that the struggle against discrimination has been futile, nor does it mean that the present is as bad as the past. Women and blacks have made impressive occupational strides as discriminatory barriers have come down (or at least have become more permeable). At the same time, many indicators show that the economic gap between women and minorities on the one hand, and white men on the other, has remained surprisingly hard to breech. This article has provided an explanation for why that might be the case.

The question of "who is to blame" for labor market discrimination in the post–civil rights era has no simple answer. The intensity and patterns of discriminatory behavior by firms can vary with social customs (organizational adaptation), the self-interested actions of capitalists (class struggle effects) or white male workers (job competition effects), the pressures of competition and government policy (flexibility), or the self-perpetuating cycle of events set in motion by discrimination (feedback). All of these elements come into play to one degree or another; discrimination has no single cause and therefore no single solution.

These elements function in different ways and carry different weights in different circumstances. As a result, the conclusions of the political economy model are contingent rather than universal. The analytical categories are designed to organize information and not to act as a substitute for it. In contrast to the deductive and determinative reasoning of neoclassical economists, political economists tell an open-ended story about discrimination that can conceivably have many different plots, characters, and conclusions.

Consider, for example, a change such as the declining power of white male workers. International flows of labor and capital, deunionization, tight money policies, corporate downsizing, and other factors have weakened the position of white male workers relative to their employers since the mid-1970s. This change can affect the discriminatory process in a variety of ways, the net effect of which cannot be predicted in an a priori fashion.

As the power of white male workers declines, their ability to influence the hiring decisions of management may also decline; however, their desire to do so may increase if their insecurity stimulates their fear of job competition. The balance of these tendencies will determine the direction of job competition effects. At the same time, class struggle effects could also go in either direction. From the perspective of management, weaker white male workers can *both* reduce the potential gains from the use of divide-and-conquer tactics (since wages are falling anyway) *and* increase the potential gains from doing so (since appeals to racism and sexism will be heard more sympathetically and can divert attention from the real causes of economic insecurity). The ultimate effect on discrimination—in terms of its intensity and composition, victims and perpetrators—can be understood only in hindsight.

The strength of this interpretation of the political economy model of discrimination is its ability to incorporate a variety of elements in the context of changing circumstances in a nonreductionist and nondeterministic fashion. What the political economy model loses with respect to formalism, it gains with respect to relevance. In the end, this is what makes it preferable to the neoclassical alternatives.

## References

Baron, James. 1991. "Organizational Evidence of Ascription in Labor Markets." In *New Approaches to Economic and Social Analyses of Discrimination*, ed. Richard Cornwall and Phanindra Wunnava. New York: Praeger.

Blumer, Herbert. 1965. "Industrialization and Race Relations." In *Industrialization and Race Relations*, ed. Guy Hunter, pp. 240–41. London: Oxford University Press.

Braverman, Harry. 1974. *Labor and Monopoly Capital: The Degradation of Work in the Twentieth Century*. New York: Monthly Review Press.

Corcoran, Mary, and Paul Courant. 1986. "Sex-Role Socialization, Screening by Sex, and Women's Work: A Reformulation of Neoclassical and Structural Models of Wage Discrimination and Job Segregation." Unpublished paper.

Doeringer, Peter, and Michael Piore. 1971. *Internal Labor Markets and Manpower Analysis*. Lexington, MA: D.C. Heath.

Greenberg, Stanley. 1976. "Business Enterprise in a Racial Order." *Politics and Society* 6 (2): 213–40.

Kanter, Rosabeth Moss. 1977. *Men and Women of the Corporation*. New York: Basic Books.

McCrate, Elaine. 1990. "Labor Market Segmentation and Relative Black/White Teenage Birth Rates." *Review of Black Political Economy* 18 (4): 37–53.

Myrdal, Gunnar. 1972 [first published 1944]. *An American Dilemma: The Negro Problem and Modern Democracy*, Volume I. New York: Random House.

Reich, Michael. 1981. *Racial Inequality: A Political-Economic Analysis*. Princeton, NJ: Princeton University Press.

Shulman, Steven. 1987. "Discrimination, Human Capital and Black-White Unemployment: Evidence from Cities." *Journal of Human Resources* 22 (3): 361–76.

Tomaskovic-Devey, Donald. 1993. *Gender and Racial Inequality at Work: The Sources and Consequences of Job Segregation*. Ithaca, NY: ILR Press.

Wilson, William Julius. 1995. "The Political Economy and Urban Racial Tensions." *The American Economist* 39 (1): 3.

Adapted from "The Political Economy of Labor Market Discrimination: A Classroom-Friendly Presentation of the Theory," *Review of Black Political Economy* 24 (4) (Spring 1996): 47–64. Reprinted with permission of Transaction Publishers, © 1996 by Transactions Publishers.

# 18

# Black Women's Breakthrough into Clerical Work

## An Occupational Tipping Model

*Mary C. King*

[B]lack women workers have experienced a dramatic improvement in their labor market status, both absolutely and relative to other workers. Since 1955, black women's earnings have increased from one-third to two-thirds those of white men. This progress was achieved by a drastic redistribution among occupations. In 1940, [over] two-thirds of black working women were employed in domestic and agricultural work, the lowest-paid rungs of the American labor market, as shown in Table 18.1. Had black women remained concentrated in these occupations, their relative earnings would be little better now. In 1988, only 3 percent of black working women were engaged in domestic and agricultural work. Now more black women are in clerical work than in any other occupation, as is true for women of all other ethnic backgrounds.

Access to occupations with better pay and promotion possibilities has been the key to economic advancement for white and minority workers. Treiman and Hartmann (1981) estimate that occupational differentiation accounts for some 35 to 40 percent of the wage gap between men and women. Cunningham and Zalokar (1992) show that differential allocation among occupations and industries has consistently accounted for about half of the earnings gap between black and white women since 1940 and that the gap has narrowed dramatically as occupational differentiation between black and white women has decreased. Blau and Beller's (1991) decomposition of the elements contributing to rising relative earnings for black women finds occupational upgrading to be the most important, particularly for older women.

Table 18.1

**Occupational Distribution of Black and White Women, 1940 and 1988**
(in percent)

|  | 1940 | | 1988* | |
|---|---|---|---|---|
|  | Black | White | Black | White |
| Managerial, professional, and technical | 4.9 | 17.6 | 19.6 | 28.6 |
| Clerical | 1.5 | 26.9 | 30.1 | 33.3 |
| Sales | 0.4 | 6.2 | 5.0 | 9.6 |
| Domestics | 57.4 | 11.0 | 3.2 | 1.4 |
| Other service | 10.0 | 11.7 | 25.1 | 15.3 |
| Farming, forestry, and fishing | 16.1 | 2.4 | 0.2 | 1.1 |
| Crafts, operatives, and laborers | 9.7 | 24.3 | 16.7 | 10.7 |

*Sources:* Public Use Microdata Sample of the 1940 Census; 1988 Current Population Survey Annual Income Extract.
*1988 clerical and sales percentages are amended to undo coding changes introduced in 1980, which switched some 10 percent of clerical workers into the sales category.

The purpose of this chapter is to discover the source of black women's recent economic advancement, with a focus on the entry of black women into clerical work. Clerical work represents the most skilled of the occupations into which large numbers of black women have moved since 1940. Furthermore, the route into clerical work is less obvious than into the service, operative, and professional occupations, which are the other primary employers of black women. Compared to clerical work, service and operative jobs are similar to black women's previous jobs in terms of qualifications and relative pay. Access to work in the "women's professions," such as teaching and nursing, is mediated by credentialing institutions and may have been facilitated by the presence of segregated schools and medical facilities.

Clerical work is not often viewed as skilled or desirable work. . . . Nevertheless, clerical jobs are unarguably better than domestic, agricultural, and most service positions in terms of wages, job security, personnel practices, and working conditions. Employment in clerical work represents a clear improvement in black women's labor market status. Attention to the mechanisms that opened clerical employment to black women may inform us what is necessary for the continued progress of black women and of other groups currently constrained in the labor market.

Researchers interested in explaining black economic progress in general have focused almost exclusively on black men. This literature has generated four competing theories to explain the advancement of black men: (1) an improvement in black men's human capital, (2) economic growth and tight labor markets, (3) government intervention in the labor market, or (4) the pressure of sociopolitical movements both directly on business and indirectly via the government. . . .

## Improved Human Capital?

Initial evidence for the first hypothesis—that improved human capital allowed black women to effectively compete for clerical jobs—appears quite strong. Black women's average educational levels increased significantly between 1940 and 1980 in both absolute and relative terms. In addition, the quality of schooling received by blacks, particularly in the South, improved markedly. Finally, the sizable migration of blacks from the rural South to northern urban areas can be interpreted as an investment in better job opportunities and therefore in human capital.

However, gaining the educational qualification for clerical work does not appear to have opened the door to clerical jobs for black women. In 1940, clerical and sales work engaged nearly 60 percent of white women with terminal high school degrees, a level of training often considered the de facto qualification for clerical work. At the time, only 7 percent of black women with terminal high school degrees were employed in clerical positions. Nearly 70 percent of the high school–educated black women held service positions, primarily domestic jobs. In fact, service occupations remained the most important source of employment for high school–educated black women until 1980, while the preponderance of high school–educated white women worked in clerical jobs throughout the period.

Furthermore, as reported by King (1991), an econometric test indicates that investments in human capital, in the form of education, experience, and relocation, explained very little of the breakthrough of black women into clerical work. This test was based on the counterfactual hypothesis that if human capital were the key to opening clerical work to black women, then growing human capital endowments should predict the increase in the proportion of black women clerical workers, even if labor market conditions remained unchanged. However, the human capital model predicted only one-sixth of black women's actual shift into clerical work from 1940 to 1988. . . .

In short, the supply-side hypothesis fails to account for the large shift of black women into clerical jobs. While improvements in educational attainment were certainly necessary for substantial representation of black women in clerical work, holding educational qualifications did not provide black women entrée to clerical positions. Black women appear to have gained the educational qualifications for clerical work well before they began to be hired into clerical positions in any numbers.

## The Access Model

The U.S. labor market is one in which a race and gender hierarchy operates via occupational segregation. Occupational segregation by gender has remained nearly constant over the last fifty years, with the exception of decreases in the 1970s. Nearly 60 percent of either men or women would have to change jobs to achieve equal representation by gender in all occupations (King 1992). . . .

Occupational differentiation by race is substantial but is currently much less than by gender. However, before the 1960s, women were far more segregated by race on the job than were men. In 1940, 60 percent of either black or white women would have had to change jobs to erase occupational differentiation by race among them, while 40 percent of men would have had to shift positions to fully integrate occupations by race among men. Occupational differentiation by race fell during the 1960s and 1970s among both women and men, though far more dramatically for women, so that by the 1980s, the level of race differentiation was about 30 percent for both women and men (King 1992).

Demographic groups gain access to different occupations in order of their position in a labor market queue. A particularly useful conception of such a queue is Strober and Catanzarite's (1988) diamond-shaped queue, with white men at the apex, black men and white women at the sides, and black women at the bottom, as illustrated in Figure 18.1. According to this construct, opportunities flow from white men to black men or white women, depending on the nature of the job, and then from either black men or white women to black women.

Unlike Thurow's queue (1975), which is based on training costs, Strober and Catanzarite's queue is predicated on social power. An economy operating within a patriarchal and racist culture allocates job opportunities (and all resources) first to white men and last to women of color. Basic tenets of an institutional view of the labor market underpin such a queue, including a recognition of chronic unemployment and underemployment and the assumption that productivity rests in the job, rather than in the individual on the job (Brown 1988).

Empirical evidence indicates that job opportunities flow more often from white women to black women than from black men to black women. Black women are even more likely to be found in women's jobs than are white women (Malveaux 1984). Black women's occupational shifts over the last fifty years, sketched broadly in Table 18.1, are from farm work and private household service to clerical work, other female service positions, retail sales, the women's professions of teaching and nursing, and some women's opera-

Figure 18.1 **Strober and Catanzarite's Diamond-Shaped Labor Market Queue**

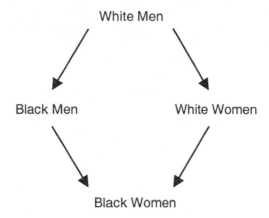

tive jobs. The hiring of black women as bus drivers and postal employees may represent examples of jobs moving down the queue from black men to black women. . . .

The access model highlights the mechanisms by which queued groups gain access to occupations previously open only to those above them in the queue. It incorporates two of the three demand-side hypotheses generated by research on black men, since tight labor markets and the enactment of civil rights legislation seem potentially important in opening clerical work to black women. The direct impact of the civil rights movement on employers is omitted from the access model due to the difficulty of assessing this phenomenon empirically. Hopefully, further work using other methods can gauge the extent to which employers changed hiring and promotion practices in response to the civil rights movement itself, rather than in reaction to government mandates.

Specific features of the access model derive from parallels apparent from studies of occupations that have tipped from male to female, such as teaching, bank telling, and clerical work, and of the process by which black men gained access to industrial jobs. Accounts of these transitions indicate that the keys to opening an occupation to a new demographic group include:

- a labor shortage in that occupation
- better opportunities for the previously preferred source of labor
- technological and organizational change affecting the occupation
- a government role, either directly as an employer or as an outside agent affecting the hiring process. . . .

## Evidence for the Access Model

Each of the elements of the access model has contributed to black women's new access to clerical jobs. Structural change, particularly the growth of the service sector and the government, as well as the increasing information needs of other industries, may have created greater demand for clerical workers than could have been met by the supply of white women. White women may have found new openings in professional, managerial, and technical positions that were more attractive than clerical work. Certainly, tremendous technological changes in clerical work occurred throughout the period, including the introduction of the duplicating machine, electric typewriters, and office computers. Technological change may have changed employers' perceptions of the qualifications necessary for clerical work in such a way that black women appeared more appropriate for clerical positions than employers had previously thought. Similarly, organizational change, particularly the development of large back-office clerical staffs, may have facilitated the hiring of black women into positions characterized by routine work, few advancement possibilities, and even physical isolation from the rest of the organization. Expanding government employment of clerical workers, based on civil service hiring procedures, may have provided black women with many clerical jobs. And, finally, government pressure on private employers to comply with equal employment legislation may have opened clerical work to black women.

### Evidence for a Clerical Labor Shortage

. . . The demand for clerical workers grew tremendously over the last fifty years, as shown in Table 18.2. Furthermore, women occupied an increasing proportion of these positions. Women accounted for 52 percent of clerical workers in 1940 and 80 percent in 1990.

The increase in clerical workers was particularly dramatic during the 1960s. Although white women's labor force participation rates rose over the entire period, the ratio of the increase in the number of white women in the labor force to the increase in the number of clerical positions in the economy fell substantially during the 1960s. In short, fewer white women were potentially available to clerical employers during the 1960s than during any other decade since 1940. The watershed for black women's access to clerical positions came about at just the same time as the rate of increase in the labor supply of white women fell significantly behind the rate of increase in clerical positions open to women. . . .

Business writers complained of a clerical labor shortage throughout the early

Table 18.2

**The Growth of the Clerical Work Force, 1940–1990** (in thousands)

|  | 1940–50 | 1950–60 | 1960–70 | 1970–80 | 1980–90* |
|---|---|---|---|---|---|
| Number of clerical workers at the end of the decade | 7,047 | 9,617 | 14,252 | 18,190 | 24,220 |
| Increase in women clerical workers over.the decade | 2,001 | 1,121 | 4,018 | 3,339 | 4,938 |
| Increase in white female workforce over the decade | 4,819 | 5,073 | 7,119 | 7,519 | 11,561 |
| Ratio of row 3/row 2 | 2.4 | 2.4 | 1.8 | 2.3 | 2.3 |

*Sources:* 1940–80 Censuses of Population; U.S. Bureau of the Census, Current Population Reports, P-60 Series #174 (1990); U.S. Council of Economic Advisors (1991).

*1980 numbers include cashiers and counter clerks in the counts of clerical workers in accordance with the pre-1980 practice. The numbers for 1990 do not include counter clerks, who comprised 1.3 percent of clerical workers in 1980.

1960s. For example, in 1962 a business consultant on the faculty of the City College of New York (CCNY) graduate business school claimed that "there is definite statistical evidence that there are fewer actual applicants for each office position today than there have been in the past few years" (Stanton 1962). The accumulation of evidence supports the idea that a relative labor shortage existed in clerical work during the 1960s. White women were not as available to employers of clerical workers as they had been in previous decades.

*Better Opportunities for White Women*

... [W]hite women do not appear to have improved their overall occupational distribution until well after black women had begun to find clerical jobs. . . . Major advances for white women did not occur until the 1970s, when the proportion of white women in professional, managerial, and technical positions jumped to 23.3 percent and then to 28.6 percent during the 1980s. . . . [C]lerical employment accounted for a consistent proportion of white women with high school educations or better over a time when white women's labor force participation rates increased rapidly and education levels were rising. Clearly then, more and better-educated white women continued to be available for clerical work, though not perhaps the lowest rungs of clerical work.

Relative wages indicate that white women gradually found jobs that paid slightly more than the average clerical job. Clerical wages slid against the wages of all white working women nearly continuously from 1961 to 1979, exactly the period during which black women were finding their way into clerical jobs in unprecedented numbers. In 1955, full-time clerical workers earned about 8 percent more than did average white women working full-time. This premium fell and then rose again in the early 1960s, before declining steadily throughout the remainder of the 1960s and 1970s. During the 1970s, clerical workers earned less than did white working women on average.

In total, the evidence does not indicate that black women's entrance into clerical positions in the mid-1960s was facilitated by a movement of white women out of clerical work into other, more desirable occupations. On the other hand, it may well be that white women moved to the top of an expanded clerical labor force and in that way left openings in the lower-paying bottom rungs of clerical work to be filled by black women.

## Technological and Organizational Change in Clerical Work

According to business consultant Randy Goldfeld (1987), "The staggering pace of technological advance has introduced office automation equipment of such sweeping variety that almost no task performed in an office 20 years ago is done today in the same way." Early studies of the impact of technological change on clerical work tended to treat the various clerical occupations as a group and to predict a single trend in change. For instance, technological change was asserted to have deskilled clerical work or reduced employment opportunities in clerical work (Glenn and Feldberg 1977; Menzies 1982). Most recent research, based largely on case studies, describes a bipolar effect, upgrading some clerical positions and downskilling others, depending both on the technology and its method of implementation (Baran and Teegarden 1987; Hughes 1989; Cappelli 1993). . . .

Both Baran and Teegarden (1987) and the authors of a congressional Office of Technology Assessment report (U.S. Congress 1985) point out that minority workers are disproportionately found in the lower rungs of clerical work, employed as file clerks or typists, and are therefore vulnerable to future displacement by office automation. This view is supported by Glenn and Tolbert (1987), who claim that the clerical jobs that women of color have entered tend to be those that are being negatively affected by new office technology.

The degree of organizational change occurring in the office during the time when black women entered the clerical workforce is more difficult to analyze with any degree of precision. However, anecdotal evidence suggests a trend toward the creation of large back-office clerical staffs to handle repetitive data-entry tasks and word processing. Nelson (1986) asserts that "back offices tend to be highly automated and employ a high proportion of low-wage clerical (or 'computerized clerical') workers." Such a reorganization, which concentrates the more routine aspects of clerical work and may accentuate or sever the clerical promotional ladder, is the sort of change that we may expect would facilitate the hiring of black women as clerical workers. In her case study of a large insurance firm, Hartmann (1987) notes the concentration of black women in back-office clerical employment.

However, economic geographers have documented the suburbanization of back offices, a move away from the inner-city labor forces, which include more minorities and more unionized workers. More recently, scholars have noted a movement to off-shore back-office clerical work to Mexico, the Caribbean, Asia, and Ireland (Posthuma 1987). . . . If further technological and organizational change reduces the number of lower-level clerical positions or relocates such work to the suburbs or even to the Third World, then black women's domestic employment in clerical work is likely to be adversely affected.

### The Role of the Government as an Employer

The government has often been the first employer of a new group in a particular occupation. . . . The public sector employs a disproportionate number of black women workers. In 1988, 26 percent of black working women were employed in the public sector, while only 16 percent of white women and 15 percent of the labor force as a whole were so employed (U.S. Bureau of Labor Statistics 1989). Historically, civil service hiring procedures allowed some black women access to clerical positions through testing, though the availability of these jobs to black women also depended upon whether or not applications required personal interviews or photos (Giddings 1984).

. . . In 1940, 25 percent of black clericals worked in the public sector, as compared to 13 percent of all women in clerical positions. In 1960, when one-fifth of clerical jobs were found in the public sector, nearly half of the black women working as clericals were employed by the government. By 1980, the public sector still employed twice the proportion of black women clericals as of white women clericals. . . .

Finally, government employment of black women in clerical positions may have facilitated their access to clerical jobs in the private sector by demonstrating that black women performed competently in clerical occupations or by accustoming people to seeing black women in these roles, while government employment of clerical workers in general may have pushed firms to hire black women by reducing the supply of clerical workers available to the private sector.

### The Role of the Government as Legislator

The Civil Rights Act, which was passed by Congress in 1964 and outlawed employment discrimination by race and sex, and President [Lyndon] Johnson's consequent Executive Order 11246, requiring affirmative action by federal contractors, are regarded as the first government interventions in the labor market to have had significant impact on employers. However, until 1972, the federal focus was almost entirely on race; little attention was paid to the issue of sex discrimination.

The impact of affirmative action and litigation brought under Title VII [of the Civil Rights Act] has been a source of substantial debate. . . . In a postmortem on affirmative action that is fairly representative of the literature as a whole, Leonard (1990) concludes that, despite poor targeting and random enforcement, affirmative action and discrimination litigation did encourage the employment of women and minorities. However, gains appear to have been modest and perhaps to have been concentrated among government contractors who were most scrutinized for compliance. Because the [President Ronald] Reagan administration gutted the agencies responsible for enforcing equal employment policies, women and minority workers have ceased to progress and, by many measures, have lost ground in the labor market.

In sum, black women's breakthrough into clerical positions may have been somewhat facilitated by the passage and enforcement of civil rights legislation, but it is very difficult to estimate how large the impact of the legislation was. Nothing in the extant research supports the hypothesis that civil rights legislation played a significant role in opening clerical positions to black women.

## Conclusion

Each element of the access model was plausibly effective during the mid-1960s, when black women were dramatically increasing their representation in clerical work. . . . The strongest evidence for the model is the relative short supply of white women to the clerical labor market during the 1960s. While white women were not yet able to find openings in professional and managerial positions, their numbers in the labor force were not increasing as rapidly as new clerical positions were being created. The finding that opportunities improved for black workers most in times of tight labor markets is not new and reinforces the notion that a call for full employment policies must be an important component of a program for the economic progress of groups low in the labor market queue.

Government employment of black women as clerical workers was also likely a crucial element in opening clerical work to black women. The public sector has consistently accounted for twice the proportion of black women working as clerical workers as of white women. The impact of civil rights legislation is very difficult to assess, but it may have played a role in opening private sector clerical jobs to black women. Consequently, public sector employment and/or public oversight of the private labor market appear to be key to the achievement of equal employment opportunity in the labor market. The "privatization" promoted by the Reagan and Bush administrations, and still occurring nationwide, bodes ill for the potential labor market progress of women and ethnic minorities.

Technological and organizational change, particularly the development of isolated back-office staffs to perform routine data-entry functions, may also have facilitated the hiring of black women into clerical positions. . . . While lower-level clerical positions do represent a foot in the door into organizations and occupations with better working conditions and better rewards to experience, tenure, and training, if black women are not able to move up from these positions, the full measure of their apparent gains will not be realized.

Of the components of the access model, the evidence is weakest that improved opportunities for white women created a vacuum among the clerical ranks. White women did not increase their proportions in managerial and professional occupations until after the big surge of black women into clerical work. However, white women may have disproportionately shifted to the top rungs of the clerical workforce, leaving room for black women at the bottom, as suggested by the wage data.

One of the most interesting findings is the correspondence of black women's shift into clerical jobs with the fall in clerical wages relative to those of white women's wages on average. An avenue of research that might prove fruitful would be to test Strober and Arnold's (1987) hypothesis that occupations become accessible to groups lower on the labor market queue only when they become less attractive, specifically by paying less for education and other human capital, than other options available to groups better placed on the queue. Clerical work as a whole might have become less rewarding than other opportunities available to white women, or the least rewarding clerical occupations may have opened first and farther to black women.

Given the indication that black women are unevenly represented among clerical occupations, research is called for that focuses on why black women gained access to the specific clerical occupations in which they are found. Job characteristics other than pay, such as the level of contact with management and customers, may be important. Such work could shed light on the question of whether the occupational segregation of black women has truly diminished or if the boundary of black women's occupations has merely shifted to a new position within the clerical classifications. . . .

# References

Baran, Barbara, and Suzanne Teegarden. 1987. "Women's Labor in the Office of the Future: A Case Study of the Insurance Industry." In *Women, Households and the Economy*, ed. Lourdes Benería and Catherine Stimpson, pp. 201–24. New Brunswick, NJ: Rutgers University Press.

Blau, Francine, and Andrea Beller. 1991. "Black-White Earnings over the 1970s and 1980s: Gender Differences in Trends." *NBER Working Paper Series* W.P. #3736. Cambridge, MA: National Bureau of Economic Research.

Brown, Clair. 1988. "Income Distribution in an Institutional World." In *Three Worlds of Labor Economics*, ed. Garth Mangum and Peter Phillips, pp. 51–63. Armonk, NY: M.E. Sharpe.

Cappelli, Peter. 1993. "Are Skill Requirements Rising? Evidence from Production and Clerical Jobs." *Industrial and Labor Relations Review* 46 (3): 515–30.

Cunningham, James S., and Nadja Zalokar. 1992. "The Economic Progress of Black Women, 1940–1980: Occupational Distribution and Relative Wages." *Industrial and Labor Relations Review* 45 (3): 540–55.

Giddings, Paula. 1984. *When and Where I Enter: The Impact of Black Women on Race and Sex in America*. Toronto: Bantam Books.

Glenn, Evelyn Nakano, and Roslyn L. Feldberg. 1977. "Degraded and De-Skilled: The Proletarianization of Clerical Work." *Social Problems* 25 (1): 52–64.

Glenn, Evelyn Nakano, and Charles M. Tolbert II. 1987. "Technology and Emerging Patterns of Stratification for Women of Color: Race and Gender Segregation in Computer Occupations." In *Women, Work and Technology: Transformations*, ed. Barbara Drygulski Wright, pp. 318–31. Ann Arbor: University of Michigan Press.

Goldfeld, Randy J. 1987. *Training in the Automated Office: A Decision-Makers' Guide to Systems Planning and Implementation*. New York: Quorum Books.

Hartmann, Heidi I. 1987. "Internal Labor Markets and Gender: A Case Study of Promotion." In *Gender in the Workplace*, ed. Clair Brown and Joseph Pechman, pp. 59–105. Washington, DC: Brookings Institution.

Hughes, Karen D. 1989. "Office Automation: A Review of the Literature." *Relations Industrielles* 44 (3): 654–77.

King, Mary C. 1991. "Occupational Mobility: Changing Boundaries for Black Women, 1940 to the Present." Ph.D. diss., University of California, Berkeley.

———. 1992. "Occupational Segregation by Race and Sex, 1940–1988." *Monthly Labor Review* 115 (4): 30–37.

Leonard, Jonathan S. 1990. "The Impact of Affirmative Action Regulations and Equal Employment Law on Black Employment." *Journal of Economic Perspectives* 4 (4): 47–63.

Malveaux, Julianne. 1984. "Low Wage Black Women: Occupational Descriptions, Strategies for Change." Unpublished paper prepared for the NAACP Legal Defense and Educational Fund, Inc.

Menzies, Heather. 1982. *Computers on the Job: Surviving Canada's Microcomputer Revolution*. Toronto: James Lorimer.

Nelson, K. 1986. "Labor Demand, Labor Supply and the Suburbanization of Low-Wage Office Work." In *Production, Work, Territory: The Geographical Anatomy of Industrial Capitalism*, ed. Allen J. Scott and Michael Storper, pp. 149–71. Boston: Allen & Unwin.

Posthuma, Annie. 1987. "The Internationalization of Clerical Work: A Study of Off-Shore Services in the Caribbean." *Science Policy Research Unit Occasional Paper Series*, no. 24, University of Sussex, United Kingdom.

Stanton, Edward. 1962. "Why Can't I Get a Good Secretary?" *Personnel Journal* 41 (2): 64–72.

Strober, Myra H., and Carolyn Arnold. 1987. "The Dynamics of Occupational Segregation Among Bank Tellers." In *Gender in the Workplace*, ed. Clair Brown and Joseph Pechman, pp. 107–57. Washington, DC: Brookings Institution.

Strober, Myra H., and Lisa M. Catanzarite. 1988. "Changes in Black Women's Representation in Occupations and a Measure of the Relative Attractiveness of Occupations, 1960–1980." Unpublished paper prepared for the National Organization for Women Legal Defense and Education Fund.

Thurow, Lester C. 1975. *Generating Inequality: Mechanisms of Distribution in the U.S. Economy*. New York: Basic Books.

Treiman, Donald J., and Heidi I. Hartmann, eds. 1981. *Women, Work and Wages: Equal Pay for Jobs of Equal Value*. Washington, DC: National Academy Press.

U.S. Bureau of the Census. 1955–1979. *Current Population Reports, P-60 Series, Consumer Income*. Washington, DC: U.S. Government Printing Office.

U.S. Bureau of Labor Statistics. 1989. *Handbook of Labor Statistics*. Washington, DC: U.S. Government Printing Office.

U.S. Congress, Office of Technology Assessment. 1985. *Automation of America's Offices*. Washington, DC: U.S. Government Printing Office.

U.S. Council of Economic Advisors. 1991. *Economic Report of the President*. Washington, DC: U.S. Government Printing Office.

Adapted from "Black Women's Breakthrough into Clerical Work: An Occupational Tipping Model," *Journal of Economic Issues* 27 (4) (December 1993): 1097–1125. Reprinted with special permission of the copyright holder, the Association for Evolutionary Economics.

# 19

# Gender as More Than a Dummy Variable

## Feminist Approaches to Discrimination

### *Deborah M. Figart*

When economists acknowledge gender in analysis, they do so
by using simple, binary indicator functions, so-called dummy
variables, to alter intercept and/or slope coefficients in
regression . . . . though they are poor analytical substitutes for
more complete models of the role gender plays in market and
non-market transactions.

—*Esther Redmount, "Toward a Feminist Econometrics"*

Variables interacting with other variables are only constructs
with no agency to do anything. Although most theories assume
some sort of process lying behind the relations between
variables, those processes are rarely directly studied.

—*Joan Acker, "Thinking About Wages"*

From the domestic labor debate to bargaining models of the household, much
of the theoretical analysis of the political economy of gender has focused on
understanding the sphere of reproduction. In some sense this is understand-
able. By asserting the social and economic significance of reproduction, feminists have demonstrated both women's economic contributions and a major
site of power inequity. In contrast, when analyzing women's labor market experiences, feminist economists have tended to respond to existing theoretical

frameworks or rely on existing analytical categories. Although exposing the limits of neoclassical approaches, segmentation theory, and other constructs for understanding women's experiences has made an enormous contribution to the literature, there is little consensus on an alternative framework.

The basis for a feminist alternative is the assertion that the social construction of gender permeates men's and women's labor market experiences. To avow that gender is more than an independent—or dummy—variable is to posit the centrality of gender (as well as race and class) in economic analysis. Conventional economic methods tend to neglect the process by which gender interacts with and shapes other social forces and institutions. Using gender as an isolated slope coefficient or measuring discrimination as an unexplained residual adds little to our understanding of the causes and nature of discrimination. While these quantitative approaches have provided important tools for feminist advocacy, they treat gender as something to be "controlled" and discrimination as "other."

Often gender and race are added as dummies in a single equation to "control for" demographic differences, ceteris paribus. The influences of human capital, industry, occupation, and union status are also incorporated as independent variables which are hypothesized to affect a dependent variable such as wages. As Joyce Jacobsen and Andrew Newman (1995) demonstrated in their survey of articles published in the top labor journals from 1947 to 1995, there is a rising trend of incorporating a dummy variable to model gender differences, while use of gender interactions with other variables such as race has decreased. Jacobsen and Newman view the use of dummy variables as an attempt to "control for" the effects of gender. The choice of language seems appropriate. "Controlling for" gender and race implies that gender and race are marginal to the analysis—that is, descriptive characteristics of individual labor market participants that do not fundamentally challenge the basic theoretical constructs. These traditional methods are useful in quantifying discriminatory outcomes, but do not provide a comprehensive understanding of discriminatory processes. Thus, a dummy variable can measure the effect of gender or race on wages, but it does not distinguish between different causal explanations. Women's earnings, for example, are influenced by processes that affect the mean values of the remaining independent variables themselves.

Neoclassical economists typically define labor market discrimination as remunerating employees differently when they have equivalent productivity, and argue that employment discrimination is not easily measurable. Discrimination is measured by a residual, the unexplained portion of the differential in wages (see, for example, Gunderson 1989). This residual technique, developed by Ronald Oaxaca (1973), estimates separate wage regressions by gender. It decomposes the gender wage gap into two parts:

- differential means or characteristics (such as education and experience), and
- differential coefficients, or returns to characteristics.

The second portion, the unexplained residual after accounting for gendered differences in measurable independent variables, is termed discrimination. This crude method itself is problematic, relegating discrimination to an amorphous status. It is measurable, but not directly, shifting researchers' focus to correct specification of the directly measurable variables. Discrimination becomes "other"; we know discrimination only by what it is not. Some mainstream economists continue to assert that the residual would be small or zero if the model could be correctly specified. Nevertheless, early research by feminist labor economists sought to estimate this unexplained residual in order to document the existence of discrimination according to the accepted definition.

Dissatisfied with the limits of this approach to discrimination, many feminist labor economists are convinced that labor market segmentation, as well as other institutional variables and nonmarket factors, exert significant influences on wage differentials and that the wage gap and women's predominance in low-paid occupations are neither productivity-based nor voluntary, individual choices to minimize atrophy over the life cycle. Donald Treiman and Heidi Hartmann (1981) were among the first to demonstrate that the percentage of female workers in an occupation was negatively associated with wages and to explore techniques to overcome such discrimination. By shifting the direction of discrimination studies to occupational segregation, feminist economists had isolated a new directly measurable variable: the impact of the percentage of female workers in an occupation on the wage. Feminist researchers (e.g., Sorensen 1989), including many noneconomists, refocused their efforts toward consideration of what explains occupational segregation by gender.

A variety of explanations for occupational segregation have been proffered. The most sophisticated approaches have focused on the power dimensions of the wage-setting process, presenting historically and even geographically and organizationally specific accounts of the process of defining labor market segments. Through occupational segregation, certain jobs have become identified as "women's work"; these jobs pay less because they are feminized and deemed "unskilled." Several studies examine the contemporary process of feminization, arguing that occupational integration leads to "tipping," resegregation, and deskilling (Strober and Arnold 1987; Reskin and Roos 1990; King 1993). This new wave of research was accompanied by an explicitly feminist campaign for equal pay for work of comparable value (or pay equity) as a public policy.

The task facing feminist economists has been to merge the lessons gained from both neoclassical economists, who have emphasized the measurable manifestations of wage discrimination, and feminist scholars, many of them in other disciplines, who have focused on historical and organizational processes in assigning jobs and wages. . . . My goal in the following discussion is not to elaborate a complete theory or model of discrimination, but rather to present a representative view of the direction of feminist research.

## Rethinking Discrimination from a Feminist Perspective

Although feminist economics places gender (and, sometimes, class, race, ethnicity, and sexuality) as the center of analysis, it is more than a study of the status of women. Feminist research in economics also points to sources of bias in traditional theory. Feminist economists support methodological and pedagogical pluralism and diverse epistemologies, emphasizing praxis (Bergmann 1987; Ferber 1995; Nelson 1995). Feminist approaches to the study of discrimination share some critiques of neoclassical discrimination models with institutionalist and radical analyses of labor markets, but also provide a unique contribution through the development of gender theory. From institutional and radical analyses, a feminist theory of discrimination recognizes that the structure of labor markets and other economic and social institutions influences individual economic actors. . . . Gender theory focuses on the process by which gender shapes social institutions, including economic institutions (see Beechey 1988; Acker 1988; Chafetz 1989; Folbre 1994). . . .

For purposes of a broad-based research agenda, I propose a feminist definition of discrimination that emphasizes process as well as outcomes and measurable as well as unquantifiable repercussions. Discrimination is not "other"; it is more than an unexplained residual and cannot be controlled for through the use of dummy variables. *Labor market discrimination is a multidimensional interaction of economic, social, political, and cultural forces in both the workplace and the family, resulting in differential outcomes involving pay, employment, and status.* This definition provides a basis for the five propositions I outline below.

## Proposition 1: Feminist Approaches Are Motivated by a Concern for Understanding and Rectifying the Discrimination Faced by Women and Other Groups

Choosing to study women and/or use women's experiences to analyze labor markets is not the easiest path to academic recognition. Feminist research implies a commitment to relating theory not only to changing consciousness but to praxis. Barbara Bergmann articulates that the task that feminist economists have set is to produce the design for a more equitable future (1987, p. 145). Thus, feminist scholarship has enormous potential for public policy and political activism. Specifically, public policies that eradicate employment and wage discrimination are central subjects of inquiry. For investigations of employment inequity, feminist research has assessed ways to reduce occupational segregation and evaluated affirmative action in hiring and promotion. . . .

Attempting to influence public policy is not simple. Sometimes, feminist viewpoints that challenge the status quo, the market, or the existing hierarchy, as in the case of comparable worth, are quickly dismissed. Further, the feminist researcher is involved with her subject matter, which can pose its own challenges. In reflecting upon her involvement with the pay equity movement, Ronnie Steinberg writes: "Throughout this work, I have juggled the explicit contradiction between the openly political and biased character of advocacy for specific policy objectives and the supposed political neutrality and biasfree assumptions of scientific inquiry. Advocacy researchers, thus, live within these and other tensions" (1996, p. 2).

## Proposition 2: Feminist Approaches Discern the Limits of Static Models of Labor Market Outcomes and Investigate the Lived Experience of Discrimination

The traditional neoclassical portrayal of discrimination as the unexplained residual in well-specified wage equations renders discrimination as a nebulous, invisible construct. Yet women's experiences of discrimination are quite concrete, and broader research methodologies (including those borrowed from or developed within other social sciences) can be used to elucidate these experiences. In economics, I would argue that qualitative methods that supplement traditional positivism strengthens research, and that is a feminist contribution.[1] Another contribution feminist economists have made to the study of discrimination is their dedication to developing innovative data sets rather than relying upon usual measures in the Current Population Survey and National Longitudinal Survey. This necessarily expands our traditional conception of data requirements and encourages us to learn from and work with sociologists and psychologists who have experience with survey research, as pointed out by both Esther Redmount and Siv Gustafsson in the economic measurement section of *Out of the Margin: Feminist Perspectives on Economics* (1995). . . .

Feminist economists have looked to and received support from other social scientists and humanities scholars in their efforts to supplement statistical studies of discrimination with qualitative analysis. . . . [For example,]

Myra Strober, Suzanne Gerlach-Downie, and Kenneth Yeager evaluate the work environment and material conditions of child care workers by interviewing them and "allowing them to tell the story of the economics of their industry and occupation" (1995, p. 94). Although the wages of child care workers need to be raised significantly, as a realistic policy priority, the authors underscore the importance of improving job satisfaction among child care workers by means other than raising wages.

Utilizing interviews as a research method in work on discrimination also opens doors to employing other qualitative evidence. Much of what we know about the practice of job evaluation and pay equity or comparable worth implementation has resulted from case studies by feminist participant observers, combined with in-depth interviews and use of original sources, especially analyses of compensation policies, personnel law, and wage data. Analyses of bargaining agreements and personnel policies can document wage and career ladder differences within internal labor markets in civil service and public sector employment (see Figart 1989). Confidential employment records with salaries and career progression information were utilized by Maryellen Kelley (1982) in her study of discrimination in seniority systems at a private employer in the Boston area. Heidi Hartmann (1987) analyzed occupational gender segregation, wage differentials, and the predominance of women in lower-paid jobs at a large insurance company. Barbara Bergmann was one of the first economists to point to structural, internal labor market barriers that impeded women's career advancement and contributed to the wage gap by exploring the discrimination suit against Liberty Mutual Insurance Company (Bergmann 1986). The case study method has yielded great advances in feminist work on wage and employment discrimination.

### Proposition 3: Feminist Approaches Focus on Relative Power in the Workplace and the Process by Which Employers and Workers Act on Their Various Competing Interests

In the United States, and even in more centralized industrial relations systems, many of the decisions that replicate or modify women's employment status occur at the level of the individual firm. The analysis of firm behavior in feminist work on discrimination does not begin and end with corporate decisions concerning the hiring of individuals, but in creating and maintaining gendered job categories and assigning wage rates to those categories. In other words, firms are not impenetrable boxes that may have tastes and preferences for white men, disconnected from societal forces and discrimination. When we look inside the box, we find specific practices, policies, and behaviors that influence occupational segregation, the social construction of skill, and pay inequality. . . . By conducting research at the level of the firm or organization, feminist researchers can avoid functionalist analyses and focus directly on the processes by which discrimination is implemented and replicated. Further, organizational studies indicate the rigidity of gender labels and wage differentials. Once jobs are gender-typed and relative pay rates are established, they are difficult to change. Even when traditionally male job categories begin integrating, there is a tendency toward resegregation as gender composition tips toward feminization (Reskin and Roos 1990). . . .

Marlene Kim (1989) also emphasizes the rigidity of wage differentials by studying the origins of pay policies within the California civil service. Her study shows how historical wage setting can influence current wages and gender inequality, contrary to neoclassical comparative statics. She finds that an explicitly gendered occupational and salary structure that developed in the 1930s persists, because the employer never altered the relative pay differentials. Kim uses historical memos and interviews to document the gendered assumptions overtly built into the original classification structure at a time before equal opportunity policies and the threat of litigation. In Kim's words, "companies that never changed their discriminatory salary structure continue to pay inequitable wages" (p. 39). . . .

## Proposition 4: Feminist Approaches Demonstrate the Integrated Analysis of Economic, Social, and Political Institutions in Maintaining Discrimination

Along with attention to firm dynamics, feminists analyze the role of larger social institutions and forces external to the firm. Feminist studies of discrimination can entail exploring the relationship between gendered employment and

- economic development and fluctuations;
- family and household institutions; and
- the state and public policy.

. . . To match the extensive research chronicling discrimination at the firm level, there is a need for more inquiry into the interrelationship between labor markets and economic, social, and political institutions—as well as the interactions between these three spheres.

### Economic Factors

Clearly the contention that economic institutions play a role in discrimination is not a new insight. . . . Indeed, many explanations of occupational segregation have been grounded in the core insight of labor market segmentation theory: that employers benefit from the persistence of labor market discrimination by race and gender. More controversial has been whether white and/or male workers gain from earnings inequality, at least in the short run (see Rubery 1978; Williams 1987).

These economic interests interact with economic trends that also affect the process of discrimination. Feminist researchers have been exploring the ways economic change and development contribute to historical variation and diversity in women's labor market experiences. Contemporary economic restructuring affords a lens for analyzing the impact of economic change on gender relations (and vice versa). Women's increased labor force participation and the concomitant growth of feminized sectors of the economy have been analyzed as central to the emerging global economy (Bakker 1988; Standing 1989). M.V. Lee Badgett and Rhonda Williams (1994) have examined the role of economic restructuring in race and gender discrimination in the United States. Comparing the costs of ending versus continuing discrimination, they analyze how these costs are influenced by labor supply, labor costs, public policy, and worker resistance; each of these factors is, in turn, affected by economic restructuring. For example, they suggest that the resistance of male workers to increased hiring of women is likely to fall during restructuring as the importance of women's earnings to families increases, but that the benefits of this decreased resistance generally accrue to white women while African American women and men are more likely to remain in the expanding low-wage economy. . . .

## Family and Household Institutions

Supply-oriented analyses of women's labor market status start by assuming a division of labor in the family as exogenous to the labor market. As Francine Blau and Marianne Ferber (1992) have pointed out, when this is coupled with Gary Becker's model of the allocation of time between household and market work, the neoclassical framework reduces to a series of feedback effects. Women's lower labor force attachment yields lower wages that yield lower labor force participation, and so on. Historical changes in women's relationship to market work are left unexplored. By considering the role of the household as an economic institution, feminist analysis asserts that the distinction between market and nonmarket discrimination is blurred. . . .

Unfortunately, much of feminist theorizing about the household has also assumed married women's limited participation in the market economy (see Glenn 1987 for a summary). Yet historical research indicates that women's lower labor force attachment is not exogenous to the economy and is socially constructed. Full-time homemaking was rarely an option for most women of color and many working-class women. Married white women's relationship to market production declined in the nineteenth-century United States, in what Claudia Goldin (1990) depicts as the downward side of a U-shaped trend reinforced by social norms, institutionalized barriers, and the process of economic development. In a cross-country study, Nilüfer Çagatay and Sule Özler (1995) also find that women's share of the labor force exhibits a U-shaped pattern over the course of development. Finally, assumptions of heterosexuality are also embedded in many feminist treatments of the household (Badgett and Williams 1992; Matthaei 1995). . . .

In feminist models of discrimination, the diversity of family structures should be recognized to avoid simplistic formulations. Furthermore, the interactions between production and reproduction must be analyzed in a way that overcomes the supply and demand dichotomy. While traditional models present us with two options—either women choose certain jobs (supply-side) or employers discriminate and segment (demand-side)—in reality, these dynamics of choice and constraint cannot be isolated from each other. Patriarchal relations within the household and society influence both suppliers and demanders of labor, and both dynamics are integral to understanding discriminatory processes and outcomes.

## The State

The state's role in maintaining class, gender, and racial hierarchies deserves greater attention in feminist analyses of discrimination. There has not been enough study by feminist economists on the role of the state in labor market inequality in industrialized countries. If one were to conduct a literature search on the keywords "women" and "state," the citations would be almost exclusively on the social welfare system. One possible exception is research on how the state as an employer develops and maintains discriminatory salary structures in the comparable worth literature. In fact, state policies can also have a tremendous impact on the direction of economic development and thus on the opportunity structures by race and gender. Thus, feminists need to evaluate the state as an agent in private-sector labor markets. . . .

Feminist macroeconomists have made a substantial contribution to comparative economics and development economics by evaluating how state economic liberalization and structural adjustment policies have affected the division of labor in the household and in the labor market. Among the published collections, two such studies, *Unequal Burden* (Benería and Feldman 1992) and *Women in the Age of Economic Transformation* (Aslanbeigui, Pressman, and Summerfield 1994), present the following arguments. The policy shift from import substitution to export-led development coupled with the demands of governments and lending institutions for free markets, privatization, and fiscal constraint is assumed to be gender neutral. In reality, these policies have reinforced patriarchy, because the costs of privatization have fallen disproportionately on women and children while the benefits of restructuring accrue to men with greater access to property, capital, and credit. Thus, liberalization policies have resulted in increased poverty among women and their families and the reliance on low-wage, primarily female labor in the export-dependent and informal sectors, while leaving women responsible for family maintenance in the household without any more decision-making authority. Although discrimination is traditionally viewed from a microeconomic perspective, macroeconomic analysis draws attention to the role of the state in shaping the direction of development, including employment opportunities by gender, class, and race.

### Proposition 5: Feminist Approaches Recognize the Intersections of Gender, Race, Class, and Other Social Forces Which Influence the Development of Labor Market Structures

This proposition may be more controversial than the others because it asserts that economic institutions do not develop autonomously of gender. Many neoclassical and Marxist approaches argue that labor market structures develop according to strictly economic rationales, either profit maximization or class-based accumulation strategies. Then, discriminatory attitudes and/or institutions give women certain places within the structure. Gender theory argues that socially constructed notions of gender shape the available places. Thus, what historian Alice Kessler-Harris calls "subjective judgment," "custom," or "tradition" contributes to women's lower wages (1990, p. 7). All of these are gendered. . . .

While radical analyses of deskilling often accept socially designated skill definitions, feminists point out that skill is also a socially contingent and gendered concept. Although jobs are frequently deskilled as they are feminized, this process occurs on both material and ideological levels. Further, Sara Horrell, Jill Rubery, and Brendan Burchell (1989) suggest that the centrality of work in men's lives and self-perceptions leads to a greater tendency to view their own jobs as skilled. Relying on a comprehensive social survey in Great Britain, the researchers uncover differences in men's and women's descriptions of the skill content of their jobs, with women understating their job attributes.

However, the social construction of gender cannot be analyzed without attention to how concepts of gender are influenced by race, class, and other social constructs. Increasingly rejected is the notion that these dynamics can be analyzed as separate and additive; instead, the simultaneity and interlocking nature of systems of oppression is being demonstrated both theoretically and empirically. [A]nalyses also point to the dangers of universalizing our conceptions of what is feminine and masculine, since these concepts are themselves different by race and class. For example, the qualities and skills frequently depicted as "male" have not been attributed to black men (Williams 1993). . . .

## Conclusion: Toward a New Feminist Economic Theory of Discrimination

Gender operates as more than a dummy variable and economic analysis cannot simply control for gender by incorporating descriptive characteristics into wage regressions. . . . [A] more dynamic analysis is needed. The propositions outlined above suggest a broad analytical framework as the way in which to proceed. They are grounded in the assertion that labor market experience is a process resulting from and contributing to the historical development of labor market outcomes. These propositions draw attention to

- the relationship between research and praxis;
- the importance of methodological pluralism for a complex understanding of economic outcomes;
- the significance of power dynamics within firms;
- the impact of economic, social, and political institutions on the process of discrimination; and
- the intersections of gender, race, class, and other social constructs.

From the feminist studies of discrimination, a vision of the labor market emerges that is quite different than the textbook view. Rather than a sign of imperfections that can be smoothly eradicated by market forces, gender inequality is extensive and adaptive. Feminist economists are developing new theories that indicate that gender is fundamental to how the economy is constituted. At the same time, we must keep in mind that getting the theory right is only one part of the project; eliminating discrimination must be our ultimate objective.

## Note

1. This is not meant to imply that quantitative research is inherently male and qualitative research inherently female.

# References

Acker, Joan. 1988. "Class, Gender, and the Relations of Distribution." *Signs* 13 (3): 473–97.

——. 1991. "Thinking About Wages: The Gendered Wage Gap in Swedish Banks." *Gender & Society* 5 (3): 390–407.

Aslanbeigui, Nahid, Steven Pressman, and Gale Summerfield, eds. 1994. *Women in the Age of Economic Transformation: Gender Impact of Reforms in Post-Socialist and Developing Countries.* New York: Routledge.

Badgett, M.V. Lee, and Rhonda M. Williams. 1992. "The Economics of Sexual Orientation: Establishing a Research Agenda." *Feminist Studies* 18 (3): 649–57.

——. 1994. "The Changing Contours of Discrimination: Race, Gender, and Structural Economic Change." In *Understanding American Economic Decline,* ed. Michael A. Bernstein and David E. Adler, pp. 313–29. Cambridge: Cambridge University Press.

Bakker, Isabella. 1988. "Women's Employment in Comparative Perspective." In *Feminization of the Labor Force: Paradoxes and Promises,* ed. Jane Jenson, Elisabeth Hagen, and Ceallaigh Reddy, pp. 17–44. New York: Oxford University Press.

Beechey, Veronica. 1988. "Rethinking the Definition of Work: Gender and Work." In *Feminization of the Labor Force: Paradoxes and Promises,* ed. Jane Jenson, Elisabeth Hagen, and Ceallaigh Reddy, pp. 45–62. New York: Oxford University Press.

Benería, Lourdes, and Shelley Feldman, eds. 1992. *Unequal Burden: Economic Crises, Persistent Poverty, and Women's Work.* Boulder, CO: Westview Press.

Bergmann, Barbara R. 1986. *The Economic Emergence of Women.* New York: Basic Books.

——. 1987. "The Task of a Feminist Economics: A More Equitable Future." In *The Impact of Feminist Research in the Academy,* ed. Christie Farnham, pp. 131–47. Bloomington: Indiana University Press.

Blau, Francine D., and Marianne A. Ferber. 1992. *The Economics of Women, Men, and Work.* Englewood Cliffs, NJ: Prentice Hall.

Çagatay, Nilüfer, and Sule Özler. 1995. "Feminization of the Labor Force: The Effects of Long-Term Development and Structural Adjustment." *World Development* 23 (11): 1883–94.

Chafetz, Janet Saltzman. 1989. "Gender Equality: Toward a Theory of Change." In *Feminism and Sociological Theory,* ed. Ruth A. Wallace, pp. 135–57. Newbury Park, CA: Sage.

Ferber, Marianne A. 1995. "The Study of Economics: A Feminist Critique." *American Economic Review* 85 (2): 357–61.

Figart, Deborah M. 1989. "Collective Bargaining and Career Development for Women in the Public Sector." *Journal of Collective Negotiations in the Public Sector* 18 (4): 301–13.

Folbre, Nancy. 1994. *Who Pays for the Kids? Gender and the Structures of Constraint.* New York: Routledge.

Glenn, Evelyn Nakano. 1987. "Gender and the Family." In *Analyzing Gender: A Handbook of Social Science Research,* ed. Beth B. Hess and Myra Marx Feree, pp. 348–80. Newbury Park, CA: Sage.

Goldin, Claudia. 1990. *Understanding the Gender Gap: An Economic History of American Women.* New York: Oxford University Press.

Gunderson, Morley. 1989. "Male-Female Wage Differentials and Policy Responses." *Journal of Economic Literature* 27 (March): 46–72.

Gustafsson, Siv S. 1995. "Economic Measurement." In *Out of the Margin: Feminist Perspectives on Economics*, ed. Edith Kuiper and Jolande Sap, pp. 223–27. New York: Routledge.

Hartmann, Heidi I. 1987. "Internal Labor Markets and Gender: A Case Study of Promotion." In *Gender in the Workplace*, ed. Clair Brown and Joseph A. Pechman, pp. 59–105. Washington, DC: Brookings Institution.

Horrell, Sara, Jill Rubery, and Brendan Burchell. 1989. "Unequal Jobs or Unequal Pay?" *Industrial Relations Journal* 20 (3): 176–91.

Jacobsen, Joyce P., and Andrew E. Newman. 1995. "Cherchez les Femmes? How Labor Economists Study Women." Paper presented at International Association for Feminist Economics Conference, Tours, France.

Kelley, Maryellen. 1982. "Discrimination in Seniority Systems: A Case Study." *Industrial and Labor Relations Review* 36 (1): 40–54.

Kessler-Harris, Alice. 1990. *A Woman's Wage: Historical Meanings and Social Consequences*. Lexington: University of Kentucky Press.

Kim, Marlene. 1989. "Gender Bias in Compensation Structures: A Case Study of Its Historical Basis and Persistence." *Journal of Social Issues* 45 (4): 39–50.

King, Mary. 1993. "Black Women's Breakthrough into Clerical Work: An Occupational Tipping Model." *Journal of Economic Issues* 27 (4): 1097–125.

Matthaei, Julie. 1995. "The Sexual Division of Labor, Sexuality, and Lesbian/Gay Liberation: Toward a Marxist-Feminist Analysis of Sexuality in U.S. Capitalism." *Review of Radical Political Economics* 27 (1): 1–37.

Nelson, Julie A. 1995. "Feminism and Economics." *Journal of Economic Perspectives* 9 (2): 131–48.

Oaxaca, Ronald. 1973. "Male Female Wage Differentials in Urban Labor Markets." *International Economic Review* 14 (3): 693–709.

Redmount, Esther. 1995. "Toward a Feminist Econometrics." In *Out of the Margin: Feminist Perspectives on Economics*, ed. Edith Kuiper and Jolande Sap, pp. 216–22. New York: Routledge.

Reskin, Barbara F., and Patricia A. Roos. 1990. *Job Queues, Gender Queues*. Philadelphia: Temple University Press.

Rubery, Jill. 1978. "Structured Labour Markets, Worker Organisation and Low Pay." *Cambridge Journal of Economics* 2 (1): 17–36.

———. 1992. "Pay, Gender and the Social Dimension to Europe." *British Journal of Industrial Relations* 30 (4): 605–21.

Sorensen, Elaine. 1989. "The Wage Effects of Occupational Sex Composition: A Review and New Findings." In *Comparable Worth: Analyses and Evidence*, ed. M. Anne Hill and Mark R. Killingsworth, pp. 57–79. Ithaca, NY: ILR Press.

Standing, Guy. 1989. "Global Feminization through Flexible Labor." *World Development* 17 (7): 1077–95.

Steinberg, Ronnie. 1996. "Advocacy Research for Feminist Policy Objectives: Experiences with Comparable Worth." In *Feminism and Social Change: Bridging Theory and Practice*, ed. Heidi Gottfried, pp. 225–55. Urbana: University of Illinois Press.

Strober, Myra H., and Carolyn L. Arnold. 1987. "The Dynamics of Occupational Segregation among Bank Tellers." In *Gender in the Workplace*, ed. Clair Brown and Joseph A. Pechman, pp. 107–57. Washington, DC: Brookings Institution.

Strober, Myra H., Suzanne Gerlach-Downie, and Kenneth E. Yeager. 1995. "Child Care Centers as Workplaces." *Feminist Economics* 1 (1): 93–120.
Treiman, Donald J., and Heidi I. Hartmann, eds. 1981. *Women, Work, and Wages: Equal Pay for Jobs of Equal Value*. Washington, DC: National Academy Press.
Williams, Rhonda. 1987. "Capital, Competition, and Discrimination: A Reconsideration of Racial Earnings Inequality." *Review of Radical Political Economics* 19 (2): 1–15.
———. 1993. "Race, Deconstruction, and the Emergent Agenda of Feminist Economic Theory." In *Beyond Economic Man: Feminist Theory and Economics*, ed. Marianne A. Ferber and Julie A. Nelson, pp. 144–53. Chicago: University of Chicago Press.

Adapted from "Gender as More Than a Dummy Variable: Feminist Approaches to Discrimination," *Review of Social Economy* 55 (1) (Spring 1997): 1–32. Reprinted with permission of the Association for Social Economics.

# 20

# Just Checking It Out

## Exploring the Significance of Informal Gender Divisions Among American Supermarket Employees

### *Martin Tolich and Celia Briar*

The ethnographic research component that informs the first part of this chapter
was conducted by Martin Tolich between 1987 and 1991. Its original focus
was on the effects of deskilling of supermarket employees as a result of the
introduction of automatic scanners at the checkouts. Because the males and
females in the group Tolich surveyed all had the same pay and job description, he assumed that gender inequalities would be at the most a minor consideration. However, it soon became clear from the interviews that there were
major gender divisions between these apparently equal workers and that this
was an overriding concern of the women in the study (as well as a source of
unease among some of the men). Tolich discussed his unexpected findings
with colleague Celia Briar, and the second part of the paper is her interpretation of his results. Informal gender discrimination is poorly understood by
those in a position to take action on it, difficult to measure and hard to act
upon in policy terms, yet has a major impact on the quality of women's
working lives. Therefore, the paper ends by suggesting how we may begin to
look at ways of addressing informal discrimination in social policy.

## The Study

The study was based on interviews with sixty-five supermarket employees in
urban northern California. The participants, of whom twenty-two were
women, were contacted through snowball sampling generated by their friends,

colleagues, and trade union representatives. In addition to conducting the interviews, Tolich was allowed systematically to observe the workers in the checkstands [checkouts] over sustained periods and to listen to the verbal exchanges that took place. He also socialized with the workers and asked informal questions in what turned out to be a most important space: the staff canteen. This was not only where staff met, at lunchtime, at the beginning and end of shifts, and at morning and afternoon teatime, but where the labor schedule was kept, which assigned workers to specific tasks.

The sixty-five participants were employed in standard 35,000–square-foot supermarkets owned by large chains—Lucky Stores, Safeway, Albertsons, and Raleys—as well as in some independent stores. These employees ranged in age from nineteen to fifty-nine. Only three of the informants were members of an ethnic minority: two were Hispanic and one was black. Ten employees had the job description "apprentice clerk" and the remaining fifty-five were classed as "journeymen clerks." It is this latter group that is the main focus of this paper.

## Organizational Structure

The supermarkets' internal occupational hierarchy was relatively flat and short for most workers (Montagna 1977, p. 319). Workers of both sexes were initially recruited at the level of "courtesy clerk." This job entailed bagging groceries, putting away "go-backs" (items that the customers did not buy), cleaning the lavatories and offices, and collecting the shopping carts from the car parks [parking lots]. Most of these workers were promoted to the next stage in the occupational structure— "apprentice clerk" —within six months. After eighteen months, most of the workers had reached the position of "journeyman clerk." It was at this point that the upward mobility of most of the employees ceased. A small number of workers were allowed to move into management. Within the supermarket occupational structure, all positions were apparently equally open to men and women. However, the degree of (unpaid) sacrifice of personal time, with no guarantee of eventual success, was a major barrier, especially to the women, who were more likely to have unpaid work responsibilities. Most of the male clerks interviewed had at some stage made attempts to climb this ladder, whereas most of the women had not.

## Task Segregation by Gender

The "journeymen clerks" were neither a numerically male-dominated nor a typically feminized group: about half of the workers eligible to be interviewed were female; all were unionized. The rates of pay were relatively good and all the employees received fringe benefits such as dental and medical insurance. However, despite this there was an informal but pervasive gender division of labor.

Tasks in the supermarket were assigned via a scheduling list. One person would be assigned to the position of "number one" checker, and when a queue of customers built up, number one would call on "number two" on the list, and so on. Thus, during the busy times in the store, staff working in the aisles pricing and replenishing stock would be called to the checkouts in a predetermined order. Anyone assigned as number one checker could expect to spend his or her entire shift in the checkout, and number two would be there for most of the time. Potentially this was a way of ensuring that the tasks were divided in an equitable manner.

In practice, however, the male clerks were routinely assigned to tasks that took them to "the floor" throughout the grocery store, replenishing shelves, pricing goods, and building displays as well as spending some time on the checkouts. They thus enjoyed considerable variety in their work. As one thirty-five-year-old male clerk, Alex, put it:

> Every two hours you're doing something else. And you're constantly doing new products. As the seasons change the produce changes: strawberry season comes, peach season comes—there's a lot of variety in that. That's one thing I like about it.

Female clerks, on the other hand, did not share this variety in their work. They were much more likely to spend their entire shift in the checkouts, and excluded from the more varied floor work—even the light work like "facing" (tidying) the shelves in the main body of the store. The only job rotation that the women had for the most part during an entire shift was during the slack times. Then they were required to "fluff up" (tidy and replenish) the displays of products such as sweets, gum, magazines, and cigarettes immediately adjacent to the checkouts. That way they were close at hand to return to checking as soon as the numbers of customers increased.

## Registering Dissatisfaction with Task Segregation

### Prospects for Promotion

Most obviously, the gender divisions affected promotion prospects. One of the criteria for promotion is knowledge of the various departments in the store, and males were able to accumulate this experience during their time out of the checkstand, whereas the women were not. Further, when the men were in the checkstand, they had the motivation to deal rapidly with the customers so that they could return to the floor. Thus the scanners recorded them as being more rapid workers than the women, who were confined to the checkouts without the prospect of any relief. Nevertheless, few of the males in this study in fact gained any long-term entry to promotion after journeyman clerk status, and the effects of gender segregation on their career prospects were not a major area of complaint raised by the women participants.

## Quality of Working Life

The effects of task segregation upon their self-esteem, sense of identity, and quality of working life were raised by the women employees as the major issue. The interviews exposed a huge amount of frustration, resentment, and disappointment. One major facet of the gender divisions was that the women workers were given the main responsibility for "emotion management." By contrast, men working on the floor were able to avoid interaction with the customers to a considerable degree (Hochschild 1983; Oghonna and Wilkinson 1988; Rafaeli 1989; Rafaeli and Sutton 1989; Tolich 1991, 1993). Several participants reported knowing men who had chosen to work on the night crew, stocking shelves, so as to avoid the checkstand completely. The women's objection tended to be less about checking per se than the fact that they had to spend so many hours being pleasant on demand, while the men did not. Sarah explained her ambivalence about checking as follows:

> I like to check. Don't get me wrong. Safeway is my social hour. The only time when I get to see people is at work. But there are times when I don't feel that good and don't want to feel happy, and I just want to get out on the floor. It doesn't have to be all the time—just once in a while. It's like day in, day out, I have to check.

There were no mixed feelings about the express lane, however. This was where customers bought nine items or less and paid by cash, making each interaction extremely brief. All of the men and women found this express checkstand to be socially estranging. It gave workers a strong sense of being constrained, and they called the express lane "the pit," the "ball and chain," and "the cage." Respondents reported that management saw the express lane as "women's work." Freda expressed her feelings about it:

> After an eight-hour shift "express" gets real tiring. And it puts you in a bad mood. I hate it. It is so antiproductive because you just end up being mean

to customers. I just stop talking. I won't say "Hi" to my customers. Like I will just check and get them out of there.

Another aspect of the job that caused the female workers dissatisfaction was that they were more physically confined and more closely monitored and supervised than the males (Cockburn 1985, p. 10). Out on the floor, male workers could be out of sight of management as well as free of the electronic monitoring of items scanned per minute in the checkstand. As a result of their relative lack of freedom of movement and variety and the al- most constant surveillance under which they worked, many of the female journeymen clerks said that they would prefer to return to being courtesy clerks if only they could earn the same money. None of the men expressed a desire to return to being a courtesy clerk, and most answered with a facial expression of disbelief at being asked.

Many of the women expressed considerable bitterness about the gender- based allocation of tasks. They could see no valid reason for it and regarded it as unfair and discriminatory. Hannah commented, "They are male chau- vinist pigs . . . that look down on you a lot." While the women acknowledged that there were tasks in the store that required physical strength (although in fact most of the heavy work was done by the male night crew), they resented not being given many jobs that were well within their capabilities.

Some male workers were aware that the discrimination soured relations between male and female workers. Nineteen-year-old José commented,

> Women hardly ever get out on the floor. But men do, and that's the reason why men and women don't really get along. They are always stuck in the checkstand, and they want to get out now and again.

Some male workers simply regarded their position as "lucky" and chose not to question it. Tom, for example, said,

> You are supposed to learn the facts of the store as you progress, but that depends whether you are a guy or a girl. . . . I was really lucky because I got out of the checkstand. It's fun to check for a while, but it gets real monoto- nous, so not having to check is a privilege. All the girls have to do is check. The guys are always out of the checkstand. It's kind of funny.

Other male clerks attempted to justify the unequal division of labor that worked in their favor, claiming that women were better at emotional man- agement. The female clerks disputed this, claiming that they, too, tired of constant interactions with customers.

Managers, who were responsible for assigning staff to particular duties, also took the view that women were more suited for emotional management than men. However, the women reported that when they complained about the gender division of labor they were given no explanation at all. One woman who had been told she could not work on the floor said, "They don't give you a reason. It's like a parent who says 'because.'" There were reports that some managers actively contributed to the sexist bias in the culture of the workplace. A male clerk reported that a manager had taught him a crude little rhyme that went, "If you squat to pee, you check before me."

Clearly, the women in the study had a strong sense of the injustice of being informally denigrated and denied power and autonomy relative to their male coworkers. Shortly after the interviews were finished, a woman brought a case of sex discrimination through her union as a result of this kind of treatment. She was successful. In 1992 a U.S. district judge in San Francisco ruled that Lucky Stores Inc. discriminated against female employees by systematically denying them promotions, training, and desirable work assignments. The decision brought to a close a four-year class action suit filed by women on behalf of 10,000 Lucky workers. Moreover, similar suits were filed against Safeway, Albertsons, and Save Mart (according to the *San Francisco Chronicle*, August 19, 1992). For now there is a legal precedent outlawing task segregation in the U.S. supermarket industry.

## Discussion

Differentiation of workers by sex is a central feature of the organization of work (Game and Pringle 1996). It may even be the central feature. Men and women are seldom found doing exactly the same work (Bradley 1989, p. 1). Although the specific kinds of work done by women and men vary between cultures and change over time, discrimination and inequalities remain intact. They predate capitalism and exist outside it (Cockburn 1985, p. 32) and have survived the upheavals of war, technological transformation, and women's increased numerical participation in paid work since World War II (Briar 1997).

Within the paid workforce, direct practices by male workers in better-paid occupations, intentionally excluding women, were commonplace in the early part of the twentieth century and only gradually diminished. These are well documented (Walby 1986). Since women have gained access to the professions and some other former male preserves, discrimination has changed its form. Women have been "included" but in less well-paid, lower-status positions in devalued supportive and helpmeet roles in relation to men (Davies 1996). For this reason, formal desegregation of the labor force through strong

equal opportunities policies is commonly regarded as the solution to the problem of gender inequality in paid work (e.g., Reskin and Roos 1990).

However, this case study of supermarket employees suggests that the problem of sex discrimination in the workplace may well be more intractable
than is commonly assumed. These women workers had obtained equal employment opportunities according to conventional definitions. Their job descriptions were formally identical to those of their male coworkers within
the same stores, with the same pay, formal promotion opportunities, and fringe
benefits. There were no reports of sexual harassment. Yet the women were
still given a very different experience and quality of working life compared
with the men, purely on account of their gender.

In order to assess the possibilities of addressing this form of discrimination, it may be useful to briefly reexamine how this occurred. As we have
seen, it was the managers across a number of supermarket chains who were
responsible for the gendered allocation of work via the scheduling lists.
Although the male employees were aware that they benefited from being
freed from the checkstands, with the consequent freedom from constant
surveillance and emotional labor, they arguably did not have the power to
initiate this sexual division of work. In some cases the male clerks were
somewhat bemused (but grateful) about the privileges they were given at
the women's expense.

However, it is not unusual for employers to discriminate against women
(Reskin and Roos 1990; Roper 1994; Adkins 1995; Briar 1997) or to accede
surprisingly willingly to working men's demands for privileges relative to
women. Reskin and Roos (1990), examining a range of American occupations over a twenty-year period, found that employers systematically discriminated in favor of men for the best jobs, even when there were financial
disadvantages in doing so. If employers and managers discriminate on the
grounds of gender, then it may be argued that capitalism and the labor market are not gender-neutral but patriarchal (Adkins 1995; Briar 1997). The
implications of this have not yet been translated into social policies affecting
working women. There is a strong assumption embedded in equal opportunities policies that employers' perceived interests lie in recruiting and retain-
ing the best employees in the most desirable positions, irrespective of gender
(or will do so once they have become enlightened). If this assumption is
incorrect, it is likely to undermine the effectiveness of efforts to promote
gender equity at work.

In fact, recent research suggests that "a job" is not a gender-neutral category, but rather reflects sex-typed expectations vis-à-vis the man or woman
admitted to the position. It is hardly surprising, therefore, that male and
female employees with the same job description find themselves expected

to carry out different work or perform the work differently. The specific kinds of gendered requirements appear nevertheless to vary among different types of occupations. In Lisa Adkins's research in the British tourist industry, the female workers were required as a condition of their job to present a smiling, (hetero)sexualized "attractive" image which the men were not (Adkins 1995). In Michael Roper's (1994) study of masculinity in organizations, women managers, unlike their male counterparts, were expected to be "motherly." As we have seen, in Tolich's study of supermarket workers, the women were obliged to perform far more emotional labor than the men (see, for example, Hochschild 1983). They also played an auxiliary, "helpmeet" role relative to the men by freeing them to do more varied and interesting work (Davies 1996).

This issue of gendered jobs has not even begun to be addressed in employment policies, where a job is seen as a neutral category. Certainly, it is not yet recognized that the requirements of a job are likely to vary according to the gender of the incumbent.

## Conclusion

The main implication of these findings is that the problem of gender discrimination in employment is likely to be more difficult to tackle than is commonly supposed. It suggests that even if women are successful in obtaining equal pay, fringe benefits, and broadly equal opportunities, that may well not be the end of the matter. Gendered task segregation can exist even among employees with the same job description, seriously affecting quality of working life. This is an important issue, and the women in this study clearly had a strong sense of injustice at being denied the levels of freedom and variety enjoyed by their male workmates.

This group of women was ultimately able to bring a successful court case through their union. This could have been made feasible by the routine nature and semiformality of the scheduling lists used by supermarket managers. However, the problem of informal sex discrimination among groups of workers with the same formal job description may well extend to groups of women who have not been able to take such action. Anecdotal evidence suggests, for example, that female lecturers are expected to spend more time attending to students' problems, leaving their male colleagues more time to do research. Precisely because of its informality, we have at present no way of knowing the full extent of gendered task segregation among apparent equals. Additional qualitative research will be needed to monitor the extent and dynamics of this type of gender discrimination and their effects on working life in different types of organizations.

## References

Adkins, L. 1995. *Gendered Work: Sexuality, Family and the Labour Marke.* Buckingham, UK: Open University Press.

Bradley, H. 1989. *Men's Work, Women's Work.* Cambridge, UK: Polity Press.

Briar, C. 1997. *Working for Women? Gendered Work and Welfare Policies in Twentieth Century Britain.* London: UCL Press.

Cockburn, C. 1985. *Machinery of Dominance.* London: Pluto Press.

Davies, C. 1996. "The Sociology of Professions and Profession of Gender." *Sociology* 30 (4): 661–78.

Game, A., and R. Pringle. 1996. "Gender at Work." In *Economics as a Social Science,* ed. G. Argyrous. Sydney: Pluto Press.

Hochschild, A.R. 1983. *The Managed Heart: The Commercialization of Human Feeling.* Berkeley: University of California Press.

Montagna, P. 1977. *Occupations and Society: Towards a Sociology of the Labour Market.* New York: John Wiley.

Ogbonna, E., and B. Wilkinson. 1988. "Corporate Strategy and Corporate Culture: The Management of Change in the Supermarket Industry." *Personnel Review* 17 (6): 10–14.

Rafaeli, A. 1989. "When Cashiers Meet Customers: An Analysis of the Role of Supermarket Cashiers." *Academy of Management Journal* 32 (2): 245–73.

Rafaeli, A., and R. Sutton. 1989. "The Expression of Emotion in Organizational Life." *Research in Organizational Behavior* 11: 1–42.

Reskin, B., and P. Roos. 1990. *Job Queues, Gender Queues: Explaining Women's Inroads into Male Occupations.* Philadelphia: Temple University Press.

Roper, M. 1994. *Masculinity and the British Organisation Man Since 1945.* Oxford: Oxford University Press.

Tolich, M. 1991. "Check It Out: Life in the Grocery Lane: A Study of Alienation among Supermarket Clerks." Ph.D. diss., University of California at Davis.

———. 1993. "Alienating and Liberating Emotions at Work: Supermarket Clerks' Performance of Customer Service." *Journal of Contemporary Ethnography* 22 (3): 361–81.

Walby, S. 1986. *Patriarchy at Work.* Cambridge: Polity Press.

---

Adapted from "Just Checking It Out: Exploring the Significance of Informal Gender Divisions Amongst American Supermarket Employees," *Gender, Work and Organization* 6 (3) (July 1999): 129–33. Reprinted with permission.

# Section 5

# Appendix

**Key Terms**

access model
crowding hypothesis
deskilling
feedback effects
gender theory
hegemony
heterodox theory
individual discrimination
institutional discrimination
intraoccupational segregation
job competition
organizational adaptation
political economy
queuing theory
segmentation theory
tipping

**Discussion Questions**

1. In a heterodox or political economy perspective on discrimination, why might occupational segregation or the wage gap persist, despite the intentions of "good employers," those who are committed to eradicating statistical discrimination?
2. Explain how Shulman's four concepts of organizational adaptation, distributional incentives, flexibility, and positive feedback might be applied to either (a) the example of the motor bus industry in Section 4 or (b) King's discussion of black women's entry into clerical occupations.
3. What roles do skill and technological change play in heterodox approaches to discrimination?
4. Does a heterodox perspective allow a role for the government and public policy in alleviating discrimination? Explain.

5. Feminists have criticized how mainstream models define as well as measure discrimination. Summarize this critique. Given this starting point, what makes a feminist perspective different from a mainstream one, and why would such an approach be interdisciplinary?

6. Discuss ways in which the study of supermarket employees by Tolich and Briar reveals issues of:
   a. intraoccupational segregation
   b. informal discrimination
   c. gender culture and stereotypes

## Exercise

1. As in Section 4, one way to organize your thoughts about the various pieces that help to build a heterodox theory explaining the economic status of women is to complete the theory matrix on the next page.

## Further Reading

Acker, Joan. 1990. "Hierarchies, Jobs, Bodies: A Theory of Gendered Organizations." *Gender & Society* 4 (2): 139–58.

Cornwall, Richard, and Phanindra Wunnava, eds. 1991. *New Approaches to Economic and Social Analyses of Discrimination*. New York: Praeger.

Nelson, Robert L., and William P. Bridges. 1999. *Legalizing Gender Inequality: Courts, Markets, and Unequal Pay for Women in America*. Cambridge: Cambridge University Press.

Reich, Michael, David M. Gordon, and Richard C. Edwards. 1973. "A Theory of Labor Market Segmentation." *American Economic Review* 63 (2): 359–65.

Reskin, Barbara F., and Patricia A. Roos. 1990. *Job Queues, Gender Queues: Explaining Women's Inroads into Male Occupations*. Philadelphia: Temple University Press.

Sorensen, Elaine. 1990. "The Crowding Hypothesis and Comparable Worth." *Journal of Human Resources* 25 (1): 55–89.

## Heterodox Theory Matrix

|  | Crowding | Queuing | Segmentation | Gender |
|---|---|---|---|---|
| Key names? |  |  |  |  |
| Discrimination? In the short run? In the long run? |  |  |  |  |
| Causes of occupational segregation? |  |  |  |  |
| Causes of wage gap? |  |  |  |  |
| Strengths of this theory? |  |  |  |  |
| Criticisms, omissions, or weaknesses? |  |  |  |  |

# Section 6

# Policies Affecting Women, Work, and Families

Women have made progress in achieving economic equity. Public policy has been one of several factors that have helped women in their pursuit of equity. But there is still far to go. This section explores alternative policy proposals that are designed to help women make gains in the labor market and to value the caring work necessary for social reproduction. While we cannot cover all possible public policies that would improve the economic status of women, the five chapters in this section offer a launching point for consideration and discussion.

Before turning to the proposed policies discussed by the authors, a brief summary of prior and existing policies would be helpful. The first attempts to use labor legislation to improve economic well-being in the United States came out of the Progressive Era (approximately 1900–1920). Individual states passed minimum wage laws and health and safety regulations providing for maximum hours and other protections. However, the laws were gender-specific, covering only female, not male workers. Although it was very restrictive about intervening in labor markets, the U.S. Supreme Court permitted these regulations because it acknowledged a larger social purpose in protecting the health and well-being of women as future mothers.

Feminists were divided about gender-specific protective legislation. While some advocates for women lobbied for the legislation as realistic in light of women's different position in society and consequent weaker bargaining position with employers, they were opposed by those who focused on the achievement of political rights (suffrage) and the demand for equal treatment. The division was partly marked by class interests, with working-class women's organizations concerned about sweatshop conditions in factories and shops. Educated, middle-class career women, better poised to benefit from equal opportunities, viewed protective legislation as a barrier to access to men's jobs. The differences between these two groups of stakeholders—

sometimes labeled the "equality-versus-difference debate"—continue to influence feminist discussion of public policy. Many contemporary feminists seek a middle ground, acknowledging historically based differences in men's and women's situations while asserting their fundamental equality.

During the post-World War II period, as more and more women gained access to education, stayed in the labor force after marriage and children, and defined the scope of their societal contributions beyond the private sphere, policies based on "equality" (rather than "difference") principles found more fertile soil. The Equal Pay Act of 1963, mandating "equal pay for equal work," passed after an eighteen-year fight in Congress. Originally written to legislate the broader principle of equal pay for work of a "comparable quality or quantity," the compromise that passed targeted women who work side-by-side with men in the same job. Pay for female-dominated occupations remained untouched. A year later, Title VII of the Civil Rights Act of 1964 guaranteed equal opportunity and equal treatment by race, sex, religion, and national origin (later amended to include disability, age, and pregnancy). Affirmative action is required for federal contractors and permissible for other employers, though fixed quotas are illegal. While the United States relies upon these two pillars of equality legislation originally passed in the 1960s, industrialized countries all over the world, from Canada to South Africa and members of the European Union, have adopted further policies to buttress support for part-time, contingent, and other low-wage workers; to provide paid leave for new mothers and fathers; to untie access to health care from having a breadwinner job; and to embrace equal pay for work of equal value. In contrast, the United States has weakened enforcement of equality policies and drastically reduced economic support for poor mothers. The Family and Medical Leave Act of 1993, which provides job protection but not paid leave, has been virtually the only national public policy victory in recent years.

Increased inequality among women has highlighted the problems of low-income women, both the working poor and welfare recipients. In fact, these two groups overlap, since many welfare recipients cycle in and out of jobs or supplement their benefits with paid work. In the opening policy chapter of Section 6, Randy Albelda and Chris Tilly cite what they call "the triple whammy" as the reasons behind the poverty of single-mother families. These families are poor because (1) discrimination means women earn less than men at their jobs, even when they are providers; (2) caregiving is still difficult to combine with full-time breadwinning; and (3) any household with only one adult earner will be disadvantaged compared with two-earner households. Recent "welfare reform," as described in their chapter "Single, with Children," has failed as an antipoverty strategy because it provides an incomplete response to a three-part problem. The promarriage aspects of the bill also fail to recognize the degree to which single parenthood reflects broad social trends that resist government modification.

Albelda and Tilly briefly summarize a policy agenda that addresses the first two whammies by raising women's wages and providing support services to assist with caring work. These are policies that can benefit many low-income women. Some key elements of this agenda are explored in subsequent chapters. "The Minimum Wage Increase: A Working Woman's Issue" by Jared Bernstein, Heidi Hartmann, and John Schmitt demonstrates how a seemingly gender-neutral policy aimed at low-income workers can, in fact, be construed as a "women's issue." Janice Peterson, in her chapter on "The Challenge of Comparable Worth," examines an unfinished item on policy agendas: recognition of the institutionalized discrimination against female-dominated occupations. The potentially affected occupations range in socioeconomic status from service jobs such as nursing home aides to professional occupations such as librarians; men as well as women in these fields are affected by unequal pay for work of comparable value. Comparable worth (also known as *pay equity*) is an issue that unites both "equality" and "difference" perspectives by demanding equal treatment for men and women in feminized jobs while recognizing the value of traditionally female skills and tasks.

Simply relying upon jobs paying good wages does not address the problem, identified in Section 3, of how society should organize and value the work of social reproduction. Such policies are also an incomplete response to the problem of poverty. Barbara Bergmann argues that it is unrealistic to expect "good jobs" to fully answer the needs of single mothers and their children. In "Curing Child Poverty in the United States," she defends the need for and the affordability of comprehensive child care, not just for poor families, but for the middle class as well. Betty Holcomb, in "Why Americans Need Family Leave Benefits and How They Can Get Them," focuses on situations in which commodified care may not be an ideal solution, proposing that the goals of the 1993 Family and Medical Leave Act be extended to incorporate federally subsidized paid leave.

The contributions in this section cover only a few of the policies that might foster economic equity by gender. They leave many other questions unaddressed. Under what conditions should society continue to offer income support for caregiving in the home? How can jobs be restructured to accommodate all workers with family responsibilities without stigma or prolonged economic penalties? Are reducing the standard workweek and offering flexible work schedules viable options? What is the impact of seemingly gender-neutral policy proposals such as Social Security privatization or health care reform? How do we degender the images of breadwinners and caregivers so that both men and women can make unbiased life choices?

# 21

# Single, with Children

## The Economic Plight of Single Mothers

*Randy Albelda and Chris Tilly*

> It's not just thinking about whether or not you can afford to go
> to a movie, but you have to think about can the kids and I stop
> and get a soda if we've been out running errands. It's a big
> decision, 'cause we just don't have much spending money.
>
> —*Single mother of two in Wisconsin, cited in Mark Rank*,
> Living on the Edge

As of 2000, 33 percent of single-mother families lived in poverty, as opposed to 7 percent of other families with children (U.S. Bureau of the Census 2001). And while the people in single-mother families account for only 6 percent of the U.S. population, they account for close to 30 percent of all poor people. The high rate of poverty among single-mother families has been under intense scrutiny over the last two decades, and the policies intended to alleviate that poverty—usually referred to as "welfare" in the United States—have come under attack and been radically transformed by the states and the federal government. This chapter discusses the reasons why single mothers fare so poorly, dispels some of the powerful myths used to justify harsh welfare policies, and discusses what alternative policies might look like.

### The Triple Whammy

Poverty among single mothers is not new: women raising their children alone have always been poor. Four decades ago, in 1959, 60 percent of single-mother families were poor, compared to 16 percent of other families with children. Despite all the sound and fury around the issue since the early 1980s, the basic reasons why single mothers and their children are poor have not changed. We call them the "triple whammy."

### The Gender Wage Gap

The first strike against single mothers is that the one working-age adult of the family is a woman, and women still earn only about two-thirds as much per hour as do men. While the vast majority of women who work could support themselves, only about half could support an entire family. The Institute for Women's Policy Research found that, nationwide, 45 percent of all women would earn too little to bring a family of three up to the poverty threshold (including day care costs for one child) *even if they worked full-time, year-round* (Spalter-Roth, Hartmann and Andrews 1993).

### Cradles to Rock, Mouths to Feed

Having children affects families' economic well-being. Young children add to the family's needs without contributing to its earning power. Caring for them claims time, energy, and money. Child care imperatives limit many mothers to part-time work, workplaces close to home, and/or jobs that offer flexibility—usually at a cost in terms of compensation and promotion opportunities. In a recent survey of women in four cities, child care constraints prevented almost one-third of women from seeking a job, prompted one in eight to turn down a job, and caused one in ten job-holding women to quit or be fired (Moss and Tilly 2001). Recent research by Jane Waldfogel (1997) finds that mothers earn less than women who are not mothers, while lone mothers earn less than married mothers, after adjusting for age, experience, and educational levels.

### Not Enough Hands

The simple fact is that families with more adults can earn more. Single-mother families, by definition, have one adult to both earn income and take care of children. This completes the triple whammy.

## Why Aren't "They" Married? New Choices, Old Problems

In 2000, one out of four families with children was a female-headed household, compared to one out of every ten in 1960 (U.S. Census Bureau 2001). The trend of a growing proportion of women who are single mothers—in-

cluding those who were once married and those who were never married—
holds for black, white, and Latino women; for middle-class as well as poor
women; and in all parts of the country. In fact, the trend is growing in Europe
as well—and the United States is far from the extreme case. In Denmark, for
example, births out of wedlock increased from 8 percent of all births in 1960
to 45 percent in 1988! In fact, rates of out-of-wedlock births in France, Britain, Norway, and Sweden all exceeded U.S. rates (Lewis 1993). Of course,
having a child out of wedlock is only one source of single motherhood; separation, divorce, and the death of a spouse are others. In the United States,
only one-quarter of single parents have never been married.

Why are more women becoming single mothers? Women have more
choices than they once did. Divorce has become easier, tolerance for domestic violence has decreased, and there is far more acceptance of a woman
raising a child alone. Men have more choices, too, with fewer strictures against
divorce or abandonment, and fewer pressures to marry the mothers of their
children. Shifting patterns of labor force participation and wages have also
influenced family structure. As more women become economically active in
the paid labor force, their ability to be self-supporting increases, making
marriage less of an economic necessity, even though earning enough to raise
children as a single mother is far from easy. Men's falling wages and employment rates have also contributed to diminishing marriage rates. Men are
reluctant to get married when their incomes are low—although they are not
hesitant about becoming fathers. Other reasons for women ending up single
include high rates of incarceration and early death in the poor communities
where single motherhood is most common, as well as the simple inability to
find the right match.

## Single Motherhood, Welfare, and Teen Motherhood:
## Debunking the Myths

In the current political climate, many are prepared to brand single mothers as
bad mothers. But is this fair? To be sure, single mothers face a formidable set
of economic obstacles, and these economic disadvantages have costs for their
children. But single mothers have their reasons for being single. Denouncing
single mothers as a group implies that if only they could find a man—any
man—they and their children would be better off. This preposterous claim
potentially leads to a very distasteful set of policy proposals, including forced
marriage or the forced removal of children from single mothers, regardless
of their ability to parent. Instead, we should acknowledge that poverty, not
single motherhood, is the problem.

One source of confusion is that discussions often tangle single motherhood with welfare recipiency, teen pregnancy, and out-of-wedlock childbearing. But although there are overlaps, these are *not* all the same thing, nor the same group of people. Prior to the elimination of the Aid to Families with Dependent Children (AFDC) program in 1996 (the federal program was replaced by state programs funded by a federal block grant called Temporary Assistance to Needy Families, or TANF), only one-third of single mothers received AFDC. Only one AFDC household in twelve was headed by a teen mother; only one-quarter of single mothers had never been married. Out-of-wedlock births have increased among *all* women, not just among those eligible for welfare. Women of *all* income groups are less likely to marry and stay married. While the childbearing rates of single women have changed very little, single women are now a larger percentage of all women, so births to single women are a larger percentage of all births (Blank 1995). Despite a large volume of research, the myths persist, holding that teen pregnancy is an epidemic (actually, teen birth rates are declining) and that overly generous welfare benefits encourage unwed motherhood (in fact, research shows no connection).

Even divorced mothers are under attack. But the claims that divorce is bad for children do not take into account that they might have fared worse if their parents had remained together in a loveless, angry, or even violent marriage (Stacey 1994; Hetherington 2001). Poverty and the public stigma that has always been attached to receiving public assistance are far more harmful to children than their mother's marital status. The most important factor accounting for the difficulties experienced by children from mother-only families, divorced or otherwise, is low income (McLanahan 1994). Just as poverty and unemployment make providing for basic needs more difficult, they put strains on marriages and family life.

## Differences Among Single Mothers

While single mothers as a group face formidable economic disadvantages, single mothers are *not* all the same. Close to two-thirds of single mothers were white in 2000, and 88 percent did *not* receive welfare during that year. Comparing welfare recipients with nonrecipients gives some clues about why those who opt for welfare have little alternative. Single mothers who receive cash assistance look very different from those who do not. They are less educated and younger—both factors leading to lower wage potential. Recipient mothers are more likely to be Latino or black, which also depresses earnings due to discrimination. They more commonly live in a large city or rural area—again, locations associated with reduced earnings.

Furthermore, welfare recipients face more constraints on their working time than do single mothers not receiving aid. Recipient mothers are much more likely to have young children—a factor that makes it difficult to do large amounts of paid labor without reliable child care. Over half of women receiving welfare have never been married. The great majority of nonrecipient single mothers were once married, giving them better prospects of collecting child support or alimony.

By comparison, married mothers are more educated, older, and more likely to be white, non-Latino, and suburban, than single mothers, especially single mothers on welfare. In short, the single mothers who resort to public assistance do so because of a whole series of limitations on their earnings opportunities.

## Struggling to Survive

Public assistance to single mothers and their children has become far less generous. The inflation adjusted (in 1996 dollars) AFDC benefits for a typical family of four in a typical state plummeted from $910 [per month] in 1970 to $403 in 1998 (U.S. House of Representatives 2000, pp. 381–82). Over 80 percent of the states went on to overhaul their welfare policies during the 1990s. The new state reforms are a mixed bag. In some cases they incorporate sensible changes that work in the direction of reducing poverty, such as allowing welfare recipients to keep more of the money they earn. But on the whole, such positive initiatives are being overwhelmed by an avalanche of misguided, punitive policies [including] time-limited benefits and workfare. The federal reform, passed in 1996, is as bad or worse. It emphasizes compelling recipients to work for pay or else lose assistance. The new law gives states full authority with virtually no accountability, eliminating any federal guarantee of assistance for those in need. And it imposes a lifetime five-year limit on welfare receipt. Overall, it signals a low point in U.S. poverty policy. Neither the federal nor state approaches hold promise for significantly diminishing poverty; they amount to new ways to punish welfare recipients and bully them off the welfare rolls.

But being on welfare is punishment enough. The benefits are remarkably low. The median benefit in 1998 was $388 a month for a family of three. Women scrape through by piecing together a variety of income sources in a precarious patchwork. They scrimp and go without things that many of us would consider necessities. And an unexpected expense—for example, for a medical problem—or a delay in any income source can precipitate a household financial crisis.

States and the federal government have been largely promoting jobs— any jobs—as the route out of welfare. However, this strategy without solid supports for going to work (such as child care, health care, and transportation), is [a] tenuous one at best. The dilemma of welfare versus paid work is most clearly seen in research done by sociologists Kathryn Edin and Laura Lein (1996). They constructed average budgets based on multiple interviews with 450 low-income single mothers in Boston, Charleston, Chicago, and San Antonio. They found that these women were subsisting on extremely low incomes: $10,700 a year among welfare mothers, and $14,900 among working single mothers—including food stamps and the Earned Income [Tax] Credit, which supplements the income of very low-income families. While conservatives like to claim that welfare creates a cycle of dependency, Edin and Lein found that on average government aid (including AFDC and Supplemental Security Income grants as well as food stamps) does not cover even half of recipients' expenses. The inadequate levels of benefits force mothers to find alternative forms of income, even if some of these sources are not legal under current welfare rules. Women do so in order to clothe, house, and feed their children. And here's the rub: employment offers only a limited route out of poverty for single mothers. Compared to women on welfare, low-wage working mothers end up taking one step forward and two steps back. Edin and Lein found that the average wage-earning mother made an added $758 a month on her main job compared to the average welfare-reliant mother. But the wage-reliant mother lost $505 in government aid and took on $190 in added work-related expenses. What's more, on average, the wage-earning mothers pay $128 more per month on housing, because they have less access to housing subsidies. Bottom line, the main job leaves these mothers $65 *behind* where they would have been on welfare! It takes added earnings from a second job or overtime just to break even. Like welfare mothers, low-wage working mothers cannot meet all of their families' needs with their own wages, continuing to depend on government aid (especially food stamps) and above all on aid from family and friends. It's not surprising that while 86 percent of the AFDC recipients in this study planned to leave welfare for paid work at some point, 73 percent were deferring employment until they could lower the costs of work and improve their earning power.

Given the gender gap in wages and the rest of the "triple whammy," economic survival is a constant struggle for most single mothers. This is true both for those trying to support a family on meager welfare benefits and for women trapped in the low-wage labor market. Unfortunately, the ongoing process of welfare "reform" that stresses getting a job—any job—threatens to remove much of the limited support that does exist.

## An Alternative Future?

The "triple whammy"—women's lower wages, the demands of caring for children, and the limitation of having only one adult in the household—explains why single mothers and their children in the United States are so likely to be poor. But there is nothing about single motherhood that inevitably condemns lone moms to penury. Rather, it is the harsh market rules and impoverished public policies characterizing the U.S. economy that create this outcome.

Public policy changes could dramatically alter the economic plight of single mothers. Raising the minimum wage to a living wage, making it easier for workers to organize unions (which help equalize wages in the workforce), and paid family leaves (instead of the twelve-week unpaid leave mandated by current federal law) would improve jobs for single mothers, as well as many other women and men. Pay equity policies (i.e., equal pay for work requiring comparable skills) would help as well. A recent study by the Institute for Women's Policy Research and the AFL-CIO found that if employed single mothers earned as much as comparably skilled men, their income would be boosted by 17 percent and their poverty rates would be halved—from 25.3 percent to 12.6 percent (AFL-CIO 1999). But upgrading jobs is not enough. Lifting single mothers out of poverty requires rebuilding and extending the social safety net: guaranteeing universal, affordable child care, assuring health coverage for all, and, yes, providing cash assistance for the times and situations when parents must stay home to take care of their children rather than working for pay.

While this agenda seems ambitious in the current conservative policy context in the United States, most of our international counterparts have adopted many parts of it—and it shows. U.S. public policies are less effective in lifting single-parent families out of poverty than those in Canada, France, Germany, the Netherlands, the United Kingdom, and Sweden, according to one study comparing the United States with these six countries (McFate, Smeeding, and Rainwater 1995). Closer to home, U.S. policies do far better at lifting elderly families than single mothers out of poverty, since Social Security benefits are considerably more generous than welfare (though continuing attacks on Social Security may undo this as well). In fact, while the federal government and the states have slashed aid for the poor, they have preserved and expanded government aid for the middle class and wealthy, including the mortgage interest tax deduction and ever-lower capital gains taxes. Why not shift some of the assistance to those most in need?

Importantly, a policy program to aid single mothers would not help them alone. By helping to level the labor market playing field and creating an income "floor," the program would benefit all low-income families and all working people, especially women. We all deserve a better society: one where women and men receive equal treatment, where employers and the government recognize family needs, and where poverty is replaced by opportunity. Taking steps to help single mothers, the poorest of all families, would be a major stride in that direction.

## References

AFL-CIO. 1999. *Equal Pay for Working Families: National and State Data on the Pay Gap and Its Costs*. Washington, DC. Executive Summary available at www.aflcio.org/women/exec99.htm.

Blank, Rebecca. 1995. "What Are the Trends in Nonmarital Births?" In *Looking Before We Leap: Social Science and Welfare Reform*, ed. R. Kent Weaver and William T. Dickens. Washington, DC: Brookings Institution.

Edin, Kathryn J., and Laura Lein. 1996. *Making Ends Meet: How Single Mothers Survive Welfare and Low-Wage Work*. New York: Russell Sage Foundation.

Hetherington, Mavis. 2001. *For Better or For Worse: Divorce Reconsidered*. New York: W.W. Norton.

Lewis, Jane. 1993. "Introduction." In *Women and Social Policies in Europe: Work, Family and the State*, ed. Jane Lewis. Aldershot, UK: Edward Elgar.

McFate, Katherine, Timothy Smeeding, and Lee Rainwater. 1995. "Markets and States: Poverty Trends and Transfer Effectiveness in the 1980s." In *Poverty, Inequality, and the Future of Social Policy: Western States in the New World Order*, ed. Katherine McFate, Roger Lawson, and William Julius Wilson, pp. 29–66. New York: Russell Sage Foundation.

McLanahan, Sara. 1994. "The Consequences of Single Motherhood." *The American Prospect* 18 (Summer) pp. 48–58.

Moss, Philip, and Chris Tilly. 2001. "Hiring in Urban Labor Markets: Shifting Labor Demands, Persistent Racial Differences." In *Sourcebook of Labor Markets: Evolving Structures and Processes*, ed. Ivar Berg and Arne Kalleberg. New York: Plenum.

Rank, Mark. 1994. *Living on the Edge: The Realities of Welfare in America*. New York: Columbia University Press.

Spalter-Roth, Roberta, Heidi Hartmann, and Linda Andrews. 1993. "Combining Work and Welfare." In *Sociology and the Public Agenda*. Newbury Park, CA: Sage.

Stacey, Judith. 1994. "The New Family Values Crusaders." *The Nation*, July 25/August 1, 119–21.

U.S. Bureau of the Census. 2001. *Poverty in the United States 2000*. P-60–214. Washington, DC: U.S. Government Printing Office.

U.S. House of Representatives, Committee on Ways and Means. 2000. *Background Material and Data on Major Programs*. Washington DC: U.S. Government Printing Office.

Waldfogel, Jane 1997. "The Effects of Children on Women's Wages." *American Sociological Review* 62: 209–17.

Wilson, William J., and Kathryn M. Neckerman. 1986. "Poverty and Family Structure: The Widening Gap Between Evidence and Policy Issues." In *Fighting Poverty: What Works and What Doesn't*, ed. Sheldon Danziger and Daniel Weinberg, pp. 232–59. Cambridge: Harvard University Press.

---

Updated by the authors from "Single, with Children: The Economic Plight of Single Mothers," in *Political Economy and Contemporary Capitalism*, ed. Ron Baiman, Heather Boushey, and Dawn Saunders. Armonk, NY: M.E. Sharpe, 2000, pp. 124–29. Reprinted with permission.

# 22

# The Minimum Wage Increase

## A Working Woman's Issue

*Jared Bernstein, Heidi Hartmann*
*and John Schmitt*

As Congress considers raising the federal minimum wage from its current level of $5.15 per hour to $6.15, it is important to understand who will benefit from this increase. An analysis of low-wage workers shows that the main beneficiaries of this one-dollar increase would be working women, almost one million of whom are single mothers. In fact, of the 11.8 million workers who would receive a pay increase as the result of this higher minimum wage, 58 percent would be women, simply because, as a group, they earn lower wages than men. As a result, a minimum wage increase would reduce the overall pay gap between women and men.

Since the minimum wage is not indexed to inflation, when Congress fails to raise the minimum wage, these workers' purchasing power declines, as was the case over the 1980s. Even with the two increases thus far in the 1990s, the minimum wage remains 19 percent below its inflation-adjusted 1979 level. This decline in the minimum wage helps to explain the growth of wage inequality and the diminished earnings of low-wage female workers over the last two decades.

In 1979, a woman working at the minimum wage earned 70 percent of the hourly wage of the median female worker (the woman right in the middle of the female wage scale). By 1998, that ratio had fallen to 52 percent. Similarly, in 1979, a single mother working full-time at the minimum wage earned enough to lift a family of three (herself and two children) above the poverty line. By 1998, however, the same family would be 18 percent below the poverty line.

. . . About 7 million women nationally—12.6 percent of all working

Table 22.1

## Characteristics of Female Workers by Wage Range, 1998

| Characteristic | Affected directly by increase ($5.15–$6.14) | Other low-wage workers ($6.15–$7.14) | $7.15 and above | All |
|---|---|---|---|---|
| Average wage (dollars) | 5.64 | 6.70 | 14.65 | 12.18 |
| Employment | 6,976,792 | 5,668,877 | 40,076,797 | 55,497,227 |
| Share of total (percent) | 12.6 | 10.2 | 72.2 | 100.0 |
| Demographics (percent) | | | | |
| Teens (16–19) | 24.7 | 11.0 | 1.4 | 6.2 |
| 20+ | 75.3 | 89.0 | 98.6 | 93.8 |
| White | 65.4 | 67.5 | 76.6 | 73.6 |
| Black | 16.2 | 16.2 | 12.0 | 13.1 |
| Hispanic | 14.4 | 12.2 | 7.1 | 9.0 |
| Work hours (percent) | | | | |
| Full-time (35+) | 44.9 | 63.8 | 82.2 | 74.0 |
| Part-time | | | | |
| 20–34 hours | 35.0 | 25.6 | 13.1 | 18.1 |
| 1–19 hours | 20.0 | 10.5 | 4.7 | 7.9 |
| Industry (percent) | | | | |
| Manufacturing | 8.4 | 10.3 | 12.3 | 11.4 |
| Retail trade | 44.0 | 31.2 | 11.4 | 18.6 |
| Occupation (percent) | | | | |
| Sales | 28.3 | 20.2 | 8.7 | 12.7 |
| Cashiers | 16.4 | 8.5 | 1.3 | 4.2 |
| Services | 32.5 | 25.9 | 9.3 | 15.0 |
| Food preparation | 16.1 | 9.9 | 3.1 | 6.1 |
| Union membership (percent) | | | | |
| Union | 3.9 | 6.5 | 16.2 | 13.1 |
| Nonunion | 96.1 | 93.5 | 83.8 | 86.9 |

*Source:* Economic Policy Institute analysis of 1998 Current Population Survey data.
*Note:* "Affected directly by increase" indicates those workers who earn between the minimum wage in their state and the proposed new level ($6.15).

women—earn between $5.15 and $6.14, the wage range that would be directly affected by an increase in the federal minimum wage.[1] In lower-wage states, the share of women that would benefit from the proposed increase is typically higher than the national average. For example, one-fifth or more of working women would receive a raise after a one-dollar increase in the federal minimum in the following states: West Virginia (22.5 percent), Arkansas (21.9 percent), Mississippi (21.1 percent), Montana (20.8 percent), Louisiana (20.2 percent), and Oklahoma (20.0 percent). The states with the largest numbers of working women who would benefit from the increase are Texas (669,000), California (572,000), Florida (414,000), New York (372,000), Ohio (345,000), and Pennsylvania (338,000).

Table 22.1 provides a clearer picture of the low-wage women who would benefit from the proposed increase (see column 1). The vast majority (75.3 percent) of these women are adults (age twenty or older). Although most low-wage women workers are white (65.4 percent), African American and Hispanic women are overrepresented in low-wage jobs. African American women are 13.1 percent of all women workers (see the last column of Table 22.1), but 16.2 percent of those in the range affected by the minimum wage increase; Hispanic women are 9.0 percent of all women workers, but 14.4 percent of low-wage women. Close to half (44.9 percent) of the female workers in the affected range work full-time (thirty-five or more hours a week), and another 35.0 percent work between twenty and thirty-four hours per week.

The next few rows of Table 22.1 show the industries and occupations where low-wage women tend to find work. An analysis by industry shows that most low-wage females are concentrated in retail trade, which employs 44.0 percent of those in the affected range. In contrast, a much smaller share of low-wage women work in the higher-paying manufacturing sector (8.4 percent). An analysis by occupation reveals that 28.3 percent of low-wage women are sales workers, with 16.4 percent working as cashiers. One-third of these women (32.5 percent) work in service occupations such as food preparation (16.1 percent). Finally, just under 4 percent of low-wage women are covered by collective bargaining through a union, in contrast to 16.2 percent of women earning $7.15 or more per hour. . . .

All of the evidence suggests that the minimum wage increase is well targeted, providing significant benefits to poor and middle-income households. Table 22.2 shows that about 18 percent of the benefits of a one-dollar increase would go to households with incomes below $10,000 per year; another 32 percent of the benefits would go to households with annual incomes between $10,000 and $25,000. In total, households making less than $25,000 a year would receive half of the benefits of a one-dollar increase. Among affected single mothers, 85 percent have household incomes below $25,000, underscoring the importance of the policy for these low-wage and low-income families.

Those who oppose raising the minimum wage typically argue that the increase will force employers to fire, or hire fewer of, those workers affected by the increase. The evidence, however, fails to support this claim. Since the last increase, in late 1996 and 1997, employment rates of low-wage workers, and particularly single mothers, have increased dramatically, as the strong economy has bolstered demand in the low-wage labor market. In this regard, one of the main policy lessons from the current recovery is that the macroeconomy is the key determinant of employment opportunity for low-wage workers, most of whom are women. But, as the above evidence shows,

Table 22.2

**Share of Gains from Proposed Minimum Wage Increase by Household Income Level, 1998**

| Income level | Gain (in percent) |
|---|---|
| Less than $10,000 | 18.1 |
| $10,000–25,000 | 32.0 |
| $25,000–35,000 | 14.9 |
| $35,000–50,000 | 13.6 |
| $50,000+ | 21.4 |

*Source:* 1998 Current Population Survey data.
*Note:* Sample excludes nonworkers. For those in the affected range, gains are calculated as the difference between current earnings and the new level (by state). This value is multiplied by weekly hours and summed across each income group.

the wage that these women receive is very much a function of where the minimum wage is set by Congress. Disregarding this reality can only serve to swell the ranks of the working poor. Raising the minimum wage will raise the incomes of many low-income families, especially those headed by single mothers.

**Note**

1. More precisely, affected workers in this report are those who earn between the maximum of either their state's minimum or $5.15, at the lower end, and the proposed new minimum wage, at the upper end. About 4.8 million men, or 7.9 percent of all working men, are in this range.

Adapted from "The Minimum Wage Increase: A Working Woman's Issue," Issue Brief #133, Economic Policy Institute, Washington, DC. Reprinted with permission of the Economic Policy Institute (see www.epinet.org).

# 23

# The Challenge of Comparable Worth

## An Institutionalist View

*Janice Peterson*

The concept of "comparable worth" would seem to be a simple one: it calls for "equal pay for jobs of comparable worth." This says that an employer should pay men and women equally for jobs that are of equal value to the firm. It aims to cause employers to equalize wage rates for women in traditionally female jobs with the wage rates of men in traditionally male jobs requiring equivalent ability.

A comparable worth policy assumes that the "worth" of a job can be measured through the process of job evaluation. Job evaluation involves measurement procedures designed to establish pay differentials between jobs on the basis of such factors as required skill, training, responsibility, and working conditions.

The concept of comparable worth has evoked a wide variety of responses. . . . Many argue that it is a necessary step in the fight against entrenched labor market discrimination. Others have condemned it as the "looniest idea since looney toons" and the "feminist road to socialism." Neoclassical economists have been particularly virulent in their attacks on comparable worth, pointing to the heresy of suggesting that wage determination be removed from its "natural" setting, the market. The debate over comparable worth is extensive and far from being resolved. The purpose of this article is to bring out some of the important issues raised in the comparable worth debate that are particularly interesting from the perspective of institutionalist analysis. . . .

### The Comparable Worth Debate

Much of the debate over comparable worth has focused on the source of the male-female "wage gap" and the ability of a comparable worth policy to close this gap. Neoclassical economists have generally argued that comparable worth is a fundamentally flawed and ill-conceived policy. They argue that advocates of such a policy misunderstand the causes of women's low wages, and thus, their policy is inappropriate.

Neoclassical critics believe that the labor market operates in accordance with the competitive forces of supply and demand. This is a world where rational, profit-maximizing employers hire labor on the basis of its marginal productivity. In such a world, labor market discrimination is deemed irrational and, therefore, cannot persist in the long run. Thus, observed differences in occupations and earnings are seen to be productivity-based.

In explaining women's inferior labor market status, neoclassical economists stress the role of choice—women choose to invest less in human capital, women choose to work in part-time jobs, women choose to work in the low-wage service sector. Thus, it is argued, women's inferior status is no one's problem but their own. Women are not underpaid; they have simply chosen to work in low-paying jobs. It is argued that if women want to earn men's wages, they should simply choose to work in men's jobs.

The neoclassical critics of comparable worth ridicule the notion that work has a "value" or "worth" other than that determined in the market. The labor market determines the value of a job through the establishment of the equilibrium wage. Comparable worth advocates are criticized for trying to replace this "natural" process with an arbitrary wage-setting regime, dependent on the value judgments of an individual or group. These critics argue that because labor resources respond to wage signals, interfering with the market will lead to inefficiencies and distortions. Thus, critics argue that comparable worth will be impossible to implement and will have disastrous results.

Advocates of comparable worth argue that the neoclassical perspective provides an incorrect view of the way labor markets actually work. In particular, they argue that differences in earnings and occupations cannot be explained entirely by productivity and choice. Thus, the neoclassical focus on these issues is seen to lead to incorrect policy conclusions.

Comparable worth advocates stress the role of labor market discrimination and occupational segregation in lowering the wages earned by women. It is argued that the labor market is stratified by discrimination, which has divided workers into jobs held predominantly by women ("women's jobs") and jobs held predominantly by men ("men's jobs"). Women workers are concentrated in a restricted number of jobs that tend to offer low pay and little opportunity for advancement.

Under these conditions, it is argued that a comparable worth policy could bring wages closer to what they would be in a nondiscriminating market, thus increasing efficiency and productivity. Discrimination is presented as a form of market failure, creating "barriers to free movement in the labor market" resulting in "incorrect prices" (Hartmann 1988, p. 220). Thus, in the presence of discrimination, male and female labor is not used in the most efficient way. In this view, "it is not comparable worth that interferes with a free market, but discrimination" (Hartmann 1984, p. 11).

Comparable worth advocates conclude that intervention in the labor market is necessary to correct the market wage to remove the distortions caused by discrimination. They argue that they are merely asking that wages be paid on the basis of the worth of the job done, not the sex of the person performing it. It is argued that comparable worth will not disrupt the functioning of the market, but will simply cleanse it of the external, distorting influence of discrimination.

While this debate has raised many important issues, appreciating the significance of many of these issues requires looking at labor markets and wage setting from a broader perspective. Institutionalist analysis, with its emphasis on process and the importance of culture and power, provides a useful way to look at these issues. It provides insight into the nature of labor markets and the actual wage determination process. This allows us to better evaluate the challenges of a comparable worth policy.

## The Nature of Labor Markets and Wage Determination

The labor market is a social institution. Wages are not determined in the abstract, but in the context of the laws, traditions, ideologies, and power relationships that shape society. The labor market does not operate as a function of "natural law," but is a social and historical artifact. It has developed historically in the social context of gender discrimination and male power. Thus, the wage bargain cannot be understood outside of the social environment and power relationships surrounding it.

Markets themselves are not value-free, but steeped in value judgments, including those regarding the "proper" roles of women. Traditional gender ideology shapes and constrains the choices available to women in the labor market. It permeates the labor market and the underlying structure of power.

The concept of power is critical to an understanding of the operation of labor markets and the status of individuals within these markets. Power may be defined as the ability to make and implement decisions involving control over others. The structure of power organizes and controls the economy, determining whose interests will count and whose will not (see Samuels 1979; Dugger 1980; Woodbury 1987).

The exercise of power can take a variety of forms. Some forms of power are very visible, requiring force or coercion. Other forms of power are more subtle, and their exercise is often unnoticed. Of particular importance to the economic status of women is this subtle form of power, referred to by John Kenneth Galbraith (1983) as "conditioned power."

Conditioned power is exercised through the belief system of a society. Submission to such power is secured through "the social commitment to what seems natural, proper or right" (Galbraith 1983, p. 5). The exercise of such power is hidden, and submission to such power is often unconscious. That is, people "choose" to behave in ways that are socially acceptable, proper, and natural. Thus, traditional gender ideology, defining the socially acceptable, proper, and natural role of women, is a system of values and beliefs through which conditioned power over women is exercised.

The conclusions of neoclassical economics, based so strongly on the assumption of "free choice," are seriously challenged by the recognition of conditioned power. The existence and exercise of power are closely linked to the ability to make choices. Those who are powerless cannot participate in genuine choice.

To the extent that women are defined by their roles, or potential roles, as wives and mothers, their "choices" are constrained. Occupational choice and other labor supply decisions, as well as the hiring decisions of employers, take place within the existing structure of power, which is heavily influenced by traditional gender ideology. Relative wages and the occupational distribution, traditionally accepted as economic outcomes, must be interpreted and evaluated in this context.

Thus, it is important to recognize that markets are socially constructed, defined for and by a particular set of rules, laws, and socially acceptable behaviors. There is no one market outcome, but a variety of possible outcomes associated with different institutional frameworks. Different market outcomes reflect different distributions of power. To argue that the existing outcome is the socially optimal one implies acceptance of the status quo distribution. It legitimates a highly unequal distribution of power in the name of market efficiency.

From this perspective, a comparable worth policy is more than a correction of market failure. It is not merely an "intervention" to correct a distortion in an otherwise adequately functioning market. It attempts to change the rules, to alter the institutional framework in which the process of wage determination takes place.

In addition to raising important theoretical questions about the nature of labor markets, the comparable worth debate has drawn attention to how wages are actually determined in the economy. In particular, the discussion has emphasized the role of social norms regarding the fairness of different wages, and the pervasiveness of nonmarket evaluation systems in the wage-setting process.

The labor market as it operates is not independent of the customs and norms of society. These include customary notions of fairness and what constitutes a fair wage. Historian Alice Kessler-Harris argues that such social norms have been important in shaping the operation of the labor market.

> Justice, equity and fairness have not been its natural outcomes. Rather, market outcomes have been tempered by customary notions of justice or fairness. The specific forms these take have been the object of struggle. And just as ideas of fairness influence our response to the market, so, too, do they influence how the market works. (1988, p. 239)

Beliefs as to what constitutes a fair wage have differed for men and women. The assumption of different roles within the family for men and women—the male "breadwinner" and the female "homemaker"—has led to different norms for women and men regarding the fairness of established wages (Sorensen 1984, pp. 468–69). This is illustrated by the acceptance of the "family wage" for male workers. It has been widely accepted that it is fair for men to earn more than women because they need it to support families, while women are seen to work only for "pin money."

Historically, nonmarket concerns have clearly shaped the wage-setting process, and these concerns have been influenced by the presumption of traditional gender roles. Thus, comparable worth policies are not really adding the notion of fairness to the wage determination process, but are calling for a reevaluation of the meaning of fairness in labor markets.

In addition, the comparable worth debate has brought attention to the fact that the wages of many workers are not being determined by the "free market," but are already determined by some form of job evaluation system (see, for example, Treiman and Hartmann 1981). Thus, in many cases, it is not a matter of replacing the market with job evaluation, but reforming an already existing system of job evaluation. Comparable worth advocates acknowledge that job evaluation, particularly as it is done now, has many problems. In fact, much of the recent research in this area focuses on the technical aspects of job evaluation, trying to identify problems and establish procedures to avoid them.

## The Challenges of Comparable Worth

Comparable worth appears to be a fairly limited policy in many ways. The focus of the policy, as it has been pursued in the United States, is at the level of individual employers. Thus, it will not lead to the national wage setting feared by many critics. Nor, on the other hand, will it eradicate the entire earnings gap. It will not address the job segregation that takes place across, as opposed to within, firms and industries.

Despite this, comparable worth continues to elicit extremely negative responses from many economists. The strength of the reaction against it suggests that something very important is being questioned; it suggests that perhaps more than the sanctity of market equilibria is at stake.

Wages do more than merely allocate scarce resources among competing ends. Wages are closely linked to status—they define the place of individuals relative to others in society. By questioning the manner in which compensation is assigned, comparable worth calls into question existing status relationships. By making explicit the gendered nature of the labor market and status hierarchy, comparable worth challenges the status quo.

Wages both define and are defined by the existing status hierarchy. Comparable worth draws attention to the link between status and the value assigned to different types of work. Comparable worth advocates argue that much of the work done by women is devalued because women do it. Contrary to the neoclassical theory, "value is determined not by measurements of output, but by the status of the person providing the inputs" (Greenwood 1984, p. 461). Thus, women's work is accorded low status and low wages because women are accorded low status in society. Thorstein Veblen (1899, 1943) attributed this devaluation of women and women's work to the triumph of predatory values over workmanship.

Comparable worth challenges this cultural devaluation of women and their work. It challenges the assumption that women's work is worth less than men's, and it challenges the belief that it is appropriate and natural for women's wages to be lower than men's. It is a plan of action that tells women workers that they are, in fact, worth as much as men.

Neoclassical labor economics is centered on the notion that wages are based on the worker's productivity or "merit." Substantial inequality is justified and rationalized on the basis of this argument. Comparable worth charges that this neoclassical "meritocracy" is a myth. Wages are not based on merit alone, but reflect other characteristics of workers, including gender. Comparable worth exposes how far actual wage-setting practices deviate from the standards defined by the neoclassical economists themselves.

In addition, comparable worth has the potential to substantially increase the wages of many women workers (see Steinberg 1987, p. 470; Amott and Matthaei 1989, p. 108). Increased earnings would contribute to increased independence of women. Thus, comparable worth ultimately challenges the notion that women should be dependent on men. This is perhaps the most serious challenge and the real source of much of the controversy. As argued by Heidi Hartmann:

> I suspect that much of the heat generated in opposition to comparable worth, on both the right and the left, is really a displaced response to this much more fundamental challenge to the status quo. The right vocally defends the free market, and the left assails technocracy—but the problem is really women's economic independence. (1988, p. 231)

## References

Amott, Teresa, and Julie Matthaei. 1989. "The Promise of Comparable Worth." *Socialist Review* 10 (April–June): 101–17.
Dugger, William. 1980. "Power: An Institutionalist Framework for Analysis." *Journal of Economic Issues* 14 (4): 6–13.
Galbraith, John Kenneth. 1983. *The Anatomy of Power*. Boston: Houghton Mifflin.
Greenwood, Daphne. 1984. "The Institutional Inadequacy of the Free Market in Determining Comparable Worth." *Journal of Economic Issues* 18 (2): 457–64.
Hartmann, Heidi. 1984. "The Case for Comparable Worth." In *Equal Pay for Unequal Work*, ed. Phyllis Schlafly, pp. 11–24. Washington, DC: Eagle Forum.
———. 1988. "The Political Economy of Comparable Worth." In *Three Worlds of Labor Economics*, ed. Garth Mangum and Peter Phillips, pp. 217–34. Armonk, NY: M.E. Sharpe.
Kessler-Harris, Alice. 1988. "The Just Price, the Free Market, and the Value of Women." *Feminist Studies* 14 (Summer): 235–50.
Samuels, Warren, ed. 1979. *The Economy as a System of Power*. New Brunswick, NJ: Transaction Books.
Sorensen, Elaine. 1984. "Equal Pay for Comparable Worth: A Policy for Eliminating the Undervaluation of Women's Work." *Journal of Economic Issues* 18 (2): 465–72.
Steinberg, Ronnie. 1987. "Radical Challenges in a Liberal World: The Mixed Success of Comparable Worth." *Gender & Society* 1 (4): 466–75.
Treiman, Donald, and Heidi Hartmann, eds. 1981. *Women, Work, and Wages: Equal Pay for Jobs of Equal Value*. Washington, DC: National Academy Press.
Veblen, Thorstein. 1899. *The Theory of the Leisure Class*. New York: Macmillan.
———. 1943. *Essays in Our Changing Order*. New York: Viking.
Woodbury, Stephen. 1987. "Power in the Labor Market: Institutionalist Approaches to Labor Problems." *Journal of Economic Issues* 21 (4): 1781–1807.

---

Adapted from "The Challenge of Comparable Worth: An Institutionalist View," *Journal of Economic Issues* 24 (2) (June 1990): 605–12. Reprinted with special permission of the copyright holder, the Association for Evolutionary Economics.

# 24

# Curing Child Poverty in the United States

## *Barbara R. Bergmann*

Millions of American children, more than one in five, live in deprivation, with sharply reduced chances of developing into reasonably happy, productive, and law-abiding citizens. Single parenthood, highly conducive to childhood poverty, is growing among all racial and ethnic groups. In the United States, as indeed in most of the developed countries, long-term marriage—the institution that has in the past been depended upon to channel economic resources toward child-raising—is sheltering an ever-shrinking proportion of the children that are born (Folbre 1993).

Rhetorical appeals for a return to "family values" are unlikely to make headway against the problem of child poverty. Charles Murray's (1984) suggestion that we force a return to near-universal child rearing within marriage by eliminating government support for single parents would, at least in the short run, bring a huge and probably unacceptable increase in the outright destitution of young children and would force the separation of many children from their mothers. A more efficacious and humane approach to the cure of child poverty would be to take the weakening of marriage as a given and to look for politically acceptable ways of capturing more economic resources for children in single-mother families. Such policies may further weaken the incentives to marriage, but that may be unavoidable.

Potential methods include getting single parents into substantial jobs, increasing wage subsidies, increasing transfer payments to at-home single mothers, and better enforcing child support payments from absent parents. Another way to direct major resources toward child raising, one that has had relatively little discussion, would be the provision by government of high-quality child care, not merely as a temporary help for the mother in leaving welfare, but as a permanent benefit to all lower-income children. With child care provided free, mothers in even the lowest-wage jobs would retain enough of their earnings to attain a minimally decent standard and would be substantially better off than those currently on welfare.

## Accounting for Needed Resources

In thinking about the pros and cons of the various ways one might capture resources for the nurture of children in single-parent families, it is useful to look at expenditure budgets for single-mother families, including taxes, that would allow a standard of minimal decency. That permits one to see what would have to be provided and to consider the sources from which these provisions might come. The official poverty line is not appropriate for this use, because it was derived without attention to differences in the needs of at-home and on-the-job single mothers (Orshansky 1978). Trudi Renwick and I (Renwick and Bergmann 1993) provide a detailed method for building basic-needs budgets (BNBs) that do attend to such differences.

The BNB includes specific allowances for minimally decent food, shelter, clothing, medical care, transportation, and child care that are tailored to the ages of the children and the work behavior of the parents (see Table 24.1). Some out-of-pocket medical expenses are allowed for in the adaptation of the BNB that is used here, but nothing for health insurance, assuming that all single parents will in the future have that provided. For single mothers with jobs, the standard of life envisioned in the BNB includes safe, high-quality full-day care for their preschool children and after-school care for their elementary school children.

It would not do to assume (as commonly is tacitly done) that all single mothers have relatives capable of giving free, high-quality child care who could provide it at little or no sacrifice to themselves. Child care choices among mothers with jobs suggest that a substantial proportion of mothers do not have such relatives (Presser 1989). Some mothers get child care services from relatives, who, seeing no alternative, feel compelled to give it at considerable financial and psychological cost to themselves. Other mothers get no free child care services at all; many have their children in substandard care.

Accordingly, the family of the mother with a job has been assigned money in the BNB ($400 per child per month in this adaptation)[1] to purchase licensed child care, as well as additional amounts for transportation to work. If a mother goes from welfare to work, these additional costs raise the amount needed to buy goods and services under the BNB by 94 percent, as seen in Table 24.1.

Table 24.1

**Three Methods of Providing the Level of Living Prescribed in the Basic-Needs Budget for a Single-Parent Family with Two Preschool Children, 1993**

| Budget items | Full welfare solution | Good-job solution | Wage-supplement solution |
|---|---|---|---|
| Food | $3,508 | $3,508 | $3,508 |
| Housing | 4,280 | 4,280 | 4,280 |
| Clothing, health care, personal care | 2,596 | 2,596 | 2,596 |
| Child care | 0 | 9,600 | 9,600 |
| Transportation | 463 | 1,024 | 1,024 |
| Costs of goods and services | $10,847 | $21,008 | $21,008 |
| Social Security tax | 0 | 1,856 | 676 |
| Federal income tax | 0 | 1,816 | 0 |
| Dependent care credit | 0 | −1,056 | 0 |
| Earned Income Tax Credit | 0 | 0 | −1,384 |
| State income tax | 0 | 638 | 175 |
| Total required | $10,847 | $24,262 | $20,476 |
| Annual wage | 0 | 24,262 | 8,840 |
| AFDC, 1993 level in median state | 4,404 | 0 | 0 |
| Food stamps, 1993 levels | 2,690 | 0 | 1,890 |
| Child care provided | 0 | 0 | 9,600 |
| Additional cash inflow required | 3,753 | 0 | 146 |
| Government benefits less taxes | $10,847 | −$3,254 | $12,168 |

## Alternative Ways to End Child Deprivation

Table 24.1 has been constructed to show three alternative ways in which a single mother with two preschool children might attain the standard of decency prescribed by the BNB. The first column of figures shows what can be called the "full welfare solution." A mother with two children on welfare in a state with median benefits received $7,094 in AFDC (Aid to Families with Dependent Children) and food stamp benefits in 1994. She could achieve the BNB standard if given an additional $3,753 in benefits. The second column displays what can be called the "good-job solution." In order to provide the $21,008 that allows the mother to purchase the goods and services that make up the BNB standard, without government help beyond what is currently mandated, she needs a job paying $24,262 before taxes.

The third column, the "wage-supplement solution," shows a set of benefits that would allow a mother earning the minimum wage full-time year-round to meet that standard. In addition to the currently mandated Earned Income Tax Credit (EITC) and food stamp benefits, she would need additional benefits totaling $9,746.

Obviously, the problem of child poverty would be more tractable if a high proportion of single mothers could do well enough in the labor market to achieve the good-job solution. Unfortunately, there are large numbers of single mothers for whom that is not currently possible, no matter how well motivated they might be. The 1993 median weekly wage for full-time women workers who head families provides a 52-week income of $20,540. Thus only a minority of single mothers already holding jobs earn enough to finance the BNB for a family of three. It is a reasonable conjecture that an even smaller proportion of the single mothers currently on AFDC would be able to earn that much if they took jobs, even after training.

Since the good-job solution is out of reach for a majority of single mothers, eliminating child deprivation would entail a choice between the other two alternatives. The full welfare solution has its adherents. However, prevailing sentiment appears to be that the government should not offer a comfortable life, exempt from job-holding, to women who lack private support for themselves and their babies, unless they are widows.

The wage-supplement solution is more costly to the public purse than the full welfare solution, but it has the selling point that it requires the mother to hold a job. Another major selling point is that it could be formulated to deliver most of its benefits directly to the children, with little cash to the parents beyond benefits currently offered, as shown in Table 24.1. Programs with government-supplied child care as a centerpiece are in effect in some of the European countries, and in conjunction with national health insurance, child allowances, and child support enforcement these programs keep poverty among children low (OECD 1990, 1994; Bradshaw et al. 1993; Bergmann 1994). Fertility does not appear to vary with the generosity of these programs.

Of course, all of the benefits in the wage-supplement solution package could be provided in cash, contingent on job-holding by the mother. However, child care services cannot be exchanged, as cash can, for items that do not benefit the child. Providing such services puts a floor under the quality of the care that the child gets.

In-kind child care benefits (through public facilities or vouchers) would go directly to the children themselves, rather than to their parents. High-quality child care that is free to parents could provide a safe, nurturing, and comfortable daytime environment for the children. It could insulate them for most of their waking hours from the stresses of a poverty-stricken milieu and could serve to acculturate them to mainstream values and habits. In public facilities, or publicly regulated facilities, children can receive preventive health care, nutritious meals, and attention to cognitive and behavioral development. Abuse would be more likely to be detected than now.

The provision of child care could be accompanied by time limits on welfare or its outright abolition. However, there would have to be provision of jobs for mothers in high unemployment areas and support for mothers disabled from work.

Government child care help to a family would increase with additional births, but nobody could argue, as many now do, that women would have additional children with the purpose of gaining additional benefits. Providing child care and severely restricting or ending welfare might not be as discouraging to out-of-wedlock births as simply ending welfare and providing no help with child care. However, the public desire to prevent such births must be weighted against the public's interest in the well-being of whatever children will in any case be born.

## Costs of the Child Care Solution

The provision of child care, if it were to be instrumental in solving the problem of child deprivation, could not be restricted to people coming off welfare. Nor could it be restricted to one year per child, nor be a half-day program, as Head Start now is. It could be restricted to single-parent families, but only at the expense of discouraging marriage and ignoring the well-being of poor children of married couples. It would be desirable for at least some child care subsidies to be extended to the middle-income groups to establish political support for the program and to bring in a constituent group that would be effective in demanding high-quality standards. To avoid "notch" effects and to reduce costs, sliding-scale fees could be established.

One can easily make a rough estimate of the cost of providing care to children of low- and middle-income families. There are 19 million children under the age of five in the United States. If high-quality child care for preschoolers (averaging the costs of providing care for infants and for the older children) can be procured at $4,800 per child per year, then providing the lowest-income fifth with free care and the next two-fifths with partially subsidized care on a sliding scale would cost $36 billion annually. There are 29 million children between ages five and twelve. Providing three-fifths of them with care on the same basis before and after school, and in the summer, at a cost of $3,400 each, would cost an additional $39 billion. As more mothers went to work, there would also be a rise in expenditures for the EITC. Any resultant increase in the unemployment rate would mean somewhat higher outlays for unemployment insurance for the experienced unemployed, who would now be competing with the former welfare mothers for job vacancies. There would be some savings: costs for AFDC and the food stamps single mothers get, running at about $32 billion [in 1994], would decline; not all children of mothers in the middle income ranges would participate.

The additional expenditures required by the wage-supplement solution are large. However, society could easily "afford" them in the sense that items amounting to that much could surely be found in the federal budget which most citizens would consider to be of lower priority than a program that successfuly attacked child deprivation. While the expense would be a difficulty, the main difficulties in enacting such a program probably lie elsewhere.

In the eyes of some, enacting a sizable child care program that extends subsidies to the middle classes would constitute an improper and unwise enticement for even more mothers to leave off full-time care of their children at home. Those who hope for a return to a system in which almost all women are housewives would resent it deeply and fight it bitterly. Another difficulty is the widespread doubt that American governmental entities would be capable of delivering excellent services to children, as European governments manage to do (Bergmann 1994). After all, American public schools have done a notoriously bad job with poor children. In this country, however, vouchers acceptable by nongovernmental providers would probably have to play a major part.

Suggestions that it would be good policy to get large numbers of single mothers off welfare and into work are frequently met with the objections that there are no jobs for them or only very poor ones. On the latter issue, concern for poor children should motivate better enforcement of the laws against race and sex discrimination. However, even the poorest job would support a standard of living above that allowed by current welfare grants, as long as child care is provided. Those who offer the "no jobs" objection assume that new entrants to the labor force must endure unemployment until the number of jobs grows to accommodate them. In fact, there is considerable turnover, particularly in low-wage jobs, and new entrants compete with those previously in the labor force for the vacancies that result. Moreover, the provision of child care to them and to other low-income families would create several million jobs in child care centers, and some jobs in public service employment would have to be provided to take care of those who are difficult to place.

## Conclusion

Child deprivation in the United States could not be eliminated simply by motivating single mothers to put forth work effort by cutting them off welfare and giving them at most transitional help with training and child care. Substantial additional funds would have to be spent, because the problem is that under current conditions sufficient economic resources are not available to nurture these children.

A program to end child poverty whose main ingredient is the provision of services to the children themselves avoids some of the political liabilities that characterize other kinds of antipoverty programs. Benefits to adults perceived as improvident are unpopular. But small children, even those born to improvident mothers, are not yet themselves guilty of improvidence. Rescuing them from deprived childhoods by providing them with high-quality care while their mothers work may command a far greater degree of public assent than allowing their mothers to raise them at home. The provision of child care may be the only politically possible way to devote enough public resources to child rearing to end the widespread deprivation of American children.

## Note

1. A study relating costs of private and public child care centers to measures of quality (Helburn 1994) suggests that costs this high or higher would be required if good-quality care were to be provided.

## References

Bergmann, Barbara R. 1994. "Can We Afford to Save Our Children? Cost and Structure of Government Programs for Children in the U.S. and France." Working paper, American University.

Bradshaw, Jonathan, John Ditch, Hilary Holmes, and Peter Whiteford. 1993. *Support for Children: A Comparison of Arrangements in Fifteen Countries.* London: HMSO.

Folbre, Nancy. 1993. *Who Pays for the Kids? Gender and the Structures of Constraint.* New York: Routledge.

Helburn, Suzanne W. 1994. "Cost of Quality Child Care." Unpublished manuscript, University of Colorado, Denver.

Murray, Charles. 1984. *Losing Ground: American Social Policy, 1950–1980.* New York: Basic Books.

OECD. 1990. "Child Care in OECD Countries." In *OECD Employment Outlook,* pp. 123–51. Paris: Organization for Economic Cooperation and Development.

———. 1994. *Measurement of Low Incomes and Poverty in a Perspective of International Comparisions.* Labor Market and Social Policy Occasional Papers No. 14. Paris: Organization for Economic Cooperation and Development.

Orshansky, Molly. 1978. "Measuring Poverty: A Debate." *Public Welfare* 36 (2): 46–55.

Presser, Harriet B. 1989. "Some Economic Complexities of Child Care Provided by Grandmothers." *Journal of Marriage and the Family* 51 (3): 581–91.

Renwick, Trudi J., and Barbara R. Bergmann. 1993. "A Budget-Based Definition of Poverty, with an Application to Single-Parent Families." *Journal of Human Resources* 28 (1): 1–24.

Adapted from "Curing Child Poverty in the United States," *American Economic Review* 84 (2) (May 1994): 76–80. Reprinted with permission of the American Economic Association.

# 25

# Why Americans Need Family Leave Benefits and How They Can Get Them

*Betty Holcomb*

For Sara Dotson, the nightmare began on a warm August evening, when her twelve-year-old daughter, Carissa, began to complain of pain in her legs. By the next day, Carissa's fever was spiking and the pain was excruciating. Even then, Dotson had no idea of the crisis that would unfold, nearly costing Carissa her life and making Dotson miss several months of work—with no guarantee of a paycheck during that time.

"One day, she was totally healthy, the next she was critically ill and no one knew what was wrong," says Dotson, a probation counselor for Thurston County in Washington State. The first week, Dotson shuttled her daughter from doctor to doctor in her hometown of Olympia, Washington. No one could control the fever or offer a diagnosis. "Finally, the local hospital told us to get her up to Children's Hospital in Seattle, immediately," she says. Seattle was an hour's drive north, and a world away from Dotson's job and usual support network. But she had no choice. After a few days, Carissa's condition stabilized and doctors identified the problem: osteomyelitis, an infection of the hip bone. The treatment? Intravenous antibiotics. Carissa would have to stay in the Seattle medical center for up to three months. That was when Dotson fell apart.

"Up until then, I was just dealing with the emergency. I didn't have time to think about anything else. But when they told me she'd have to be hospitalized in Seattle for three months, I panicked," she says. "I knew I needed to be there with her. But my job was back in Olympia. I couldn't do both."

What would they do for income? Dotson's husband, Randy, had lost his high-tech job the winter before, when his company downsized. Since then, he'd taken odd jobs, even driving a truck for a while, while he kept searching for work in his field. Without Sara's salary, they'd quickly go broke. Sara had only a few weeks of paid time off coming to her that year. "I just remember sitting there in that hospital in Seattle, thinking: Three months? Even if they held my job, we wouldn't have my paycheck. What would we do?" At that moment, Dotson, like so many American workers, saw that her fate depended entirely on the generosity of her employer, Thurston County.

She soon learned that she would be one of the lucky ones. Her boss was sympathetic, and the county had a system that allowed employees to donate unused paid time off to others in need. Dotson's boss put out an alert, and offers started rolling in. And happily, Carissa made a quicker-than-expected recovery. She was able to go home in six weeks, rather than the expected twelve. "We've definitely been tested," Sara says of the experience. "But it could have been much worse. I don't know what families do who don't have a paid leave."

### So Many Families at Risk

It's certainly a tough question—and one that this country has yet to address. Just listen to Sharon McDougle, a technician for an aerospace company in Texas. "When I was getting ready to have my baby, I just didn't have enough vacation and sick leave to take a real maternity leave—and my husband got laid off when I was seven months pregnant."

Her solution? "I was back on the job at two weeks after I had the baby," she says. "And it was terrible. I was the walking dead. It was like I was sleepwalking. I look back now and I don't know how I did it. I guess I just did it because I had to. There was no other choice," she says. "Without my paycheck, we had no money." In fact, she and her husband had to depend on the generosity of coworkers who took up a collection for them when she learned she was going to have to miss a third week's pay. . . .

Aside from the fund-raising coworkers, McDougle's experience is far from uncommon among workers who cut their family leave short or simply skip the time off altogether, even though they have a pressing need and the legal right to take one. Two-thirds of the workers who need, but do not take, family leave say it is because they can't afford to. Each year, that translates into more than 2.3 million people. In addition, two out of five who do take a leave cut it short because of lost pay. . . .

Advocates who work closely with the millions of workers who struggle with these issues put the matter simply. "Family leave has helped millions of people in this country," says Judith L. Lichtman, president of the National Partnership for Women & Families. "But without a paycheck coming in, too many people simply can't use it at all, or must cut it far too short."

## New Campaign for Paid Leave

That's why a new movement has begun to expand and improve family leave benefits across the nation. The effort, led by the National Partnership for Women & Families, brings together a nonpartisan, wide-ranging group of labor, women's, children's, faith-based, and health groups, academicians, and policy makers, who see a desperate need to make it easier for America's workers to balance their work and family duties. "Our goal is to see that more parents can spend precious time with their babies, fewer children will have to face hospital stays alone, and more workers are able to care for their spouse or parents in an emergency," adds Lichtman.

Without benefits during leave, American workers must depend on vacation or sick time—if they are lucky enough to have such benefits. Yet new research shows that many workers, especially the ones who need it the most, lack any paid sick leave or paid vacation days. One third of all Americans who are above the poverty line, and two-thirds of the working poor, lack such benefits, according to Jody Heymann, director of policy for the Harvard University Center for Society and Health.

Even relatively well-to-do workers in America have very little paid time off a year. Those who work in large companies have only about three weeks of paid time off a year, outside of holidays. That's the combination of sick days, vacation, and personal leave—certainly not long enough to see workers through medical emergencies, recovery from childbirth, or care for a seriously ill spouse or elderly parent. "It's cruel to make workers choose between a sick relative and a paycheck," adds Lichtman, "yet that's exactly what we are asking far too many people to do right now."

The federal Family and Medical Leave Act (FMLA), signed into law in 1993, offers many workers some important protections when they have to deal with family medical emergencies or care for a new baby or adopted child. Those who work at companies with fifty or more employees can take up to twelve weeks of unpaid leave—and still get their jobs back. Under that law, covered workers also retain their health insurance and any seniority they've earned. To date, some 35 million workers have taken leaves under this law. "It's definitely progress from the bad old days when American workers were simply fired or had to quit when they had a baby, adopted a child, or had to care for a sick child or an elderly parent," says Lissa Bell, senior policy associate for the National Partnership for Women & Families. Still,

Bell would be one of the first to concede that much more needs to be done to help workers who need a family leave.

For starters, because the federal law covers only employees at companies with fifty or more workers, that translates into only 57 percent of the private workforce, leaving the rest to face down such crises as best they can. A few more workers can find help in state leave laws—Vermont, for example, extends job-protected leave to workers at firms with as few as ten employees.

The bottom line? Millions of men and women still have no guarantee that their job will be held for them when they face a medical crisis, or even when they have a new baby or adopt a child. These cold facts have sparked the movement to see that more workers are protected and that all workers entitled to leave have some income while they are out on leave.

## A Vast Unmet Need

Most certainly, demographers and policy makers see a pressing need for paid leave that will only grow in the years to come. In 1997, one in four Americans had an elderly relative to care for, and many reduced their work hours or took at least a brief leave to care for that person.

Or they muddled along, torn between the competing demands of a job and a family member desperately in need of care. Such was the case for Kathleen Duffus, who was working for a financial services firm when her fifty-six-year-old father was diagnosed with Alzheimer's disease. Duffus couldn't afford to go without her paycheck. For eight long years, she struggled to keep up at work and keep up with her father's care. It was difficult, given that he lived an hour and a half away and needed constant attention. Even when she found a decent nursing home, she had to be available for conferences with doctors and other medical support staff—and to simply visit with him. "A lot of this time I was in crisis mode, working in overdrive and struggling with being so far away from my dad. It definitely took a toll on me. Paid family and medical leave would have allowed me to plan a little better for things, and it also would have given me more time with my dad."

In the coming years, the need for this type of family leave will only become more urgent. Nearly two-thirds of American women and men under the age of sixty believe they will have to care for an older relative in the next decade. The situation is already dire when it comes to infant care. Without a paycheck, too many parents must rush back to work and leave their babies in less than optimal care. Polls show most parents would prefer to be home with their babies, if only they could afford to be.

When babies are six or even eight weeks old, it's simply impossible to find care for them in a licensed center. Most states prohibit centers from taking babies under six weeks old, and with good reason. A young infant's immune system is not yet mature, making babies highly susceptible to infection. On this very point, Faith Wohl, president of the Child Care Action Campaign and another advocate who has joined the national campaign for paid family leave, says, "We could go a long way toward providing babies with the care they need by creating a paid leave that made it possible for more parents to be home during the early, critical months."

**Paid Leave Around the World**

The United States lags behind nearly every other industrialized nation in the world in terms of paid leave. These countries already grant paid leave to new parents, based on the philosophy that parents are a child's best caregivers, new mothers need time to recover from childbirth, and all families need help raising the nation's future workers and citizens.

A new mother in Chile, for example, can take up to eighteen weeks off after childbirth, at full pay. French mothers are entitled to sixteen weeks; German mothers, fourteen weeks; and Italian mothers twenty weeks—all at 100 percent of pay. In Norway, mothers can take up to a year off at 80 percent of pay. And [in 2001], Canadian mothers won the right to take off a full year from work after the birth of a baby at 60 percent of pay. Several countries extend paid leave to both mothers and fathers.

"Other countries have long had paid and job-protected leaves for new parents, and more are including men in their policies, as a way of encouraging fathers to get more involved with their children," says Sheila Kamerman, head of the Cross-National Studies Program of the School of Social Work at Columbia University. "And the leave is just one of the components that other countries have deemed necessary support to families with young children. They also get child allowances, to help defray the cost of raising children, health insurance, and even free health care for new babies. Many also support early childhood and education programs." "You have to really feel sorry for the American working mother when you learn what other countries have to offer," says Kamerman. "I think that working families who attempt to balance work and family life in the United States with so little help from the society at large are under enormous stress."

Given all these issues for workers and their families, it's no surprise that Americans overwhelmingly support proposals to create paid leave, as revealed in polls and surveys in recent years. In 1998, the National Partnership for Women & Families found that 82 percent of women and 75 percent of men favored the idea of developing a new insurance program that would give families some income when a worker takes a family or medical leave. In

1999, support for the idea remained strong: 83 percent of women said expanding FMLA and providing paid leave is important to them. In 2000, several polls found equally enthusiastic support. . . . "There's very little question that family leave benefits and expansion of the current family leave law are popular," says Lichtman of the National Partnership. "The question now is really how do we make that happen. Other countries use their unemployment systems or disability insurance plans. What system will we use here?"

## Blueprints for Change

Existing private and public policies do offer a vision of how family leave benefits could be provided in this country. In 2001, some twenty-five states had proposals under active consideration. Many of these models would build on existing disability insurance or unemployment systems. A few are completely new, innovative proposals, such as establishing independent family leave funds, tax credits for families and employers, and allowances for new parents who stay home with their babies.

At present, five states utilize temporary disability insurance systems to help provide paid leave—California, Hawaii, New Jersey, New York, and Rhode Island (as well as Puerto Rico). Some 22 percent of the private workforce, or one out of every five workers, is covered by one of these state plans. Under these programs, all employers provide disability insurance, either as part of a state plan or via private insurance, through which workers out on disability leave receive income. Disabled pregnant women and women recovering from childbirth are covered as part of these programs. The income that workers receive under these programs varies from state to state. It is generally awarded on a sliding scale, depending on an employee's salary, up to a state-imposed ceiling. California recently raised its ceiling to $492 a week, making it the most generous; the average payment is just $229 a week. . . . Because these state insurance systems already exist, work well, and are generally seen as affordable by employers, many advocates see them as an ideal vehicle for providing family leave benefits. . . .

There are other promising ways to provide such benefits, and many are now included in proposals before state legislatures. The most popular to date has been to expand the unemployment insurance (UI) system—a method also used in other countries—to cover workers out on family leave. "Letting employees collect unemployment insurance while they are on parental leave is consistent with both the history and purpose of the unemployment compensation system," says Bell of the National Partnership. "When the unemployment system was first established, most workers were male breadwinners and most reasons for their temporarily not working were economic downturns. Today, breadwinners are both male and female, and their reasons for temporarily not working include compelling family needs. It makes sense to update the UI system to reflect the reality of today's workforce."

The U.S. Department of Labor gave life to this idea in June 2000, when it published a rule that explicitly permits state law to allow new parents to collect unemployment insurance while out on leave (known as "Baby UI").... The UI model is especially appealing since every state already has an unemployment benefits system in place, and it requires only direction from state lawmakers to expand it. Unemployment insurance is supported by small payroll taxes, and estimates show that it would take only a minimal increase in most states to add a benefit for new parents. . . .

Advocates in other states have proposed creating entirely new family leave funds, paid for by small increases in payroll taxes. "With just a penny an hour increase in the employer's contribution and a penny an hour from workers, we figure we could fund a paid family leave of up to five weeks," says Marilyn Watkins of the Economic Policy Institute in Seattle, which has been leading the campaign there. "We could provide up to $250 a week to workers out on leave, which would make a huge difference to many families." Other, more limited initiatives have surfaced in other states. . . . Given such momentum, advocates think it is only a matter of time before family leave is more affordable. "It took us a decade to get the Family and Medical Leave Act passed," says Lichtman. "We know this is a multiyear campaign, but a lot of progress has already been made. It's amazing to have so many states with so many active proposals."

**Good for Business**

To date, some 35 million American workers have taken advantage of the provisions of the federal Family and Medical Leave Act. The vast majority of employers—84 percent—find that the benefits of providing leave offset or outweigh the costs. Nearly 42 percent reported a positive return on their leave programs, and another 42 percent said the costs were neutral.

Interestingly, one third of American companies now offer thirteen or more weeks for maternity leave, and 15 percent offer that same generous leave to new fathers, adoptive parents, or workers who must take time off to care for a seriously ill child. In part this may be due to companies' perceptions that they are more attractive to potential employees with such a policy and that they will reduce staff turnover. Surveys at IBM show, for example, that family-friendly benefits rank second only to pay as the reason that top-performing employees stay at the corporation. IBM was one of the first companies in America to offer a fully paid leave for eight weeks or longer, as well as a part-time return to work, along with a job guarantee of up to several years.

Companies in industries where the fight for top talent is fierce, such as high-tech, drugs, and telecommunications, have adopted generous leaves in order to become the employer of choice. . . . Companies can also realize an increase in profits due to family friendly policies. Giving workers the time they need to tend to family matters saves money by keeping them on the payroll.

Many private employers already carry disability insurance voluntarily because it's a benefit that workers have come to expect. Most employees do not expect to suffer through a heart attack, broken bone, or gall bladder removal without a paycheck. It's just part of the benefit package, one that covers women recovering from childbirth as well. In other words, it's widely accepted as a cost of doing business. . . . In some cases, especially at large corporations, such insurance can provide substantial income—even a full paycheck—to workers out on leave, including women recovering from childbirth and men and women recovering from an illness. . . .

**Progress Slow, But Steady**

Given the current energy and activity devoted to creating paid leave at the state level, many advocates believe it's only a matter of time before federal lawmakers get on board. Senator Christopher Dodd (D-CT) hopes to add fuel to that fire with a bill coauthored by [then] Senate majority leader Tom Daschle (D-SD) that would make $400 million available for state demonstration projects that showcase effective ways to create benefits during family leave. In the meantime, they have also proposed extending unpaid leave to workers at smaller companies—those with as few as twenty-five workers—so that 14 million more workers would have the right to take at least a job-protected leave.

No wonder advocates are so optimistic. "When I first started to report on my research findings in the early 1970s about the benefits of paid and job-protected leave, people used to think I was from someplace else, like Mars. When I first testified in Congress in the mid-1970s, there was complete disbelief," says Professor Kamerman. "But now, no one dismisses the ideas anymore. In fact, we are making progress. It's slow, but we are making progress." Lichtman of the National Partnership notes: "It does take time, but the support for family leave benefits is so large that we think it is inevitable that Americans will get what other workers around the world already have—some pay and peace of mind when they have a new baby or must deal with a family health emergency."

Adapted from "Why Americans Need Family Leave Benefits and How They Can Get Them," from the National Partnership for Women & Families. For a copy of the full report and information about the campaign for paid family leave, see www.nationalpartnership.org. Reprinted with permission of the author and the National Partnership.

# Section 6

# Appendix

## Key Terms

Aid to Families with Dependent Children
basic-needs budget
comparable worth/pay equity
conditional power
equality versus difference
job evaluation
minimum wage
poverty, and how it is measured
protective legislation
Temporary Assistance for Needy Families

## Discussion Questions

1. Albelda and Tilly argue that "poverty, not single motherhood, is the problem." Explain and evaluate this statement.
2. Suggest three specific ways in which an increase in the federal minimum wage would disproportionately help employed women and people of color.
3. In seeking to improve women's labor market prospects, why is focusing on curing child poverty relevant and important?
4. What are the arguments for and against a comparable worth policy? Why do neoclassical economists oppose comparable worth and institutionalists support it?
5. The United States is one of the few industrialized countries that does not offer paid leave for caring for new infants or other family members. How has this affected women workers?
6. Some policy proposals focus on integrating women into the labor market on the same terms as men (equality) while others seek recognition for women's traditional contributions (difference). How do we strike a balance between these two goals?

## Exercises

1. How many states have set their state minimum wage higher than the federal minimum wage? Is your state's minimum higher than the federal standard? To investigate, visit the U.S. Department of Labor, Employment Standards Administration's web site at www.dol.gov/esa/welcome.html. Click on State Minimum Wages.

2. *"Do the Q."* Poverty rates and poverty lines are set by the U.S. Census Bureau, a division of the Department of Commerce. Go to the Census Bureau web site at www.census.gov/hhes/www/poverty.html to compare the most recent poverty rates by demographic group. The publication is titled "Poverty in the United States." (Be sure to read about "How the Census Bureau Measures Poverty.") Try creating bar charts in a spreadsheet program such as Microsoft Excel in order to contrast poverty rates by:

   a.    marital or family status
   b.    age, e.g., adult versus child poverty
   c.    race of adult and household head

3. *"Do the Q."* Calculate how much a full-time, year-round worker would earn at the current federal minimum wage. (You may need to make assumptions about what constitutes year-round, full-time work.) Compare this annual amount with the poverty lines for families of different sizes. Poverty thresholds for each year are found on the U.S. Census Bureau web site at www.census.gov/hhes/www/poverty.html. Can a worker support a family by working in a minimum wage job?

4. Write a sample "Letter to the Editor" to your local newspaper making a case for paid family leave that would resonate with both business executives and legislators.

## Further Reading

Bergmann, Barbara R. 1996. *In Defense of Affirmative Action.* New York: Basic Books.

Figart, Deborah M. 2002. "Race and Pay Equity: Policy Brief." Washington, DC: National Committee on Pay Equity. Available online: www.feminist.com/fairpay/brief.htm.

Figart, Deborah M., Ellen Mutari, and Marilyn Power. 2002. *Living Wages, Equal Wages: Gender and Labor Market Policies in the United States.* London: Routledge.

Fraser, Nancy. 1997. *Justice Interruptus: Critical Reflections on the "Postsocialist" Condition.* London: Routledge.

Helbrun, Suzanne W., ed. 1999. *The Silent Crisis in U.S. Child Care,* Vol. 563 of *The Annals of the American Academy of Political and Social Science.* Thousand Oaks, CA: Sage Periodicals Press.

King, Mary C., ed. 2001. *Squaring Up: Policy Strategies to Raise Women's Incomes in the United States.* Ann Arbor: University of Michigan Press.

Vogel, Lise. 1993. *Mothers on the Job.* New Brunswick, NJ: Rutgers University Press.

# Section 7

# The Gendered Impact of Economic Development and Globalization

The final section of the reader looks beyond the borders of the United States to examine the contemporary global economy. At the end of the twentieth century, the world economy underwent a period of restructuring, as new technologies and industries combined with globalization to transform political, economic, and social institutions. As we begin the twenty-first century, technological improvements in transportation and communication have virtually eroded borders between countries. Production spans the globe as raw materials from one country are shipped elsewhere to be processed, to yet another country to be manufactured into an input, and then assembled into a final product in yet another location.

For advanced industrialized countries such as the United States, this global production line has meant that many of the manufacturing jobs that once represented the heart of the economy, pumping out the economic lifeblood of the nation, have been moved overseas. This process is called *deindustrialization.* As we saw in Section 2, many of these manufacturing jobs were male-dominated and the service sector employment that rose to replace them has been female-intensive. Occupations in service-sector industries constituted roughly half of U.S. employment following World War II and grew to three-fourths by the mid-1980s. Demand for women's labor expanded. However, women workers in textiles, apparel, and other industries also lost their footholds in manufacturing.

In feminist analyses of economic restructuring, *feminization of the labor force*, described in Section 2, is inextricably connected to the *feminization of labor,* that is, the transformation of "good" jobs (gendered male) into "bad" jobs (gendered female). Thus, gender is an important dimension of structural change that alters the conditions of work for both women and men. Many service sector jobs in the postindustrial period have been less unionized, lower paid, and had less employment stability. Contingent employment (temporary help and contracted services) has replaced full-time, year-round jobs. Part-time and home-based work has grown. Income inequality among families rose during the 1980s as the rich grew richer and the middle class and poor struggled to get by. Even the economic boom of the 1990s was fueled by escalating consumer debt, as families used credit cards, second mortgages, and lines of credit to finance their purchases.

The end of the twentieth century was also marked by dramatic changes in the political economy, especially in the social consensus on the proper role of the state. We have seen a return to laissez-faire principles regarding market forces, economic arguments that seemed less persuasive when memories of the Great Depression were close at hand. Economic liberalization, meaning less government regulation and a shift away from macroeconomic stabilization policies, has accompanied globalization. International organizations such as the World Bank and International Monetary Fund (IMF) and international trade agreements such as the General Agreement on Tariffs and Trade (GATT) and the North American Free Trade Agreement (NAFTA) have actively promoted economic liberalization policies.

Another side of globalization and liberalization can be seen by taking the standpoint of women in developing countries who have assumed new roles in the global assembly line. In order to obtain loans from international lending organizations, many developing countries have been pressured to adopt programs of export-oriented manufacturing, focused on producing goods for consumption in advanced industrial nations. Women are employed in relocated industries such as garment manufacturing, sewing designer clothes for affluent women in the United States and other advanced industrialized countries. High-tech assembly jobs making semiconductors, computer chips, and electronics rely on women's "nimble fingers." In fact, jobs as diverse as agricultural production and data entry employ women in the developing world.

Export-oriented development is one aspect of *structural adjustment policies* aiming to restructure the political economies of developing nations. The economic concept of comparative advantage, which was applied in Section 3 to the division of labor within households, is used to argue that countries with cheap, available labor can promote economic growth by attracting labor-intensive industries. Attempts to raise wages and improve labor standards would undermine the primary reason why global companies choose to relocate to the developing world.

Structural adjustment programs, however, have been controversial. Many of the trends associated with the feminization of labor described above, including the proliferation of "bad" jobs with poor working conditions, are even more serious problems in developing countries where informal sector employment is extensive. Workers, in the worst instances, are treated as disposable commodities, to be replaced as global capital moves on to the next underdeveloped region. Economist Guy Standing has referred to this process as "global feminization through flexible labor." The first three chapters in this section explore some of these controversies associated with this combination of globalization and liberalization.

In the first selection, Nilüfer Çagatay contrasts two attitudes toward globalization, grounded in alternative theoretical economic approaches. "Gender and International Labor Standards in the World Economy" echoes one of the themes of this reader: the debate between those who believe free market forces enhance the quality of life for both men and women and those who see a need for government intervention in the economy to mitigate some of the inequities generated by "free" markets. Çagatay maintains that both neoclassical and institutionalist approaches to globalization overlook the specific impact on women. Specifically, like most economic analyses, policy debates over globalization neglect the interaction between paid and unpaid contributions to economic well-being.

The institutionalist analysis of globalization is treated in greater depth by Lourdes Benería and by Eiman Zein-Elabdin in their two chapters. These authors also address the role of feminism in attempts to humanize the global economy and make economic processes more responsive to the concerns of women, families, and environmental activists. In "Globalization, Gender, and the Davos Man," Benería examines the parallels between the historic industrialization process in Europe and the United States and the contemporary experience of developing countries, using the work of institutionalist writer Karl Polanyi as an interpretive lens. In both instances, the so-called "free" market was a creation of political forces and state action. In both cases, the harsh side effects of industrialization generated social critics who sought to limit the power of business to organize peoples' lives.

Zein-Elabdin contrasts two efforts to incorporate gender into development models: women in development and ecofeminism. Incorporating themes that were discussed in Section 6, she notes that these models suggest different concepts of gender equity; the first attempts to integrate women into male economic norms while the latter asserts that women have an essentially different character than men, rendering women more in sync with nature and the environment. Like Benería, Zein-Elabdin is searching for a third position, in which women, specifically Third World feminists, can contribute to well-being based on a historically specific standpoint. In many respects, the Convention on the Elimination of All Forms of Discrimination Against Women (CEDAW), reprinted as the final chapter in this reader, provides a comprehensive policy agenda that balances these equality and difference perspectives.

# 26

# Gender and International Labor Standards in the World Economy

*Nilüfer Çagatay*

Several trends have recently stimulated a renewed interest in discussions of international labor standards or worker's rights. Among these are the transition from a "mass production for mass consumption" economy to the "flexible production" system, rising globalization of production, and increasing global mobility of capital. These tendencies are all the more enhanced by the neoliberal structural adjustment policies carried out in developing countries where governments compete to attract capital by lowering labor standards, thereby also threatening labor standards for workers in the industrialized countries.

There are two frequently mentioned positions with respect to discussions of labor standards: the "neoclassical" and the "institutionalist" perspectives. These two schools disagree on whether labor standards help or hurt the constituencies that they are intended to empower as well as whether labor standards help or hinder growth and trade. Recent discussions have also generated disagreements between these schools of thought in terms of whether there should be a linkage between labor standards and trade agreements, as in the context of discussions of the Uruguay Round and the World Trade Organization (WTO). Another point of disagreement is whether greater globalization will lead to downward harmonization of labor standards. Institutionalists tend to argue that without regulation, there will be downward harmonization. They advocate regulation, and some among them propose trade-linked schemes such as "social tariffs" to ensure "upward harmonization," while neoclassicals argue that labor conditions can best be improved in the long run by deregulating labor markets.[1]

The purpose of this chapter is to briefly examine these two approaches from a feminist perspective and elaborate on what that perspective might be. Even though the institutionalist and neoclassical perspectives disagree on a number of important questions, as I argue below they tend to share a common gender-biased definition of labor.[2]

## Alternative Perspectives on Labor Standards

The neoclassicals generally view labor standards as impediments to labor market clearing (see, for example, Fields 1990; Bhagwati 1994; Srinivasan 1994). "Excessive labor standards" increase labor costs, cause unemployment and allocative inefficiency, jeopardize growth, and drive a wedge between "protected" and "unprotected" workers, benefiting protected workers at the expense of the unprotected. In this view, there is a trade-off between labor standards and employment. The major income distributive concern is the distribution of income among workers or wage structures.

Neoclassicals advocate relying on market forces to bring about improvements in labor conditions. They argue that such improvements follow from growth or come about as a result of increased demand for labor standards by consumers. The industrializing economies' comparative advantage lies in their relatively abundant labor. Thus comparative advantage can be made use of only if wages reflect the forces of supply and demand without interference from the government or other "market distorting" entities like labor unions. In the long run, outward orientation and the resulting high growth rates translate into increasing wages and better labor conditions. Neoclassicals, therefore, advocate delinking trade agreements and labor standards. They also fear that labor standards might be used for protectionist purposes by industrialized countries.

While there is no or little discussion of *gender* as such, neoclassicals discuss women workers generally in terms of the negative impact of market distortions and regulations on women. Protective legislation is seen as an impediment to women's full participation in labor markets. Likewise, maternity benefits and child care provisions are usually seen as disadvantaging and limiting women's employment. Deregulation is beneficial to women since they are seen as the "main victims" of regulation.

According to the alternative view, usually referred to as institutionalist, the causal link between standards and outcomes runs contrary to the neoclassical arguments (see, for example, Piore 1990; Singh 1991; Wilkinson 1994). In this view, standards encourage the adoption of new technologies that enhance productivity. According to Piore (1990), for example, the original development of labor standards was based on the rationale for getting rid of sweatshops and a switch to a higher productivity regime under mass production systems. In an example from the industrializing economies, Standing (1991) has found that in Malaysia unions contributed to both productivity enhancement and a narrowing of the gender gap in wages.

Institutionalists, therefore, advocate the adoption and observation of labor standards. There are also variants of this approach that argue that corporatist bargaining systems (such as in Sweden) are more successful in both protecting workers' rights and leading to better macroeconomic outcomes. Singh (1991) argues that a new expansionist, macroeconomic regime can be founded on the basis of a new social consensus reached by corporate institutional arrangements between employers, governments, and workers. Given the erosion of standards within more flexible production systems, Standing (1991) advocates new forms of organizing that are more appropriate in the context of flexible production.

Some institutionalist writers have addressed gender issues in the context of discussions of feminization as well as in discussions on standards with regard to discrimination. For example, Standing (1989) views global feminization and flexibility (in the context of supply-side macroeconomic policies) as interlinked phenomena that undermine labor standards. Within this framework, women are sometimes viewed as a "vulnerable" segment of workers who are recruited by capital in ways that undermine existing labor standards. In contrast to the neoclassicals, the institutionalists locate the central power relations in the capital-labor relationship. More recently, Howes and Singh (1995) have argued that the new social consensus generated by a corporatist regime referred to above must include specifically "women's voice" as distinct from having only unions represent women workers' interests. Institutionalists also advocate upholding antidiscrimination laws and other regulations such as minimum wage laws and maternity benefits, whose costs, they argue, must be socialized.

## Toward a Feminist Approach to Labor Standards

Feminist views on workers' rights are more complicated than the neoclassical or institutionalist approaches, which share the commonality of defining labor primarily as "paid labor" and, therefore, focus on paid labor. While both approaches tend to view women as a vulnerable segment of workers, the bases of vulnerability, which need to be located in gender as well as class relations, are not systematically addressed. A feminist approach to labor standards would start with the introduction of the concept of gender as an analytical tool in understanding both the rise and evolution of labor standards.

Feminist economists view the basic gender division of labor as that division between productive/reproductive labor activities. Further, women's responsibilities for social reproduction performed in the form of unpaid domestic labor influence their position in labor markets as paid laborers. Women's labor force participation rate is lower than men's. However, women tend to have a greater combined labor burden consisting of paid and unpaid activities in the world economy. Occupations and industries tend to be gender-typed, and those that are associated with the female gender tend to be lower paying and of lower social status. Women also often receive lower wages for the same work. They tend to engage more frequently in part-time, casual, flexible, or informal labor activities as a result of their unpaid domestic labor responsibilities. These gender-based inequalities in markets, in turn, reinforce men's power vis-à-vis women within households and other institutions. For feminists, therefore, a fundamental goal is the elimination of the "traditional" gender division of labor within households, since this division reinforces the gender inequalities within labor markets and vice versa. Focusing on a narrow definition of labor as "paid labor" is insufficient.

Given the gender-based division of labor and the patterns of gender segregation and differentiation in labor markets, feminists question what labor standards have meant for women and men historically (as opposed to an ungendered category of workers).

Feminist scholars have argued that in industrialized economies, various forms of protective legislation, restrictions of child labor, and the demands of unions concerning the "family wage" in the nineteenth century helped create the gender-based division of labor between (women's) unpaid domestic labor and (largely men's) paid laboring activities. Thus, traditional union strategies that have been predicated upon a "male breadwinner ideology" must change and take into account both the breakdown of this ideology and the reality of feminization of the labor force in the post-World War II period in most regions of the world economy.

Furthermore, the conditions associated with flexible production had defined the conditions of women's paid labor activities before the arrival of flexible production for male workers. Hence, historically and at present, women tend to engage more frequently in unpaid family labor and casual, part-time, or home work arrangements and are overrepresented in the informal sector compared to men. For example, women frequently work for subminimum wages in many informal or home work types of activities because such forms of work allow them to care for their children as they engage in paid work. This has meant that they are in sectors or in types of activity that are more difficult to organize. There may be no employer to negotiate with, or those who employ them may be male family members, as in the case of women who perform unpaid family labor. Under such conditions, what is at issue is not only the unequal power relation between capitalists and workers, but also the unequal power relations based on gender (within and outside the family). These mean that women have not benefited from some labor standards, such as collective bargaining, to the same degree as men.

Even for women who work in "organizable" sectors such as manufacturing, problems persist. Feminists have argued that the freedom to associate and bargain over the conditions of work has a gender-bias in that women, due to their (unpaid) domestic labor responsibility, cannot fully participate in collective bargaining or unionizing activities. Hence the degree of unionization of women is generally lower compared to that of men. The fact that unions are dominated by men, especially at the higher ranks, has meant that unions historically have not been as concerned with work conditions that affect women more, *given the present state of gender relations*. For example, they have not been as sensitive to harassment issues or child care provisions at the workplace.

However, feminists and others have shown that in industries or firms that are unionized, the gender gap in wages is narrower compared to nonunionized sectors. This is because unions are effective in enforcing equal pay for equal work provisions and other labor standards for their members. Moreover, it is evident from cross-country studies of industrialized economies that in countries with more centralized bargaining systems the gender earnings gap is lower compared to those with more decentralized bargaining systems (Blau and Kahn 1992; Howes and Singh 1995). Feminists also view minimum wage laws as a possible way of alleviating (especially but not exclusively) women's poverty. They see maternity benefits and child care facilities as mechanisms that offset "pre-existing distortions that arise because the costs of women's unpaid work in having and rearing children are not taken account of by markets" (Elson 1991). They also see pay equity schemes as important policy tools. Thus feminists advocate regulation of labor markets, notwithstanding the historical gender biases embedded in the formation of labor standards in the age of "male breadwinner" ideology.

In spite of all the gender bias against women's ability to benefit from labor standards as discussed above, recently women have been organizing themselves in innovative ways that have proven to be empowering (Martens and Mitter 1994). Such innovative forms of organizing include national and international networks, credit unions, and other types of associations such as SEWA (Self Employed Women's Association in India). These networks tend to be organized horizontally rather than vertically. They provide training, credit, and empowering knowledge. Such forms of organizing are important and crucial for all workers, especially in the changing conditions of work toward greater flexibility.

Feminists have been pursuing their goals of gender equity in a wide variety of international forums, such as the United Nations conferences on women. Such conferences have led to the Convention on the Elimination of All Forms of Discrimination Against Women (CEDAW) and various other platforms for action geared toward empowerment of women. Such international conferences have encouraged rethinking the concept of labor from women's perspectives. One such important step was taken at the recent Beijing conference on women with the recognition of unpaid domestic labor as work.

## Conclusion

The neoclassical and institutionalist approaches rely on a gender-biased definition of labor, since the debates generally take market-related work as the appropriate definition of labor, leaving out unpaid domestic labor. Redefining labor along feminist lines means that we also need to rethink the nexus of productivity, wages, trade, and labor standards. The nonfeminist approaches either ignore the gender biases historically embedded in *some* standards (the neoinstitutionalists) or the gender biases that are produced or reproduced by markets (the neoclassicals).

It is the contention of this paper that neither a simple reliance on "deregulated markets," nor on labor standard regulations defined in terms of "market-related work," or on mechanical trade-linked schemes can bring about an improvement in the conditions of work. A feminist perspective fundamentally challenges the meaning of labor and worker assumed by both schools of thought, helping us rethink the theoretical parameters of the debate and come up with new policies and politics that can be more conducive to attaining "upward harmonization" for both genders across the development divide in the context of the changing world economy.

## Notes

1. See Herzenberg and Perez-Lopez (1990) and Schoepfle and Swinnerton (1994) for examples of such debates. Needless to say, the neoclassical and neoinstitutionalist schools are not monolithic. A third approach, the Marxist one, as discussed by Dorman (1995), argues that worker rights are an aspect of the struggle of workers against capital via the state apparatus. Some Marxists support trade-linked schemes, while some oppose them.

2. In these discussions, there is generally a distinction between "core standards," including freedom from forced labor and slavery and the right to associate freely, which are seen to be human rights–related and expected as absolute conditions by everyone, versus those standards that are viewed as being linked to the level of economic development and therefore as relative conditions. The most frequently cited and ratified standards include the above standards, minimum age laws, collective bargaining laws, and freedom from discrimination.

## References

Bhagwati, Jagdish. 1994. "Policy Perspectives and Future Directions: A View from Academia." In *International Labor Standards and Global Economic Integration:*

*Proceedings of a Symposium*, ed. Gregory K. Schoepfle and Kenneth A. Swinnerton. Washington, DC: U.S. Department of Labor.

Blau, Francine D., and Lawrence Kahn. 1992. "The Gender Earnings Gap: Learning from International Comparisons." *American Economic Review* 82 (2): 533–38.

Dorman, Peter. 1995. "Policies to Promote Labor Rights: An Analytical Review." Unpublished paper, James Madison College, Michigan State University, East Lansing.

Elson, Diane. 1991. "Appraising Recent Developments in the World Market for Nimble Fingers: Accumulation, Regulation, Organization." Unpublished paper, Department of Economics, University of Manchester, UK.

Fields, Gary. 1990. "Labor Standards, Economic Development and International Trade." In *Labor Standards and Development in the Global Economy*, ed. Stephen Herzenberg and Jorge Perez-Lopez. Washington, DC: U.S. Department of Labor.

Herzenberg, Stephen, and Jorge Perez-Lopez, eds. 1990. *Labor Standards and Development in the Global Economy*. Washington, DC: U.S. Department of Labor.

Howes, Candace, and Ajit Singh. 1995. "Long-Trends in the World Economy: The Gender Dimension." *World Development* 23 (11): 1895–1911.

Martens, Margaret Hosmer, and Swasti Mitter, eds. 1994. *Women in Trade Unions: Organizing the Unorganized*. Geneva: International Labour Office.

Piore, Michael. 1990. "Labor Standards and Business Strategies." In *Labor Standards and Development in the Global Economy*, ed. Stephen Herzenberg and Jorge Perez-Lopez. Washington, DC: U.S. Department of Labor.

Schoepfle, Gregory, K. and Kenneth A. Swinnerton, eds. 1994. *International Labor Standards and Global Economic Integration: Proceedings of a Symposium*. Washington, DC: U.S. Department of Labor.

Singh, Ajit. 1991. "Labor Markets and Structural Adjustments." In *Towards Social Adjustment*, ed. Guy Standing and Victor Tokman. Geneva: International Labour Office.

Srinivasan, T.N. 1994. "International Labor Standards and International Trade: International Labor Standards Once Again!" In *International Labor Standards and Global Economic Integration: Proceedings of a Symposium*, ed. Gregory K. Schoepfle and Kenneth A. Swinnerton. Washington, DC: U.S. Department of Labor.

Standing, Guy. 1989. "Global Feminization Through Flexible Labor." *World Development* 17 (7): 1077–95.

———. 1991. "Do Unions Impede or Accelerate Structural Adjustment? Industrial Versus Company Unions in an Industrializing Labour Market." *Cambridge Journal of Economics* 16: 327–54.

Wilkinson, Frank. 1994. "Equality, Efficiency and Economic Progress: The Case for Universally Applied Equitable Standards for Wages and Conditions of Work." In *Creating Economic Opportunities: The Role of Labour Standards in Industrial Restructuring*, ed. Werner Sengenberger and Duncan Campbell. Geneva: International Labour Office.

Adapted from "Gender and International Labor Standards in the World Economy," *Review of Radical Political Economics* 28 (3): 92–101. Reprinted with permission of Elsevier Science.

# 27

# Globalization, Gender, and the Davos Man

## Lourdes Benería

Much has been said over the past fifteen years about global markets. The process of accelerated globalization that we have witnessed during recent decades has been a powerful source of change—driving national economies, deepening their international connections, and affecting many aspects of social, political, and cultural life. Despite the debate over the extent to which the degree of globalization is higher today than in other historical periods, few of us doubt that powerful forces are working toward the formation of "global villages." From an economic perspective, the basic features of globalization are the transformations linked to ever expanding markets and the rapid technological change in communications and transportation that transcend national boundaries and shrink space. The expansion of markets has taken place within the context of the neoliberal model of development, which has returned to a laissez-faire discourse and practice that characterized nineteenth-century capitalism. One argument presented in this chapter is that, despite its different framework, the current global expansion exhibits similarities to the earlier expansion of markets. This is the case for both high- and low-income countries, including those in transition to market economies from the centralized planning of the former Soviet Union. . . .

### The Self-Regulated Market

*The Great Transformation* [by Karl Polanyi] was first published in 1944. It is an analysis of the construction and growth of the self-regulated market and of laissez-faire capitalism from the beginning of the industrial revolution up to the early twentieth century. Polanyi's "great transformation" was the "taming" of the market. It was represented by what he calls the "collectivist countermovement" that, beginning in the late nineteenth century and continuing through the twentieth, took refuge in "social and national protectionism" against "the weaknesses and perils inherent in a self-regulating market" (1957 [1944], p. 145).

Polanyi's analysis centers on the profound change in human behavior represented by market-oriented choices and by decisions in which gain replaced subsistence as the center of economic activity. Gain and profit, Polanyi argues, had never before played such important roles in human activity. Critical of Adam Smith's suggestion that the social division of labor depended upon the existence of markets and "upon man's propensity to barter, truck and exchange one thing for another" (p. 43), Polanyi argues instead that the division of labor in earlier societies had depended on "differences inherent in the facts of sex, geography, and individual endowment" (p. 44). For Polanyi, production and distribution in many earlier societies were ensured through reciprocity and redistribution, two principles not currently associated with economics. These principles were part of an economic system that was "a mere function of social organization," that is, at the service of social life. Capitalism, however, evolved in the opposite direction, leading to a situation in which the economic system determined social organization. Commenting on Smith, Polanyi argues that "no misreading of the past ever proved to be more prophetic of the future" (p. 43), in the sense that one hundred years after Adam Smith wrote about man's propensity to barter, truck, and exchange, this propensity became the norm—theoretically and practically—of industrial capitalist/market society. Although Polanyi may not always persuade us that the pursuit of economic gain is a result of market society, its fundamental role in a market economy—and in the theoretical models that sustain that economy—is unarguably central.

For Polanyi, a crucial step in this gradual transformation toward the predominance of "the economic" was the one "which makes isolated markets into a [self-regulated] market economy." Contrary to conventional wisdom, Polanyi argues, this change was not "the natural outcome of the spreading of markets" (p. 57). On the contrary, the market economy was socially constructed and accompanied by a profound change in the organization of society itself. . . .

Polanyi mentions also the enormous increase in the administrative functions of a state newly endowed with a central bureaucracy, the strengthening of private property, and the enforcement of contracts in market exchange and other transactions. . . . He also ascribes the formation of a competitive national labor market in eighteenth- and nineteenth-century England to a series of policies that dislocated labor and forced the new laboring classes to work for low wages. In this sense, Polanyi's analysis suggests the seemingly contradictory notion of laissez-faire liberalism as "the product of deliberate state action," including "a conscious and often violent intervention on the part of the government" (p. 250). As he points out, "all these strongholds of government interference were erected with a view to the organizing of some simple [market] freedom."

On the other hand, Polanyi points out that the "collectivist countermovement" or "great transformation"—the subsequent great variety of (re)actions taken against some of the negative consequences of the expanding market—started spontaneously as the critiques of capitalism led to political organizing and a variety of citizens' actions. Many of them constituted defensive actions on the part of different social groups. The left movements and social planning of the twentieth century were part of this transformation, although Polanyi sees its origins not in "any preference for socialism or nationalism" but in "the broader range of the vital social interests affected by the expanding market mechanism" (p. 145). . . .

The profound change represented by the gradual construction of a market society found a key expression in the changes in human behavior that led to the prevalence of rational economic man. As Polanyi puts it, "a market economy can only exist in a market society." That is, it can only exist when accompanied by changes in norms and behavior that enable the market to function. Economic rationality is based on the expectation that human beings behave in such ways as to achieve maximum gains. As any course in introductory economics emphasizes, while the entrepreneur seeks to maximize profit, the employee seeks to attain the highest earnings possible, and the consumer to maximize his or her utility. At the theoretical level, Adam Smith linked the selfish pursuit of individual gain to the maximization of the wealth of nations through the invisible hand of the market. He saw no contradiction between the two, and the orthodox tradition in economics continues to rely on this basic link.

In that tradition, and as feminist economists have often pointed out, the basic assumption of rational economic man has been embodied in neoclassical economic theory (Ferber and Nelson 1993; Folbre 1994). Economic rationality is assumed to be the norm in human behavior and the way to ensure the healthy functioning of the competitive market. This is expected to result in the most efficient allocation of resources and the maximization of production at the lowest possible costs. Feminist economists have also pointed out that most orthodox analysis excludes behavior based on other types of motivation, such as altruism, empathy, love, the pursuit of art and beauty for their own sake, reciprocity, and care. Selfless behavior is viewed as belonging to the nonmarket sector, such as the family. . . .

## The Construction of the National and Global Market

> "Capitalism without bankruptcy is like Christianity without hell."[1]

As the twentieth-century nears its end, many parallels can be traced between the social construction of national market economies analyzed by Polanyi for nineteenth-century Europe and the expansion and deepening of both national and transnational markets across the globe. To be sure, a debate exists about the extent to which globalization represents a new historical trend; various authors, for example, have pointed out that some indicators of the degree of globalization are similar to those reached in earlier historical periods—such as before World War I. Yet the intensification of integrative processes during the past thirty years—for example, in terms of increasingly rapid movement of goods, communications, and exchange among countries and regions—has been unprecedented. The financial sector has led in the degree to which its markets have transcended national boundaries, while trade liberalization and the internationalization of production have accelerated the global integration of markets in goods and services.

At the national level, these processes have been facilitated by numerous efforts on the part of governments, which have played an active role in the globalization of domestic economies and of their social, political, and cultural life. This time, however, the construction of global markets has taken place in particular through the interventions of international forces beyond national boundaries, such as the regional formation of free-trade areas and common markets, the growth of multinational corporations, the role of international organizations such as the World Bank and the International Monetary Fund, and the influence of foreign governments and other international actors, such as private banks, in determining policy in developing countries. . . .

Although these policies have clearly increased the economic freedom of many actors involved in the market, they have also represented the use of a strong hand on the part of national governments and international institutions intent on building the neoliberal model of the late twentieth century, that is, achieving the great leap forward in the construction of national and global markets. To invoke Polanyi, these policies have been the product of deliberate state intervention—often carried out in the name of market freedoms—imposed from the top down and without a truly democratic process of discussion and decision making among all affected parties. As the *Wall*

*Street Journal* put it for the case of Argentina, "[T]he reforms were largely accomplished by the political will of a presidential strongman who invoked executive decrees over 1,000 times" (O'Grady 1997). . . .

At the same time, the expansion of markets, associated also with the intensification of "modernization" across the globe, has been accompanied with triumphalist (re)statements and affirmations of discourses emphasizing the norms and behavior associated with economic rationality. These must be seen as part of the process of constructing markets à la Polanyi. We have witnessed this process in different forms, ranging from a strong emphasis on productivity, efficiency, and financial rewards, to shifts in values and attitudes—typified by the yuppies in the 1980s—such as a new emphasis on individualism and competitive behavior, together with an apparent tolerance and even acceptance of social inequalities and greed. The neoliberal weekly *The Economist* sees this set of factors as symbolized by the "Davos Man" who has replaced the "Chatham House Man" in his influence in the global marketplace.[2] The Davos Man, according to the weekly, includes businessmen, bankers, officials, and intellectuals who "hold university degrees, work with words and numbers, speak some English and share beliefs in individualism, market economics and democracy. They control many of the world's governments, and the bulk of its economic and military capabilities." The Davos Man does not "butter up the politicians; it is the other way around . . . finding it boring to shake the hand of an obscure prime minister." Instead, he prefers to meet the Bill Gateses of the world. Written as a critique of Samuel Huntington's thesis in *The Clash of Civilizations and the Remaking of the World Order*, the praise of Davos Man by *The Economist* turns into an ode to the global and more contemporary version of economic man:

> Some people find Davos Man hard to take: there is something uncultured about all the money-grubbing and managerialism. But it is part of the beauty of Davos Man that, by and large, he does not give a fig for culture as the Huntingtons of the world define it. He will attend a piano recital, but does not mind whether an idea, a technique or a market is (in Mr. Huntington's complex scheme) Sinic, Hindu, Islamic or Orthodox. ("In Praise of the Davos Man" 1997, p. 18)

Thus, *The Economist* expects that Davos Man, through the magic powers of the market and its homogenizing tendencies, is more likely to bring people and cultures together than force them apart. In many ways, he is the rational economic man gone global.

What *The Economist* does not recognize is that the commercialization of everyday life and of all sectors of the economy generates dynamics and values that individuals and cultures might find repulsive. In many ways, we have witnessed, in Polanyi's terms, the tendency for society to become "an accessory to the economic system" rather than the other way around. . . .

## Gender and the Market

This section argues that Polanyi's analysis of the social construction of markets has important gender-related implications that he did not take into consideration. A central argument in this chapter is that the links to the market have been historically different for men and women, with consequences for their choices and behavior. Although Polanyi points out that all production in a market society is for sale, he fails to discuss the fact that, parallel to the deepening of market relations, a large proportion of the population engages in unpaid production, only indirectly linked to the market. Women are disproportionately concentrated in this type of work, which includes agricultural family labor, particularly but not solely in subsistence economies, domestic work, and volunteer work. In contemporary societies, women perform by far the largest proportion of unpaid activities. According to the United Nations Development Program's (UNDP's) "rough estimates" at the global level, if unpaid activities were valued at prevailing wages, they would amount to $16 trillion or about 70 percent of total world output ($23 trillion). Of this $16 trillion, $11 trillion, or almost 69 percent, represents women's work (UNDP 1995). . . .

Thus, to a large extent, men and women have been positioned differently with respect to both market transformations and the linkages between gender and nature (Merchant 1989). While the market has been associated with public life and "maleness," women have been viewed as closer to nature—often in essentialist ways instead of as a result of historical constructions. This perspective has in turn had an impact on the meaning of gender, a subject analyzed, for example, in the feminist literature dealing with the construction of femininity and masculinity (Gilligan 1982; Bem 1993; Butler 1993), and on our notions of the market itself (McCloskey 1993; Strassmann 1993). Clearly, Polanyi's 1944 analysis needs to be expanded to incorporate gender dimensions.

The norms and behavior associated with the market do not apply to the sphere of unpaid work that produces goods and services for use rather than for exchange. To the extent that unpaid work is not equally subject to the competitive pressures of the market, it can respond to motivations other than gain, such as nurturing, love, and altruism, or to other norms of behavior, such as duty and religious beliefs/practices. Without falling into essentialist arguments about men's and women's motivations, and keeping in mind the multiple differences across countries and cultures, we can conclude from the literature that there are gender-related variations in norms, values, and behavior (England 1993; Nelson 1993; Seguino, Stevens, and Lutz 1996). Likewise, the literature has discussed extensively women's concentration in caring/ nurturing work, either unpaid or paid (Folbre and Weisskopf 1996). Women have also concentrated in the service sector. To illustrate, the average proportion of women in this sector in the Organization for Economic Cooperation and Development (OECD) countries has been reported to be as high as 95 percent (Christopherson 1997).

Although the UNDP-type data show that the current predominance of women in unpaid work and that of men in paid activities is beyond dispute, engagement in nongainful activities is no more the exclusive domain of women than is market work the exclusive domain of men. In earlier societies, the principles of reciprocity and distribution described by Polanyi did not necessarily function according to the rules of market rationality. Instead, tradition, religion, kin, and community played an important role in setting up norms and affecting collective and individual values. But nonmaximizing behavior can also be found in contemporary societies. In subsistence economies, production is not geared to the market, and family labor is motivated primarily by needs rather than gain. Likewise, in market economies, behavior following norms of solidarity and choices between work and leisure, not necessarily pursuing gain or following the dictates of efficiency, competition, and productivity associated with economic rationality, has certainly not disappeared. This is symbolized by the large numbers of volunteer workers performing countless unpaid activities and by those engaged by choice in creative and/or in poorly remunerated work. In the case of volunteer work, such as that carried out at the community level, the motives might be associated with a sense of collective well-being, empathy for others, or political commitment; in the case of artistic work, they might result from the pursuit of beauty and creativity, irrespective of their market value.

Feminist economists have written extensively about the way economic rationality, even in capitalist economies, may not be as prevalent as mainstream economics assumes. Their work has led them to recognize the need to develop alternative models based on assumptions of human cooperation, empathy, and collective well-being (Ferber and Nelson 1993; Strober 1994; Folbre 1994). In seeking alternative models, they join other scholars who have also questioned neoclassical assumptions on the grounds that they are predicated upon the Hobbesian view of self-interested individuals.

These authors argue that the numerous exceptions to this rule suggest that human behavior responds to a complex set of often contradictory tendencies (Marwell and Ames 1981; Frank, Golovich, and Regan 1993). Thus, neoclassical assumptions seem to contradict "real-life experiments in which collective action and empathetic connected economic decision-making are observed" (Seguino, Stevens, and Lutz 1996). Adopting a gender perspective, some authors have pointed out that this type of behavior is more frequently encountered among women than among men (Guyer 1980; Gilligan 1982; Benería and Roldan 1987). . . .

The claim on the part of feminist economists that models of free individual choice are inadequate for the analysis of issues of dependence/interdependence, tradition, and power (Ferber and Nelson 1993) is particularly relevant for cultures in which individualistic, market-oriented behavior is more often the exception than the norm. Feminists have also pointed out that neoclassical analysis is based on a "separate self model" in which utility is viewed as subjective and unrelated to that of other people. As Paula England has argued, this model is linked to the assumption that individual behavior is selfish, since "emotional connection often creates empathy, altruism, and a subjective sense of social solidarity" (England 1993). Thus, to the extent that women are more emotionally connected than men, in large part because of their roles in child rearing and family care as well as because of the prevalent gender ideology, the separate self model has an androcentric bias. Moreover, to the extent that this model typifies Western individualism, it shares a Western bias and is foreign to societies with more collective forms of action and decision making. Neoclassical economic analysis has had little to say about these alternative modes of behavior and their significance for different forms of social organization and for policy and action.

We might ask if women's behaviors are changing as they enter the labor market in increasing numbers and as globalization intensifies the feminization of the labor force. Many studies have documented women's role in processes of industrialization in a variety of countries and their participation in production for global markets. During the past quarter century, we have witnessed the rapid formation of a female labor force in many countries. This labor force is often tied to the service sector and to production for export, even in countries where women's participation in paid work was traditionally low and socially unacceptable (Pyle 1982; Hein 1986; Ong 1987; Feldman 1992). In addition, the feminist movement, in its quest for gender equality, has contributed to this trend by emphasizing the need for women to increase their financial autonomy, bargaining power, and control over their lives. . . .

The extension and deepening of markets across the globe raises many questions. What is the effect on individual behavior of being integrated in market activities? More specifically, what is the effect on women as the weight of their paid labor time increases relative to their domestic work? Does it imply that they are increasingly adopting the norms of economic rationality à la "economic man"? Are women becoming more individualistic, selfish, and less nurturing? Is market behavior undermining "women's ways of seeing and doing"? Are gender identities being reconstituted? The answers to these questions are not clear-cut. To begin with, a nonessentialist view of gender differences implies that social change influences gender (re)constructions; as women become continuous participants in the market, it is likely their motives and aspirations will change, and they will adopt patterns of behavior traditionally observed more frequently among men. Casual observation and anecdotal evidence may persuade many of us that this is already happening. In addition, there remain areas of ambiguity, tension, and contradiction in the answers to these questions. These are rooted in different variables, some of which are historical and related to other factors.

The market can have positive effects, such as the breaking up of patriarchal traditions or the curtailment of arranged marriages that limit individual autonomy. On the cultural side, it can accelerate the diffusion of both "liberating" and "sexist" practices. It can also have negative consequences for those who suffer from discrimination and market exploitation. The literature on female labor in export-processing industries has provided examples of how an increase in women's autonomy and bargaining power can run parallel to discriminatory practices against them, at the workplace as well as at the community level (Pyle 1982; Hein 1986; Ong 1987; Cravey 1998). . . .

Several authors who have observed the changes in gender ideology in these countries have emphasized that the transition has exacerbated "latent and manifest patriarchal attitudes," increasing women's vulnerability both culturally and economically (Moghadan 1993). Bridger, Kay, and Pinnick note that "the initial rounds of democratic elections in Russia have virtually wiped women off the political map and their re-emergence is now painfully slow and fraught with difficulty" (1996, p. 2). In some Central Asian republics, new restrictions on women's lives have been imposed, such as barring them from appearing in public without a male or an elder woman, wearing pants, and driving cars (Tohidi 1996). A key question, however, will be the extent to which market forces will transform these norms and how the process of "modernization" spread through the market might shatter or erode patriarchal forms.

Ambiguity can also be found in feminist discourses themselves. For example, feminists have emphasized gender equality as a key goal, including the importance of women having the same access to the public sphere as men. In this sense, it is often assumed that women can behave as men do. Yet much feminist research has emphasized women's "difference." Gilligan, for example, documents the "different modes of thinking about relationships and the association of these modes with male and female voices." These different modes arise, she argues, "in a social context where factors of social status and power combine with reproductive biology to shape the experience of males and females and the relationship between the sexes" (1982, p. 2). Although Gilligan's work has been criticized for its essentialist overtones, it suggests that a key issue for feminism is how to combine an emphasis on difference with the pursuit of equality and how to preserve gender traits that contribute to individual, family, and human welfare without generating or perpetuating gender inequalities based on unequal power relations. One danger, for example, is to perceive difference in essentialist ways—a danger that is often encountered by those who view gender differences in oppositional ways, such as idealizing women's goodness and female superiority while viewing men as their opposite. This is different from understanding the extent to which it is important to maintain and even to foster, among men and women, what are identified as women's ways of knowing and doing, and the extent to which these can contribute to transforming knowledge and determining social change. The next section will deal with these questions.

## Beyond Self-Interest?

"I don't need money, I want the river's color back."

*—Silas Natkime, son of the Waa Valley chief, Irian Jaya, Indonesia[3]*

These words, a ringing affirmation of the value of a clean river over that of money, symbolizes one of the dilemmas of development, for it expresses an individual's desire to give priority to ecological over economic outcomes. It could also be interpreted as a reaction against the water-polluting outcome of "development." To return to Polanyi: his criticism of market society was that it is based on self-interest, leading to "disruptive strains" and "varied symptoms of disequilibrium," such as unemployment, class inequalities, "pressure on exchanges" and "imperialist rivalries" (1957 [1944]). We might now add environmental degradation to his list of disruptive strains. . . .

For Polanyi, this tendency led to the need for planning or toward forms of market intervention that would counteract not only disruptive strains but also the domination of economic self-interest over all aspects of political and social life. This is not just history. As we observe the unfolding of global markets in the late twentieth century, we see these strains reappear. To be sure, the global market has displayed its dynamism and ability to supply unprecedented amounts of goods and services and to generate new forms of wealth. However, it has also generated new imbalances and economic and social crises, particularly in Africa and Latin America during the 1980s and in Eastern Europe and Asia during the 1990s. Evidence linking globalization

with increasing inequalities and maldistribution of resources within and between countries has been growing (ECLAC 1995; Freeman 1996; Benería
1996; UNDP 1996, 1998, 1999).

Analogously, high unemployment or underemployment in many areas,
including high-income countries such as in Europe, disrupts the social fabric
of communities and countries. As Dani Rodrik (1997) has argued, globalization undermines social cohesiveness, requiring compensatory policies and
the design of social insurance systems. In some Latin American circles, the
tendencies of the past decade have been viewed as leading toward what some
authors have called "socially unsustainable development" in the long run. In
the same way, Asian, Russian, and Brazilian economic crises have raised
new questions about the instability of financial markets, and they have begun
to change course, initiating a new debate on global reforms and national
controls over capital flows. Fifty years after *The Great Transformation*,
Polanyi's call for subordinating the market to the priorities set by democratic
societies resonates urgently, even though to achieve this goal we will have to
accommodate new, late twentieth-century realities.

This prospect poses challenging questions for feminism, which could in
fact be viewed as one of Polanyi's countermovements, representing an emphasis on gender equality but linked also to wider social issues. Can feminism make a contribution to the quest for new directions in human
development? Can the alternative models discussed by feminists provide
useful guidelines for constructing alternative societies? Can women offer
different voices as they become more integrated in the market and public
life? Can "difference" be maintained, and can it be a source of inspiration for
those who work toward progressive social change? . . .

Far from seeing this mode as "backward" or "irrational," we can perceive
it as a source of inspiration leading to alternative ways of organizing society
based on nonhegemonic conceptual/theoretical tools and models. This means,
for example, not taking rational economic man's objectives as the desired
norm, which does not necessarily imply a rejection of markets as a way to
organize production and distribution of goods and services. As Polanyi stated,
"the end of market society means in no way the absence of markets" (1957
[1944], p. 252). However, this view calls for subordinating markets to the
objectives of truly democratic communities and countries. The goal is to
place economic activity at the service of human or people-centered development and not the other way around; or to reach an era in which productivity
and efficiency are achieved not for their own sake but as a way to increase
collective well-being. Hence, in the same way that it is possible to think of
Christianity without hell, it is also possible to design ways to reduce the
social costs of bankruptcy. All of this implies placing issues of distribution,

inequality, ethics, the environment, and the nature of individual happiness, collective well-being, and social change at the center of our agendas. It follows that an urgent task for economists and social scientists is to translate these general objectives into specific policies and action. . . .

Feminism has played an important part in the struggle for solutions at the decentralized, local, and institutional level: it has fought discrimination and inequalities across countries; it has changed institutions and decision-making processes; it has incorporated new agendas in the politics of daily life; it has affected national policies; it has made an impact on international agendas; and it has been influential in bringing human welfare to the center of debates on economic and social policy. It now has to meet the further challenges posed by globalization.

Polanyi wrote that the endeavor of thinking of people first "cannot be successful unless it is disciplined by a total view of man and society very different from that which we inherited from market economy" (1957 [1944]). The principal message of this chapter is that this effort must be transformative and based on a "total view of wo/man and society." Rather than diminishing this view as "soft," "idealistic," and "female," we must dare to take up the challenge and continue to follow the concrete, bottom-up strategies that have made feminism such a powerful agent of social change.

## Notes

1. From a refrain attributed to Westerners in a *New York Times* article that argues that, during the Asian crisis, corporations in Asia failed in record numbers but without disappearing from the market (WuDunn 1998), that is, without "going to hell."
2. The reference is to the annual meeting in Davos, Switzerland, of "people who run the world." The Chatham House is the "elegant London home" of the Royal Institute of International Affairs, where "diplomats have mulled the strange ways of abroad" for "nearly 80 years" ("In Praise of the Davos Man" 1997).
3. See Shari and McWilliams (1995, p. 66.)

## References

Bem, Sandra Lipsitz. 1993. *The Lenses of Gender: Transforming the Debate on Sexual Inequality*. New Haven, CT: Yale University Press.

Benería, Lourdes. 1996. "The Legacy of Structural Adjustment in Latin America." In *Economic Restructuring in the Americas*, ed. L. Benería and M. J. Dudley. Ithaca, NY: Cornell University, Latin American Studies Program.

Benería, Lourdes, and Martha Roldan. 1987. *The Crossroads of Class and Gender: Industrial Homework, Subcontracting and Household Dynamics in Mexico City*. Chicago: University of Chicago Press.

Bridger, Sue, Rebecca Kay, and Kathryn Pinnick. 1996. *No More Heroines? Russia, Women and the Market*. London: Routledge.

Butler, Judith. 1993. *Bodies That Matter: On the Discursive Limits of "Sex."* London: Routledge.

Christopherson, Susan. 1997. "The Caring Gap for Caring Workers: The Restructuring of Care and the Status of Women in OECD Countries." Paper presented at the Conference on Revisioning the Welfare State: Feminist Perspectives on the U.S., and Europe, Ithaca, NY: Cornell University, October 3–5.

Cravey, Althaj. 1998. *Women and Work in Mexico's Maquiladoras.* Totowa, NJ: Rowman & Allenheld.

ECLAC (Economic Commission for Latin America and the Caribbean). 1995. *Social Panorama of Latin America.* Santiago de Chile: ECLAC.

England, Paula. 1993. "The Separative Self: Androcentric Bias in Neoclassical Assumptions." In *Beyond Economic Man: Feminist Theory and Economics,* ed. Marianne A. Ferber and Julie A. Nelson, 37–53. Chicago: University of Chicago Press.

Feldman, Shelley. 1992. "Crisis, Islam and Gender in Bangladesh: The Social Construction of a Female Labor Force." In *Unequal Burden: Economic Crises, Persistent Poverty and Women's Work,* ed. Lourdes Benería and Shelley Feldman, 105–30. Boulder, CO: Westview Press.

Ferber, Marianne A., and Julie A. Nelson, eds. 1993. *Beyond Economic Man: Feminist Theory and Economics.* Chicago: University of Chicago Press.

Folbre, Nancy. 1994. *Who Pays for the Kids? Gender and the Structures of Constraint.* London: Routledge.

Folbre, Nancy, and Thomas Weisskopf. 1996. "Did Father Know Best? Families, Markets, and the Supply of Caring Labor." Paper presented at the Conference on Economics, Values and Organization, Yale University, New Haven, CT, April 19–21.

Frank, Robert, Thomas Golovich, and Dennis Regan. 1993. "Does Studying Economics Inhibit Cooperation?" *Journal of Economic Perspectives* 7 (2): 159–71.

Freeman, Richard. 1996. "The New Inequality." *Boston Review* (December–January): 1–5.

Gilligan, Carol. 1982. *In a Different Voice.* Cambridge: Harvard University Press.

Guyer, Jane. 1980. "Households, Budgets and Women's Incomes." Boston University, Africana Studies Center Working Paper No. 28.

Hein, Catherine. 1986. "The Feminization of Industrial Employment in Mauritius: A Case of Sex Segregation." In *Sex Inequalities in Urban Employment in the Third World,* ed. Richard Anker and Catherine Hein, 277–312. New York: St. Martin's Press.

"In Praise of the Davos Man." 1997. *The Economist,* vol. 342, February 1, p. 18.

Marwell, Gerald, and Ruth Ames. 1981. "Economists Free Ride, Does Anyone Else? (Experiments in the Provision of Public Goods)." *Journal of Public Economics* 15 (3): 295–310.

McCloskey, Donald N. 1993. "Some Consequences of a Conjective Economics." In *Beyond Economic Man: Feminist Theory and Economics,* ed. Marianne A. Ferber and Julie A. Nelson, 69–93. Chicago: University of Chicago Press.

Merchant, Carolyn. 1989. *The Death of Nature: Women, Ecology and the Scientific Revolution.* San Francisco: Harper & Row.

Moghadan, Valentine. 1993. *Democratic Reform and the Position of Women in Transitional Economies.* Oxford: Clarendon Press.

Nelson, Julie. 1993. "The Study of Choice or the Study of Provisioning? Gender and the Definition of Economics." In *Beyond Economic Man: Feminist Theory and Economics*, ed. Marianne A. Ferber and Julie A. Nelson, 23–36. Chicago: University of Chicago Press.

O'Grady, Mary Anastasia. 1997. "Don't Blame the Market for Argentina's Woes." *Wall Street Journal*, May 30.

Ong, Aiwa. 1987. *Spirits of Resistance and Capitalist Discipline: Women Factory Workers in Malaysia*. Albany, NY: SUNY Press.

Polanyi, Karl. 1957 [1944]. *The Great Transformation*. Boston: Beacon Press.

Pyle, Jean. 1982. "Export-Led Development and the Underemployment of Women: The Impact of Discriminatory Employment Policy in the Republic of Ireland." In *Women, Men and the New International Division of Labor*, ed. June Nash and Maria Patricia Fernandez-Kelly, 85–112. Albany, NY: SUNY Press.

Rodrik, Dani. 1997. *Has Globalization Gone Too Far?* Washington, DC: Institute for International Economics.

Seguino, Stephanie, Thomas Stevens, and Mark Lutz. 1996. "Gender and Cooperative Behavior: Economic Man Rides Alone." *Feminist Economics* 2 (1): 195–223.

Shari, Michael, and Gary McWillliams. 1995. "Gold Rush in New Guinea." *Business Week*, Issue 3451, November 20, pp. 66–67.

Strassmann, Diana. 1993. "Not a Free Market: The Rhetoric of Disciplinary Authority in Economics." In *Beyond Economic Man: Feminist Theory and Economics*, ed. Marianne A. Ferber and Julie A. Nelson, 54–68. Chicago: University of Chicago Press.

Strober, Myra. 1994. "Rethinking Economics Through a Feminist Lens." *American Economic Review* 84 (2): 143–7.

Tohidi, Nayereh. 1996. "Guardians of the Nation: Women, Islam and Soviet Modernization in Azerbaijan." Paper presented at the conference on Women's Identities and Roles in the Course of Change, Ankara, Turkey, October 23–25.

UNDP (United Nations Development Program). 1995, 1996, 1998, 1999. *Human Development Report*. New York: Oxford University Press.

WuDunn, Sheryl. 1998. "Bankruptcy the Asian Way." *New York Times*, September 8.

Adapted from "Globalization, Gender and the Davos Man," *Feminist Economics* 5 (3) (November 1999): 61–83. The web site for *Feminist Economics* can be found at www.tandf.co.uk/journals. Reprinted with permission of Taylor & Francis Ltd.

# 28

# Development, Gender, and the Environment

## Theoretical or Contextual Link? Toward an Institutional Analysis of Gender

*Eiman Zein-Elabdin*

The current discourse on development, gender, and the environment has emerged from a convergence of feminist and environmentalist critiques of economic development. This discourse is dominated by two paradigms: women in development (WID) and ecofeminism. Although the two paradigms have been influential in advancing women's issues in economics, this influence has been limited by the lack of understanding of the institutional nature of gender among the proponents of the paradigms. This lack of recognition is due to the essentialist characterization of women that underlies both paradigms. In WID, women are treated as rational beings who readily respond to economic incentives within any cultural setting; in ecofeminism, women possess a supramaterial bond with nature that endows them with a privileged understanding of the environment and an innate ability to care for it regardless of the specific institutions at work. This oversight of the institutional nature of gender obscures its economic significance, its path dependence, and its resistance to change. It also obscures power implications, thereby depriving the issue of gender of one of its most important elements.

In this chapter, I propose an alternative conceptual framework for redrawing this discourse, particularly with regard to the treatment of gender. This framework is predicated on two related points: (1) Any discussion of gender or women must be firmly grounded in an institutionalist understanding of economic and social processes. I use the term *gender specification* to refer to

the social designation of individuals to a particular gender and the historically and culturally circumscribed economic and social roles contingent upon
that designation. Gender specification defines the relative positions of women
and men in the economy and in relation to the environment. (2) Because of
the historical and cultural specificity of institutions and processes, there is
no basis for a theoretical discourse on development, gender, and the environment, but only a contextual analysis of the multiple points at which development, women, and the environment meet and interact. That is to say, the
relationship between women and the environment can be understood only
within the institutional contexts in which the two interact and in which development takes place.

So far, institutionalists have considered the convergence of institutionalist
and feminist epistemologies (Waller and Jennings 1990) but not the perti-
nence of institutional economics itself as a conceptual framework for discussing gender. I argue here that institutional economics is poised to make
important contributions to a substantive analysis of gender as well. This argument has significant implications not merely for development economics,
but for economic analysis in general. . . .

## The Discourse on Development, Gender, and the Environment

WID and ecofeminism come from different historical and philosophical origins. They differ drastically in their conception of women and women's relationship to the environment and present almost antithetical views on economic
development. Yet the two approaches share more in common than first im-
pressions suggest. Both categorize women as a monolithic group and univer-
salize their experiences across class, culture, and other differentiating
variables. Neither approach perceives of gender specification as an institution fundamental for understanding the economic and social conditions of
women in the Third World and their relation to the environment. In this chapter, the World Bank literature, particularly in the area of forestry in sub-
Saharan Africa, is taken as the leading example of the WID approach, and
the work of Vandana Shiva is taken to represent the ecofeminist one.

### Women in Sustainable Development

The WID approach unites neoclassical economic theory and liberal feminist
thought, depicting rationality and optimizing behavior as inherent attributes
of the human species; women are no different from men in that respect. Economic development is seen as the logical social outcome of that behavior;
the only problem is that development has so far almost entirely bypassed

women in the Third World. The United Nations' WID initiative was sparked by a recognition that women had not shared in most "gains" from economic growth: women received lower wages and held less property than men across the Third World (Boserup 1970). The WID prescription for correcting this flawed picture is to "integrate" women into the development process through their inclusion in decision making and through better documentation and reevaluation of their work. By the late 1980s, concern with environmental quality and ecological sustainability had intensified, and this same conception was carried over without modification in a format that can be characterized as integrating women in sustainable development.

As the leading international development institution, the World Bank has been hard at work trying to achieve this integration. In 1987, the Bank launched an initiative to make "WID issues" part of its "mainstream work" (World Bank 1987b, 1988). This was followed in 1989 by policy guidelines for "involving women in forestry projects" (Molnar and Schreiber 1989). Since then, a number of "gender and environment" projects have been introduced by the Bank in order to raise awareness among policy makers of the links between women and the environment and to increase women's participation in sustainable development (Clones 1992). Recently, the Bank released a blueprint for a comprehensive forestry strategy in sub-Saharan Africa that calls for expanding the role of women in development (World Bank 1994).

The Bank's approach to women and development in each of these ventures is based on a doctrine that stresses efficiency and the importance of human capital. This doctrine typically emphasizes the need to raise women's productivity as a means of raising rates of return on development projects and proclaims the cost-effectiveness of investment in women, for example, through education and better health care (World Bank 1984, 1989). However, by proceeding as though women can be imported into preconceived structures—in this case development projects—this approach assumes that women will easily adjust their "decision matrices" to take into account new variables. This assumption, in my view, is symptomatic of the neoclassical tendency to overlook the extent to which people's behavior is shaped by entrenched institutions. Indeed, this oversight partly explains the Bank's unsatisfactory record in forestry management in sub-Saharan Africa, where the Bank has admitted that its forestry projects have had little impact on the rate of deforestation (World Bank 1994). Some of the reasons for this outcome, according to the Bank, are that it made few attempts to involve the local population and paid little attention to local conditions such as land tenure systems. In other words, it overlooked the institutional nature of change.

## Development and Ecofeminism

The first attempt to tie together issues of development, women, and the environment was perhaps that of Carolyn Merchant (1989). Merchant's classic *The Death of Nature* investigated the association between women and nature in Western European thought and the impact of industrialization in Europe on dominant perceptions of nature and on the economic and social status of women. Inspired in part by Merchant's work, Vandana Shiva has become a leading voice in the ecofeminist critique of development and its consequences for both women and the environment in the Third World.

Shiva characterizes development as a Western, masculine project of modernization that has involved the subjugation of women and nature.

> The violence to nature, which seems intrinsic to the dominant development model, is also associated with violence to women who depend on nature for drawing sustenance for themselves, their families, their societies. This violence against nature and women is built into the very mode of perceiving both, and forms the basis of the current development paradigm. (Shiva 1989, p. xvi)

Shiva also attacks development and technological progress as reductionist. In her view, development has resulted in environmental destruction, thereby reducing nature's capacity to sustain life. This destruction is most obvious, she argues, in the area of forestry, where the practice of establishing timber plantations, introduced by colonial administrations and later carried on by independent governments under the sponsorship of international development agencies, has led to soil erosion, elimination of indigenous species, and destruction of the water cycle in many areas. Development has also reduced "other" epistemologies by denying the wisdom of "traditional societies" and replacing it with modern science. Shiva argues that women's leadership of environmental struggles and a return to "traditional" knowledge and practices provide the key to transforming development from an oppressive, destructive process to a more equitable, sustainable one.

The value of Shiva's work derives mainly from her critique of economic development. Her critique profoundly highlights the stranglehold that the logic of the market and faith in untrammeled economic growth has on people in less developed countries. She particularly faults development for having altered the primary function of economic systems from provisioning for local people to producing for international markets. This, of course, is in stark contrast to the WID position, whose underlying theme of modernization makes it insufficiently critical of economic development. However, by this sweeping condemnation of Western science and technology, Shiva falls into a trap of her own reductionism, attributing all the problems of poor countries to modernity and "progress." More to the point, Shiva's attempt to draw universal parallels between women and nature overlooks the specific institutional milieus where women interact with nature.

**Women and Nature: Theoretical or Contextual?**

The fundamental question underlying the discourse on development, gender, and the environment is that of the relationship between women and nature. On this question, WID and ecofeminism diverge significantly. Indeed, they create two extreme views of how women and nature are related, based on general assumptions and theories held by each approach. The WID position, represented in the World Bank literature and operations, tends to disproportionately implicate women in environmental degradation, whereas the ecofeminist position tends to present women's attitudes toward the environment as largely benign. In reality, women's experiences everywhere represent a vast continuum between these two extremes, conditioned in each case by different economies, histories, and cultures expressed in different institutions.

In the WID position, women hold the same anthropocentric attitudes toward nature as men; there is no claim of a singular relationship between women and nature. Women's engagement in environmental destruction is interpreted as a manifestation of their poverty and lack of resources rather than their gendered identity. In the case of deforestation in sub-Saharan Africa, inadequate access to financial and technological resources limits women's ability to use "less destructive energy gathering practices" (Clones 1992, p. 21). Poor women must rely on fuelwood instead of modern fuels such as oil and gas. Poor farmers, including women, resort to extensive cultivation in lieu of yield-boosting complementary inputs such as fertilizers. Forest destruction then is interpreted as a rational decision by the poor in the face of limited access to modern energy sources and agricultural inputs (World Bank 1991). This interpretation of poverty as a primary cause of environmental degradation forms the basic premise of the sustainable development paradigm and is well articulated in major Bank documents (World Bank 1987a, 1992a).

Since women are overly represented among the poor, this premise tends to unwittingly implicate women in environmental degradation to a greater extent than is borne out by the evidence. For example, in Africa the Bank has largely focused on forest destruction as a result of firewood gathering—mostly done by women (World Bank 1983, 1988). But the male-dominated charcoal industry that supplies urban centers with fuel contributes more to deforestation in the region than the sparse collection of firewood by women in rural areas (Zein-Elabdin 1993). Although the Bank has recently acknowledged this fact (World Bank 1994), it continues to focus on the role of women in forest destruction. This disproportionate implication of women in environmental degradation is articulated in what the Bank calls the "poverty-gender-environment nexus" (World Bank 1993), where women are linked to ecological destruction through their poverty. In fact, the only instances where gender is explicitly mentioned in relation to environmental problems usually involve women. In effect, women's gender becomes a vector for ecological destruction. Having said all that, the Bank's position still has the desirable characteristic of locating women's relationship to the environment in the material conditions under which women live and obtain their livelihood.

By contrast, the ecofeminist position as articulated in Shiva's work generally emphasizes the "intimate" relationship between women and nature.

> In the perspective of women engaged in survival struggles which are, simultaneously, struggles for the protection of nature, women and nature are intimately related, and their domination and liberation similarly linked. (1989, p. 47)

Shiva argues that this relationship exists on a symbolic as well as a material level. On a symbolic level, she relates that, in Indian cosmology, nature (Prakriti) is considered to be the embodiment of the "feminine principle." On a material level, she stresses the role of Indian women as the "primary sustainers of society," providing food, water, and fuel and tending to animals. On both levels, environmental problems represent the loss of the feminine principle: "The ecological crisis is, at its root, the death of the feminine principle, symbolically as well as in contexts such as rural India, not merely in form and symbol, but also in the everyday processes of survival and sustenance" (p. 42). Shiva suggests that recovery of the feminine principle is key to transforming development to a more sustainable course, thereby assigning the responsibility for ecological leadership to women.

This line of thinking seeks to establish a metaphysical, supramaterial relationship between women and nature and is therefore highly problematic. It is based on an essentialist understanding of the relationship between women and nature; therefore it does not explain this relationship. Nor does it explain the extent to which this symbolic association between women and nature in cultural imagery may be rooted in historical, material origins (Agarwal 1992; Jackson 1993). Because of this fundamental weakness, this line of thinking falls into circular reasoning to the point where one is not quite certain which domination preceded the other. Has nature been dominated because it is perceived to be female, or are women dominated because they are associated with nature?

Equally problematic is how ecofeminism accounts for the impact of modernization and development on other groups besides women, e.g., workers, Africans, and other members of nonindustrialized societies. So far the development of capitalism throughout the world has involved significant subjugation and exploitation of all these groups. There is an intractable dilemma. Acknowledging the similar impact on groups other than women considerably dilutes the ecofeminist point, whereas ignoring it is an unacceptable omission. In fact, both Shiva and Merchant acknowledge that the exploitative character of capitalist development is not limited to women, but both nonetheless go on to single out women in order to maintain the premise of their argument.

More pertinently, this line of thinking presents nature as a static, ahistorical entity while absolving women of all responsibility for environmental degradation. In this view, women seem to be blessed with an inherent cognizance of environmental phenomena. This cognizance is reflected in Shiva's accounts of women's knowledge of local ecosystems and adoption of sustainable practices. But this celebration of women's closeness to nature is not balanced by contrasting accounts of women partaking in environmental destruction, in India or elsewhere. Although she recognizes that not all women are environmentally conscious, she attributes that to the loss of a natural essence they once possessed: "The principle of creating and conserving life is lost to the ecologically alienated, consumerist elite women of the Third World and the over-consuming west" (Shiva 1989, p. 42).

The upshot is that the WID and the ecofeminist interpretations of the relationship between women and nature represent two extremes in this discourse. The former tends to disproportionately implicate women in ecological destruction, while the latter tends to exempt women from all ecological accountability. These extreme tendencies are an inevitable consequence of the absence of institutional analysis in the two approaches. Such an analysis will reveal a multiplicity of patterns of women interacting with the environment that can hardly be captured in few universal principles or assumptions.

I argue instead that women's relationship to nature is *contextual*. That is to say, this relationship is molded by the specific institutional contexts of women's interplay with their natural environments. These institutional contexts include natural resources, the technology, and the means of subsistence, as well as gender specification and other institutions that embody the history and culture of a society. These institutions establish distinct patterns of thought and behavior reflected in the organization of provisioning activities and in accumulated wisdom about the environment. Experiences of women in less developed countries indicate how these contexts are articulated in particular attitudes and responses to environmental challenges. . . .

**Redrawing the Discourse: The Institutional Nature of Gender**

. . . I argue here that only an institutional perspective is capable of fully legitimating gender as a subject of study in economics and of bringing forth its full economic, political, and cultural significance. Moreover, it will place women's relation to the environment in its historical and cultural context and therefore illuminate various policy approaches to this question.

The thrust of institutions can still be best represented by Walton Hamilton's description: an institution

> connotes a way of thought or action of some prevalence and permanence, which is embedded in the *habits* of a group or the customs of a people. . . . Institutions fix the confines of and impose form upon the activities of human beings. The world of use and wont, to which imperfectly we accommodate our lives, is a tangled and unbroken web of institutions. (Hamilton 1932, p. 84; emphasis added)

Based on this description, gender specification can be defined as an institution, a social framework that establishes distinct roles for groups and individuals, fixing the confines of and imposing form upon the activities of women and men, in a persistent, regularly observed manner. This definition is based on Veblen's concept of institutions as "habits of thought" (Veblen 1973). Gender specification is nothing but a collection of historically and culturally determined habits of thought. These habits are not gathered in one body or aspect of life, but are diffused throughout the social fiber of a society as to become implicit terms of reference for men and women. These habits are so diffused and deeply embedded in the social fiber as to render gender specification and its articulation in economic activity virtually invisible. They have become "*axiomatic* and indispensable by habituation and general acceptance" (Veblen 1923, p. 101; emphasis added).

Having characterized gender specification as a consequence of a web of institutions, its economic significance can be fully revealed only by an understanding of economic systems in their substantive meaning, that is, the actual processes of provisioning and material "want satisfaction" (Polanyi 1957). These provisioning processes are rooted in the history, culture, and environment of a society, where humans interact with these through certain institutions, hence the economy as instituted process (Polanyi 1957). As Waller and Jennings (1991) have recognized, Polanyi's ideas are most conducive to studying gender issues and by extension, the actual points of interaction between women and the environment within different economies. What is even more important is that in this institutional approach gender specification assumes equal importance to other institutions, including markets, in terms of its economic and political significance and implications. This conceptualization is best described in Polanyi's own words: "religion or government may be as important for the structure and functioning of the economy as monetary institutions or the availability of tools and machines themselves that lighten the toil of labor" (1957, p. 250). Accordingly, institutional economics is most capable of placing gender on an equal footing with other "legitimate" subjects of study in economics.

In a broad and rudimentary sense, as an institution, gender specification in any particular society defines distinct roles for women and men in production, as it also determines their relative shares in the resulting output. For example, in many countries women grow subsistence crops and derive nonmonetary income, while men grow cash crops and receive cash income, giving them greater access to property and wealth. Given that production and distribution are the primary functions of all economic systems, gender specification becomes fundamental rather than incidental. By fundamental, I do not mean that it is primordial, predating all social relations, but simply that it is as fundamental to economic processes as other institutions. It permeates all economic activities and relations and helps set the relative positions of women and men in the economy.

This discussion of gender specification should not imply that it is a universal, ahistorical construct. On the contrary, institutions are culture-specific and evolving—albeit sluggishly—in response to different economic stimuli. Considering this nature of institutions, the particular form in which gender specification helps determine the economic fortunes of men and women can be understood only within specific temporal and spatial contexts, for example, late nineteenth-century American corporations, Tamil plantation workers in colonial Sri Lanka, or contemporary households in rural Burkina Faso. . . .

That is how one can explain why women in India and Kenya organized to fight deforestation and soil erosion, while those in Mexico engaged in solid waste management in urban areas, and why, for that matter, women in the United States have organized to fight hazardous waste disposal in their towns. One cannot come up with a universal theory of gender and ecological sustainability in the tradition of neoclassical economics (i.e., rationality and choice) or the views of ecofeminists (i.e., women and nature). Neither can the environment be presented as a static, ahistorical entity. The human-environment relationship is dialectical, evolving out of certain historical sequences. "The community will make use of the forces of the environment for the purposes of its life according to methods learned in the past and embodied in these institutions" (Veblen 1973, p. 134). . . .

To be sure, it is not sufficient to merely recognize the presence of institutions. In fact, institutional reform in less developed countries is the new mandate in World Bank operations (World Bank 1994). It is more important to appreciate how these institutions govern social activity, interact with one another, and mutate over time. That is why it is imperative to distinguish the two institutional schools. The World Bank reform is based on the "new institutional" concept of institutions as the incentive structure for society—hence the Bank's notion that institutional reform is needed to allow efficient decisions by individuals. This view perceives that people uniformly respond to stimuli, thereby entirely missing the cultural idiosyncrasy and path dependence of institutions. It also misses the nature of institutions as habits of thought; therefore it recognizes land tenure systems and forestry departments as institutions but not gender specification. In consequence, the Bank calls for greater inclusion of women in development projects (to raise efficiency) but not for examining gender specification as a source of discrimination in society and bias in the outcomes of these projects against women.

The ecofeminist position, on the other hand, recognizes institutions to a greater extent than the WID position. Shiva pays considerable attention to history and cultural tradition. Indeed, her economic perspective is much akin to the "old" institutionalist one because she perceives of economies as provisioning systems and processes and blames development for having replaced this character with narrow, profit-motivated market exchange. Nevertheless, her attempt to construct a unique link between women and nature across different cultural and historical backgrounds clouds her analysis and deprives it of great validity. As mentioned earlier, even when she recognizes the different environmental attitudes among women from different economic strata, she attributes that to loss of a natural quality instead of their habitual conditioning by different institutions.

Given the limitations of the WID and the ecofeminist paradigms and on the basis of the conceptualization of gender and women's relationship to the environment presented in this chapter, the discourse on development, gender, and the environment may be redrawn along the following lines: *how gender specification as an institution is articulated in economic processes, generating certain income and wealth distribution patterns; and how this articulation determines the extent of sustainability of the natural environment within particular historical and cultural parameters.* In other words, the problem is identifying and understanding the actual institutions and economic processes that lead to gender-specific attitudes and actions toward the environment and use of natural resources within different historical and cultural confines as opposed to undertaking a theoretical dissection of development, gender, and the environment. This format neither attempts to "integrate" women (as a homogeneous group) in a process of sustainable development nor tries to ascribe a special role to them in leading environmental recovery by virtue of their unique affinity to nature. . . .

## References

Agarwal, Bina. 1992. "The Gender and Environment Debate: Lessons from India." *Feminist Studies* 18 (1): 119–58.

Boserup, Ester. 1970. *Woman's Role in Economic Development*. New York: St. Martin's Press.

Clones, Julia. 1992. "The Links between Gender Issues and the Fragile Environments of Sub-Saharan Africa." Technical Department, Africa Region. Washington, DC: World Bank.

Hamilton, Walton H. 1932. "Institution." In *Encyclopaedia of the Social Sciences*, vol. 8., ed. Edwin R.A. Seligman and Alvin Johnson, pp. 84–89. New York: Macmillan.

Jackson, Cecile. 1993. "Environmentalisms and Gender Interests in the Third World." *Development and Change* 24: 649–77.

Merchant, Carolyn. 1989. *The Death of Nature: Women, Ecology and the Scientific Revolution*. San Francisco: Harper and Row.

Molnar, Augusta, and Goetz Schreiber. 1989. "Women and Forestry: Operational Issues." Policy, Planning and Research Paper. Washington, DC: World Bank.

Polanyi, Karl. 1957. "The Economy As Instituted Process." In *Trade and Market in the Early Empires: Economies in History and Theory*, ed. Karl Polanyi, Conrad M. Arensberg, and Harry W. Pearson. Glencoe, IL: Free Press.

Shiva, Vandana. 1989. *Staying Alive: Women, Ecology and Development*. London: Zed Books.

Veblen, Thorstein. 1923 [1899]. *Absentee Ownership and Business Enterprise in Recent Times*. New York: B.W. Huebsch.

———. 1973. *The Theory of the Leisure Class*. Boston: Houghton Mifflin.

Waller, William, and Ann Jennings. 1990. "On the Possibility of a Feminist Economics: The Convergence of Institutional and Feminist Methodology." *Journal of Economic Issues* 24 (2): 613–22.

World Bank. 1987a. *Environment, Growth and Development*. Washington, DC: World Bank.

———. 1992a. *World Development Report 1992*. New York: Oxford University Press.

———. 1993. *The World Bank and the Environment*. Washington, DC: World Bank.

———. 1994. *A Strategy for the Forest Sector in Sub-Saharan Africa*. Technical Department, Africa Region, Technical Paper no. 251. Washington, DC: World Bank.

———. 1983, 1984, 1987b, 1988, 1989, 1991, 1992b. *Annual Reports*. Washington, DC: World Bank.

World Commission on Environment and Development. 1987. *Our Common Future*. Oxford: Oxford University Press.

World Resources Institute. 1985. *Tropical Forests: A Call for Action*. New York: World Resources Institute.

Zein-Elabdin, Eiman. 1993. "The Impact of Improved Cookstoves on the Demand for Fuel Wood in Sub-Saharan Africa, and its Relation to Deforestation." Ph.D. diss., University of Tennessee, Knoxville, Tennessee.

---

Adapted from "Development, Gender, and the Environment: Theoretical or Contextual Link? Toward an Institutional Analysis of Gender," *Journal of Economic Issues* 30 (4) (December 1996): 929–47. Reprinted with special permission of the copyright holder, the Association for Evolutionary Economics.

# 29

# Convention on the Elimination of All Forms of Discrimination Against Women

The States Parties to the present Convention,

*Noting* that the Charter of the United Nations reaffirms faith in fundamental human rights, in the dignity and worth of the human person and in the equal rights of men and women,

*Noting* that the Universal Declaration of Human Rights affirms the principle of the inadmissibility of discrimination and proclaims that all human beings are born free and equal in dignity and rights and that everyone is entitled to all the rights and freedoms set forth therein, without distinction of any kind, including distinction based on sex,

*Noting* that the States Parties to the International Covenants on Human Rights have the obligation to ensure the equal right of men and women to enjoy all economic, social, cultural, civil and political rights,

*Considering* the international conventions concluded under the auspices of the United Nations and the specialized agencies promoting equality of rights of men and women,

*Noting also* the resolutions, declarations and recommendations adopted by the United Nations and the specialized agencies promoting equality of rights of men and women,

*Concerned*, however, that despite these various instruments extensive discrimination against women continues to exist,

*Recalling* that discrimination against women violates the principles of

equality of rights and respect for human dignity, is an obstacle to the participation of women, on equal terms with men, in the political, social, economic
and cultural life of their countries, hampers the growth of the prosperity of
society and the family and makes more difficult the full development of the
potentialities of women in the service of their countries and of humanity,

*Concerned* that in situations of poverty women have the least access to food,
health, education, training and opportunities for employment and other needs,

*Convinced* that the establishment of the new international economic order
based on equity and justice will contribute significantly towards the promotion of equality between men and women,

*Emphasizing* that the eradication of apartheid, of all forms of racism, racial discrimination, colonialism, neo-colonialism, aggression, foreign occupation and domination and interference in the internal affairs of States is
essential to the full enjoyment of the rights of men and women,

*Affirming* that the strengthening of international peace and security, relax-
ation of international tension, mutual co-operation among all States irrespective of their social and economic systems, general and complete disarmament,
and in particular nuclear disarmament under strict and effective international
control, the affirmation of the principles of justice, equality and mutual benefit
in relations among countries and the realization of the right of peoples under
alien and colonial domination and foreign occupation to self-determination
and independence, as well as respect for national sovereignty and territorial
integrity, will promote social progress and development and as a consequence
will contribute to the attainment of full equality between men and women,

*Convinced* that the full and complete development of a country, the welfare of the world and the cause of peace require the maximum participation
of women on equal terms with men in all fields,

*Bearing in mind* the great contribution of women to the welfare of the
family and to the development of society, so far not fully recognized, the
social significance of maternity and the role of both parents in the family and
in the upbringing of children, and aware that the role of women in procre-
ation should not be a basis for discrimination but that the upbringing of children requires a sharing of responsibility between men and women and society
as a whole,

*Aware* that a change in the traditional role of men as well as the role of
women in society and in the family is needed to achieve full equality between men and women,

*Determined* to implement the principles set forth in the Declaration on the
Elimination of Discrimination against Women and, for that purpose, to adopt
the measures required for the elimination of such discrimination in all its
forms and manifestations,

*Have agreed* on the following:

## Part I

### Article 1

For the purposes of the present Convention, the term "discrimination against women" shall mean any distinction, exclusion or restriction made on the basis of sex which has the effect or purpose of impairing or nullifying the recognition, enjoyment or exercise by women irrespective of their marital status, on a basis of equality of men and women, of human rights and fundamental freedoms in the political, economic, social, cultural, civil or any other field.

### Article 2

States Parties condemn discrimination against women in all its forms, agree to pursue by all appropriate means and without delay a policy of eliminating discrimination against women and, to this end, undertake:

    (a) To embody the principle of the equality of men and women in their national constitutions or other appropriate legislation if not yet incorporated therein and to ensure, through law and other appropriate means, the practical realization of this principle;

    (b) To adopt appropriate legislative and other measures, including sanctions where appropriate, prohibiting all discrimination against women;

    (c) To establish legal protection of the rights of women on an equal basis with men and to ensure through competent national tribunals and other public institutions the effective protection of women against any act of discrimination;

    (d) To refrain from engaging in any act or practice of discrimination against women and to ensure that public authorities and institutions shall act in conformity with this obligation;

    (e) To take all appropriate measures to eliminate discrimination against women by any person, organization or enterprise;

    (f) To take all appropriate measures, including legislation, to modify or abolish existing laws, regulations, customs and practices which constitute discrimination against women;

    (g) To repeal all national penal provisions which constitute discrimination against women.

*Article 3*

States Parties shall take in all fields, in particular in the political, social, economic and cultural fields, all appropriate measures, including legislation, to ensure the full development and advancement of women, for the purpose of guaranteeing them the exercise and enjoyment of human rights and fundamental freedoms on a basis of equality with men.

*Article 4*

1. Adoption by States Parties of temporary special measures aimed at accelerating de facto equality between men and women shall not be considered discrimination as defined in the present Convention, but shall in no way entail as a consequence the maintenance of unequal or separate standards; these measures shall be discontinued when the objectives of equality of opportunity and treatment have been achieved.
2. Adoption by States Parties of special measures, including those measures contained in the present Convention, aimed at protecting maternity shall not be considered discriminatory.

*Article 5*

States Parties shall take all appropriate measures:

(a) To modify the social and cultural patterns of conduct of men and women, with a view to achieving the elimination of prejudices and customary and all other practices which are based on the idea of the inferiority or the superiority of either of the sexes or on stereotyped roles for men and women;
(b) To ensure that family education includes a proper understanding of maternity as a social function and the recognition of the common responsibility of men and women in the upbringing and development of their children, it being understood that the interest of the children is the primordial consideration in all cases.

*Article 6*

States Parties shall take all appropriate measures, including legislation, to suppress all forms of traffic in women and exploitation of prostitution of women.

## Part II

### Article 7

States Parties shall take all appropriate measures to eliminate discrimination against women in the political and public life of the country and, in particular, shall ensure to women, on equal terms with men, the right:

(a) To vote in all elections and public referenda and to be eligible for election to all publicly elected bodies;
(b) To participate in the formulation of government policy and the implementation thereof and to hold public office and perform all public functions at all levels of government;
(c) To participate in non-governmental organizations and associations concerned with the public and political life of the country.

### Article 8

States Parties shall take all appropriate measures to ensure to women, on equal terms with men and without any discrimination, the opportunity to represent their Governments at the international level and to participate in the work of international organizations.

### Article 9

1. States Parties shall grant women equal rights with men to acquire, change or retain their nationality. They shall ensure in particular that neither marriage to an alien nor change of nationality by the husband during marriage shall automatically change the nationality of the wife, render her stateless or force upon her the nationality of the husband.
2. States Parties shall grant women equal rights with men with respect to the nationality of their children.

## Part III

### Article 10

States Parties shall take all appropriate measures to eliminate discrimination against women in order to ensure to them equal rights with men in the field of education and in particular to ensure, on a basis of equality of men and women:

(a) The same conditions for career and vocational guidance, for access to studies and for the achievement of diplomas in educational establishments of all categories in rural as well as in urban areas; this equality shall be ensured in preschool, general, technical, professional and higher technical education, as well as in all types of vocational training;

(b) Access to the same curricula, the same examinations, teaching staff with qualifications of the same standard and school premises and equipment of the same quality;

(c) The elimination of any stereotyped concept of the roles of men and women at all levels and in all forms of education by encouraging coeducation and other types of education which will help to achieve this aim and, in particular, by the revision of textbooks and school programmes and the adaptation of teaching methods;

(d) The same opportunities to benefit from scholarships and other study grants;

(e) The same opportunities for access to programmes of continuing education including adult and functional literacy programmes, particularly those aimed at reducing, at the earliest possible time, any gap in education existing between men and women;

(f) The reduction of female student drop-out rates and the organization of programmes for girls and women who have left school prematurely;

(g) The same opportunities to participate actively in sports and physical education;

(h) Access to specific educational information to help to ensure the health and well-being of families, including information and advice on family planning.

## Article 11

1. States Parties shall take all appropriate measures to eliminate discrimination against women in the field of employment in order to ensure, on a basis of equality of men and women, the same rights, in particular:

(a) The right to work as an inalienable right of all human beings;

(b) The right to the same employment opportunities, including the application of the same criteria for selection in matters of employment;

(c)  The right to free choice of profession and employment, the right to promotion, job security and all benefits and conditions of service and the right to receive vocational training and retraining, including apprenticeships, advanced vocational training and recurrent training;

(d)  The right to equal remuneration, including benefits, and to equal treatment in respect of work of equal value, as well as equality of treatment in the evaluation of the quality of work;

(e)  The right to social security, particularly in cases of retirement, unemployment, sickness, invalidity and old age and other incapacity to work, as well as the right to paid leave;

(f)  The right to protection of health and to safety in working conditions, including the safeguarding of the function of reproduction.

2.  In order to prevent discrimination against women on the grounds of marriage or maternity and to ensure their effective right to work, States Parties shall take appropriate measures:

(a)  To prohibit, subject to the imposition of sanctions, dismissal on the grounds of pregnancy or of maternity leave and discrimination in dismissals on the basis of marital status;

(b)  To introduce maternity leave with pay or with comparable social benefits without loss of former employment, seniority or social allowances;

(c)  To encourage the provision of the necessary supporting social services to enable parents to combine family obligations with work responsibilities and participation in public life, in particular through promoting the establishment and development of a network of child-care facilities;

(d)  To provide special protection to women during pregnancy in types of work proved to be harmful to them.

3.  Protective legislation relating to matters covered in this article shall be reviewed periodically in the light of scientific and technological knowledge and shall be revised, repealed or extended as necessary.

## Article 12

1.  States Parties shall take all appropriate measures to eliminate discrimination against women in the field of health care in order to ensure, on a basis of equality of men and women, access to health care services, including those related to family planning.

2. Notwithstanding the provisions of paragraph 1 of this article, States Parties shall ensure to women appropriate services in connection with pregnancy, confinement and the post-natal period, granting free services where necessary, as well as adequate nutrition during pregnancy and lactation.

## Article 13

States Parties shall take all appropriate measures to eliminate discrimination against women in other areas of economic and social life in order to ensure, on a basis of equality of men and women, the same rights, in particular:

(a) The right to family benefits;
(b) The right to bank loans, mortgages and other forms of financial credit;
(c) The right to participate in recreational activities, sports and all aspects of cultural life.

## Article 14

1. States Parties shall take into account the particular problems faced by rural women and the significant roles which rural women play in the economic survival of their families, including their work in the non-monetized sectors of the economy, and shall take all appropriate measures to ensure the application of the provisions of this Convention to women in rural areas.
2. States Parties shall take all appropriate measures to eliminate discrimination against women in rural areas in order to ensure, on a basis of equality of men and women, that they participate in and benefit from rural development and, in particular, shall ensure to such women the right:

(a) To participate in the elaboration and implementation of development planning at all levels;
(b) To have access to adequate health care facilities, including information, counselling and services in family planning;
(c) To benefit directly from social security programmes;
(d) To obtain all types of training and education, formal and non-formal, including that relating to functional literacy, as well as, *inter alia*, the benefit of all community and extension services, in order to increase their technical proficiency;

   (e) To organize self-help groups and co-operatives in order to obtain equal access to economic opportunities through employment or self-employment;

   (f) To participate in all community activities;

   (g) To have access to agricultural credit and loans, marketing facilities, appropriate technology and equal treatment in land and agrarian reform as well as in land resettlement schemes;

   (h) To enjoy adequate living conditions, particularly in relation to housing, sanitation, electricity and water supply, transport and communications.

## Part IV

### Article 15

1. States Parties shall accord to women equality with men before the law.
2. States Parties shall accord to women, in civil matters, a legal capacity identical to that of men and the same opportunities to exercise that capacity. In particular, they shall give women equal rights to conclude contracts and to administer property and shall treat them equally in all stages of procedure in courts and tribunals.
3. States Parties agree that all contracts and all other private instruments of any kind with a legal effect which is directed at restricting the legal capacity of women shall be deemed null and void.
4. States Parties shall accord to men and women the same rights with regard to the law relating to the movement of persons and the freedom to choose their residence and domicile.

### Article 16

1. States Parties shall take all appropriate measures to eliminate discrimination against women in all matters relating to marriage and family relations and in particular shall ensure, on a basis of equality of men and women:

   (a) The same right to enter into marriage;

   (b) The same right freely to choose a spouse and to enter into marriage only with their free and full consent;

   (c) The same rights and responsibilities during marriage and at its dissolution;

(d) The same rights and responsibilities as parents, irrespective of their marital status, in matters relating to their children; in all cases the interests of the children shall be paramount;

(e) The same rights to decide freely and responsibly on the number and spacing of their children and to have access to the information, education and means to enable them to exercise these rights;

(f) The same rights and responsibilities with regard to guardianship, wardship, trusteeship and adoption of children, or similar institutions where these concepts exist in national legislation; in all cases the interests of the children shall be paramount;

(g) The same personal rights as husband and wife, including the right to choose a family name, a profession and an occupation;

(h) The same rights for both spouses in respect of the ownership, acquisition, management, administration, enjoyment and disposition of property, whether free of charge or for a valuable consideration.

2. The betrothal and the marriage of a child shall have no legal effect, and all necessary action, including legislation, shall be taken to specify a minimum age for marriage and to make the registration of marriages in an official registry compulsory.

---

# Section 7

# Appendix

## Key Terms

deindustrialization
deregulation
ecofeminism
globalization
harmonization
informal sector
labor standards
modernization
neoliberal model
rationality
self-interest
structural adjustment policies
sustainable development
transnational entities

## Discussion Questions

1. Summarize the differences between neoclassical and institutionalist approaches to globalization and the role of markets in the international economy. How does a feminist perspective on globalization and international labor standards differ from more traditional perspectives?
2. How does globalization improve the lives of women in developing countries? How does it make their lives more difficult? Compare your responses with what you know about the impact of industrialization on women in the United States.
3. What was Polanyi's "great transformation"? What does Bencría think is the role of feminism in the next "great transformation"?
4. Is the quality of the environment a feminist issue? Is government regulation of markets a feminist issue? Why or why not?
5. Reviewing the forms of discrimination and rights listed in articles in Convention on the Elimination of All Forms of Discrimination Against Women (CEDAW), which would you consider the priority

areas for women in the United States today? List four or five specific articles. Where have U.S. women made progress in the past
hundred years?

6. Based on your readings on globalization and development, which of
the articles in CEDAW seem most important for women in developing nations?

7. What aspects of CEDAW do you think are the most controversial?
Are there any areas where you would disagree with the wording in
CEDAW?

## Exercise

1. What countries ("parties") of the United Nations have signed on to
the Convention on the Elimination of All Forms of Discrimination
Against Women? To learn more about who has (and, surprisingly,
has not), visit www.un.org/womenwatch/daw/cedaw/.

## Further Reading

Aslanbeigui, Nahid, Steven Pressman, and Gale Summerfield, eds. 1994. *Women in
the Age of Economic Transformation: Gender Impact of Reforms in Post-Socialist
and Developing Countries*. New York: Routledge.

Carr, Marilyn, Martha Alter Chen, and Jane Tate. 2000. "Globalization and Home-
Based Workers." *Feminist Economics* 6 (3): 123-42.

Date-Bah, Eugenia, ed. 1997. *Promoting Gender Equality at Work: Turning Vision
into Reality*. London: Zed Books.

Jackson, Cecile, and Ruth Pearson. 1998. *Feminist Visions of Development*. New York:
Routledge.

Standing, Guy. 1999. "Globalization Through Flexible Labor: A Theme Revisited."
*World Development* 27 (3): 583-602.

# About the Editors and Contributors

**Joan Acker** is Professor Emerita of Sociology at University of Oregon.

**Randy Albelda** is Professor of Economics and Director of the Ph.D. Program in Public Policy at the University of Massachusetts–Boston.

**Lourdes Benería** is Professor in the Department of City and Regional Planning at Cornell University.

**Barbara R. Bergmann** is Professor Emerita of Economics at The American University and the University of Maryland.

**Jared Bernstein** is Economist and Codirector of the Research Department at the Economic Policy Institute in Washington, DC.

**Suzanne M. Bianchi** is Professor of Sociology and Director of the Center on Population, Gender, and Social Inequality at the University of Maryland.

**Celia Briar** is Senior Lecturer in the School of Sociology, Social Policy, and Social Work at Massey University in Palmerston North, New Zealand.

**Nilüfer Çagatay** is Economics Advisor on Poverty and Gender at the United Nations Development Program.

**Philip N. Cohen** is Assistant Professor of Sociology at the University of California–Irvine.

**Marianne A. Ferber** is Professor Emerita of Economics at the University of Illinois–Champaign/Urbana.

**Deborah M. Figart** is Professor of Economics at Richard Stockton College. She has taught courses such as Women and Work in economics departments and in interdisciplinary general studies programs in the social sciences. Her research in labor market theory and policy, pay equity, working time, and discrimination by race-ethnicity and gender has been published in numerous journals. She is the coauthor or coeditor of four previous book volumes, including *Living Wages, Equal Wages: Gender and Labor Market Policies in the United States.*

**Nancy Folbre** is Professor of Economics at the University of Massachusetts–Amherst.

**Claudia Goldin** is Professor of Economics at Harvard University.

**Heidi Hartmann** is President and CEO of the Institute for Women's Policy Research in Washington, DC.

**Betty Holcomb** is a freelance writer from Montclair, New Jersey. She is the author of *Best Friend's Guide to Maternity Leave* (Perseus Books, 2002) and *Not Guilty! The Good News for Working Mothers* (Scribner, 1998).

**Ivy Kennelly** is Assistant Professor of Sociology at The George Washington University in Washington, DC.

**Mary C. King** is Associate Professor of Economics at Portland State University in Oregon.

**Michael Levin** is Professor of Philosophy at City College of New York, CUNY.

**Wayne A. Lewchuk** is Professor of Economics and Director of the Labor Studies Program at McMaster University in Ontario, Canada.

**Martha MacDonald** is Professor of Economics at St. Mary's University in Nova Scotia, Canada.

**Ellen Mutari** is Assistant Professor in the General Studies Division of Richard Stockton College, where she teaches quantitative reasoning, writing, economics, and interdisciplinary courses. She has published on the theory and methodology of feminist political economy, women's employment during the Great Depression, working time, gender statistics, and race- and gender-based discrimination. Previously she coedited *Gender and Political Economy: Incorporating Diversity into Theory and Policy* (M.E. Sharpe, 1997).

**Julie A. Nelson** is Senior Research Associate in the Global Development and Environment Institute at Tufts University.

**Elizabeth Oughton** is a member of the Department of Geography at the University of Durham, United Kingdom.

**Janice Peterson** is Senior Analyst in Education, Workforce, and Income Security at the General Accounting Office in Washington, DC.

**Marilyn Power** is Professor of Economics at Sarah Lawrence College.

**William Rau** is Professor of Economics at Illinois State University in Normal, Illinois.

**John Schmitt** is Research Associate at the Economic Policy Institute in Washington, DC.

**Ann Schwarz-Miller** is Associate Professor of Economics at Old Dominion University in Norfolk, Virginia.

**Steven Shulman** is Professor of Economics at Colorado State University in Fort Collins.

**Myra H. Strober** is Professor of Education at Stanford University.

**Wayne K. Talley** is Beazeley Professor of Economics at Old Dominion University in Norfolk, Virginia.

**Chris Tilly** is University Professor in the Department of Regional Economic and Social Development at the University of Massachusetts–Lowell.

**Martin Tolich** is Senior Lecturer in the School of Sociology, Social Policy, and Social Work at Massey University in Palmerston North, New Zealand.

**Robert Wazienski** is Assistant Professor of Sociology and also Director of

Schroeder Hall Academic Computing at Illinois State University in Normal, Illinois.

**Catherine J. Weinberger** is an independent scholar affiliated with the University of California at Santa Barbara Department of Economics and the Institute for Social, Behavioral and Economic Research.

**Jane Wheelock** is Professor of Socio-economics at University of Newcastle-upon-Tyne in the United Kingdom.

**Lauren Young** is a student in the Graduate School of Business at Stanford University.

**Eiman Zein-Elabdin** is Professor of Economics at Franklin and Marshall College in Lancaster, Pennsylvania.

# Index